S·A
Special A

Volume 14

Story & Art by
Maki Minami

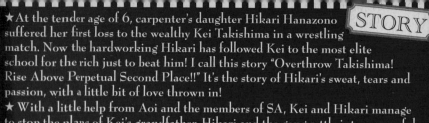

★ At the tender age of 6, carpenter's daughter Hikari Hanazono suffered her first loss to the wealthy Kei Takishima in a wrestling match. Now the hardworking Hikari has followed Kei to the most elite school for the rich just to beat him! I call this story "Overthrow Takishima! Rise Above Perpetual Second Place!!" It's the story of Hikari's sweat, tears and passion, with a little bit of love thrown in!

★ With a little help from Aoi and the members of SA, Kei and Hikari manage to stop the plans of Kei's grandfather. Hikari and the gang settle into a peaceful new school year after Kei's study camp, Valentine's Day and the discovery of Kei's big secret, but the scores for the first test of the year are just in!

Kei Takishima

Ranked number one in SA, Kei is a seemingly flawless student who not only gets perfect test scores but also runs his family business, Takishima Group, from behind the scenes. He is in love with Hikari, but she doesn't realize it.

Ryu Tsuji

Ranked number seven in SA, Ryu is the son of the president of a sporting goods company...but wait, he loves animals, too! Megumi and Jun are completely infatuated with him.

Megumi Yamamoto

Megumi is the daughter of a music producer and a genius vocalist. Ranked number four in SA, she only talks to people by writing in her sketchbook.

Jun Yamamoto

Megumi's twin brother, Jun is ranked number three in SA. Like his sister, he doesn't talk much. They have both been strongly attached to Ryu since they were kids.

S·A CHARACTERS

What is "Special A"?

Hikari goes to an elite school called Hakusenkan High School. This school divides each grade level into groups A through F, according to the students' test scores. Group A includes only the top seven students in each class. Then the top seven students from all grades' A groups are put into a group called Special A, which is considered much higher than all others. Known as SA, they are "the elite among the elite."

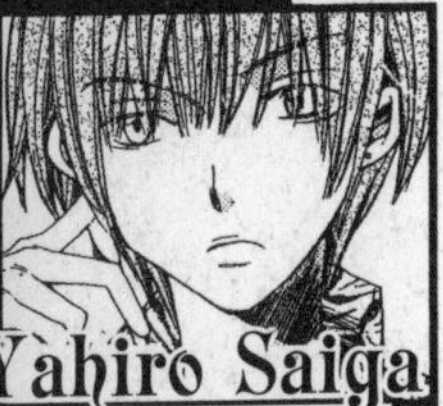

Yahiro Saiga

A childhood friend of Kei and Akira. His family is richer than the Takishima Group.

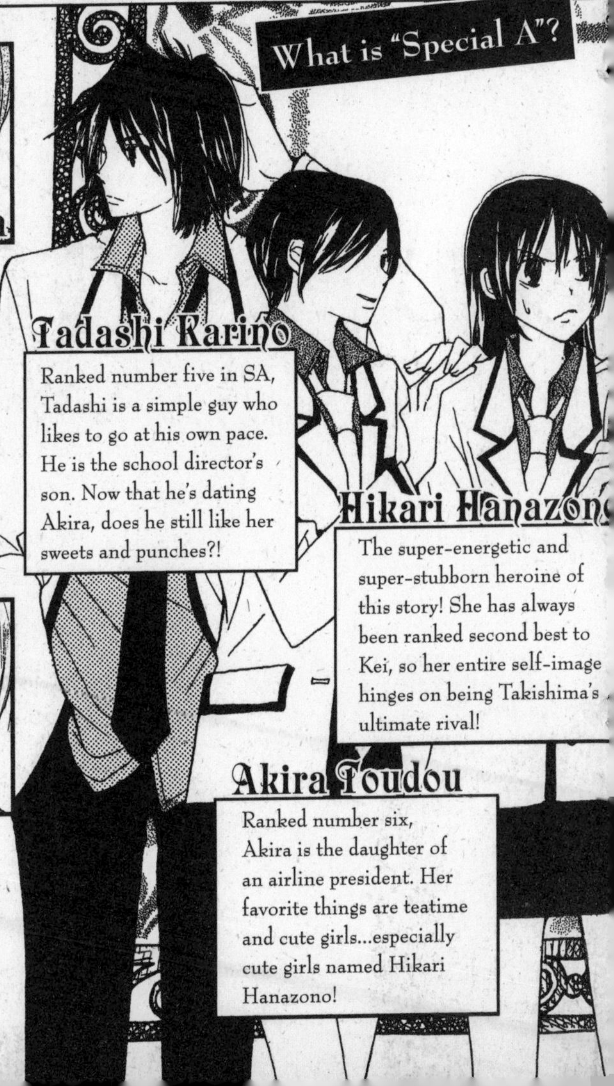

Tadashi Karino

Ranked number five in SA, Tadashi is a simple guy who likes to go at his own pace. He is the school director's son. Now that he's dating Akira, does he still like her sweets and punches?!

Hikari Hanazono

The super-energetic and super-stubborn heroine of this story! She has always been ranked second best to Kei, so her entire self-image hinges on being Takishima's ultimate rival!

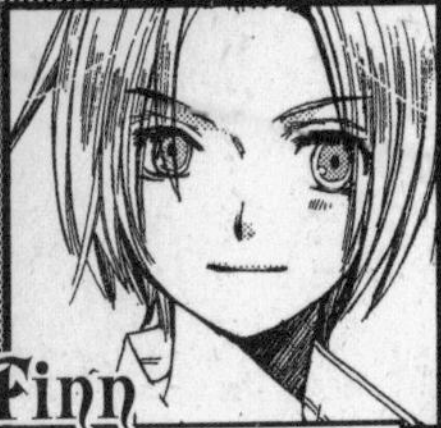

Finn

The prince of a foreign country. He traveled to Japan to make Hikari his bride. (He's really a girl.)

Akira Toudou

Ranked number six, Akira is the daughter of an airline president. Her favorite things are teatime and cute girls...especially cute girls named Hikari Hanazono!

Contents

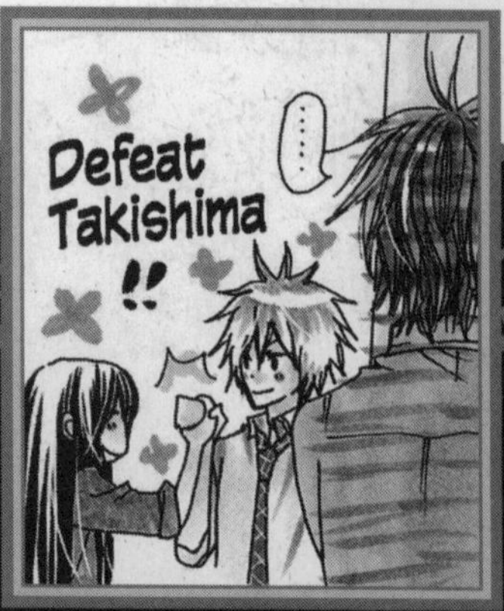

......
Defeat Takishima !!

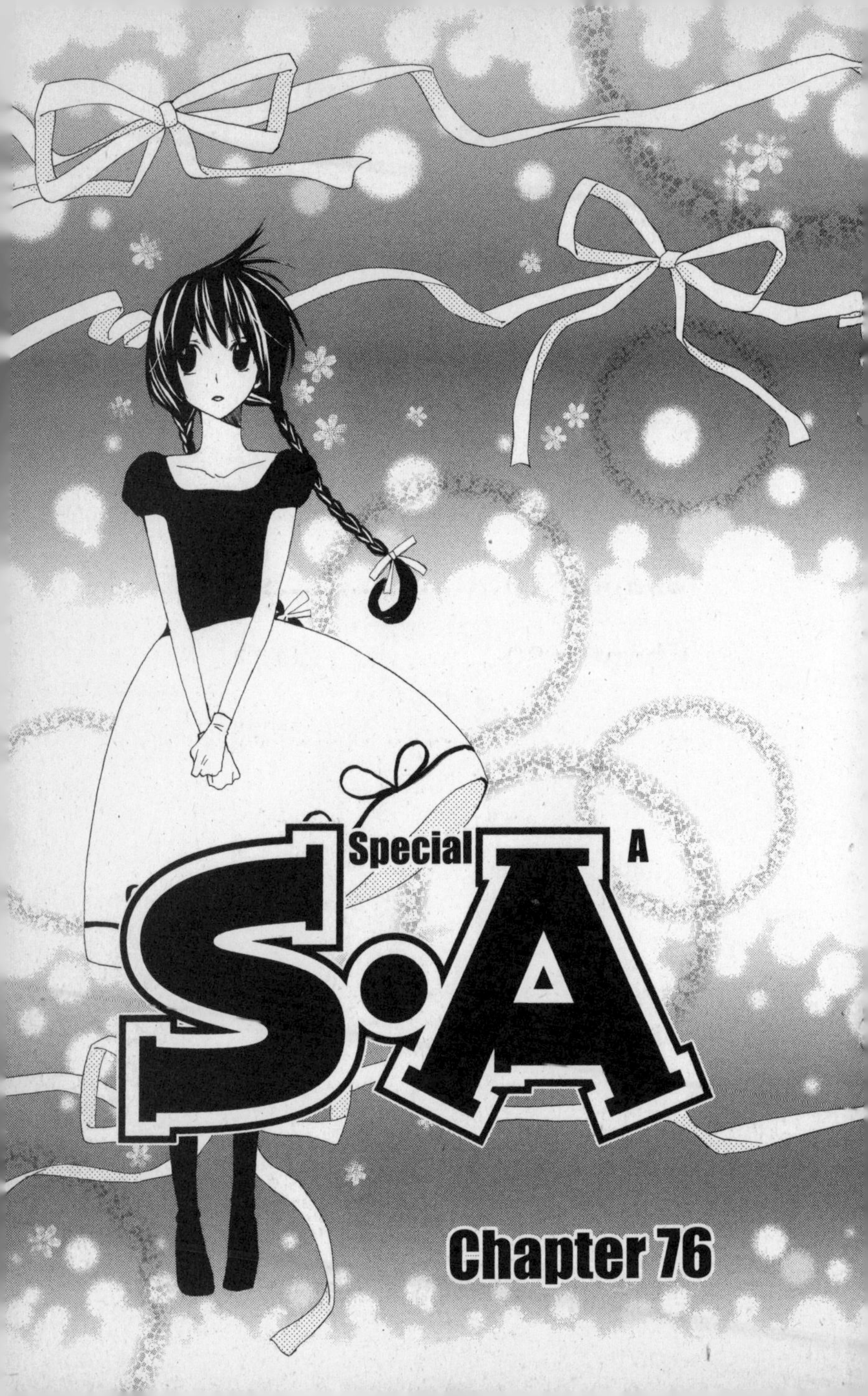
Special A
S·A
Chapter 76

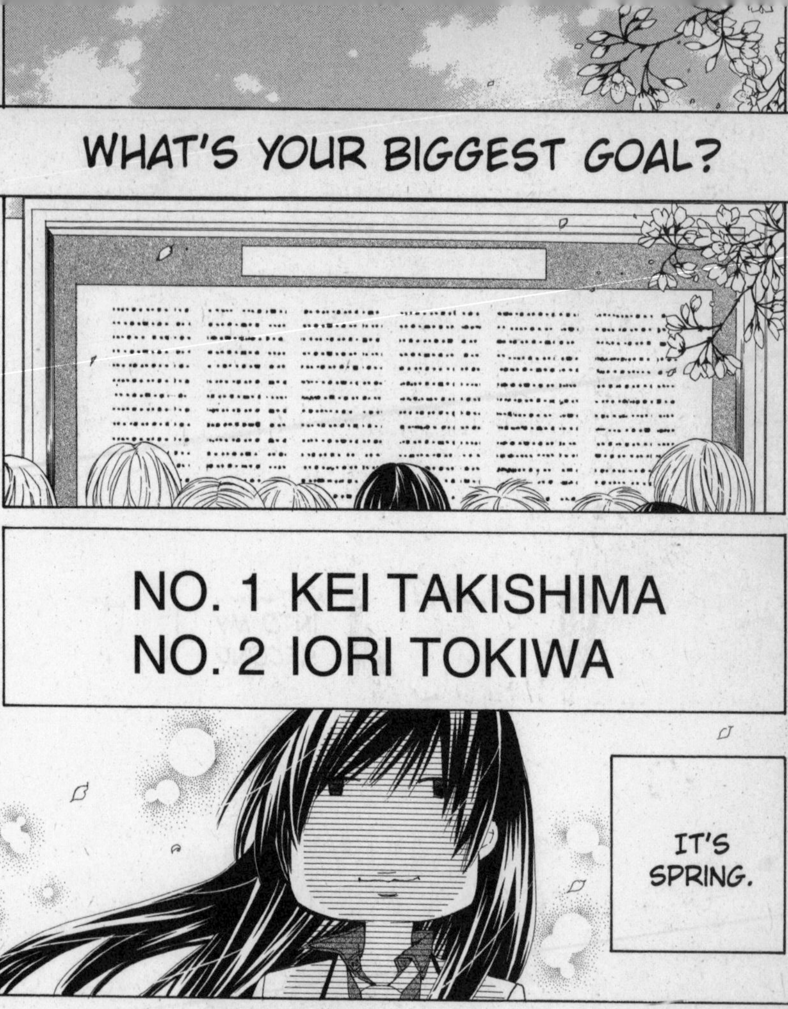
WHAT'S YOUR BIGGEST GOAL?
NO. 1 KEI TAKISHIMA
NO. 2 IORI TOKIWA
IT'S SPRING.

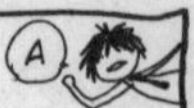

· COVER AND THIS AND THAT ·

- HIKARI AND IORI ARE ON THE COVER THIS TIME. THE WREATH AROUND THEM TURNED OUT REALLY CHRISTMAS-Y, EVEN THOUGH IT'S SUPPOSED TO BE SUMMER...
  AND NOW THAT I LOOK AT IT, I DON'T THINK I'VE EVER COLORED IN AN S.A STUDENT'S TIE LIKE THAT!!
- IORI'S A NEW CHARACTER THAT I WANT TO TRY TO USE A LOT. I HOPE I CAN WRITE SOME FUN STUFF FOR HIM!

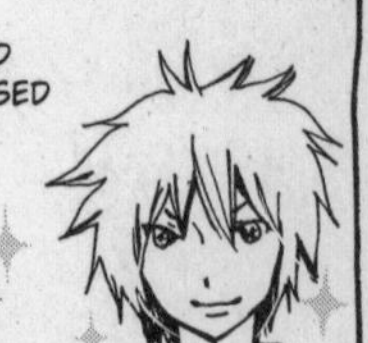

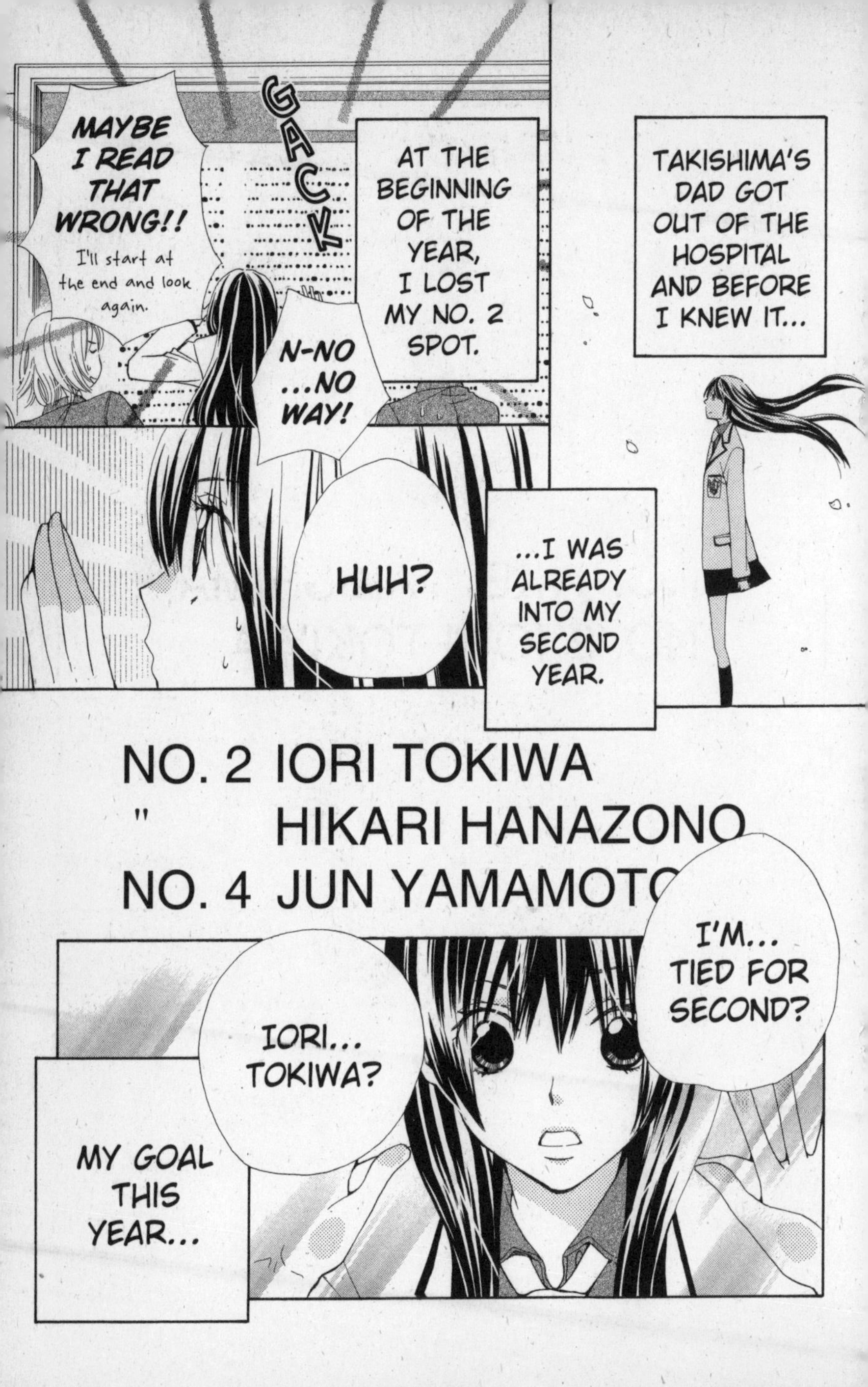
TAKISHIMA'S DAD GOT OUT OF THE HOSPITAL AND BEFORE I KNEW IT...
...I WAS ALREADY INTO MY SECOND YEAR.
AT THE BEGINNING OF THE YEAR, I LOST MY NO. 2 SPOT.
GACK
MAYBE I READ THAT WRONG!!
I'll start at the end and look again.
N-NO ...NO WAY!
HUH?
NO. 2 IORI TOKIWA
" HIKARI HANAZONO
NO. 4 JUN YAMAMOTO
I'M... TIED FOR SECOND?
IORI... TOKIWA?
MY GOAL THIS YEAR...

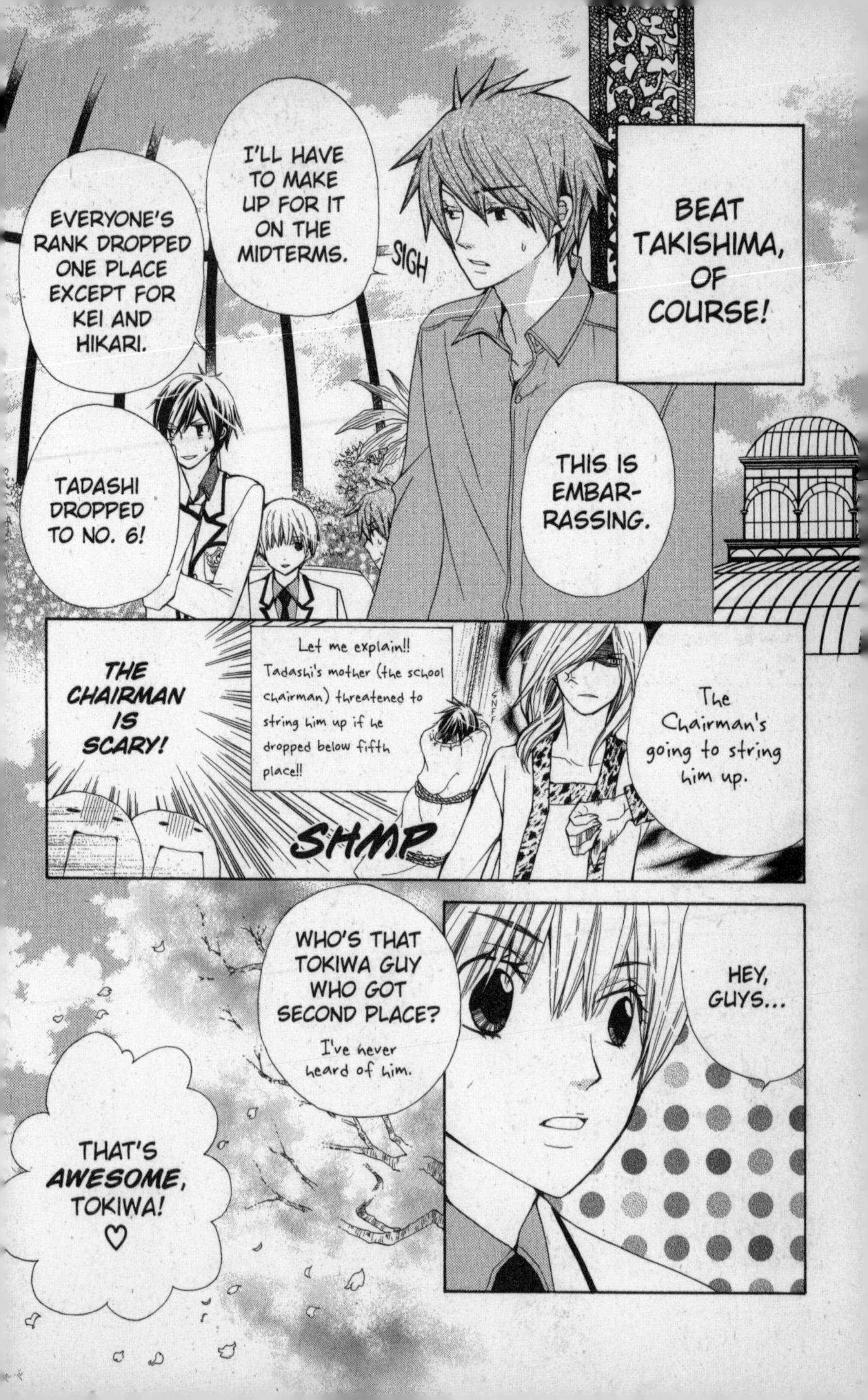
BEAT TAKISHIMA, OF COURSE!
I'LL HAVE TO MAKE UP FOR IT ON THE MIDTERMS.
SIGH
EVERYONE'S RANK DROPPED ONE PLACE EXCEPT FOR KEI AND HIKARI.
THIS IS EMBARRASSING.
TADASHI DROPPED TO NO. 6!
The Chairman's going to string him up.
SNFF
Let me explain!! Tadashi's mother (the school chairman) threatened to string him up if he dropped below fifth place!!
SHMP
THE CHAIRMAN IS SCARY!
HEY, GUYS...
WHO'S THAT TOKIWA GUY WHO GOT SECOND PLACE?
I've never heard of him.
THAT'S AWESOME, TOKIWA! ♡

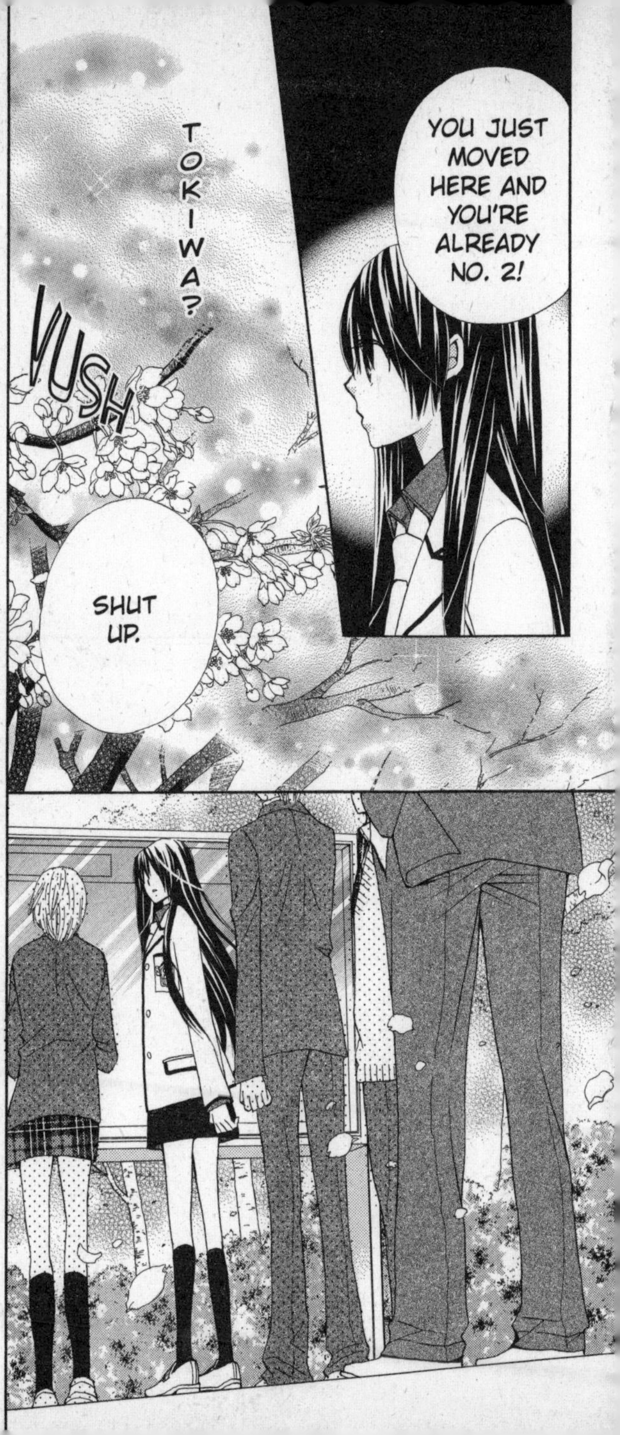
YOU JUST MOVED HERE AND YOU'RE ALREADY NO. 2!
TOKIWA?
VUSH
SHUT UP.

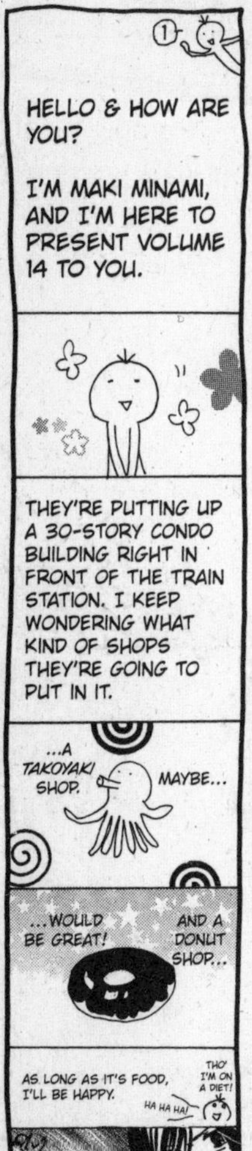
1
HELLO & HOW ARE YOU?
I'M MAKI MINAMI, AND I'M HERE TO PRESENT VOLUME 14 TO YOU.
THEY'RE PUTTING UP A 30-STORY CONDO BUILDING RIGHT IN FRONT OF THE TRAIN STATION. I KEEP WONDERING WHAT KIND OF SHOPS THEY'RE GOING TO PUT IN IT.
MAYBE...
...A TAKOYAKI SHOP.
AND A DONUT SHOP...
...WOULD BE GREAT!
AS LONG AS IT'S FOOD, I'LL BE HAPPY.
HA HA HA!
THO' I'M ON A DIET!

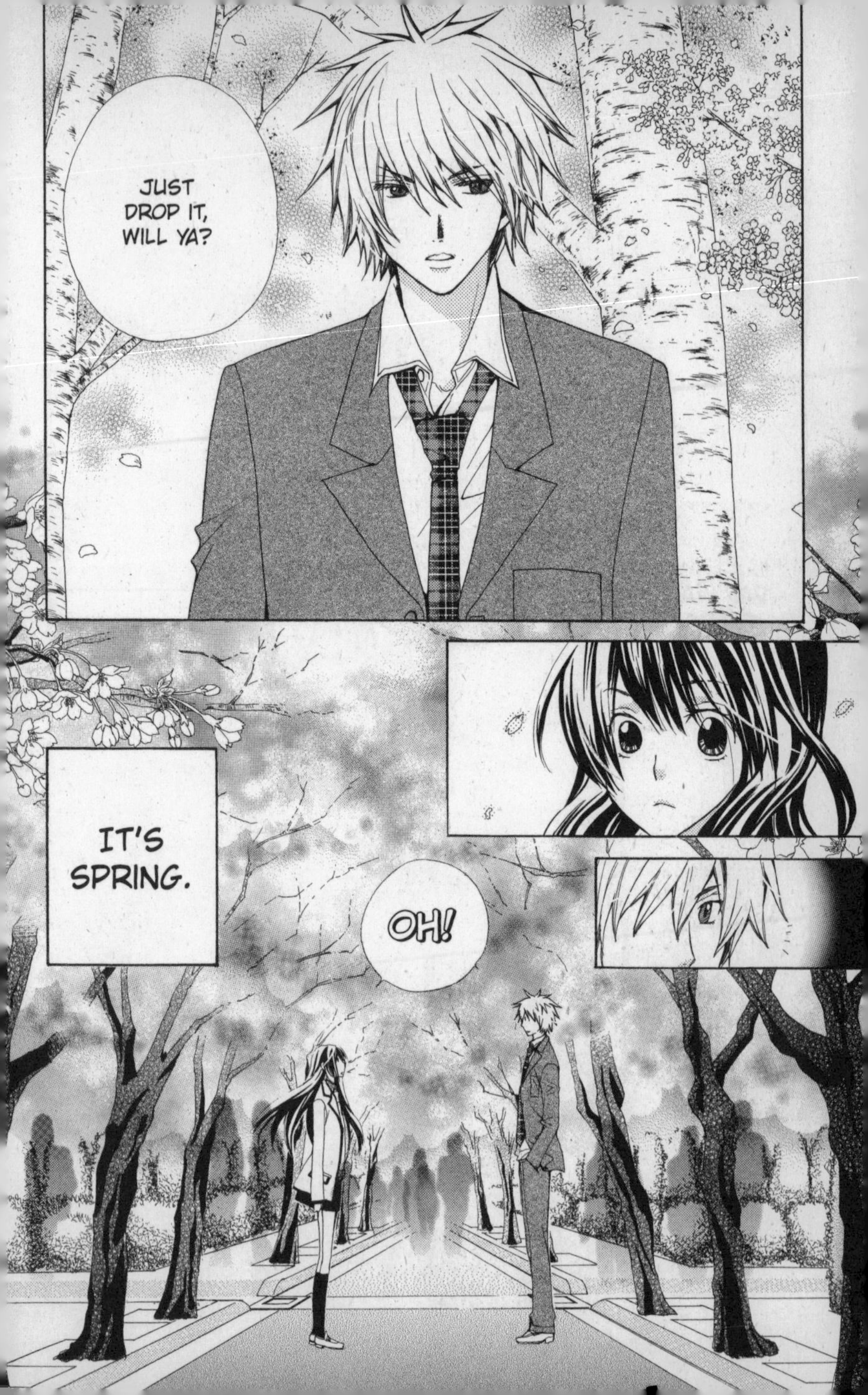
JUST DROP IT, WILL YA?
OH!
IT'S SPRING.

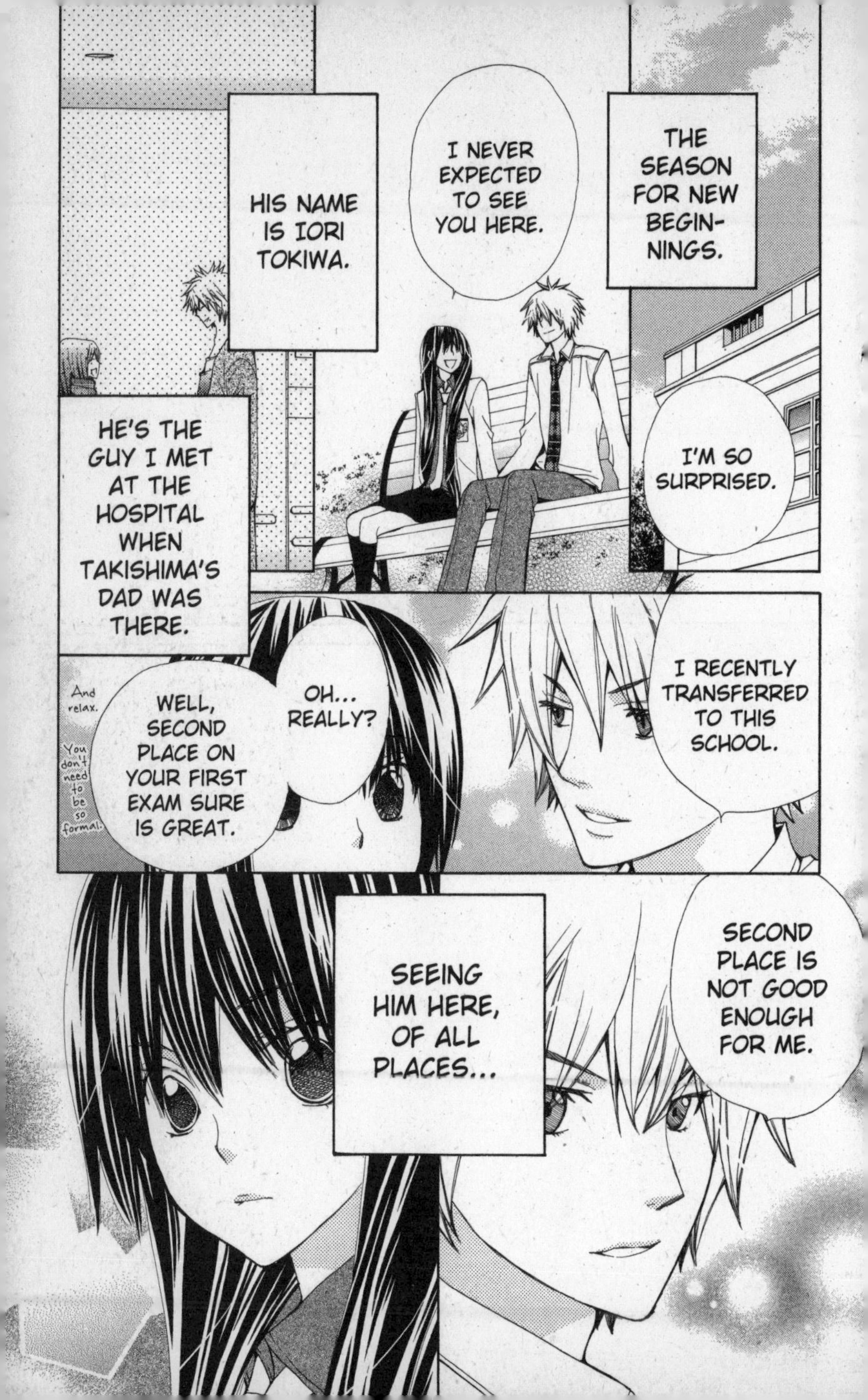
THE SEASON FOR NEW BEGIN-NINGS.
I NEVER EXPECTED TO SEE YOU HERE.
I'M SO SURPRISED.
HIS NAME IS IORI TOKIWA.
HE'S THE GUY I MET AT THE HOSPITAL WHEN TAKISHIMA'S DAD WAS THERE.
I RECENTLY TRANSFERRED TO THIS SCHOOL.
OH... REALLY?
WELL, SECOND PLACE ON YOUR FIRST EXAM SURE IS GREAT.
And relax.
You don't need to be so formal.
SECOND PLACE IS NOT GOOD ENOUGH FOR ME.
SEEING HIM HERE, OF ALL PLACES...

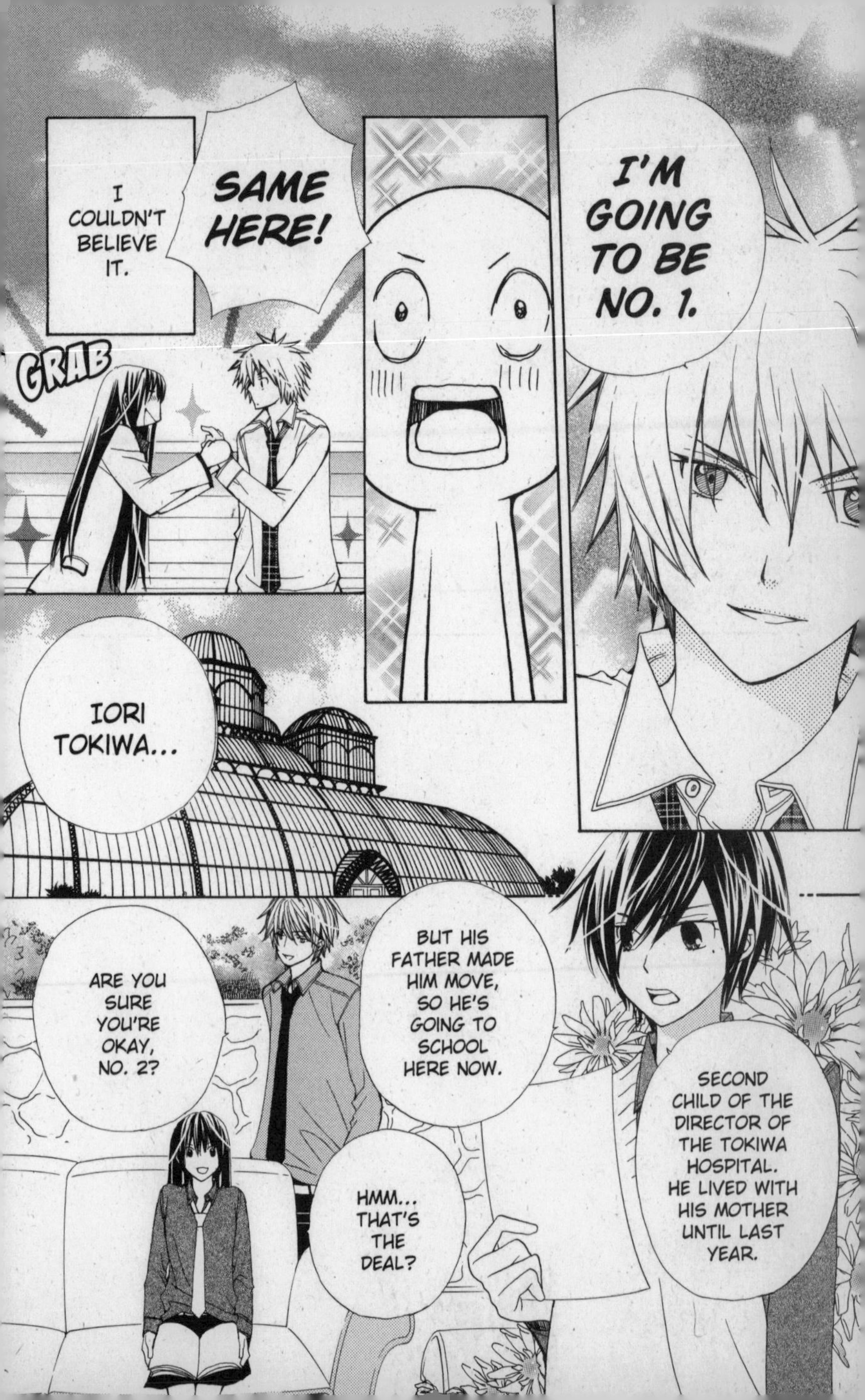
I'M GOING TO BE NO. 1.
I COULDN'T BELIEVE IT.
SAME HERE!
GRAB
IORI TOKIWA...
SECOND CHILD OF THE DIRECTOR OF THE TOKIWA HOSPITAL. HE LIVED WITH HIS MOTHER UNTIL LAST YEAR.
BUT HIS FATHER MADE HIM MOVE, SO HE'S GOING TO SCHOOL HERE NOW.
HMM... THAT'S THE DEAL?
ARE YOU SURE YOU'RE OKAY, NO. 2?

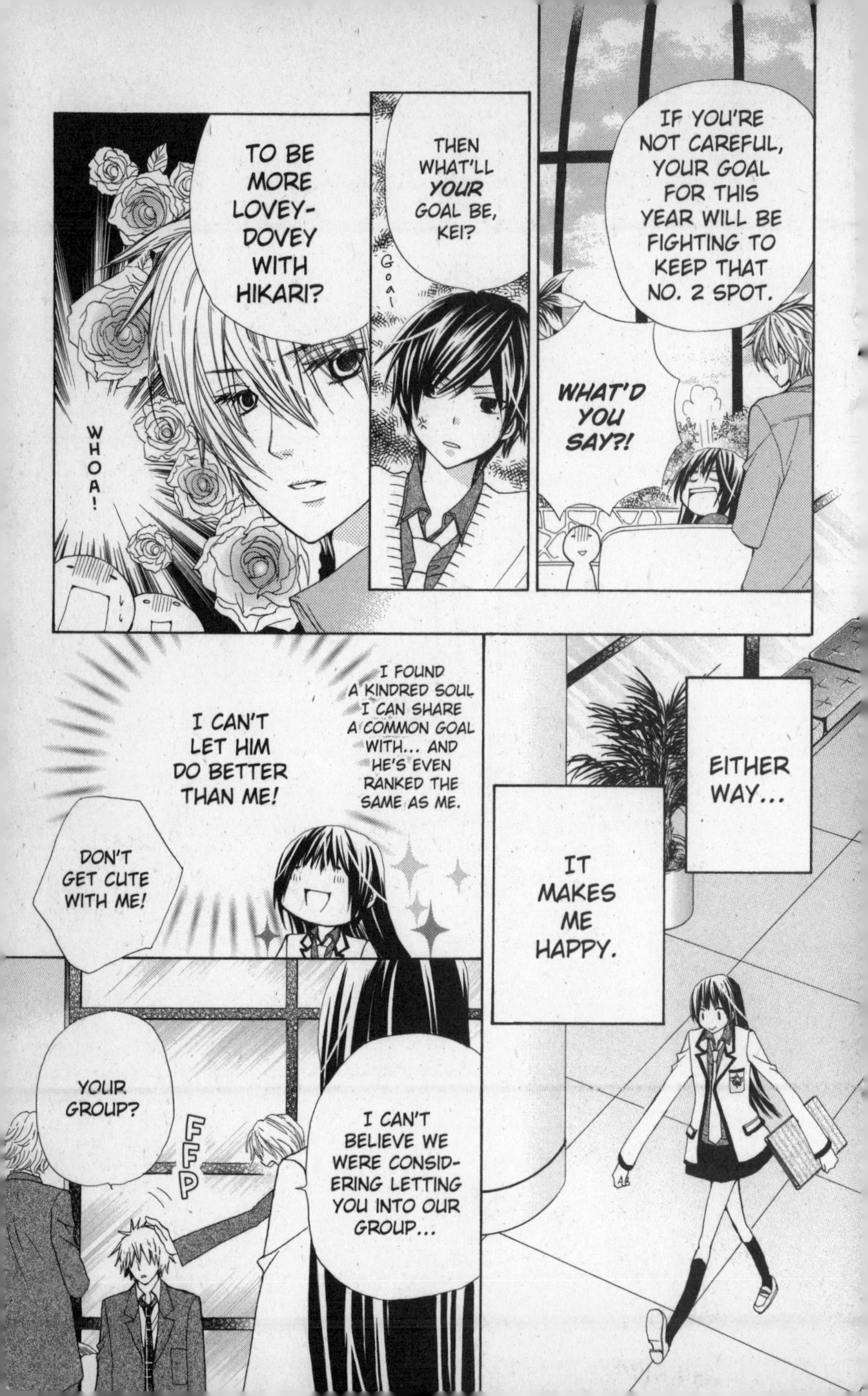
IF YOU'RE NOT CAREFUL, YOUR GOAL FOR THIS YEAR WILL BE FIGHTING TO KEEP THAT NO. 2 SPOT.
WHAT'D YOU SAY?!
THEN WHAT'LL YOUR GOAL BE, KEI?
Goal
TO BE MORE LOVEY-DOVEY WITH HIKARI?
WHOA!
EITHER WAY...
IT MAKES ME HAPPY.
I FOUND A KINDRED SOUL I CAN SHARE A COMMON GOAL WITH... AND HE'S EVEN RANKED THE SAME AS ME.
I CAN'T LET HIM DO BETTER THAN ME!
DON'T GET CUTE WITH ME!
I CAN'T BELIEVE WE WERE CONSIDERING LETTING YOU INTO OUR GROUP...
FFP
YOUR GROUP?

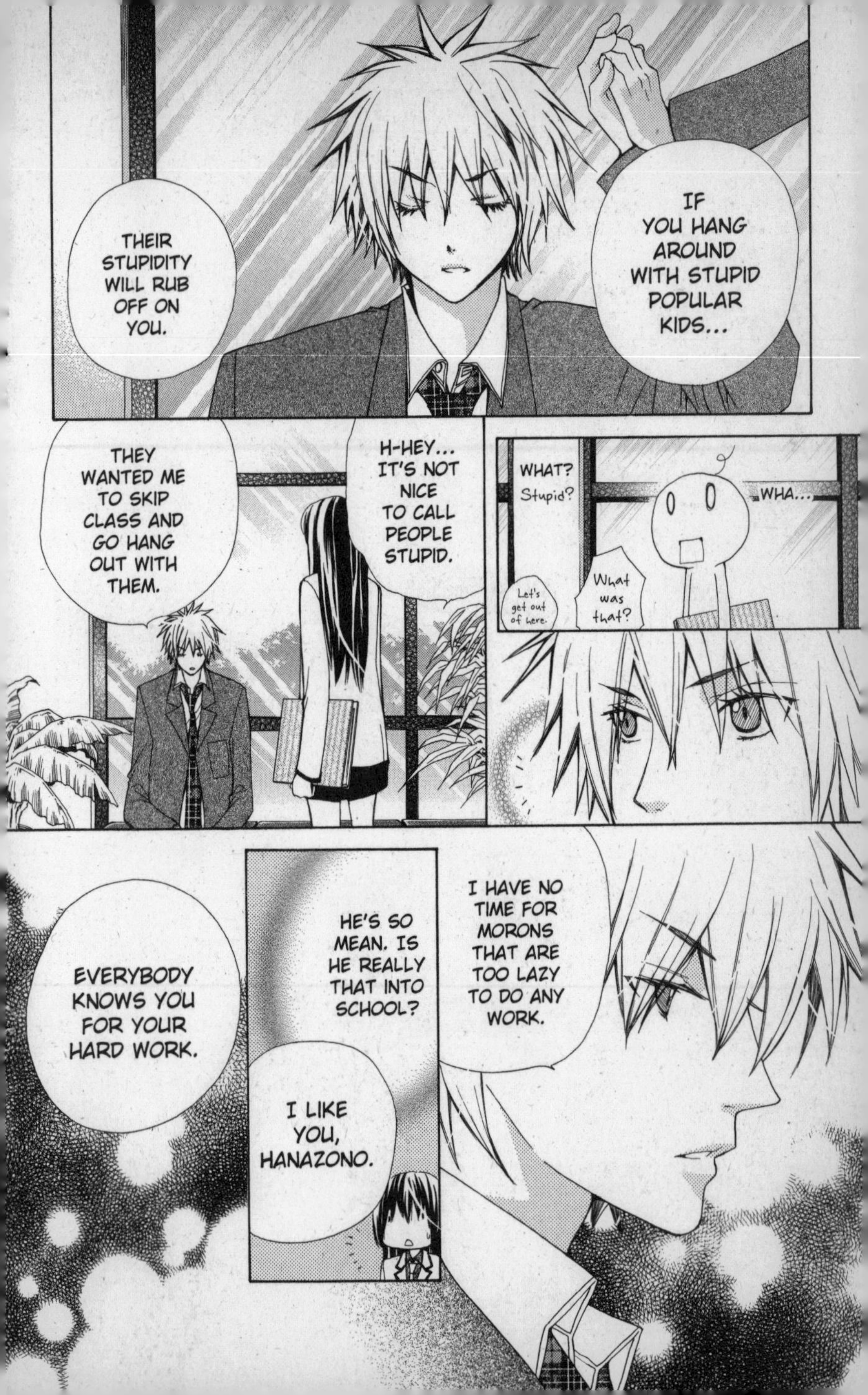
IF YOU HANG AROUND WITH STUPID POPULAR KIDS...
THEIR STUPIDITY WILL RUB OFF ON YOU.
WHA...
WHAT? Stupid?
What was that?
Let's get out of here.
H-HEY... IT'S NOT NICE TO CALL PEOPLE STUPID.
THEY WANTED ME TO SKIP CLASS AND GO HANG OUT WITH THEM.
I HAVE NO TIME FOR MORONS THAT ARE TOO LAZY TO DO ANY WORK.
HE'S SO MEAN. IS HE REALLY THAT INTO SCHOOL?
EVERYBODY KNOWS YOU FOR YOUR HARD WORK.
I LIKE YOU, HANAZONO.

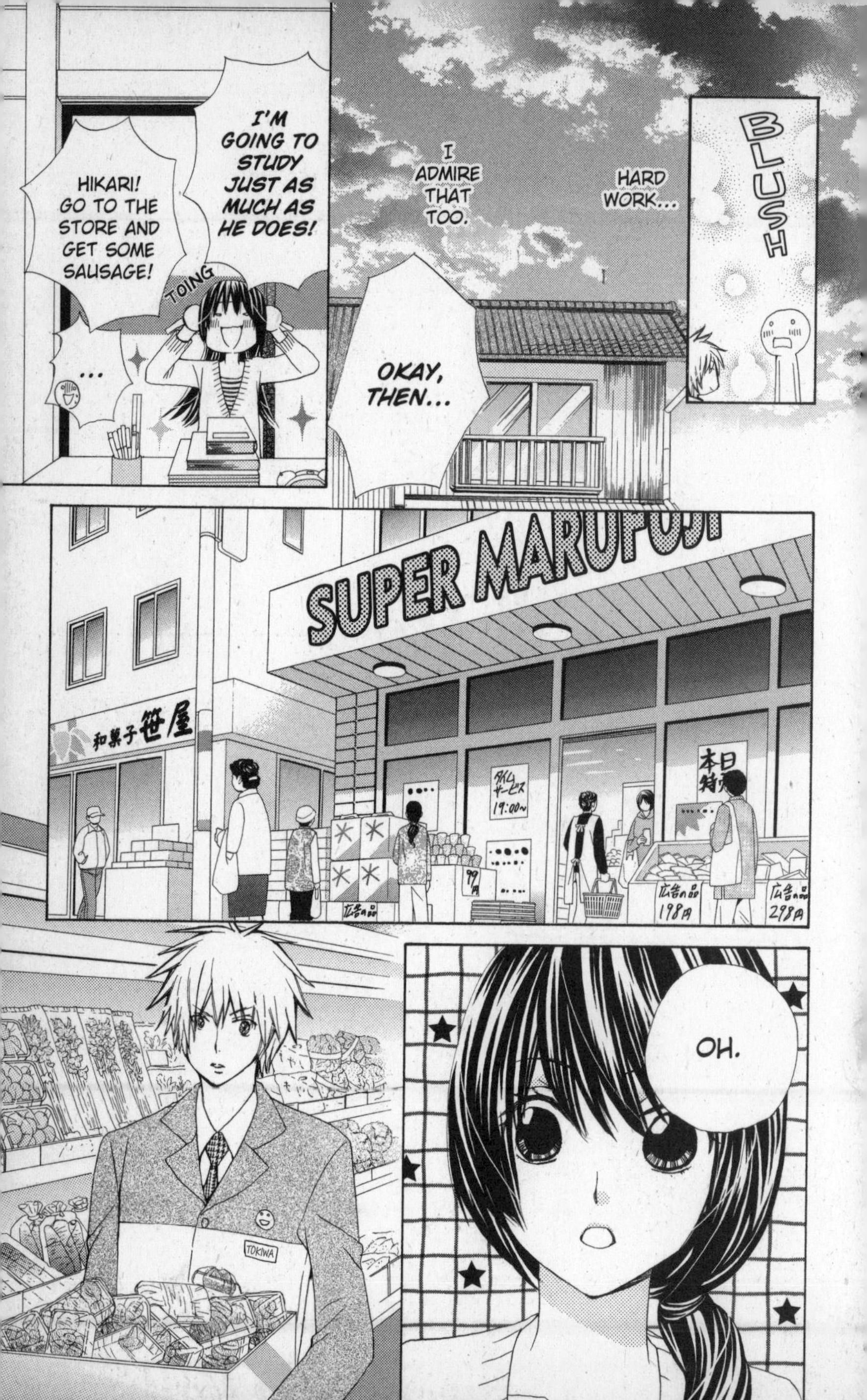
BLUSH
HARD WORK...
I ADMIRE THAT TOO.
OKAY, THEN...
I'M GOING TO STUDY JUST AS MUCH AS HE DOES!
TOING
HIKARI! GO TO THE STORE AND GET SOME SAUSAGE!
...
SUPER MARUFUJI
和菓子 笹屋
タイムサービス 19:00~
広告の品 198円
広告の品 298円
OH.
TOKIWA

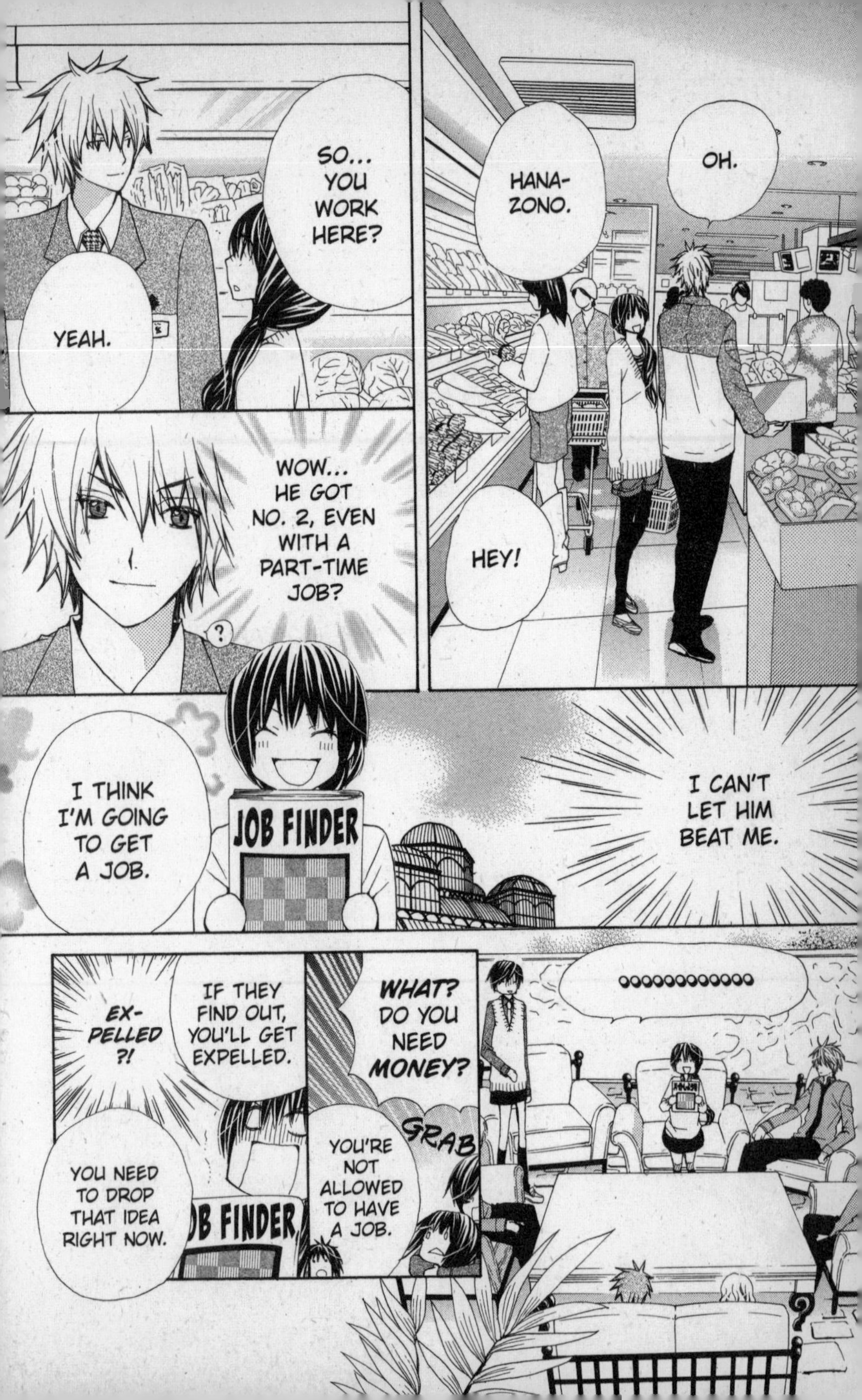

OH.
HANA-ZONO.
HEY!
SO... YOU WORK HERE?
YEAH.
WOW... HE GOT NO. 2, EVEN WITH A PART-TIME JOB?
?
I CAN'T LET HIM BEAT ME.
I THINK I'M GOING TO GET A JOB.
JOB FINDER
OOOOOOOOOOOOO
WHAT? DO YOU NEED MONEY?
GRAB
YOU'RE NOT ALLOWED TO HAVE A JOB.
IF THEY FIND OUT, YOU'LL GET EXPELLED.
EX-PELLED?!
YOU NEED TO DROP THAT IDEA RIGHT NOW.
OB FINDER

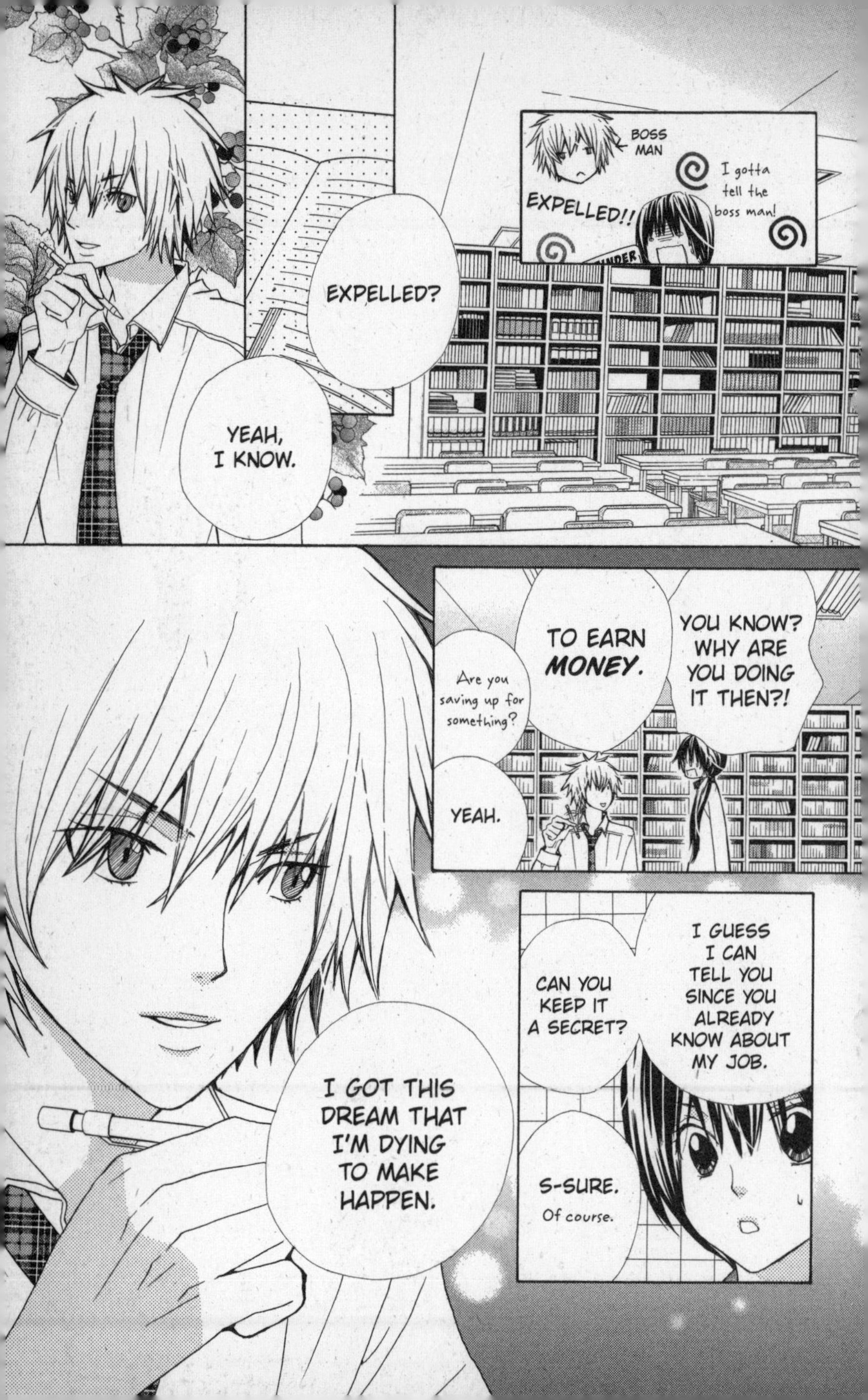

BOSS MAN
I gotta tell the boss man!
EXPELLED!!
EXPELLED?
YEAH, I KNOW.
YOU KNOW? WHY ARE YOU DOING IT THEN?!
TO EARN *MONEY*.
Are you saving up for something?
YEAH.
I GUESS I CAN TELL YOU SINCE YOU ALREADY KNOW ABOUT MY JOB.
CAN YOU KEEP IT A SECRET?
S-SURE.
Of course.
I GOT THIS DREAM THAT I'M DYING TO MAKE HAPPEN.

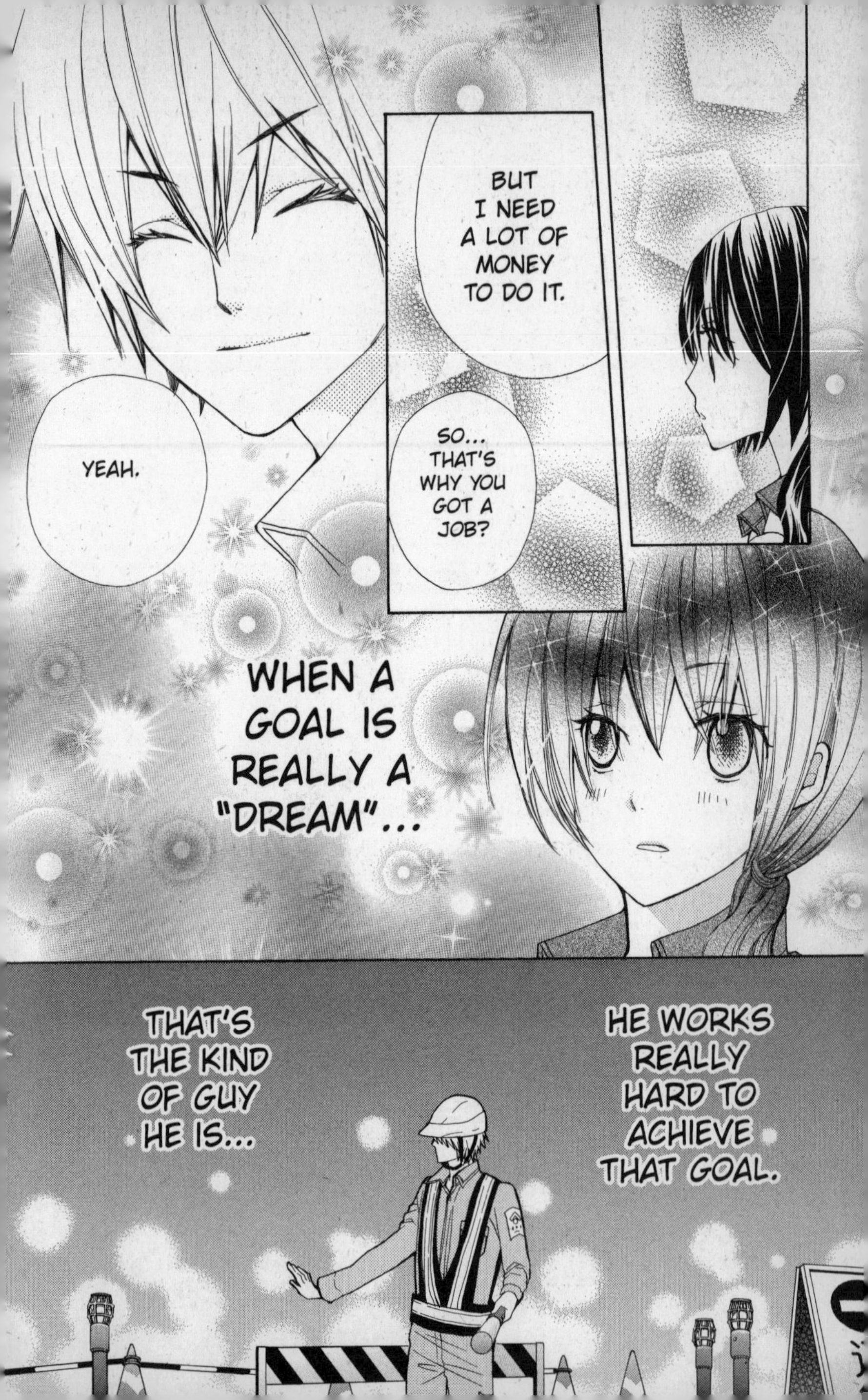
BUT I NEED A LOT OF MONEY TO DO IT.
SO... THAT'S WHY YOU GOT A JOB?
YEAH.
WHEN A GOAL IS REALLY A "DREAM"...
HE WORKS REALLY HARD TO ACHIEVE THAT GOAL.
THAT'S THE KIND OF GUY HE IS...

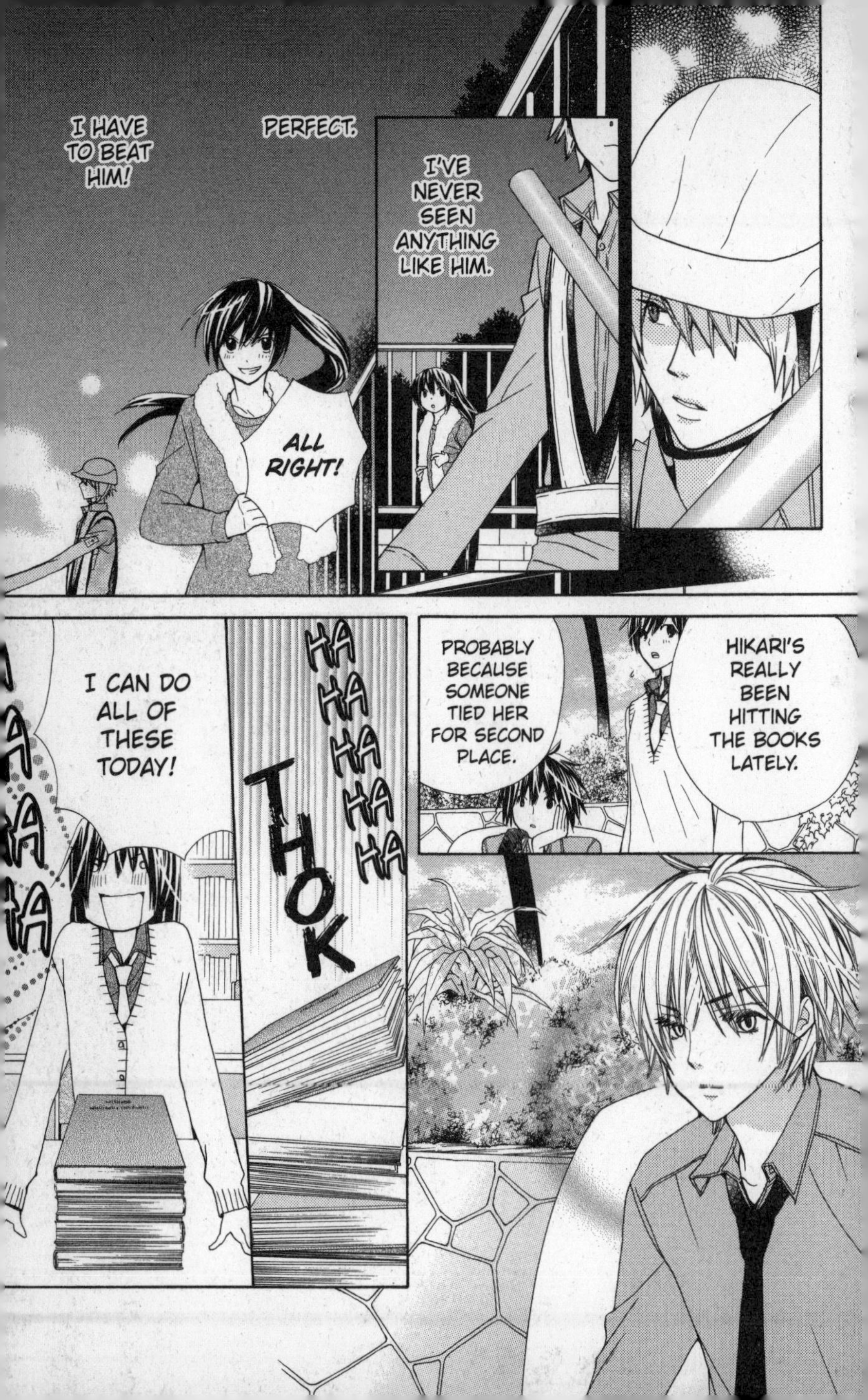
I'VE NEVER SEEN ANYTHING LIKE HIM.
PERFECT.
I HAVE TO BEAT HIM!
ALL RIGHT!
HIKARI'S REALLY BEEN HITTING THE BOOKS LATELY.
PROBABLY BECAUSE SOMEONE TIED HER FOR SECOND PLACE.
HA HA HA HA HA HA
THOK
I CAN DO ALL OF THESE TODAY!

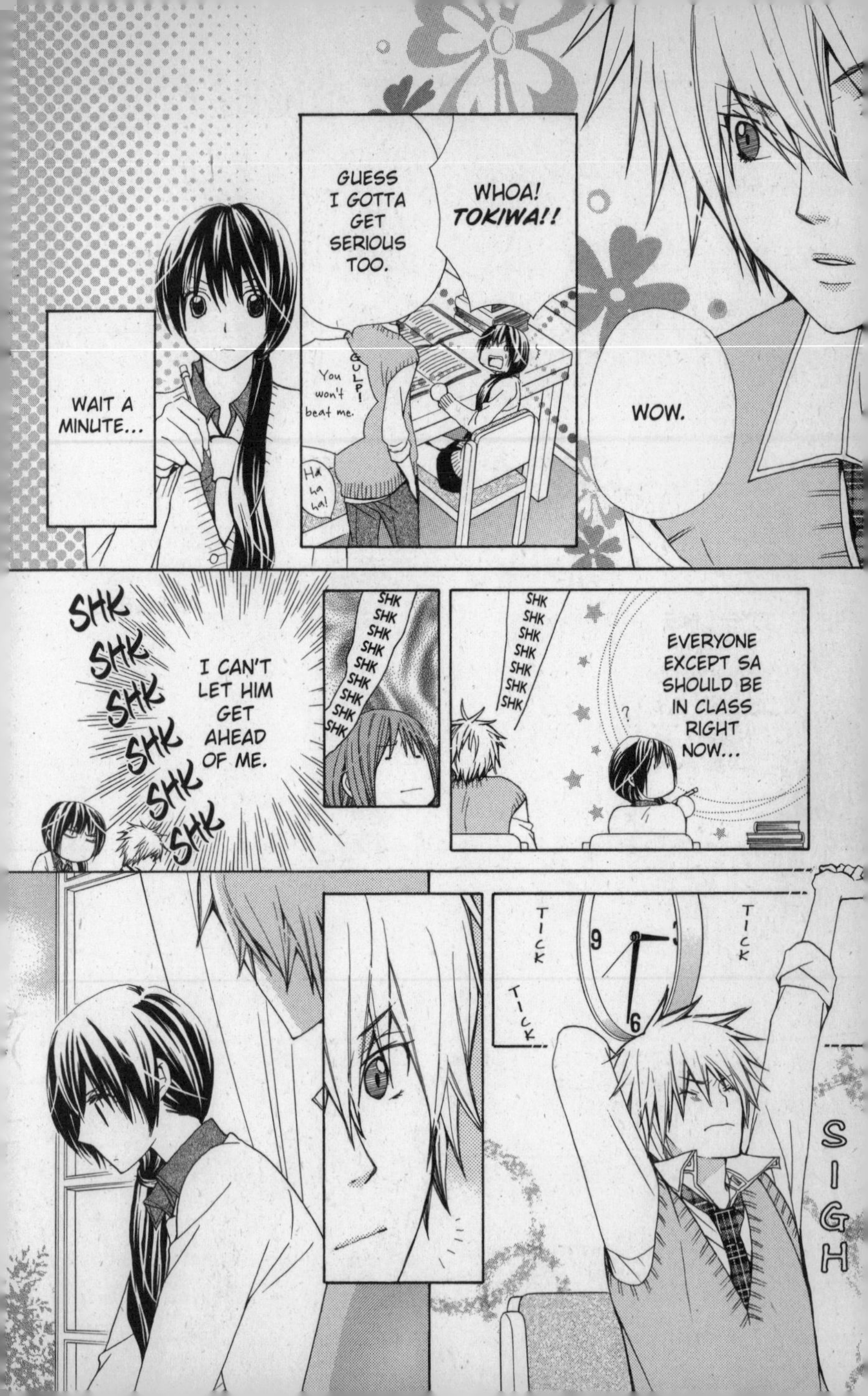
WOW.
WHOA! *TOKIWA!!*
GUESS I GOTTA GET SERIOUS TOO.
GULP!
You won't beat me.
Ha ha ha!
WAIT A MINUTE...
EVERYONE EXCEPT SA SHOULD BE IN CLASS RIGHT NOW...
SHK SHK SHK SHK SHK SHK SHK
SHK SHK SHK SHK SHK SHK SHK SHK SHK
I CAN'T LET HIM GET AHEAD OF ME.
SHK SHK SHK SHK SHK SHK
SIGH
TICK
TICK
TICK

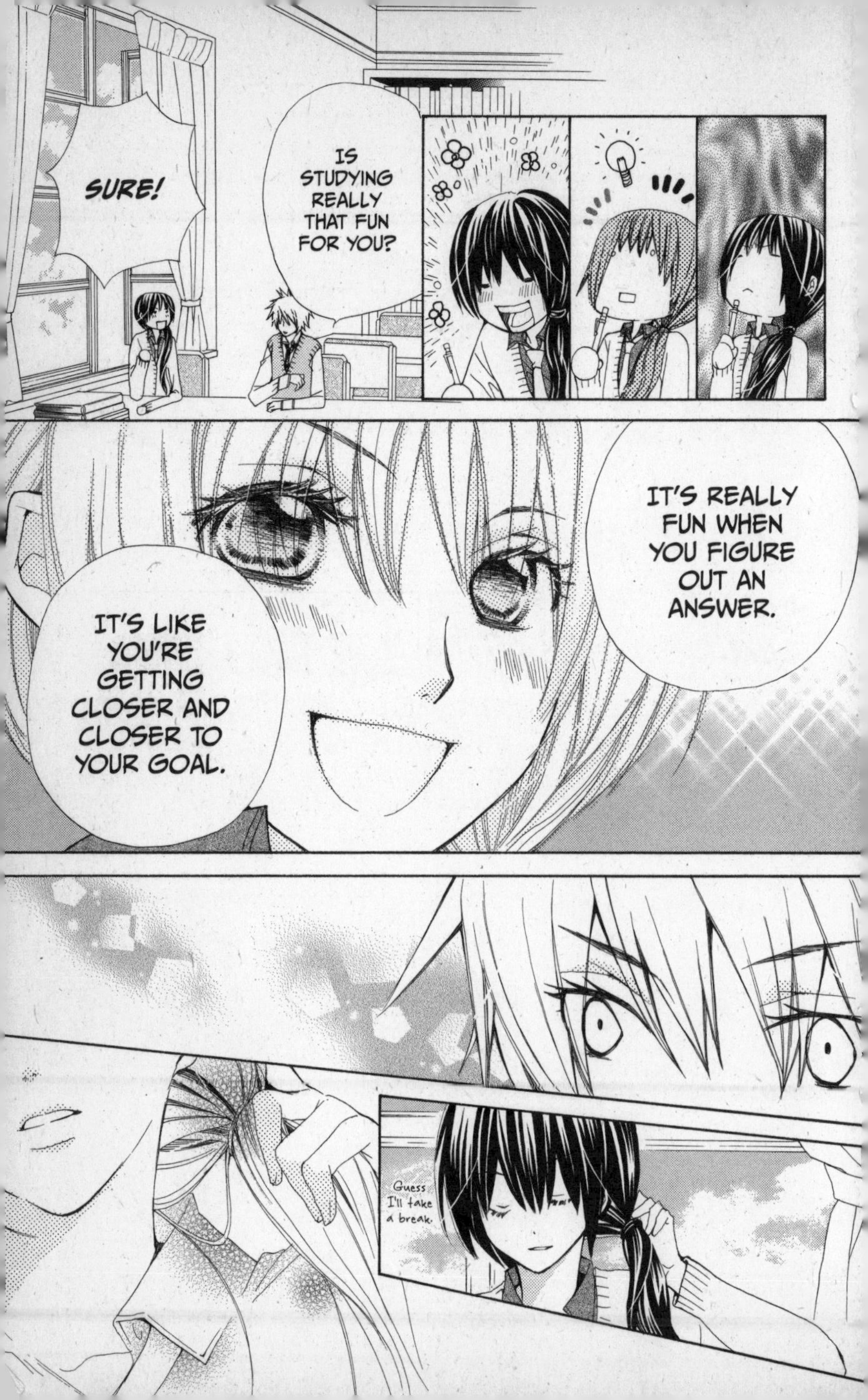
IS STUDYING REALLY THAT FUN FOR YOU?
SURE!
IT'S REALLY FUN WHEN YOU FIGURE OUT AN ANSWER.
IT'S LIKE YOU'RE GETTING CLOSER AND CLOSER TO YOUR GOAL.
Guess I'll take a break.

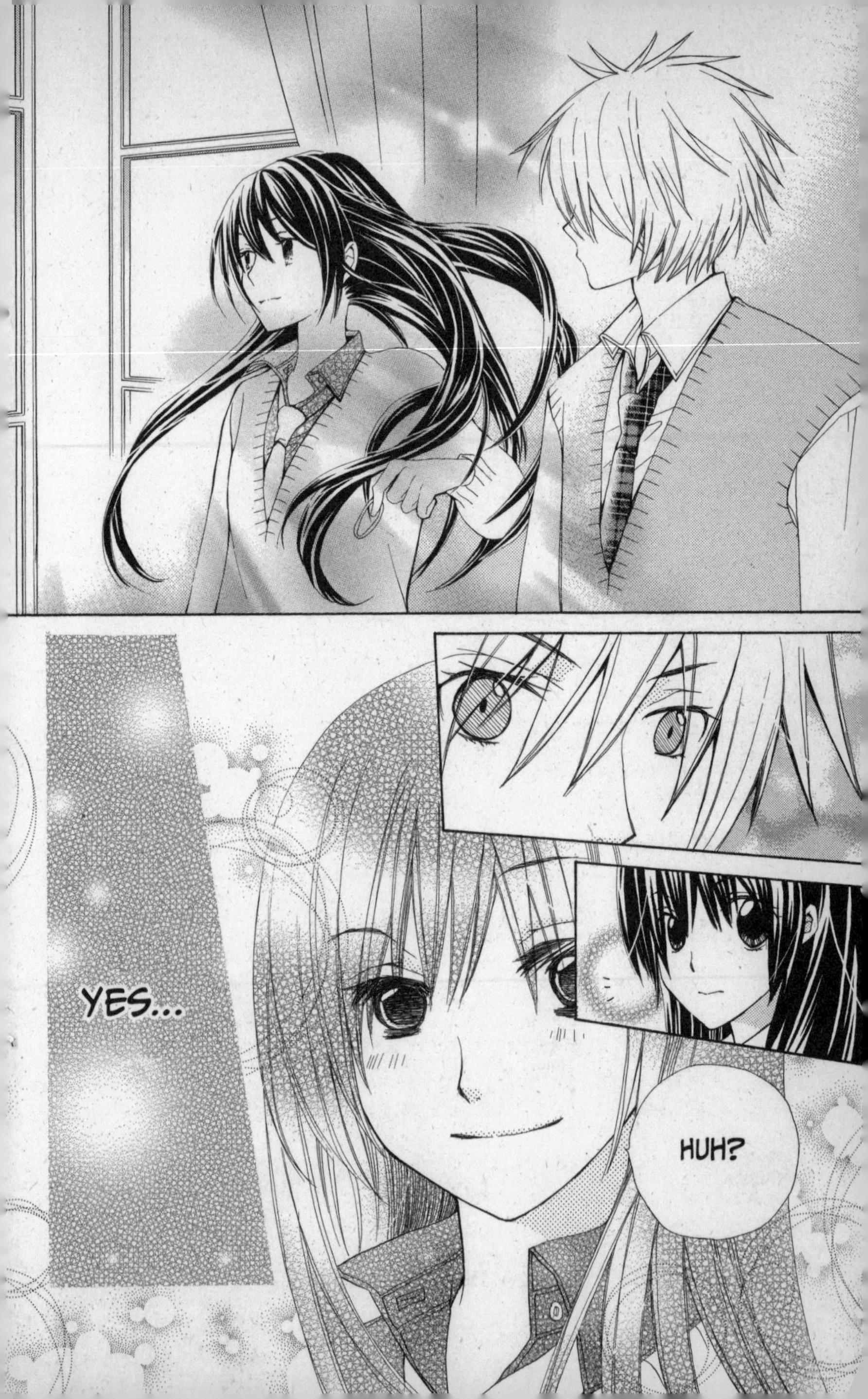
HUH?
YES...

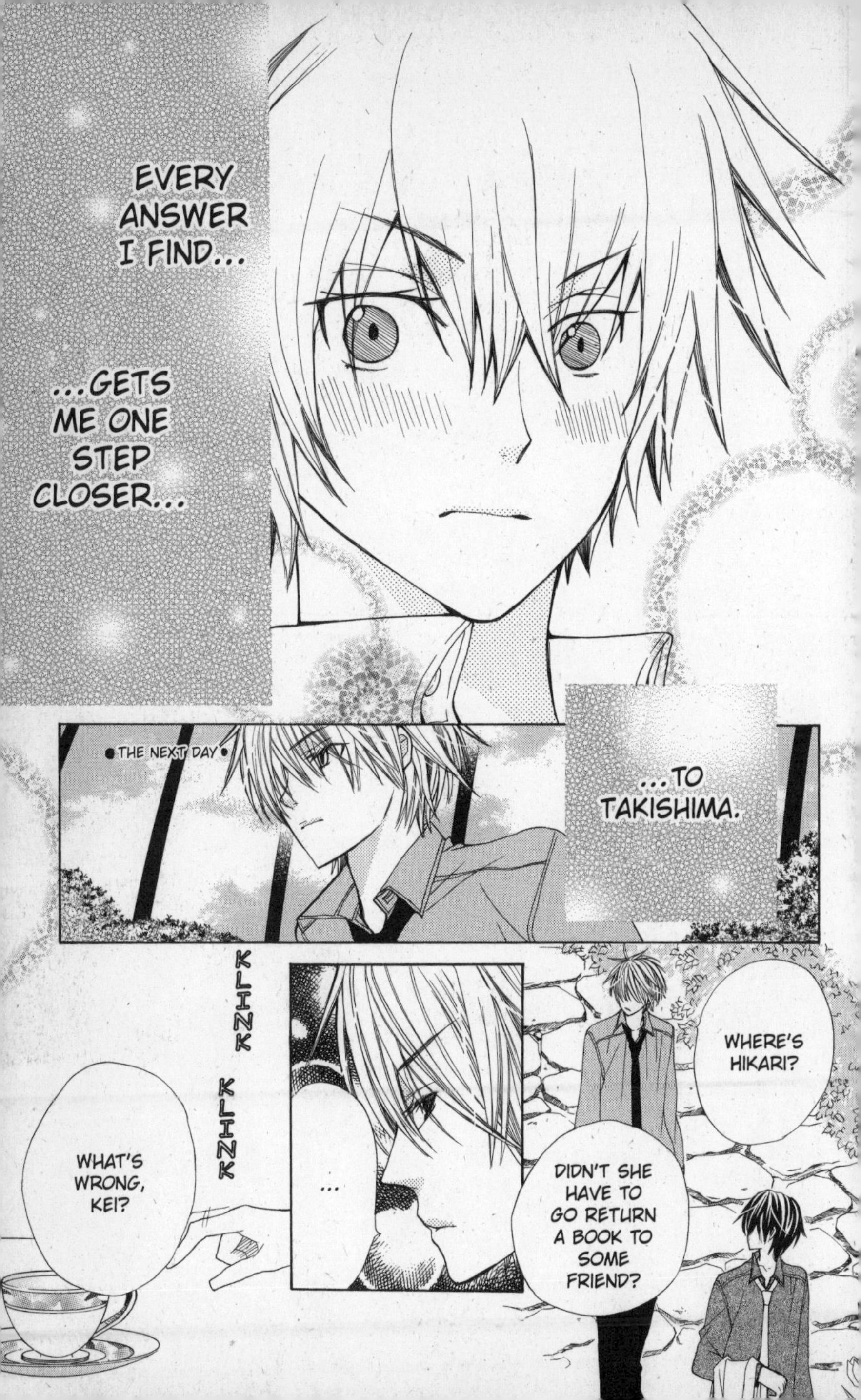
EVERY ANSWER I FIND...
...GETS ME ONE STEP CLOSER...
...TO TAKISHIMA.
THE NEXT DAY
WHERE'S HIKARI?
DIDN'T SHE HAVE TO GO RETURN A BOOK TO SOME FRIEND?
...
KLINK
KLINK
WHAT'S WRONG, KEI?

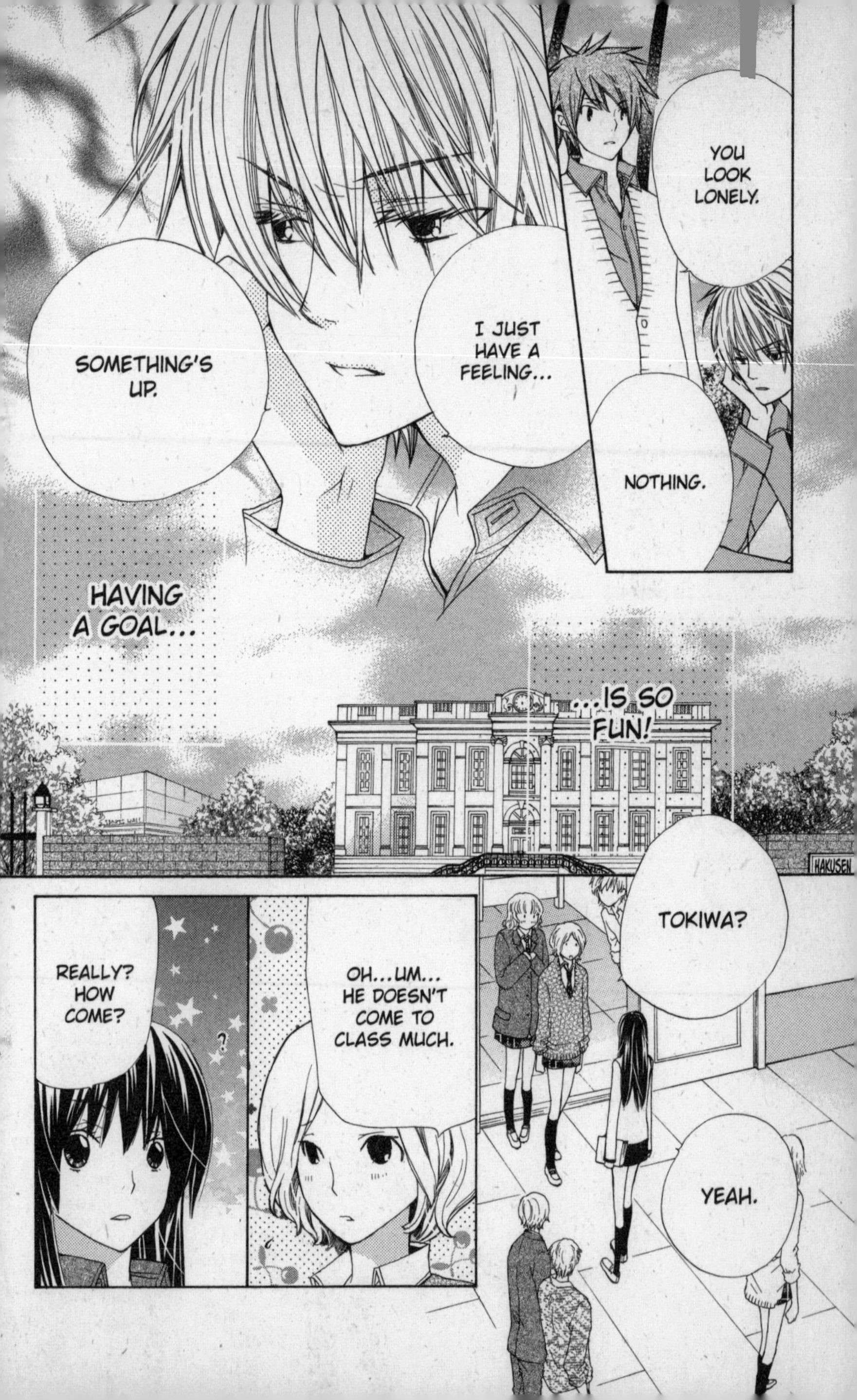
YOU LOOK LONELY.
NOTHING.
I JUST HAVE A FEELING...
SOMETHING'S UP.
HAVING A GOAL...
...IS SO FUN!
HAKUSEN
TOKIWA?
YEAH.
OH...UM... HE DOESN'T COME TO CLASS MUCH.
REALLY? HOW COME?

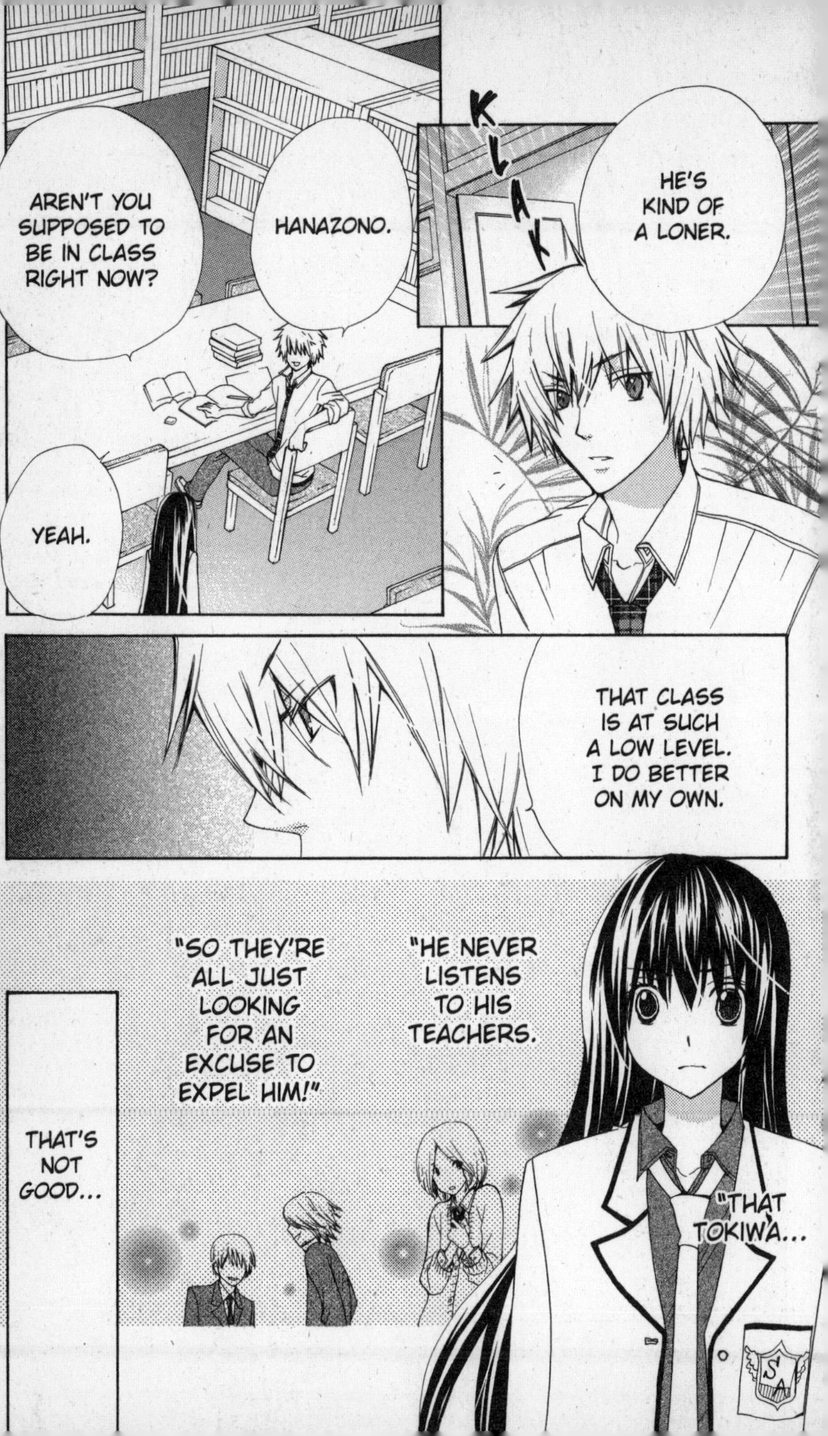
KLAK
HE'S KIND OF A LONER.
HANAZONO.
AREN'T YOU SUPPOSED TO BE IN CLASS RIGHT NOW?
YEAH.
THAT CLASS IS AT SUCH A LOW LEVEL. I DO BETTER ON MY OWN.
"THAT TOKIWA...
"HE NEVER LISTENS TO HIS TEACHERS.
"SO THEY'RE ALL JUST LOOKING FOR AN EXCUSE TO EXPEL HIM!"
THAT'S NOT GOOD...

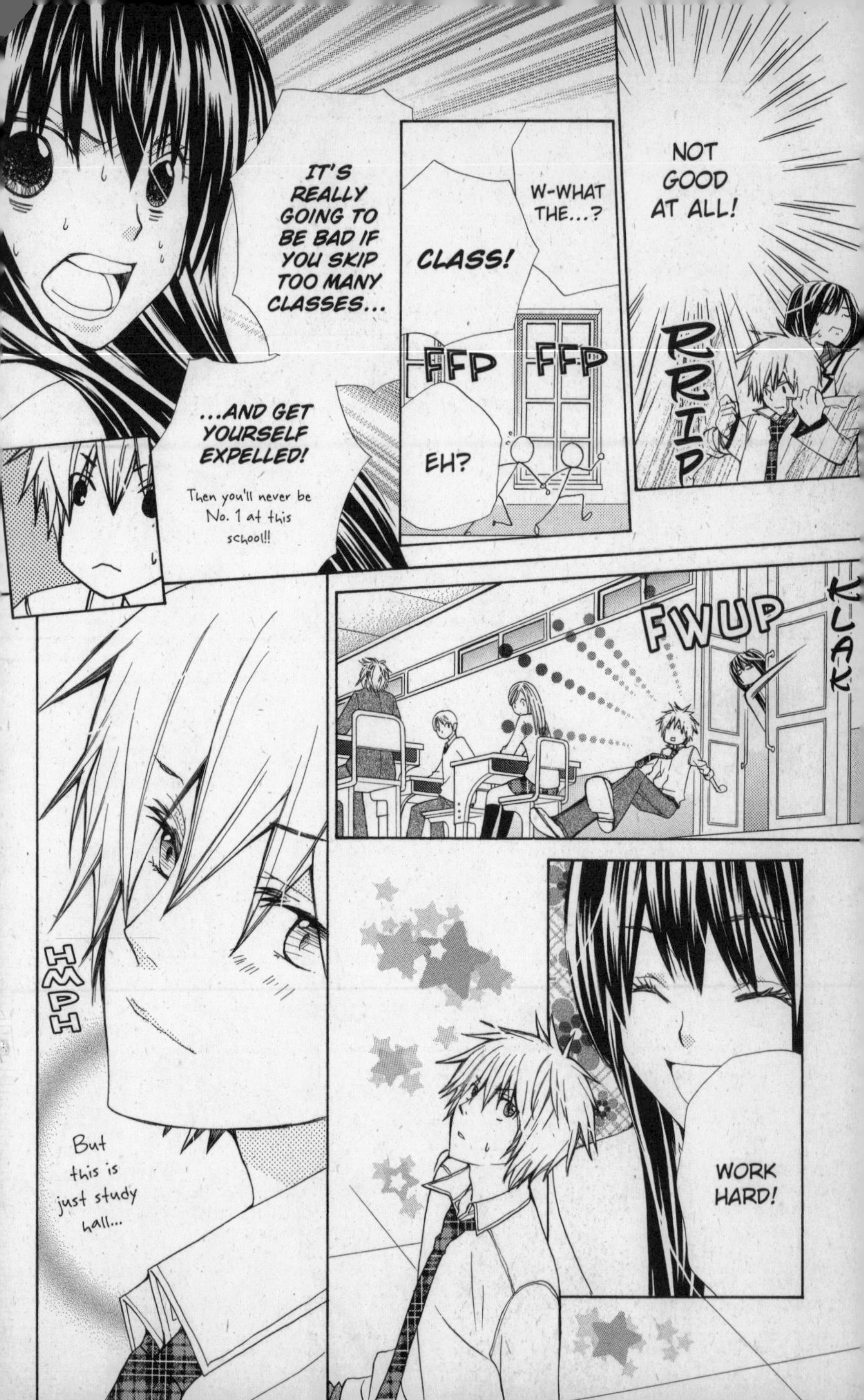
NOT GOOD AT ALL!
RRIP
W-WHAT THE...?
CLASS!
FFP
FFP
EH?
IT'S REALLY GOING TO BE BAD IF YOU SKIP TOO MANY CLASSES...
...AND GET YOURSELF EXPELLED!
Then you'll never be No. 1 at this school!!
KLAK
FWUP
WORK HARD!
HMPH
But this is just study hall...

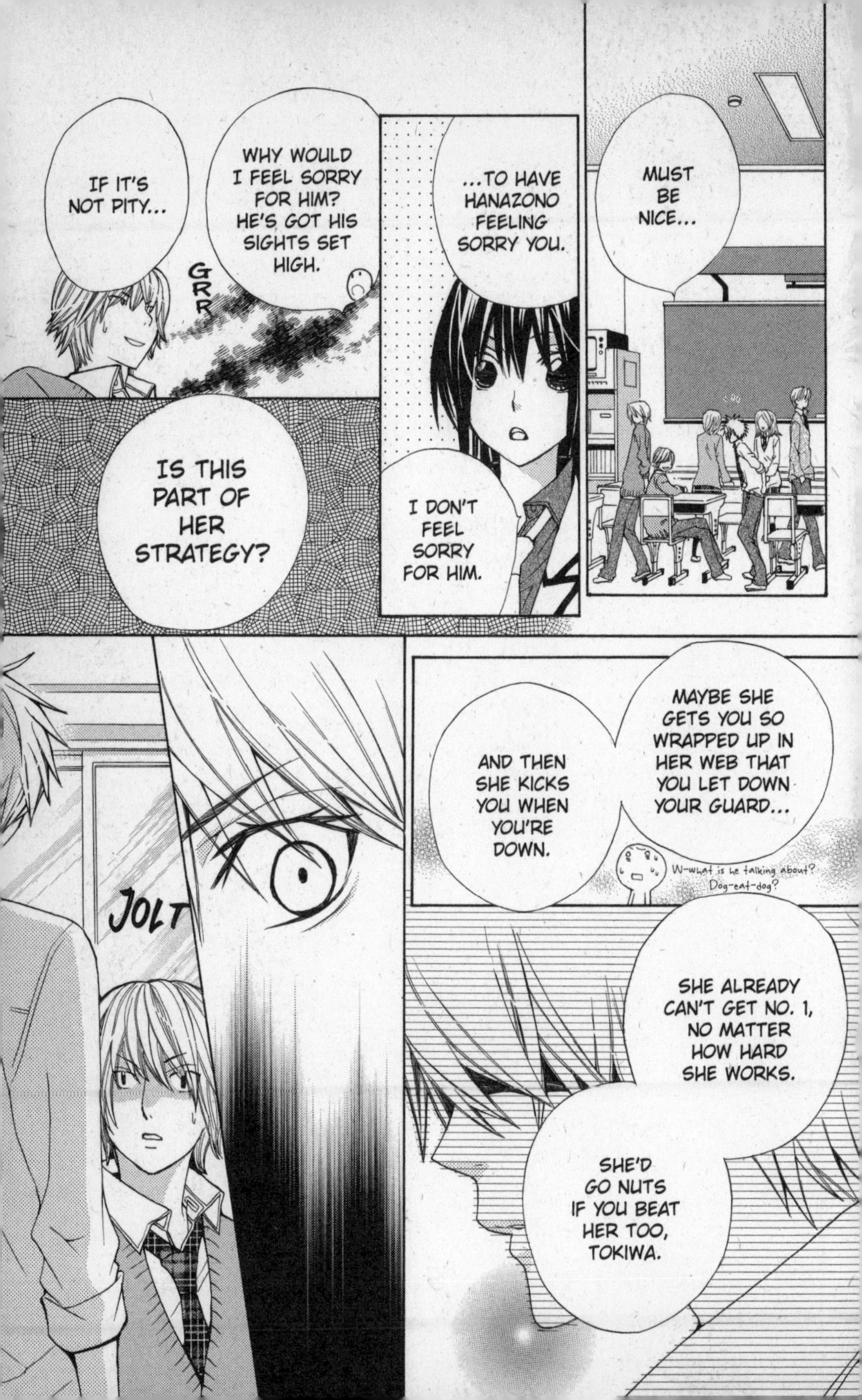
MUST BE NICE...
...TO HAVE HANAZONO FEELING SORRY YOU.
I DON'T FEEL SORRY FOR HIM.
WHY WOULD I FEEL SORRY FOR HIM? HE'S GOT HIS SIGHTS SET HIGH.
IF IT'S NOT PITY...
GRR
IS THIS PART OF HER STRATEGY?
MAYBE SHE GETS YOU SO WRAPPED UP IN HER WEB THAT YOU LET DOWN YOUR GUARD...
AND THEN SHE KICKS YOU WHEN YOU'RE DOWN.
W-what is he talking about? Dog-eat-dog?
SHE ALREADY CAN'T GET NO. 1, NO MATTER HOW HARD SHE WORKS.
SHE'D GO NUTS IF YOU BEAT HER TOO, TOKIWA.
JOLT

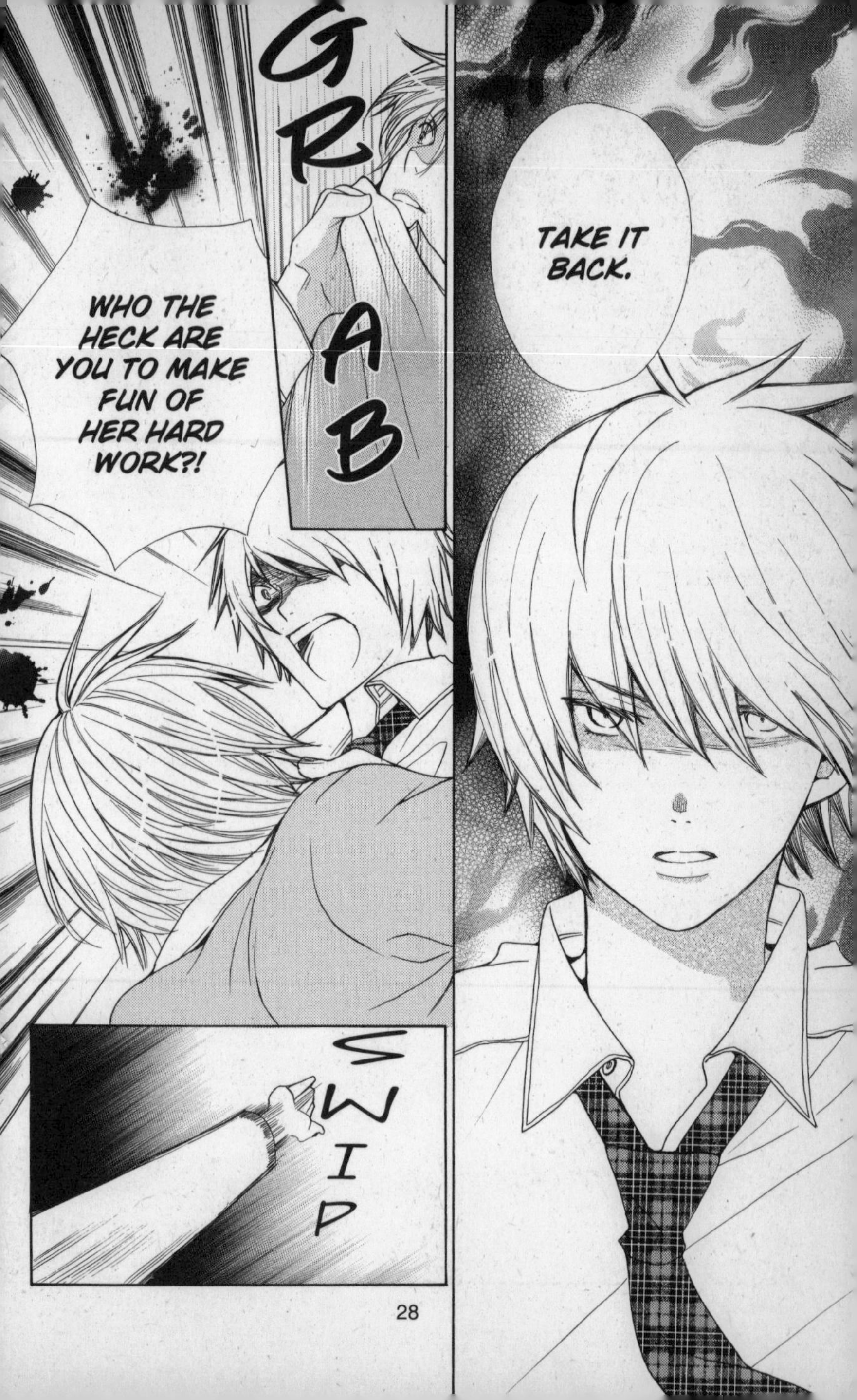
TAKE IT BACK.
GRAB
WHO THE HECK ARE YOU TO MAKE FUN OF HER HARD WORK?!
SWIP

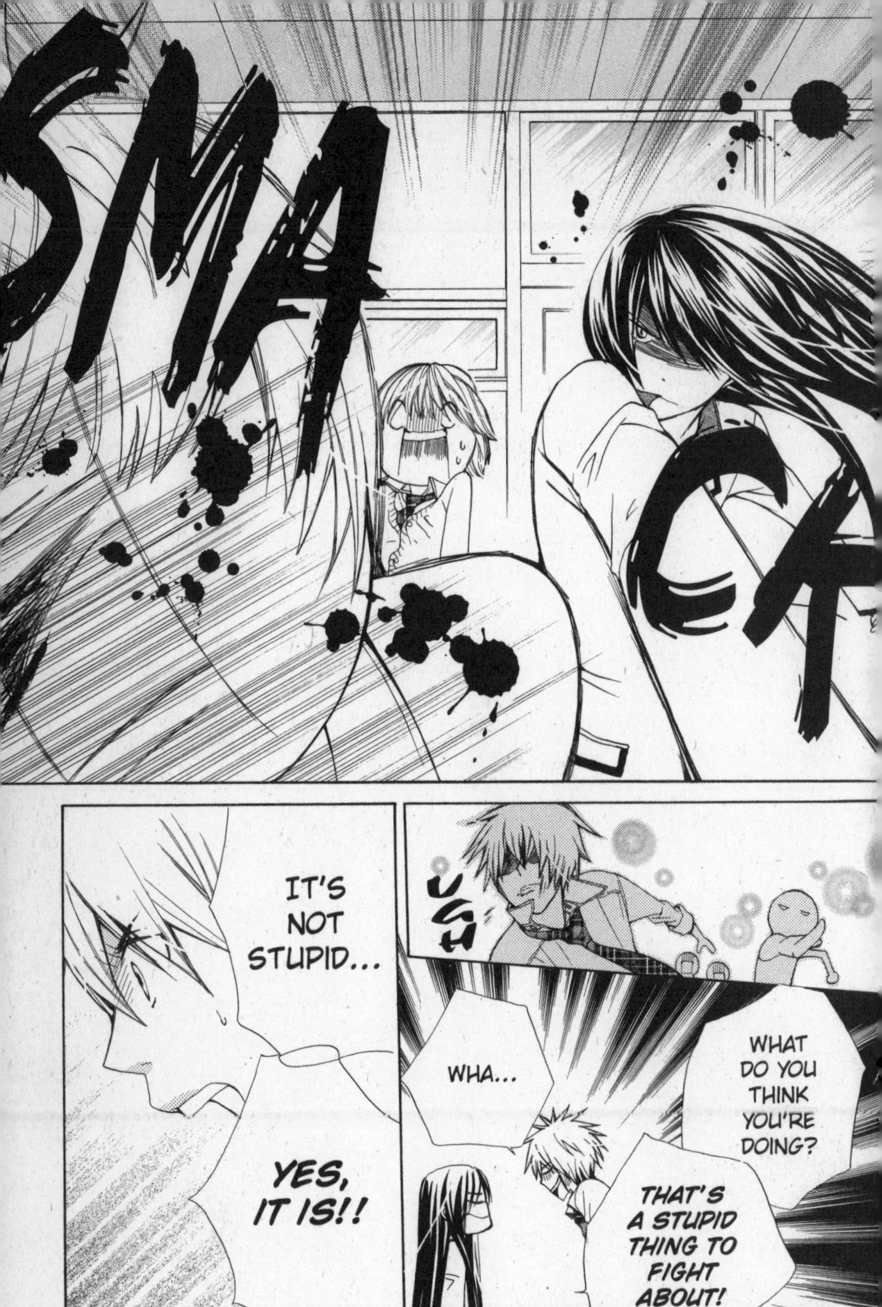
SMACK
UGH
WHAT DO YOU THINK YOU'RE DOING?
WHA...
THAT'S A STUPID THING TO FIGHT ABOUT!
IT'S NOT STUPID...
YES, IT IS!!

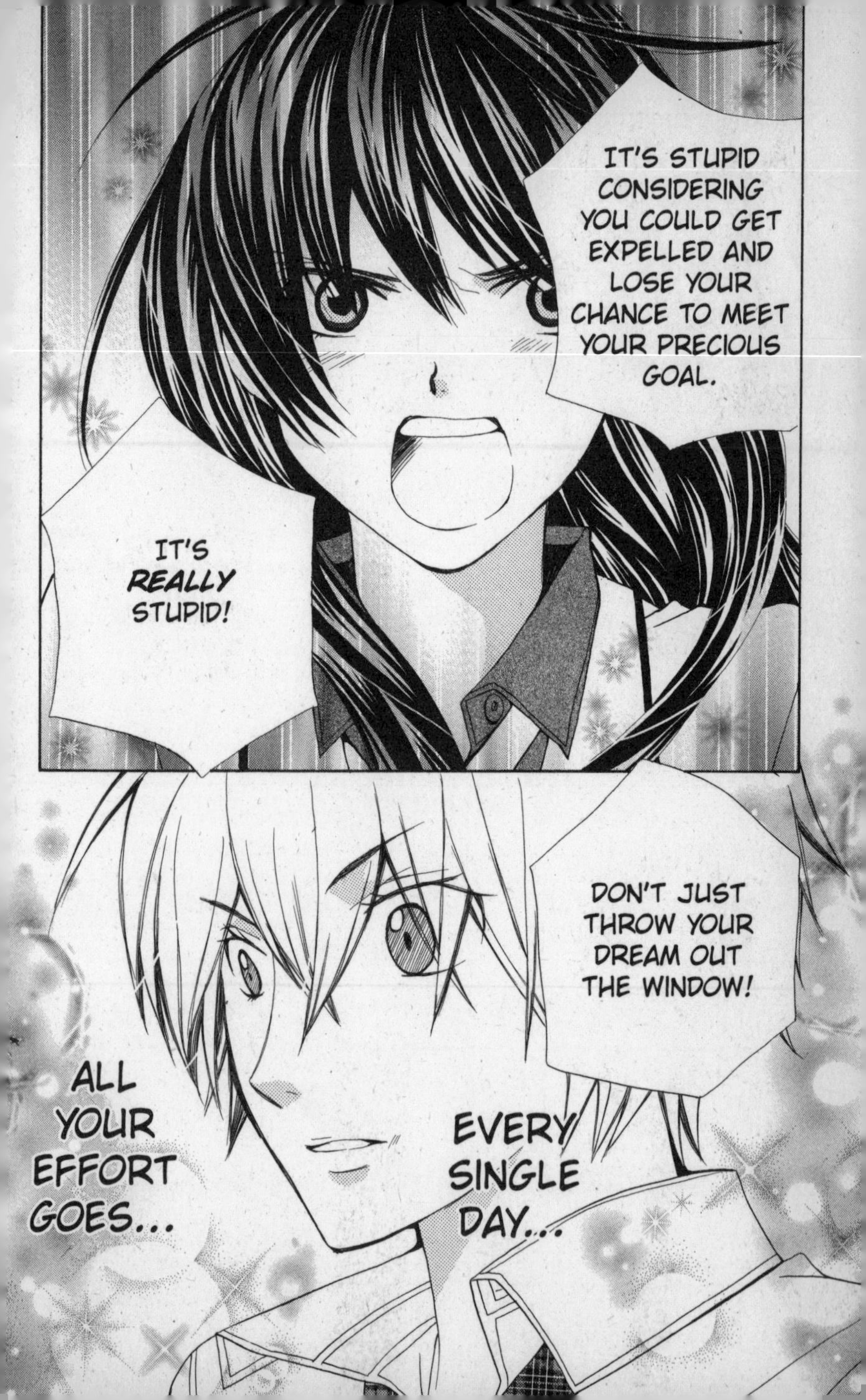
IT'S STUPID CONSIDERING YOU COULD GET EXPELLED AND LOSE YOUR CHANCE TO MEET YOUR PRECIOUS GOAL.
IT'S *REALLY* STUPID!
DON'T JUST THROW YOUR DREAM OUT THE WINDOW!
EVERY SINGLE DAY...
ALL YOUR EFFORT GOES...

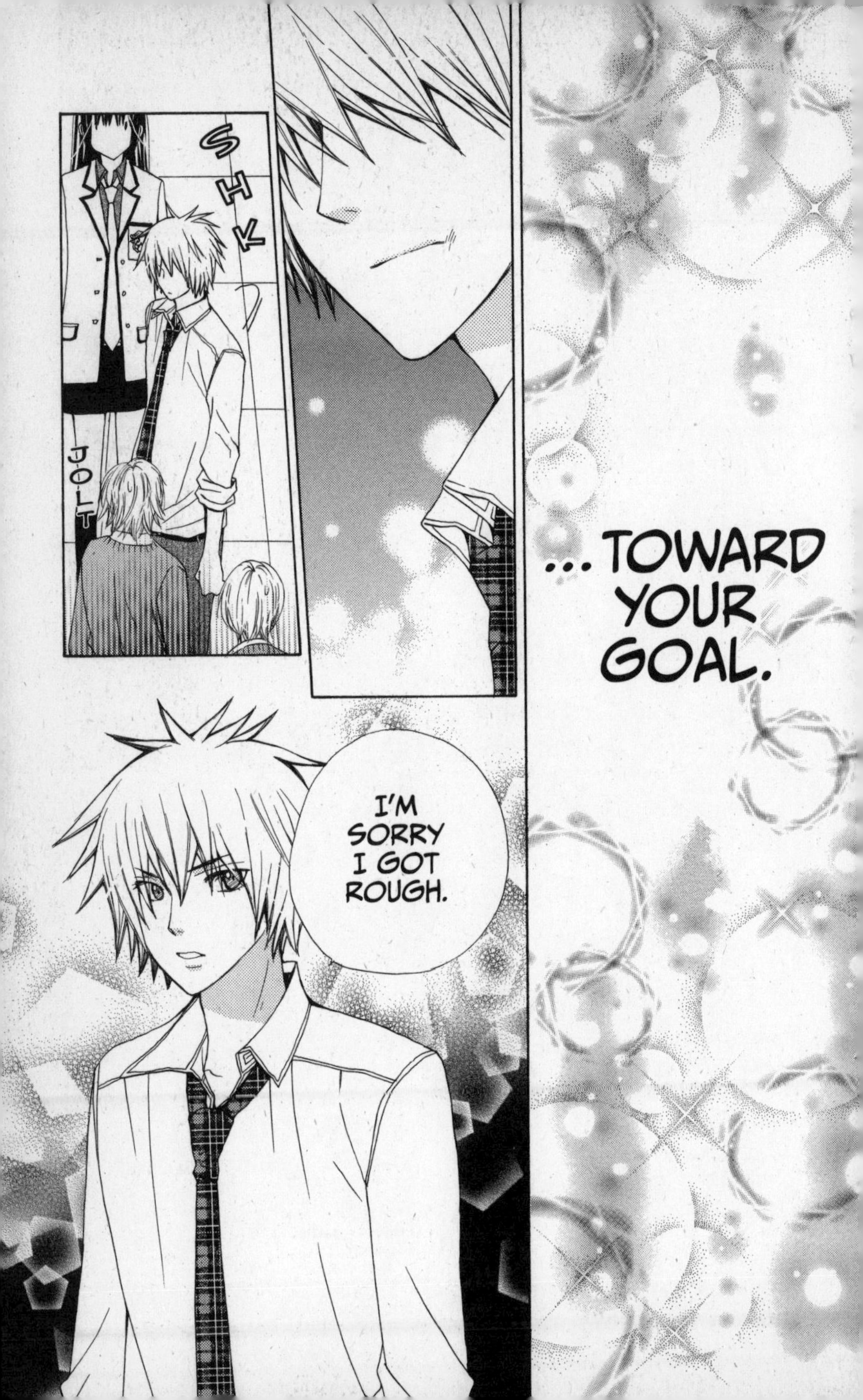
...TOWARD YOUR GOAL.
SHK
JOLT
I'M SORRY I GOT ROUGH.

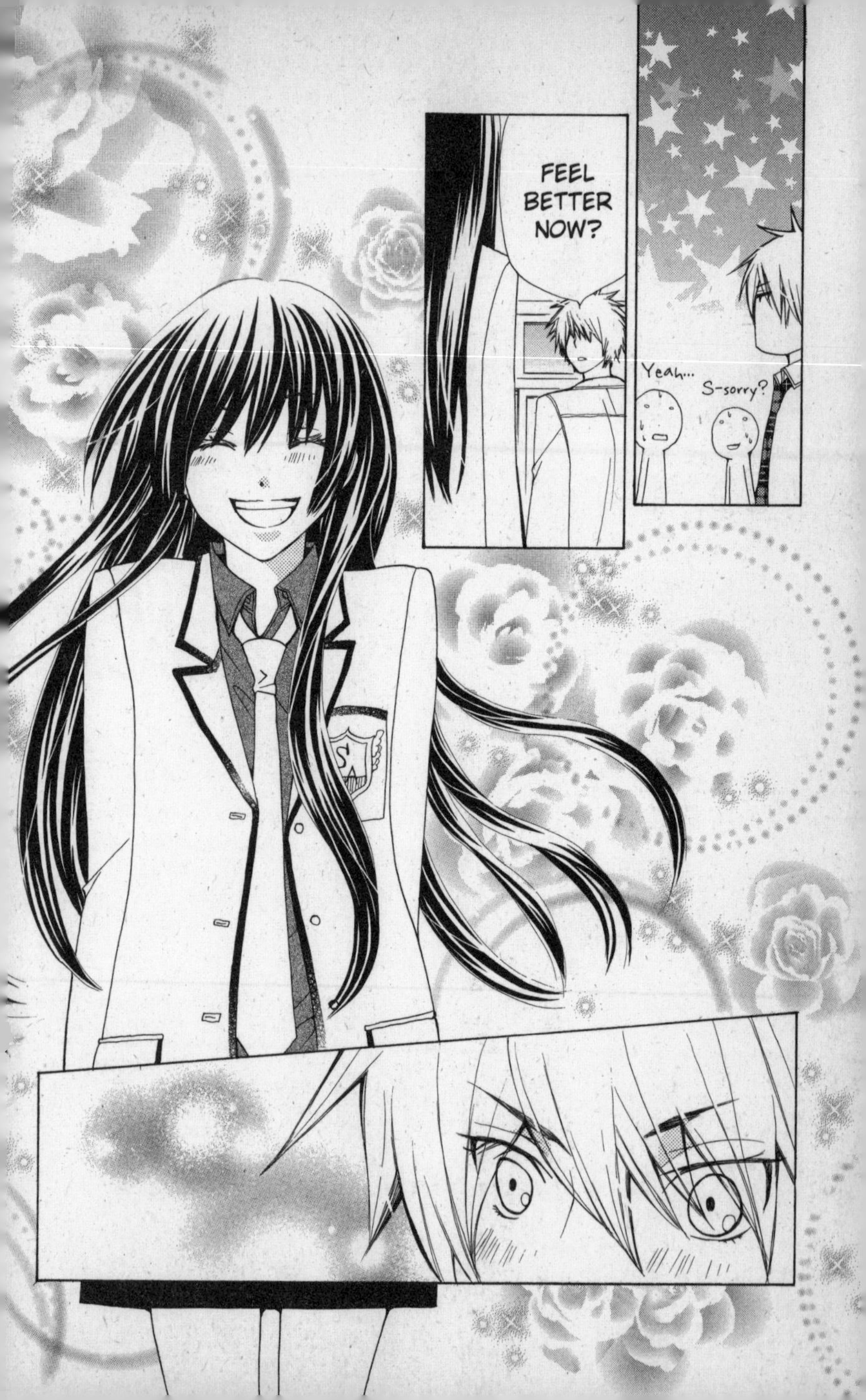
S-sorry?
Yeah...
FEEL BETTER NOW?

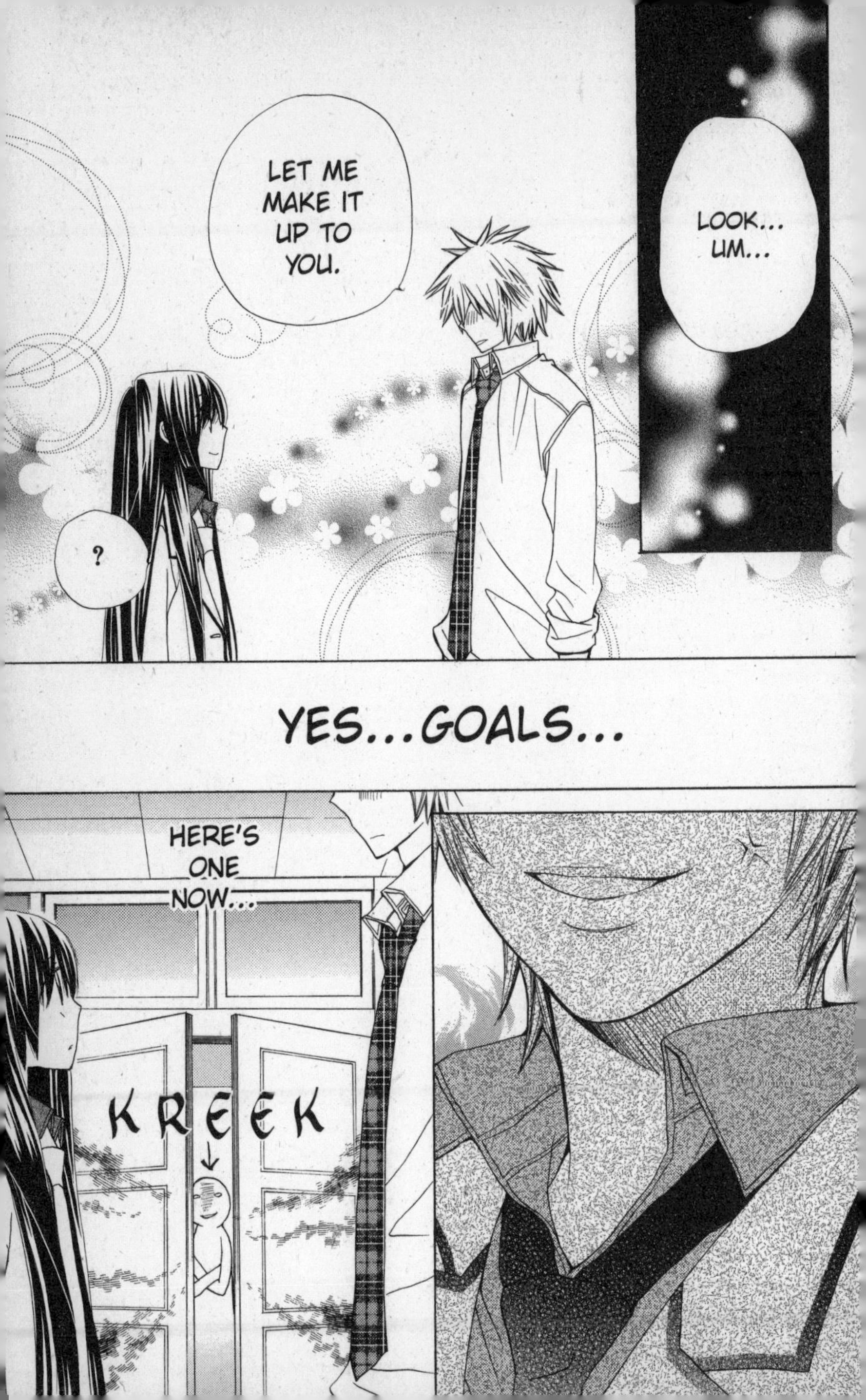
LOOK... UM...
LET ME MAKE IT UP TO YOU.
?
YES...GOALS...
HERE'S ONE NOW...
KREEK

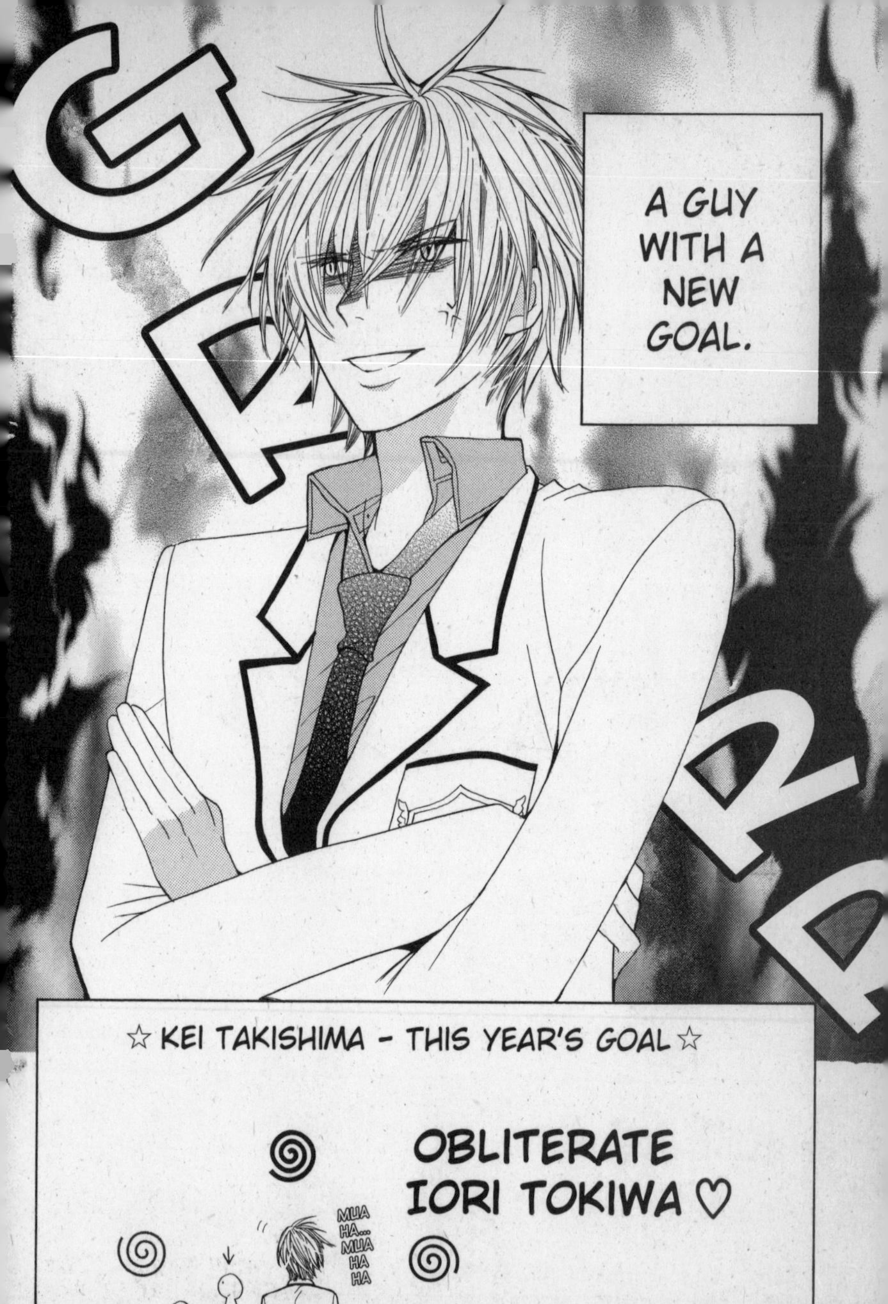

A GUY WITH A NEW GOAL.
GRRR
☆ KEI TAKISHIMA - THIS YEAR'S GOAL ☆
◎ OBLITERATE IORI TOKIWA ♡ ◎
◎
MUA HA... MUA HA HA

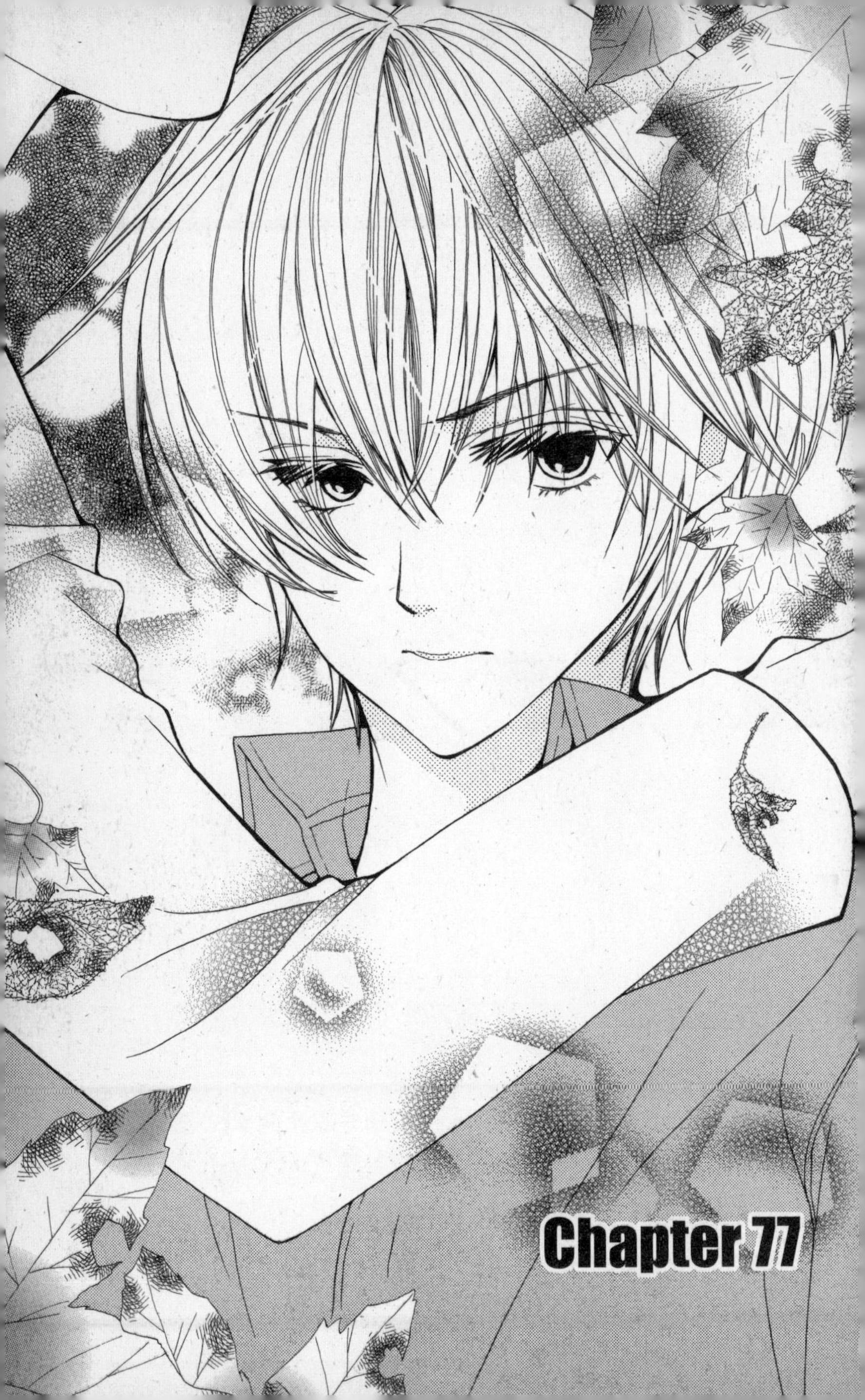
Chapter 77

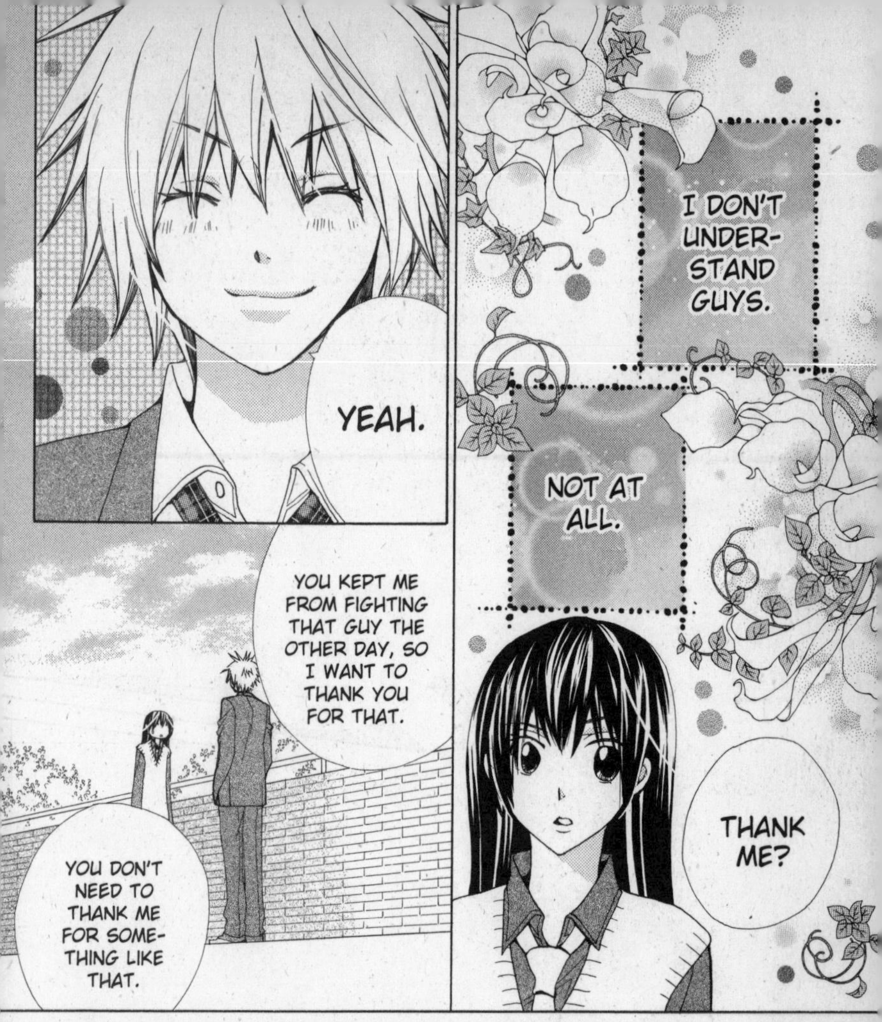
I DON'T UNDER-STAND GUYS.
NOT AT ALL.
THANK ME?
YEAH.
YOU KEPT ME FROM FIGHTING THAT GUY THE OTHER DAY, SO I WANT TO THANK YOU FOR THAT.
YOU DON'T NEED TO THANK ME FOR SOME-THING LIKE THAT.

· S.A CAFÉ ·

I GOT TO GO TO THE *S.A* CAFÉ THAT WAS OPEN ON APRIL 19 AND 20, 2008. THE IDEA WAS THAT ALL THE GUYS FROM *S.A* WERE REALLY STUDENTS AT HARAJUKU'S EDELSTEIN. I WAS SO EXCITED WHEN I WENT IN AND KEI WAS THE HOST! (EVEN THOUGH IT WAS KIND OF STRANGE.)→

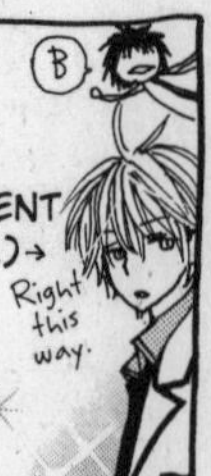
B
Right this way.

I TRIED NOT TO STARE THE WHOLE TIME, BUT I KNOW THAT I WASN'T THE ONLY ONE WHO WAS SHOCKED BY HOW MANY CUTE GUYS THERE WERE.
THANK YOU SO MUCH FOR GIVING ME THIS ONCE-IN-A-LIFETIME CHANCE TO SEE MY CHARACTERS IN REAL LIFE!!

The servers did such a great job! Everything was delicious!!

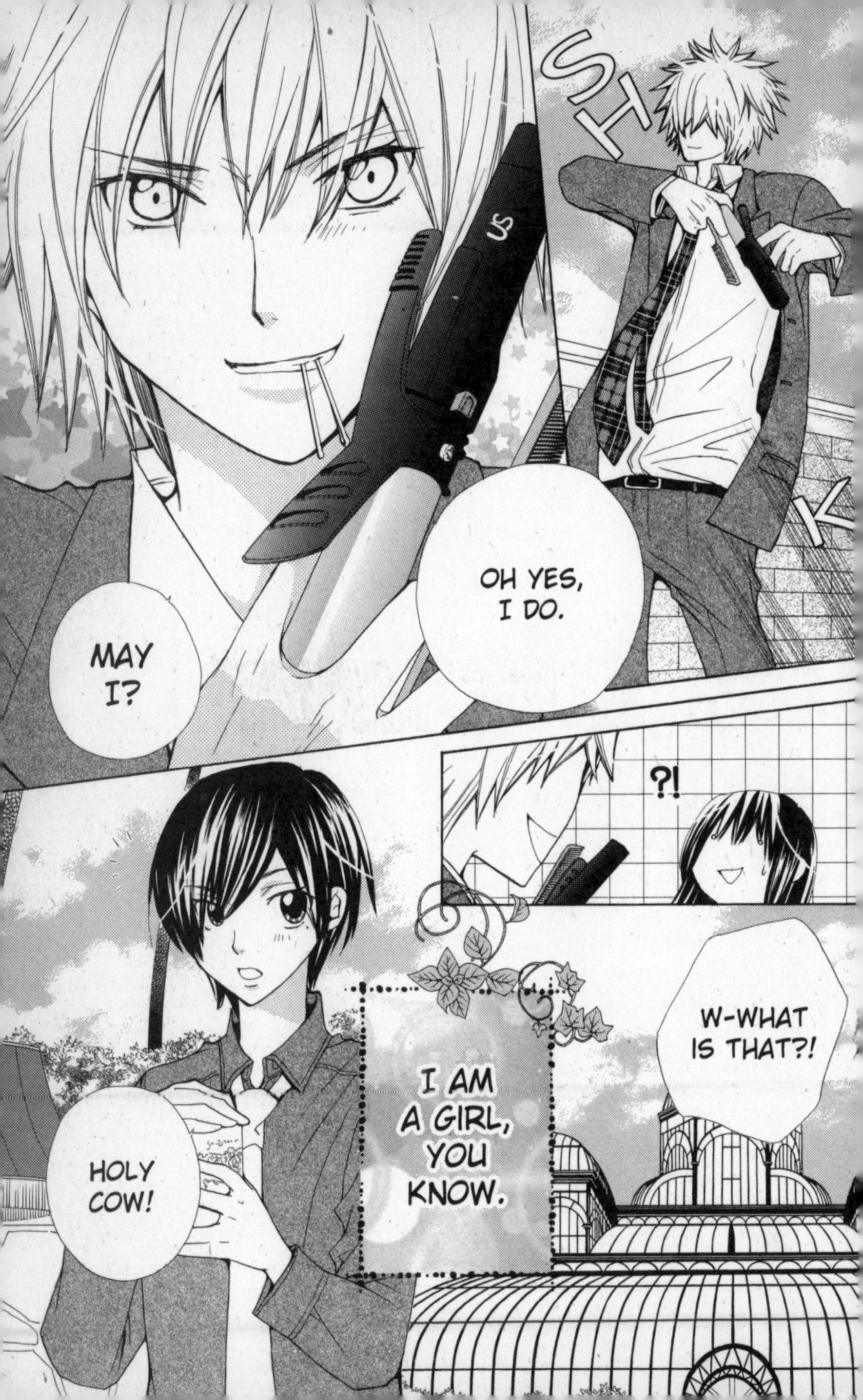
SH
K
OH YES, I DO.
MAY I?
?!
W-WHAT IS THAT?!
I AM A GIRL, YOU KNOW.
HOLY COW!

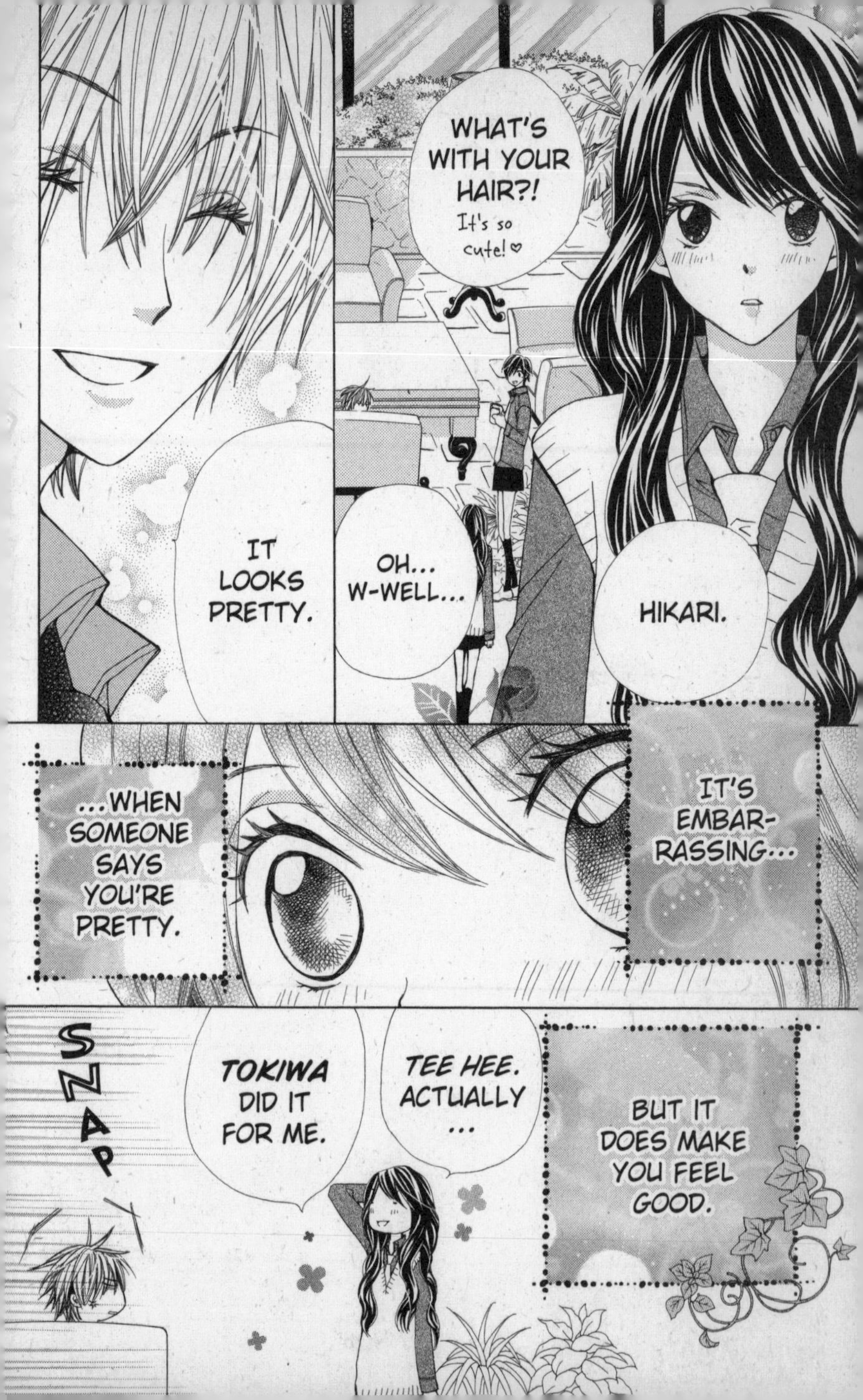
HIKARI.
WHAT'S WITH YOUR HAIR?! It's so cute! ♡
OH... W-WELL...
IT LOOKS PRETTY.
IT'S EMBARRASSING...
...WHEN SOMEONE SAYS YOU'RE PRETTY.
BUT IT DOES MAKE YOU FEEL GOOD.
TEE HEE. ACTUALLY...
TOKIWA DID IT FOR ME.
SNAP

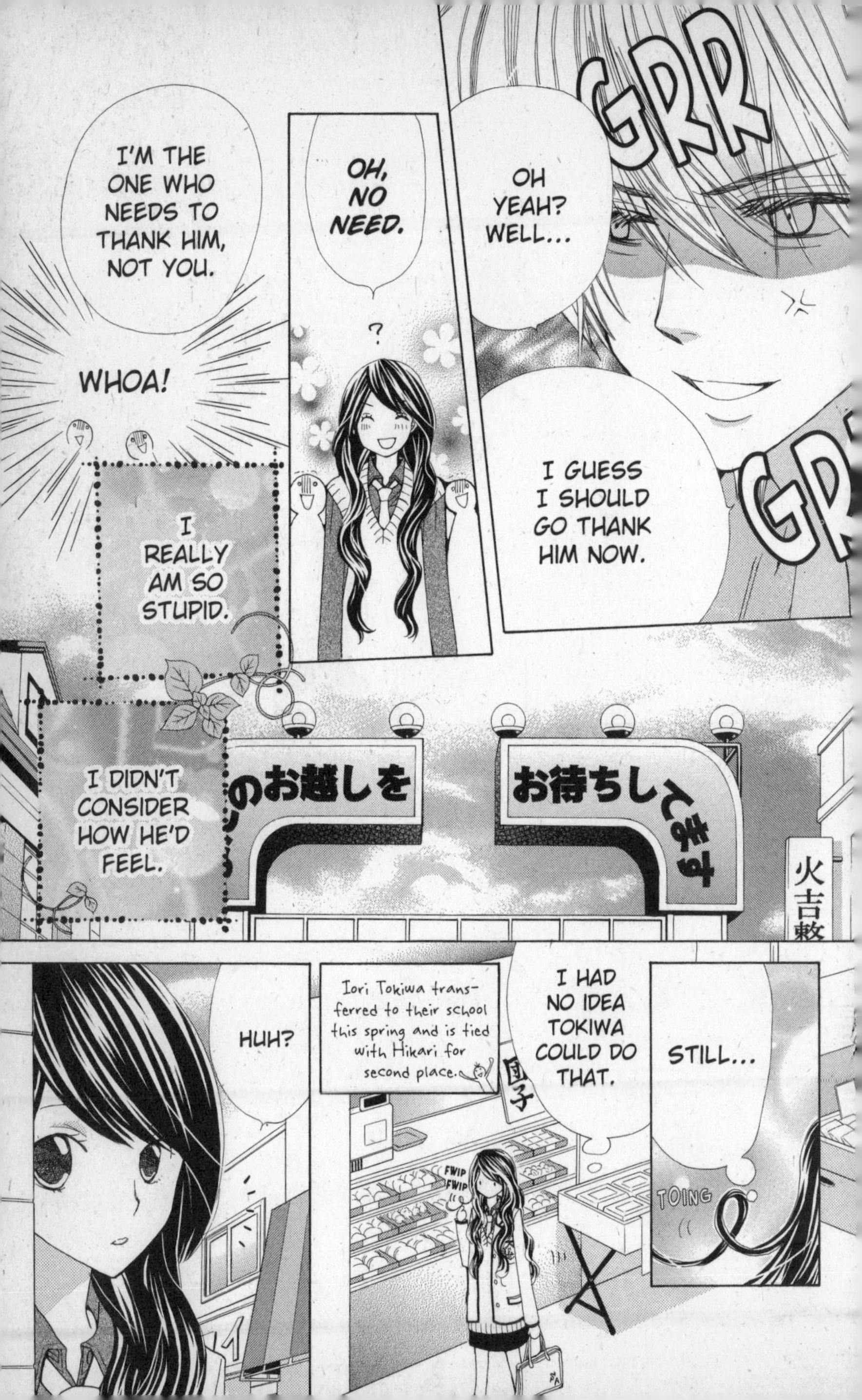
GRR
OH YEAH? WELL...
I GUESS I SHOULD GO THANK HIM NOW.
GR
OH, NO NEED.
?
I'M THE ONE WHO NEEDS TO THANK HIM, NOT YOU.
WHOA!
お待ちしてます
のお越しを
I REALLY AM SO STUPID.
I DIDN'T CONSIDER HOW HE'D FEEL.
STILL...
TOING
I HAD NO IDEA TOKIWA COULD DO THAT.
団子
Iori Tokiwa transferred to their school this spring and is tied with Hikari for second place.
FWIP FWIP
HUH?

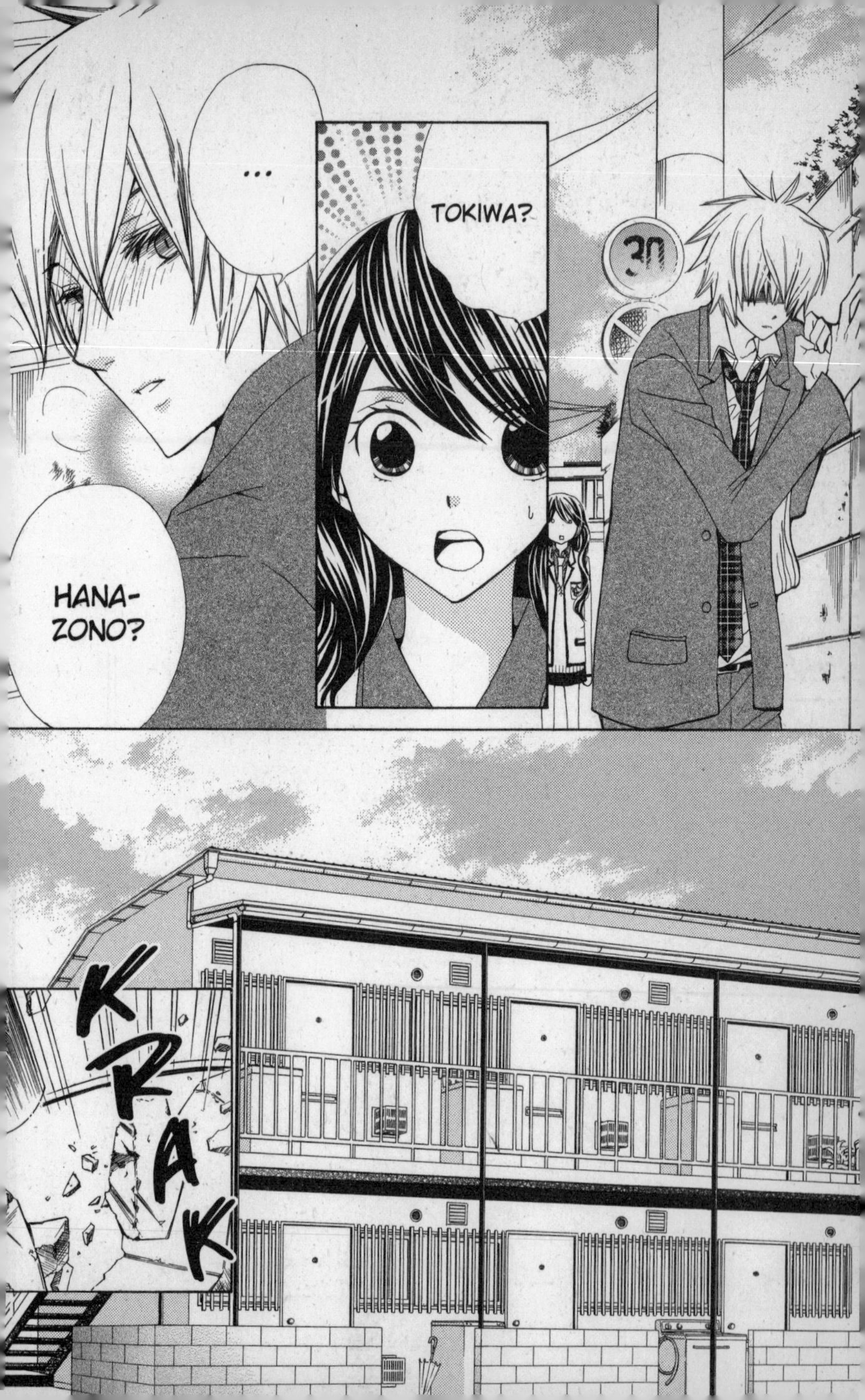
TOKIWA?
...
HANA-ZONO?
KRAK

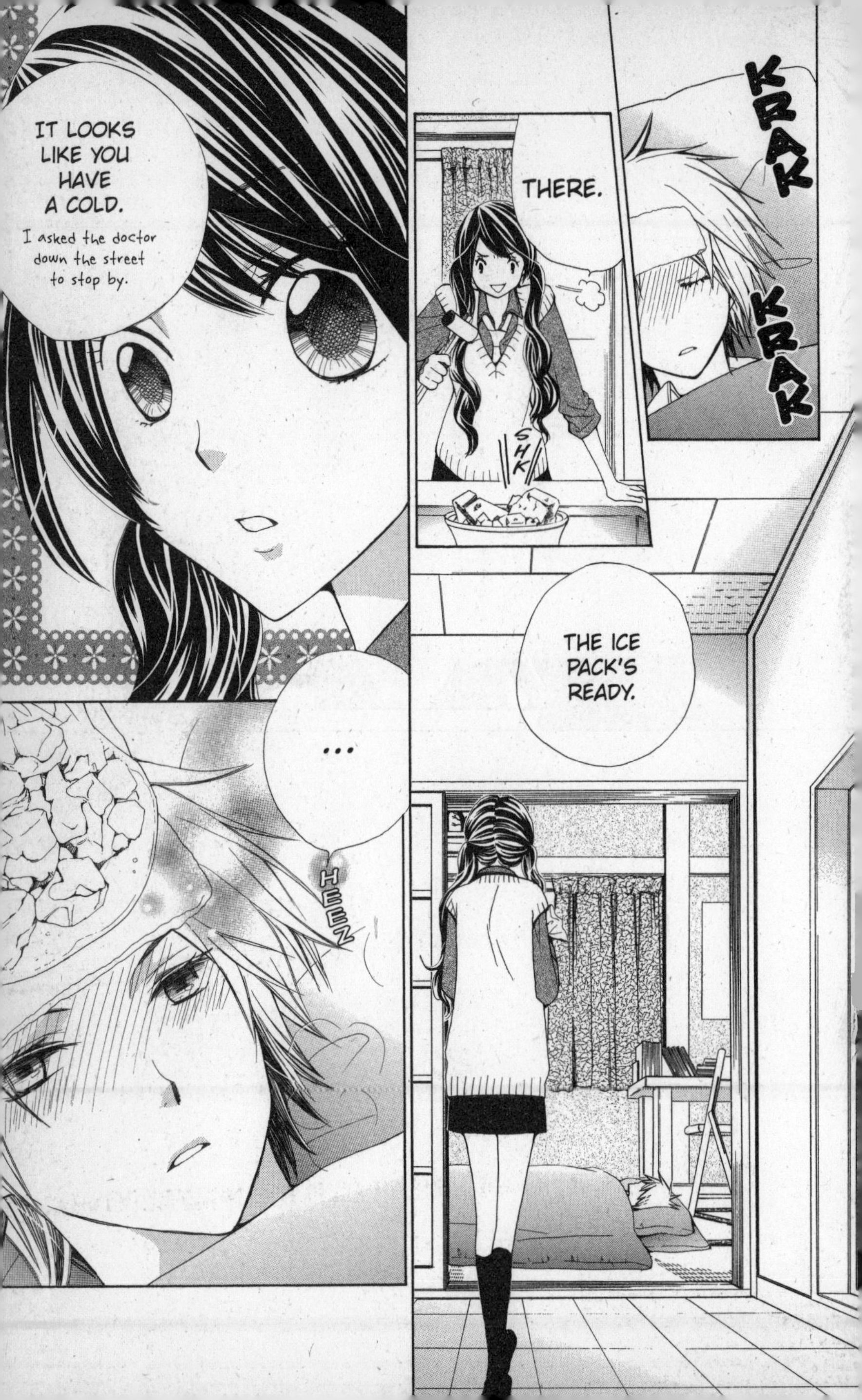
KRAK KRAK
THERE.
SHK
THE ICE PACK'S READY.
IT LOOKS LIKE YOU HAVE A COLD.
I asked the doctor down the street to stop by.
...
HEEZ

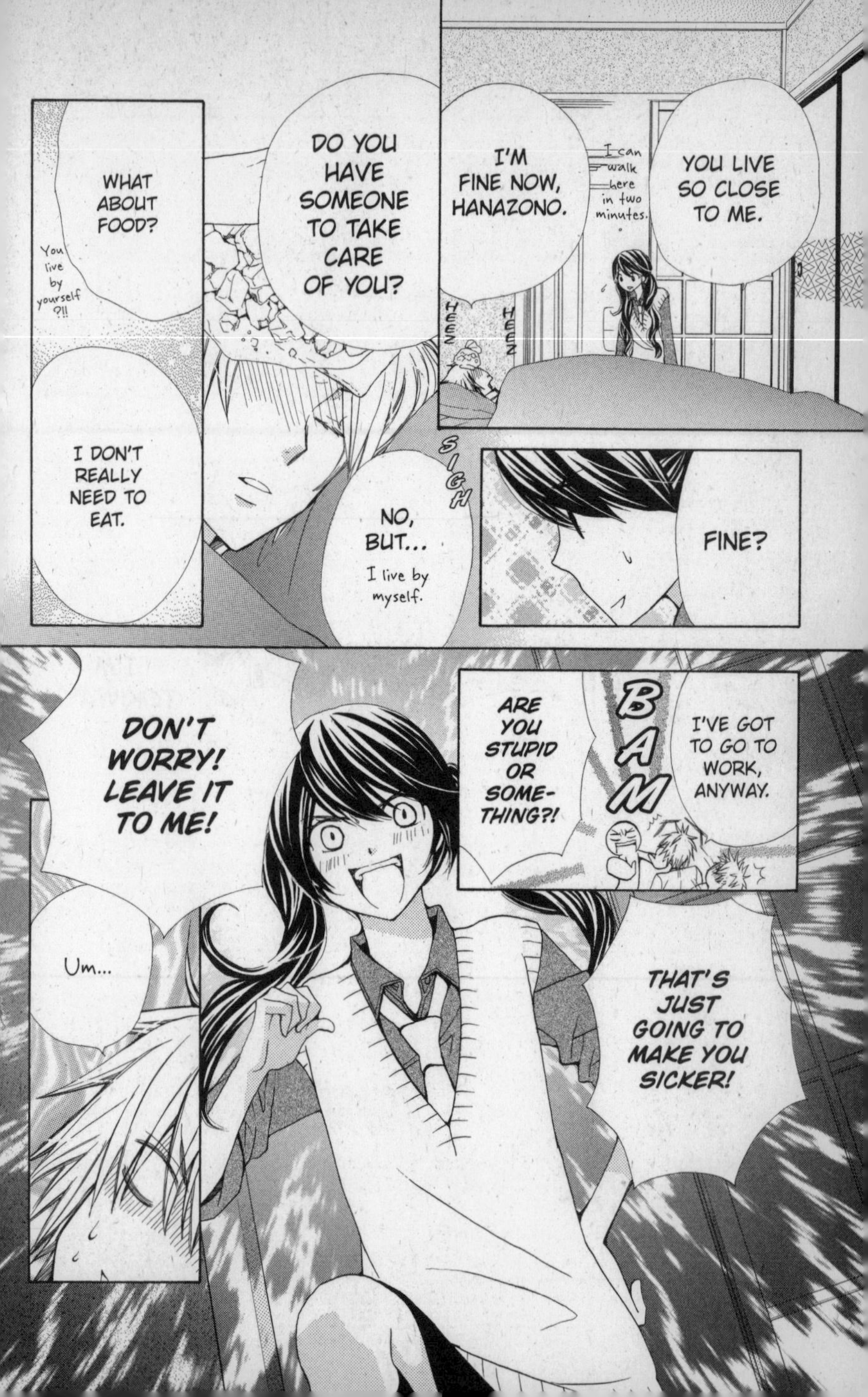
YOU LIVE SO CLOSE TO ME.
I can walk here in two minutes.
I'M FINE NOW, HANAZONO.
HEEZ
HEEZ
FINE?
SIGH
DO YOU HAVE SOMEONE TO TAKE CARE OF YOU?
NO, BUT...
I live by myself.
WHAT ABOUT FOOD?
You live by yourself?!!
I DON'T REALLY NEED TO EAT.
I'VE GOT TO GO TO WORK, ANYWAY.
BAM
ARE YOU STUPID OR SOME-THING?!
THAT'S JUST GOING TO MAKE YOU SICKER!
DON'T WORRY! LEAVE IT TO ME!
Um...

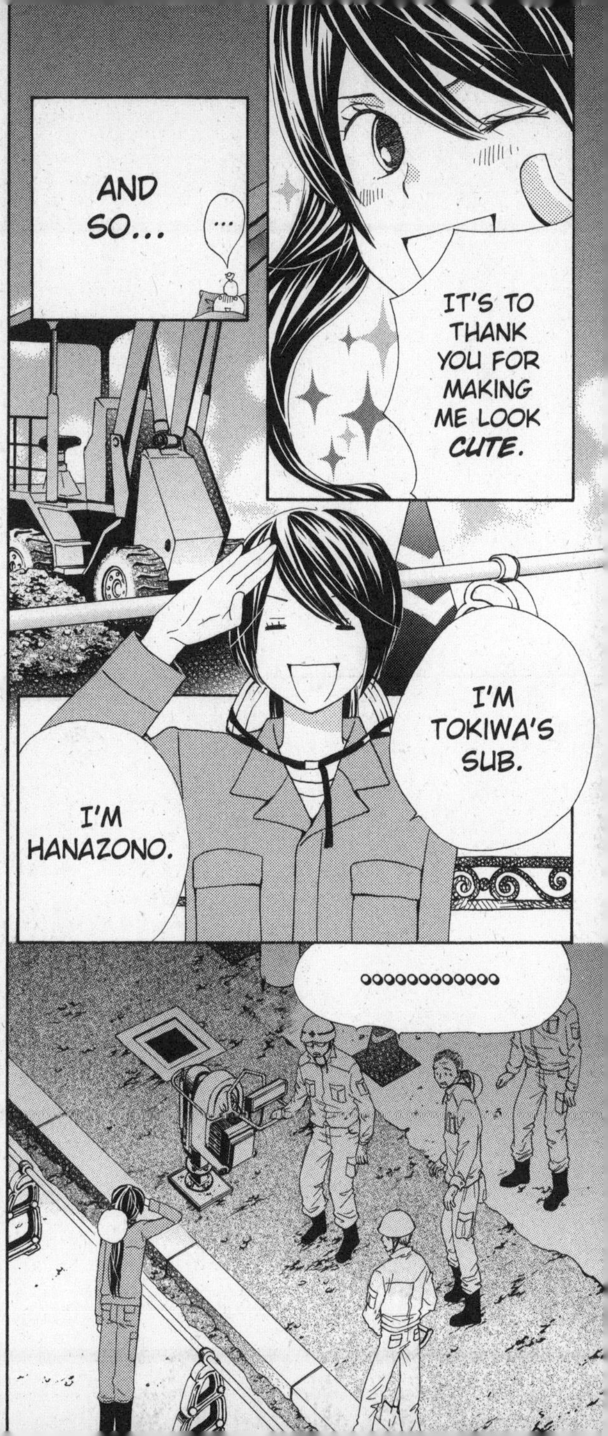
IT'S TO THANK YOU FOR MAKING ME LOOK CUTE.
AND SO...
...
I'M TOKIWA'S SUB.
I'M HANAZONO.
OOOOOOOOOOOO

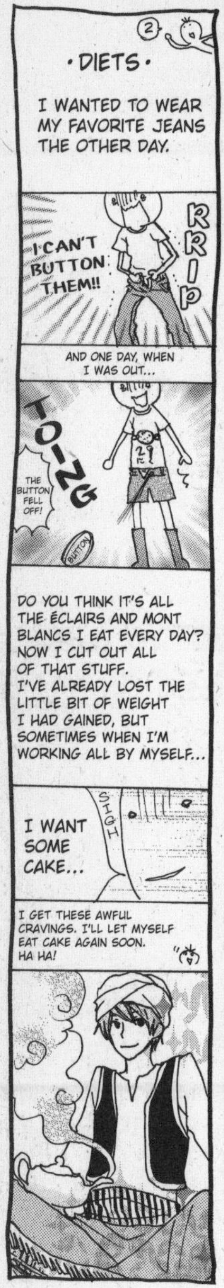
2
• DIETS •
I WANTED TO WEAR MY FAVORITE JEANS THE OTHER DAY.
RRIP
I CAN'T BUTTON THEM!!
AND ONE DAY, WHEN I WAS OUT...
TOING
THE BUTTON FELL OFF!
BUTTON
DO YOU THINK IT'S ALL THE ÉCLAIRS AND MONT BLANCS I EAT EVERY DAY? NOW I CUT OUT ALL OF THAT STUFF. I'VE ALREADY LOST THE LITTLE BIT OF WEIGHT I HAD GAINED, BUT SOMETIMES WHEN I'M WORKING ALL BY MYSELF...
SIGH
I WANT SOME CAKE...
I GET THESE AWFUL CRAVINGS. I'LL LET MYSELF EAT CAKE AGAIN SOON. HA HA!

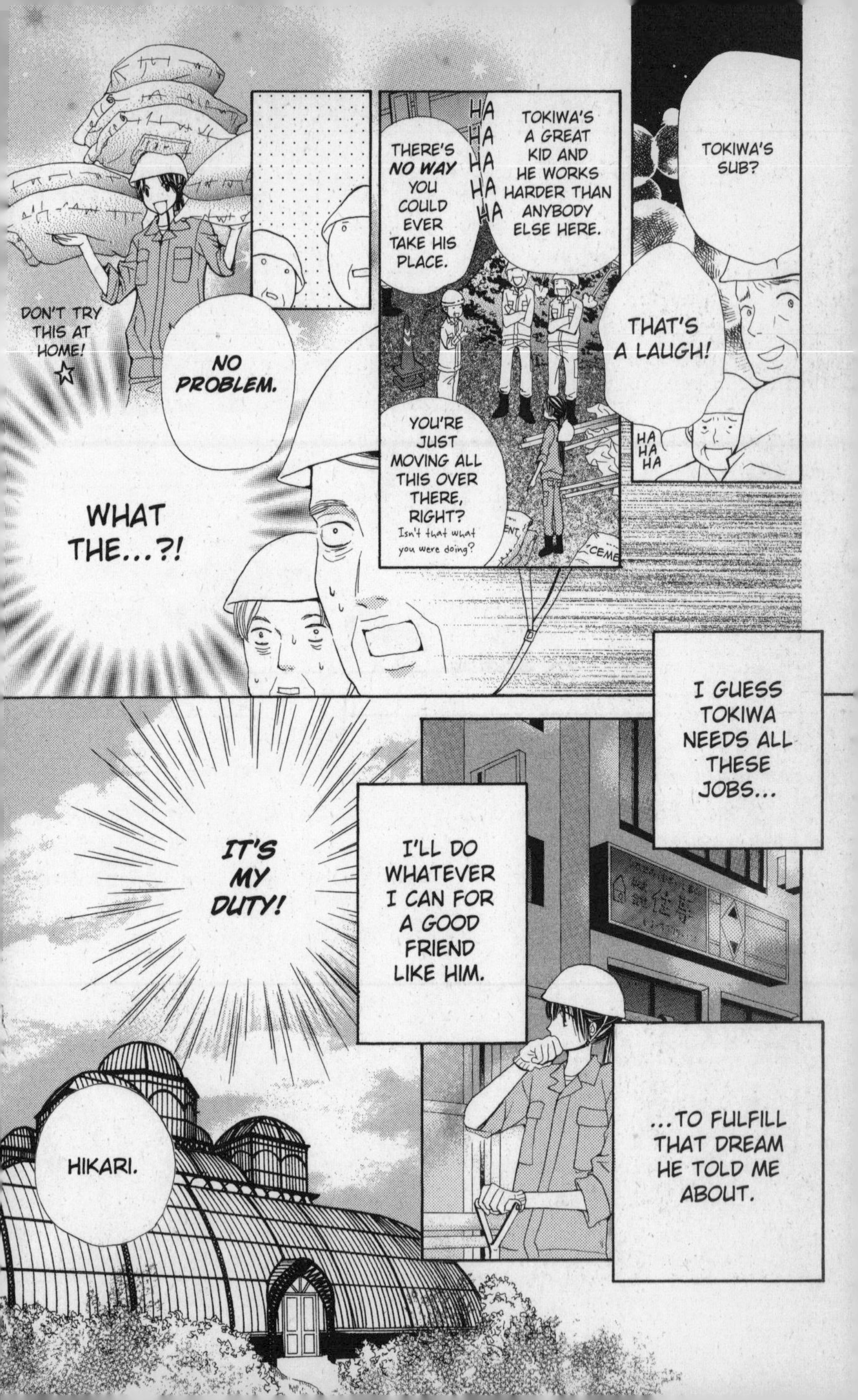
TOKIWA'S SUB?
THAT'S A LAUGH!
HA HA HA
TOKIWA'S A GREAT KID AND HE WORKS HARDER THAN ANYBODY ELSE HERE.
HA HA HA HA HA
THERE'S NO WAY YOU COULD EVER TAKE HIS PLACE.
YOU'RE JUST MOVING ALL THIS OVER THERE, RIGHT?
Isn't that what you were doing?
NO PROBLEM.
DON'T TRY THIS AT HOME! ☆
WHAT THE...?!
I GUESS TOKIWA NEEDS ALL THESE JOBS...
...TO FULFILL THAT DREAM HE TOLD ME ABOUT.
I'LL DO WHATEVER I CAN FOR A GOOD FRIEND LIKE HIM.
IT'S MY DUTY!
HIKARI.

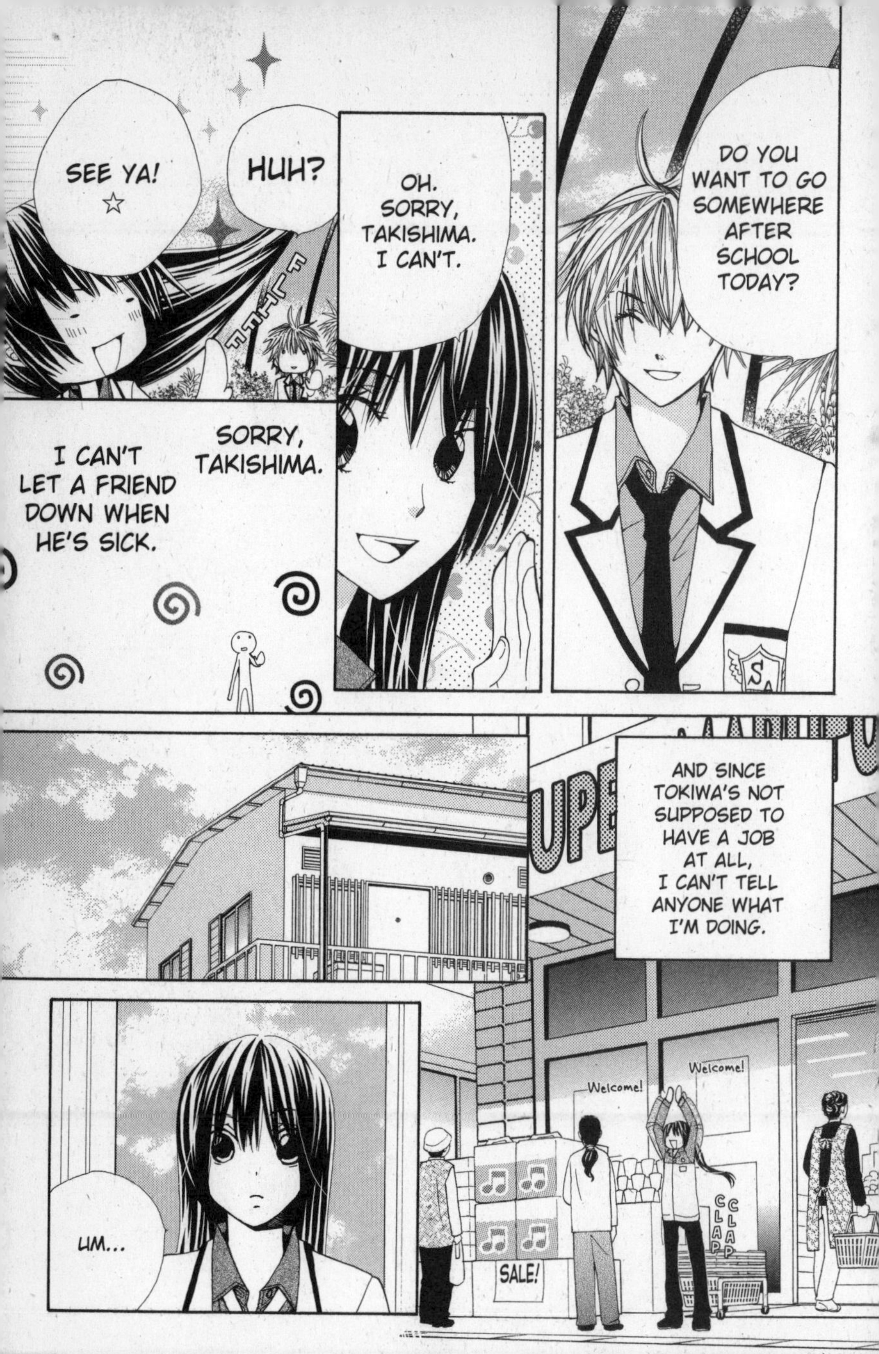
DO YOU WANT TO GO SOMEWHERE AFTER SCHOOL TODAY?
OH. SORRY, TAKISHIMA. I CAN'T.
HUH?
SEE YA! ☆
SORRY, TAKISHIMA.
I CAN'T LET A FRIEND DOWN WHEN HE'S SICK.
AND SINCE TOKIWA'S NOT SUPPOSED TO HAVE A JOB AT ALL, I CAN'T TELL ANYONE WHAT I'M DOING.
Welcome!
Welcome!
CLAP CLAP
SALE!
UM...

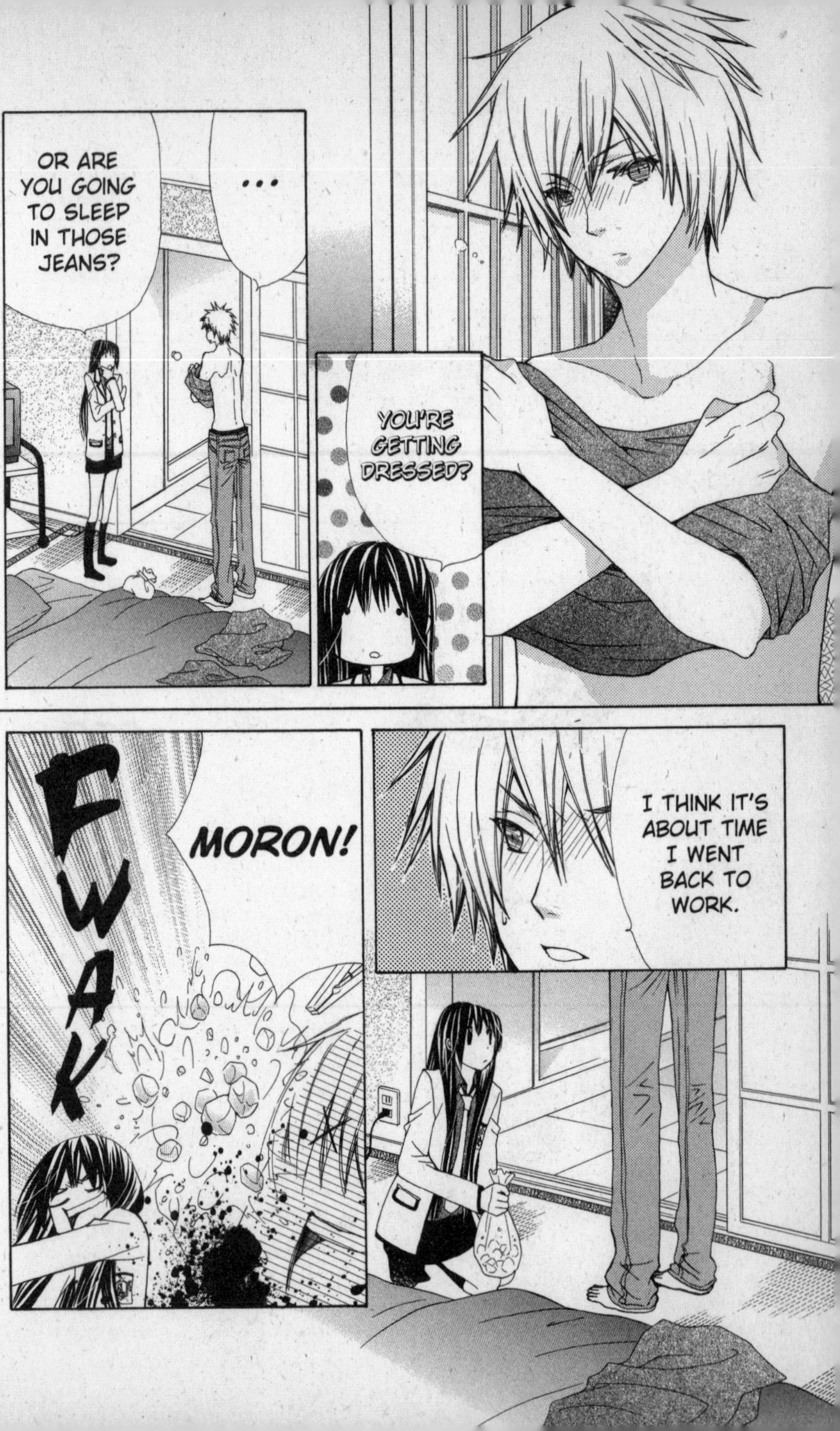
YOU'RE GETTING DRESSED?
...
OR ARE YOU GOING TO SLEEP IN THOSE JEANS?
I THINK IT'S ABOUT TIME I WENT BACK TO WORK.
MORON!
FWAK

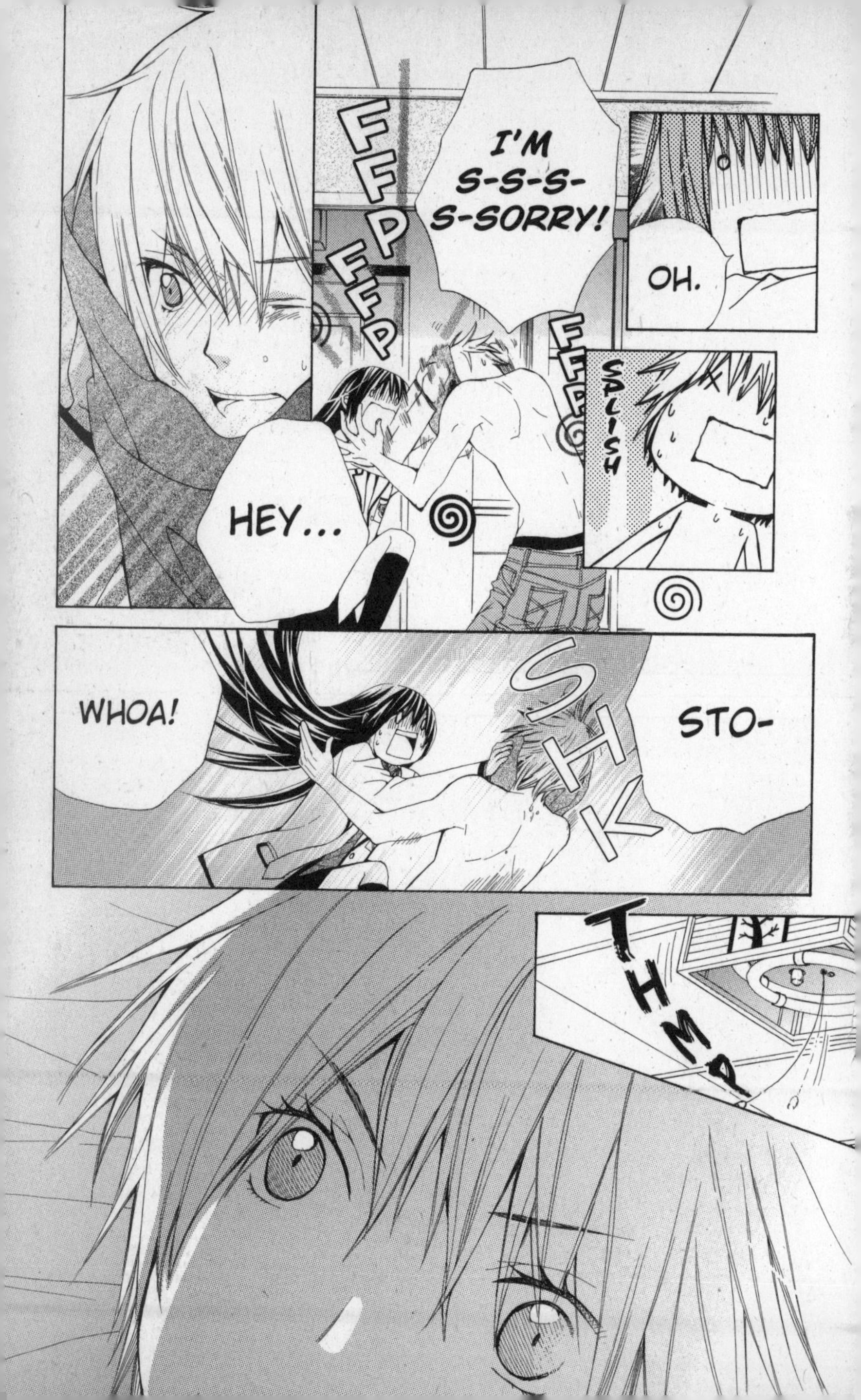
FFP
FFP
I'M S-S-S-S-SORRY!
OH.
SPLISH
FFP
HEY...
STO-
SHK
WHOA!
THMP

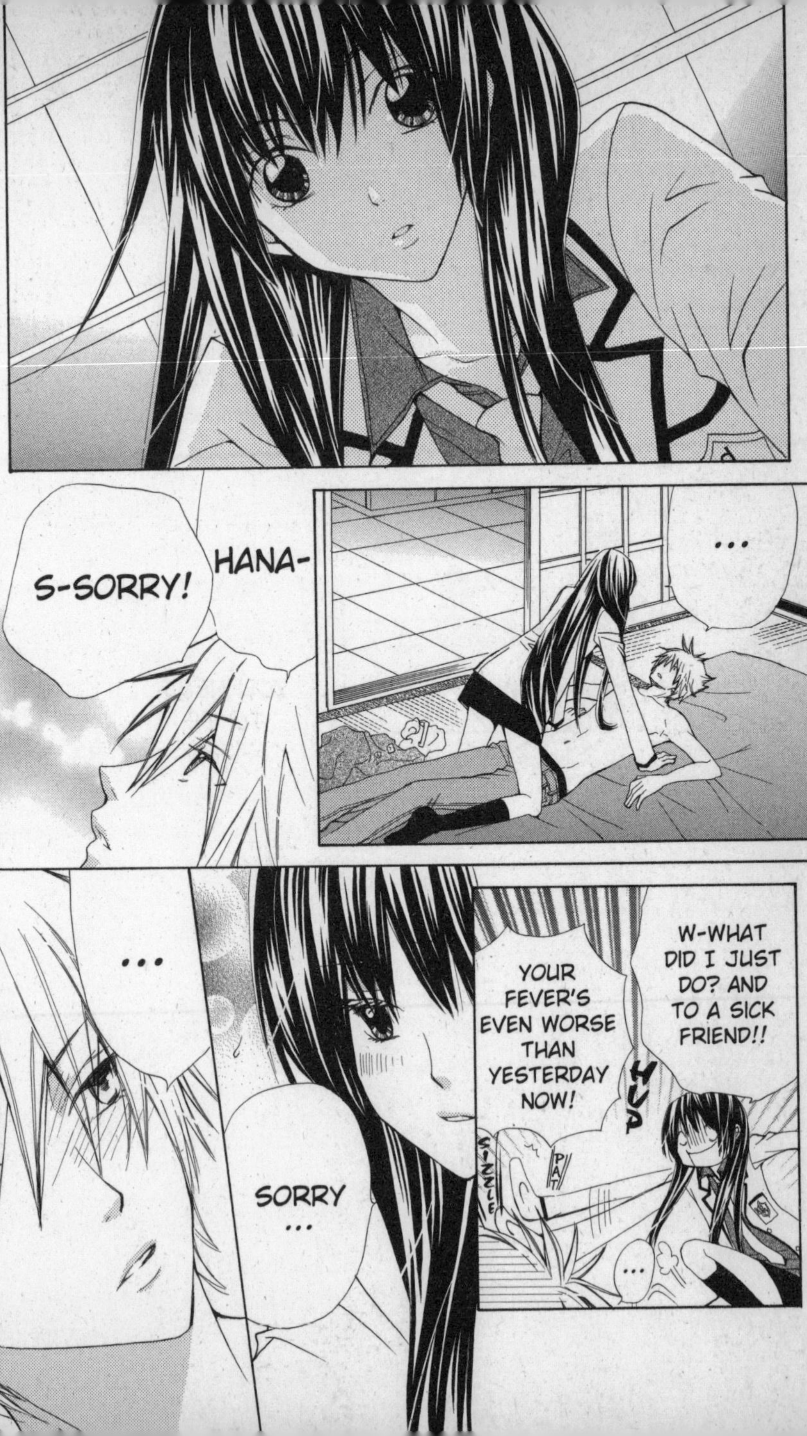
...
HANA-
S-SORRY!
W-WHAT DID I JUST DO? AND TO A SICK FRIEND!!
HUP
YOUR FEVER'S EVEN WORSE THAN YESTERDAY NOW!
PAT
SIZZLE
...
...
SORRY ...

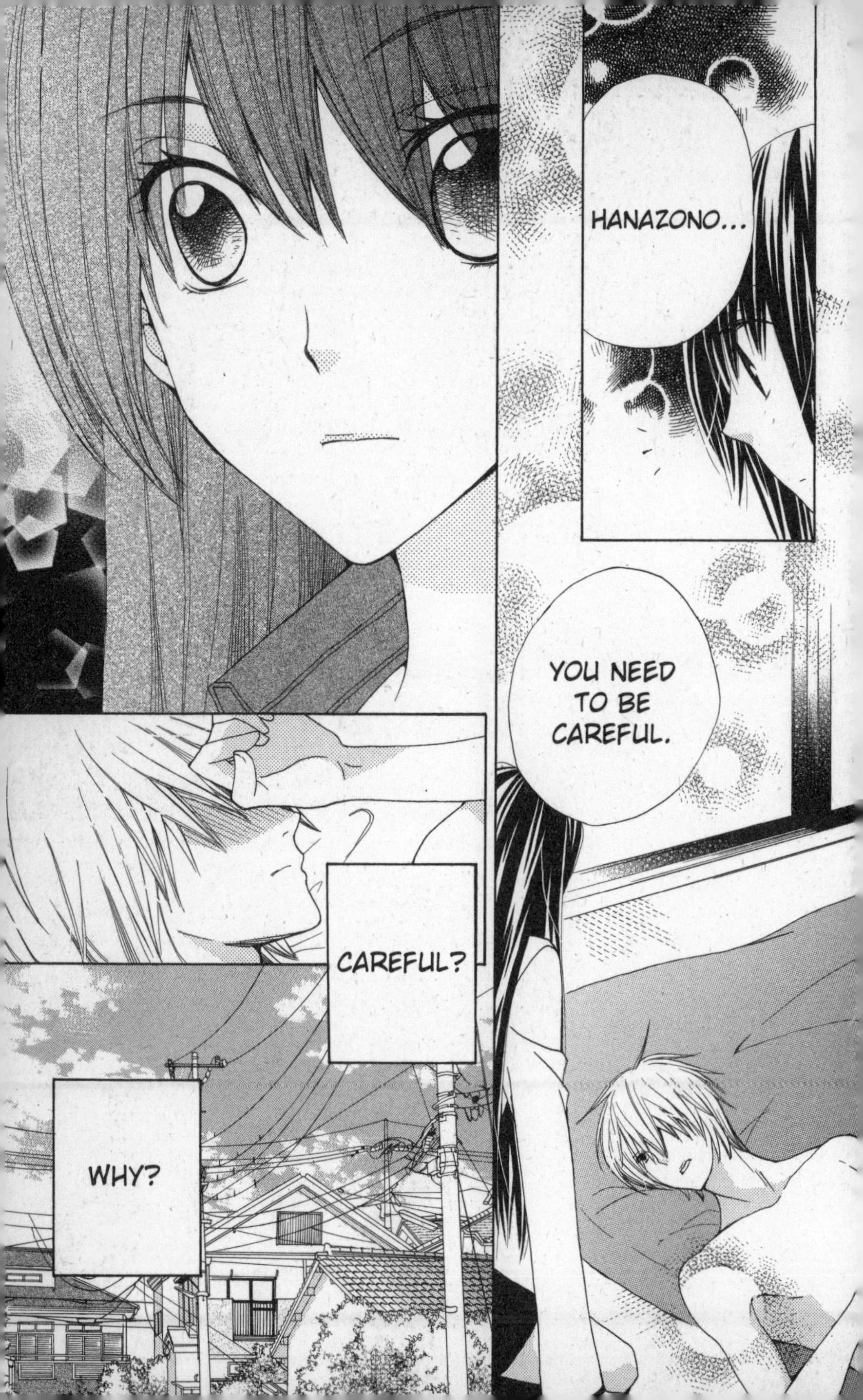
HANAZONO...
YOU NEED TO BE CAREFUL.
CAREFUL?
WHY?

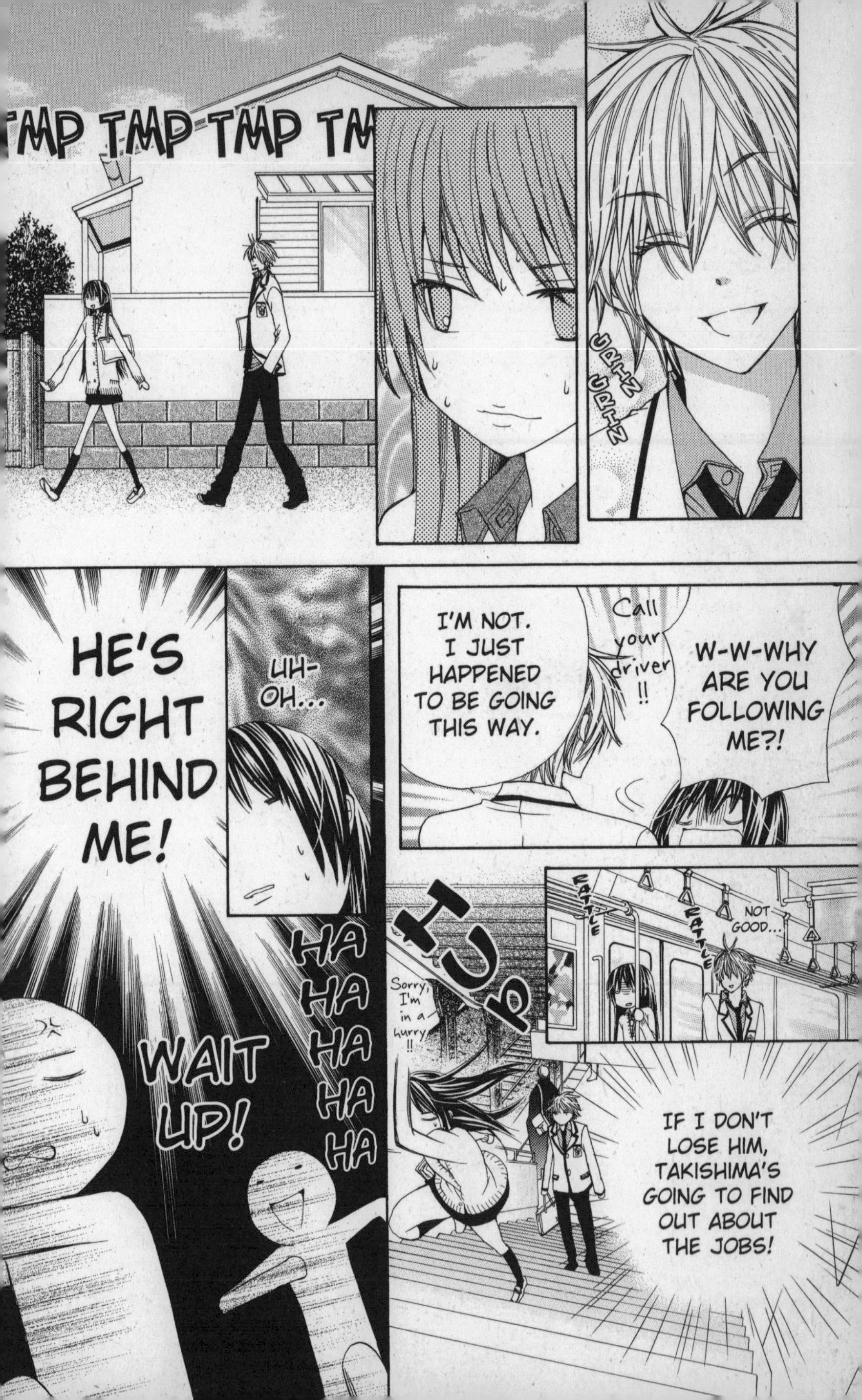
GRIN GRIN
TAMP TAMP TAMP TAM
W-W-WHY ARE YOU FOLLOWING ME?!
Call your driver!!
I'M NOT. I JUST HAPPENED TO BE GOING THIS WAY.
RATTLE
RATTLE
NOT GOOD...
IF I DON'T LOSE HIM, TAKISHIMA'S GOING TO FIND OUT ABOUT THE JOBS!
HUP
Sorry, I'm in a hurry!!
UH-OH...
HE'S RIGHT BEHIND ME!
HA HA HA HA HA
WAIT UP!

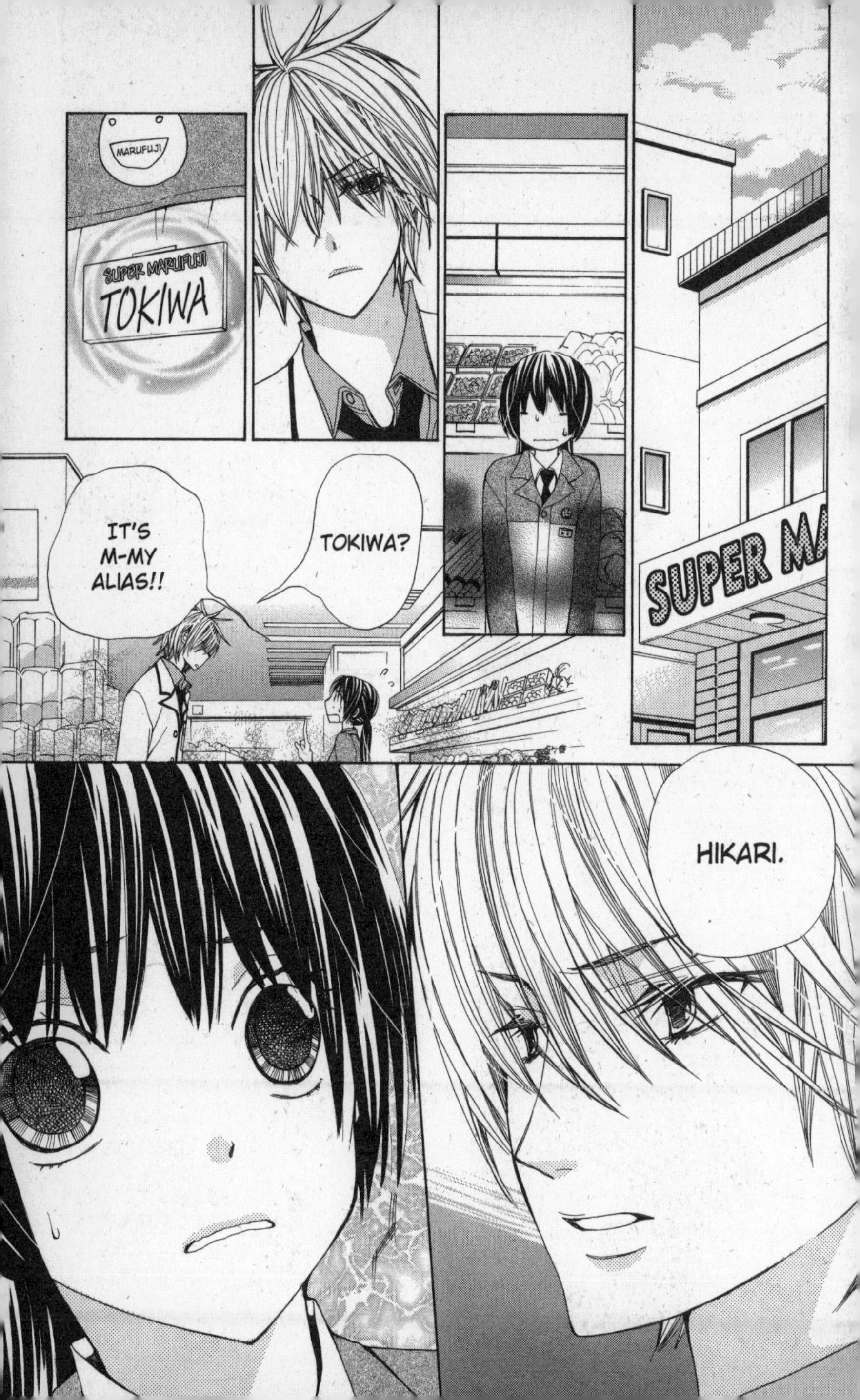
SUPER MA
MARUFUJI
SUPER MARUFUJI
TOKIWA
TOKIWA?
IT'S M-MY ALIAS!!
HIKARI.

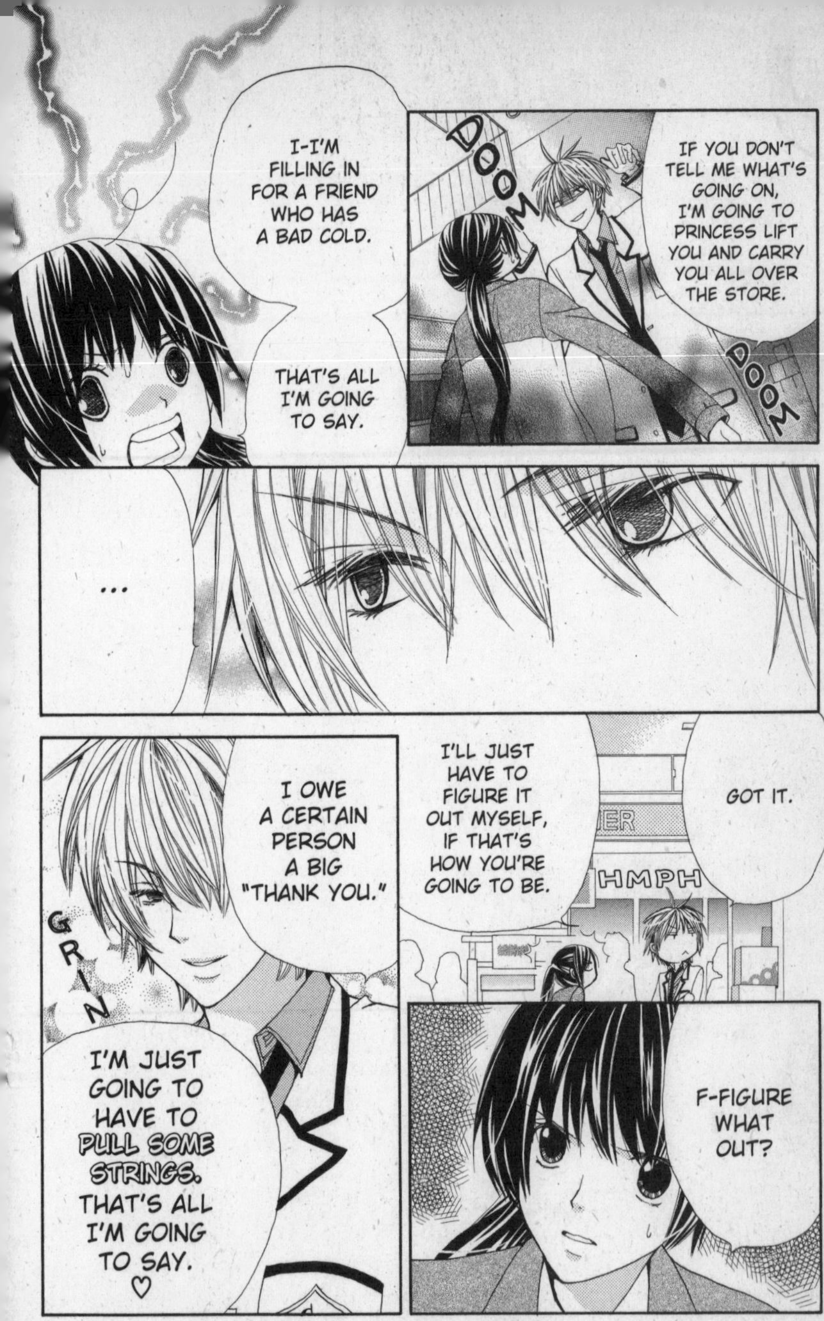
IF YOU DON'T TELL ME WHAT'S GOING ON, I'M GOING TO PRINCESS LIFT YOU AND CARRY YOU ALL OVER THE STORE.
DOOM
DOOM
I-I'M FILLING IN FOR A FRIEND WHO HAS A BAD COLD.
THAT'S ALL I'M GOING TO SAY.
...
GOT IT.
I'LL JUST HAVE TO FIGURE IT OUT MYSELF, IF THAT'S HOW YOU'RE GOING TO BE.
HMPH
F-FIGURE WHAT OUT?
I OWE A CERTAIN PERSON A BIG "THANK YOU."
GRIN
I'M JUST GOING TO HAVE TO PULL SOME STRINGS. THAT'S ALL I'M GOING TO SAY. ♡

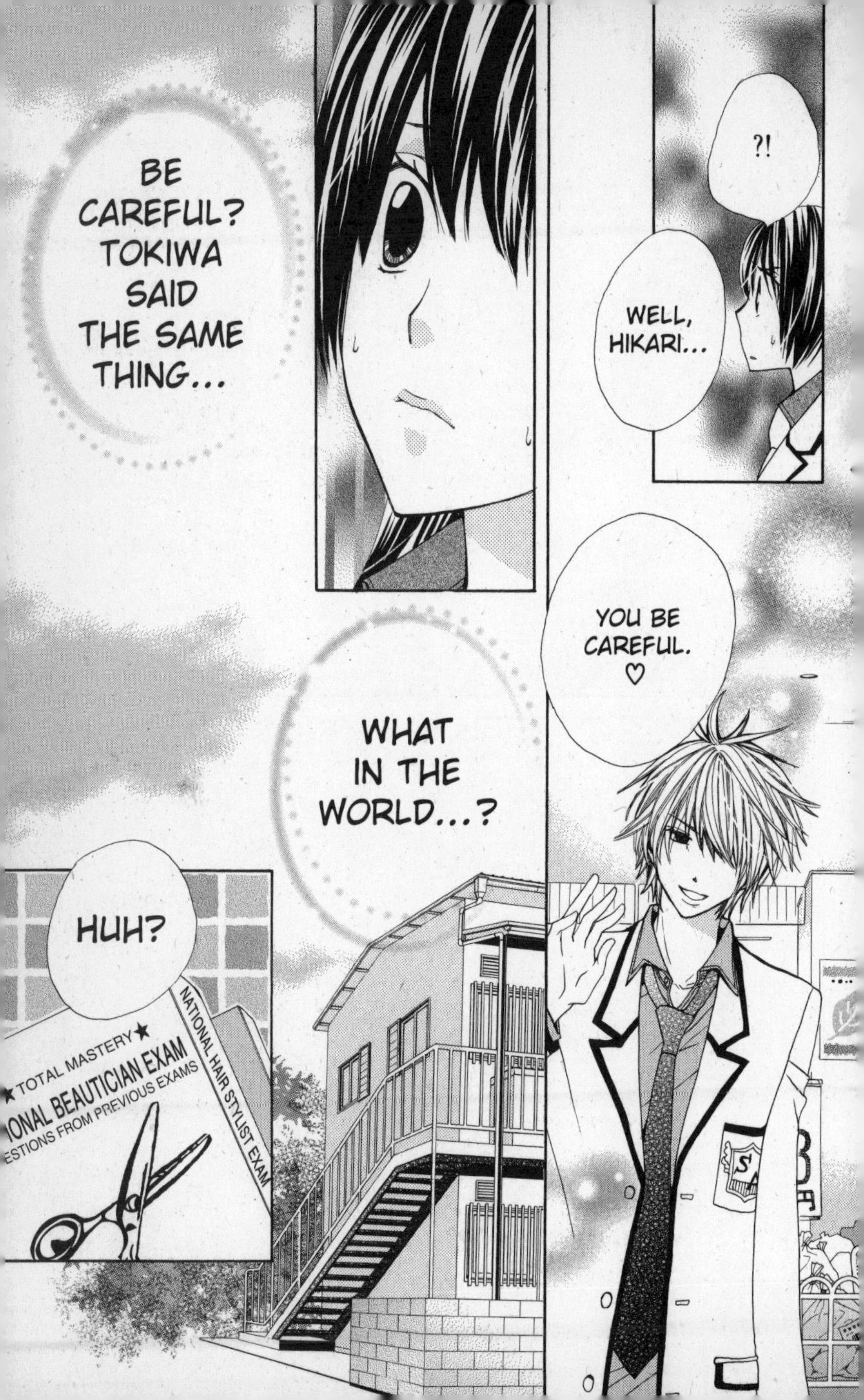
?!
WELL, HIKARI...
YOU BE CAREFUL. ♡
BE CAREFUL? TOKIWA SAID THE SAME THING...
WHAT IN THE WORLD...?
HUH?
NATIONAL HAIR STYLIST EXAM
★TOTAL MASTERY★
IONAL BEAUTICIAN EXAM
ESTIONS FROM PREVIOUS EXAMS

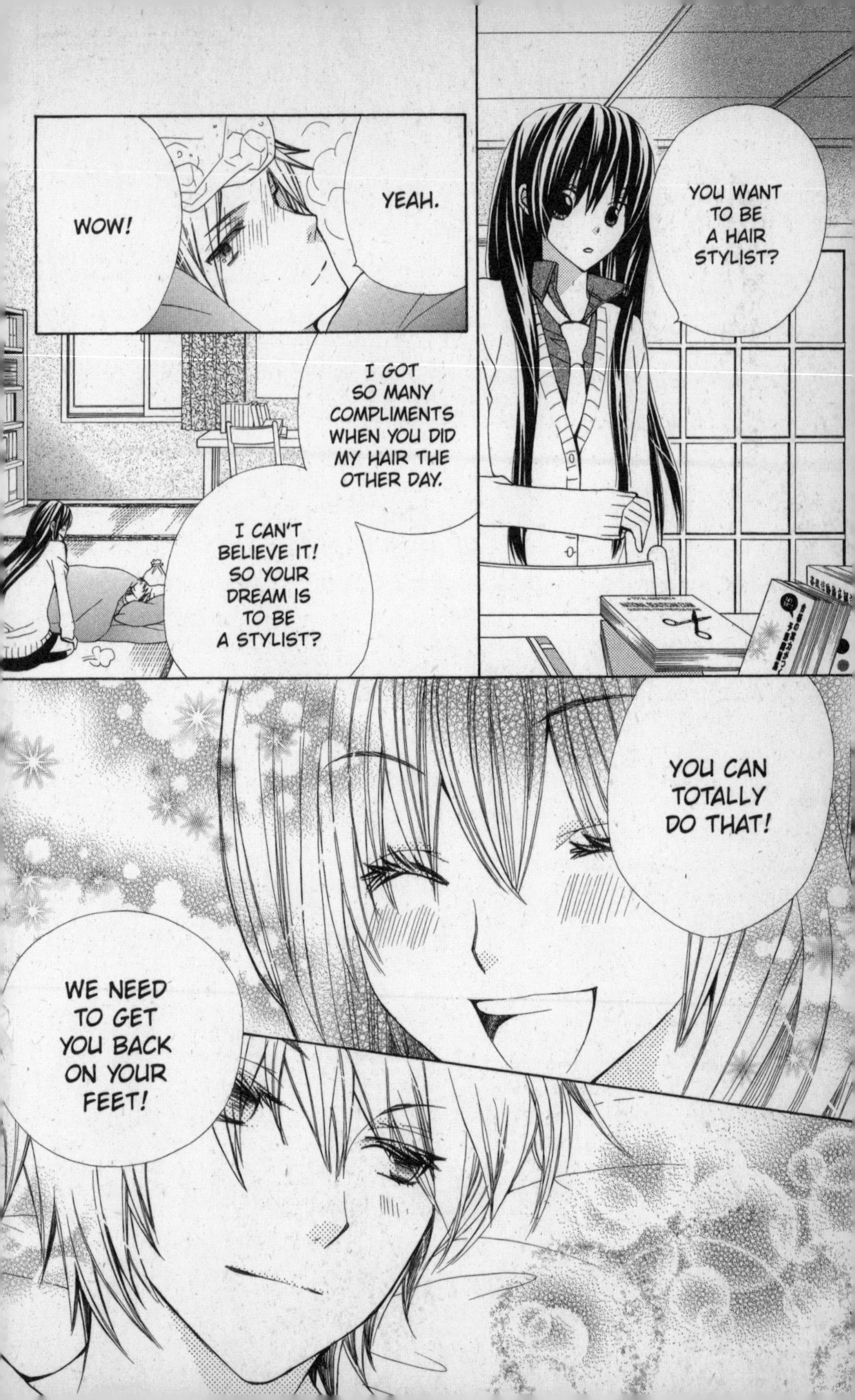
YOU WANT TO BE A HAIR STYLIST?
YEAH.
WOW!
I GOT SO MANY COMPLIMENTS WHEN YOU DID MY HAIR THE OTHER DAY.
I CAN'T BELIEVE IT! SO YOUR DREAM IS TO BE A STYLIST?
YOU CAN TOTALLY DO THAT!
WE NEED TO GET YOU BACK ON YOUR FEET!

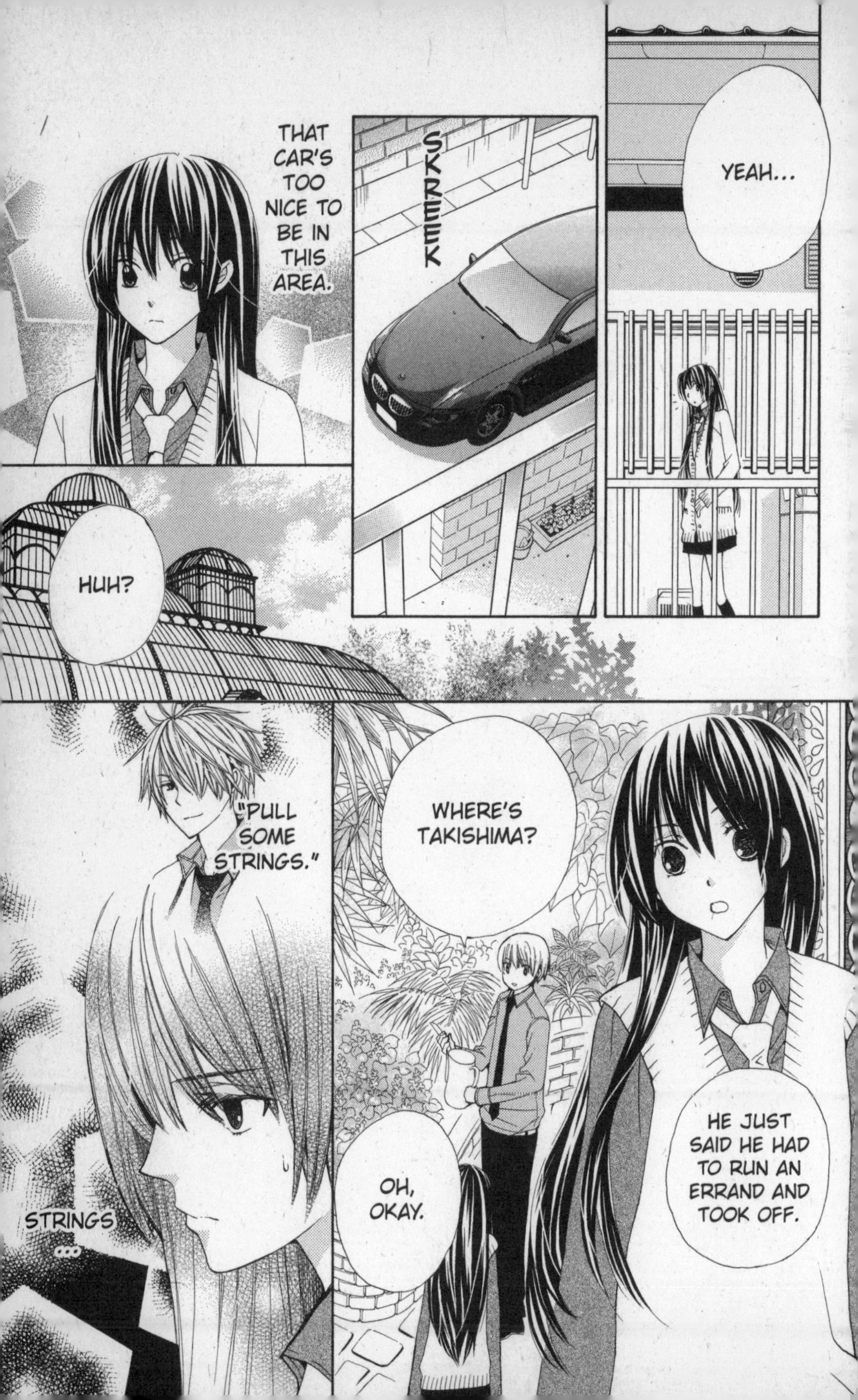
YEAH...
SKREEK
THAT CAR'S TOO NICE TO BE IN THIS AREA.
HUH?
WHERE'S TAKISHIMA?
HE JUST SAID HE HAD TO RUN AN ERRAND AND TOOK OFF.
OH, OKAY.
"PULL SOME STRINGS."
STRINGS...

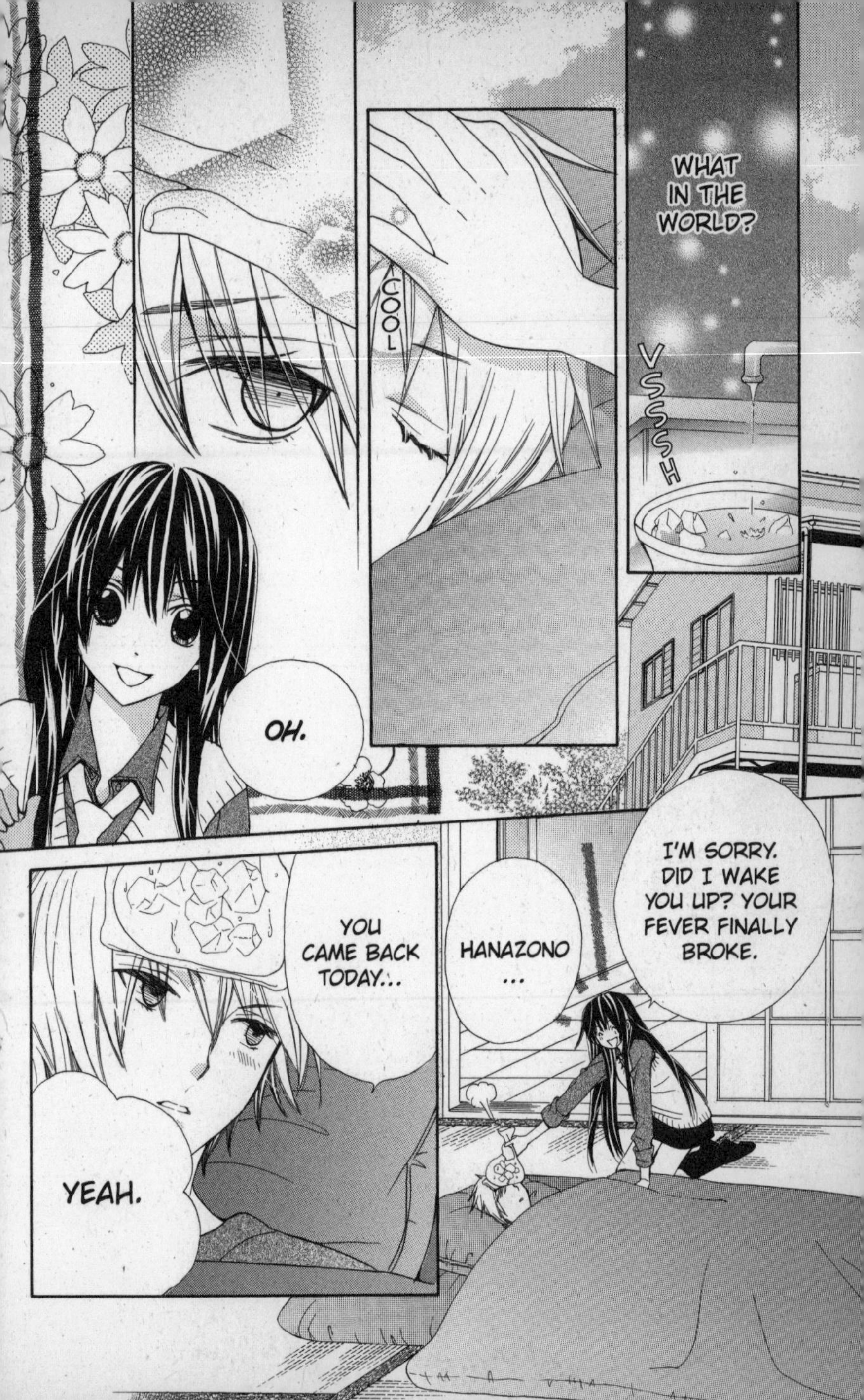
WHAT IN THE WORLD?
VSSSH
COOL
OH.
I'M SORRY. DID I WAKE YOU UP? YOUR FEVER FINALLY BROKE.
HANAZONO...
YOU CAME BACK TODAY...
YEAH.

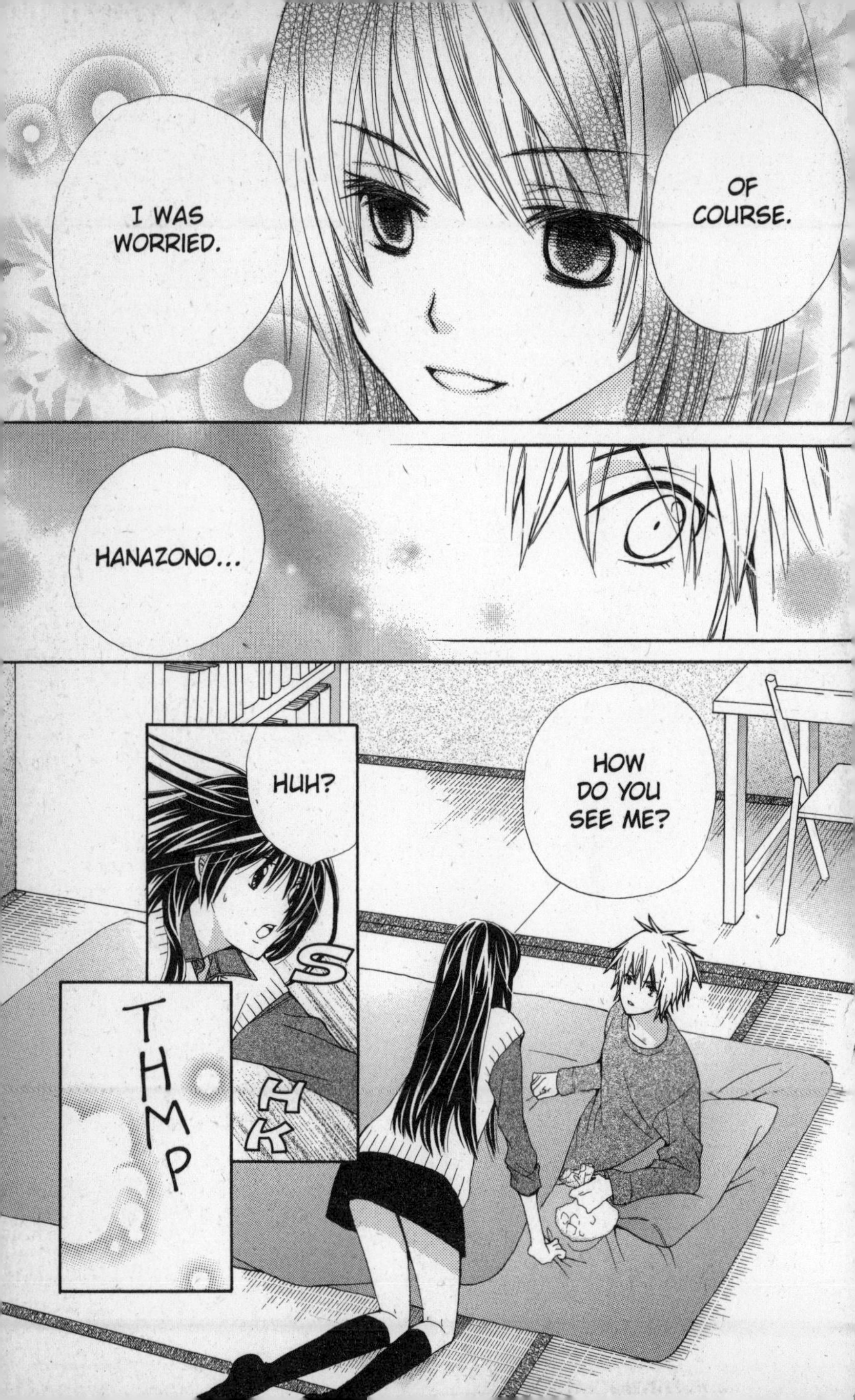
OF COURSE.
I WAS WORRIED.
HANAZONO...
HOW DO YOU SEE ME?
HUH?
SHK
THMP

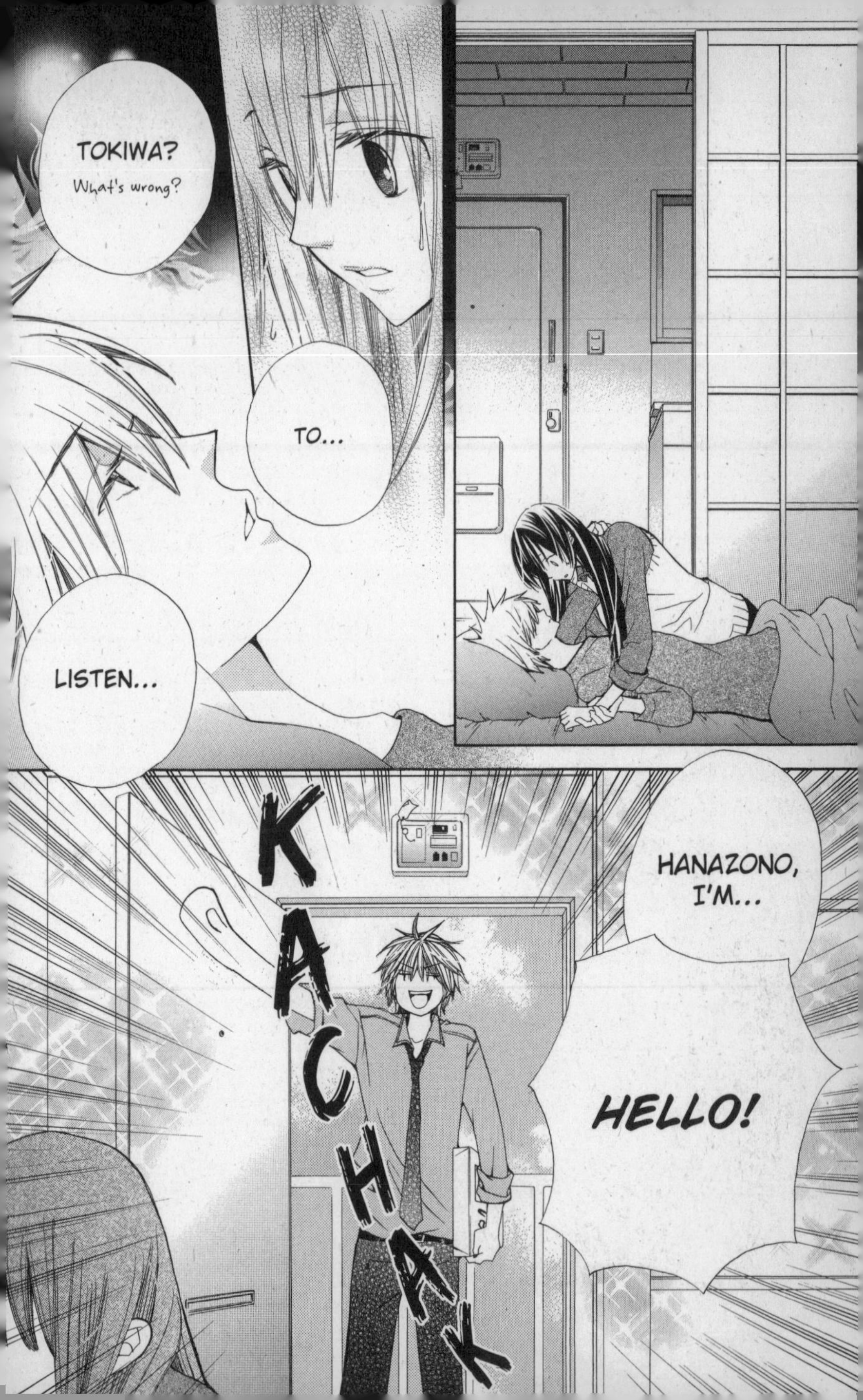

TOKIWA?
What's wrong?
TO...
LISTEN...
HANAZONO, I'M...
KACHAK
HELLO!

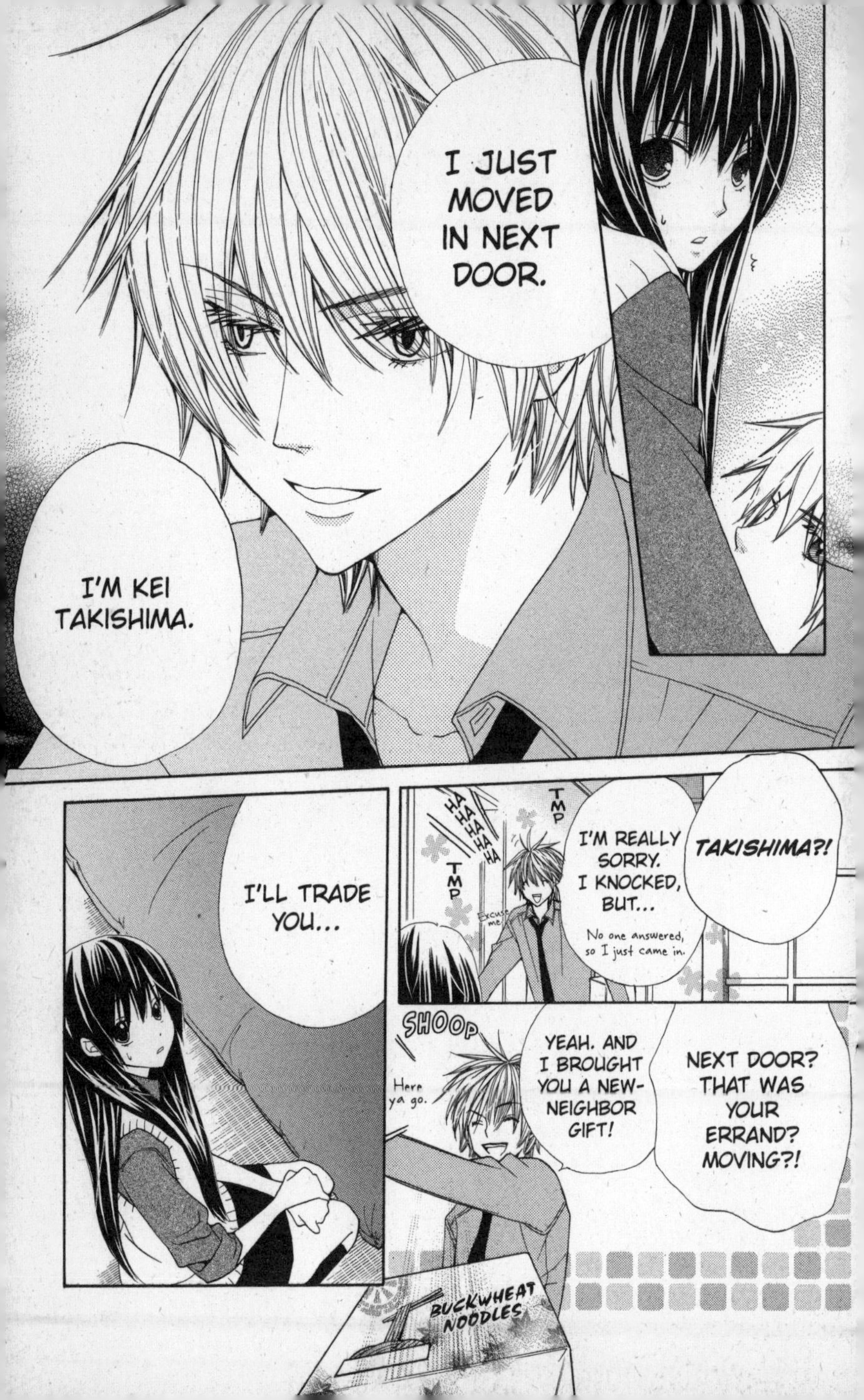
I JUST MOVED IN NEXT DOOR.
I'M KEI TAKISHIMA.
TAKISHIMA?!
HAHAHAHAHAHA
TMP
TMP
I'M REALLY SORRY. I KNOCKED, BUT...
No one answered, so I just came in.
Excuse me!
NEXT DOOR? THAT WAS YOUR ERRAND? MOVING?!
YEAH. AND I BROUGHT YOU A NEW-NEIGHBOR GIFT!
SHOOP
Here ya go.
BUCKWHEAT NOODLES
I'LL TRADE YOU...

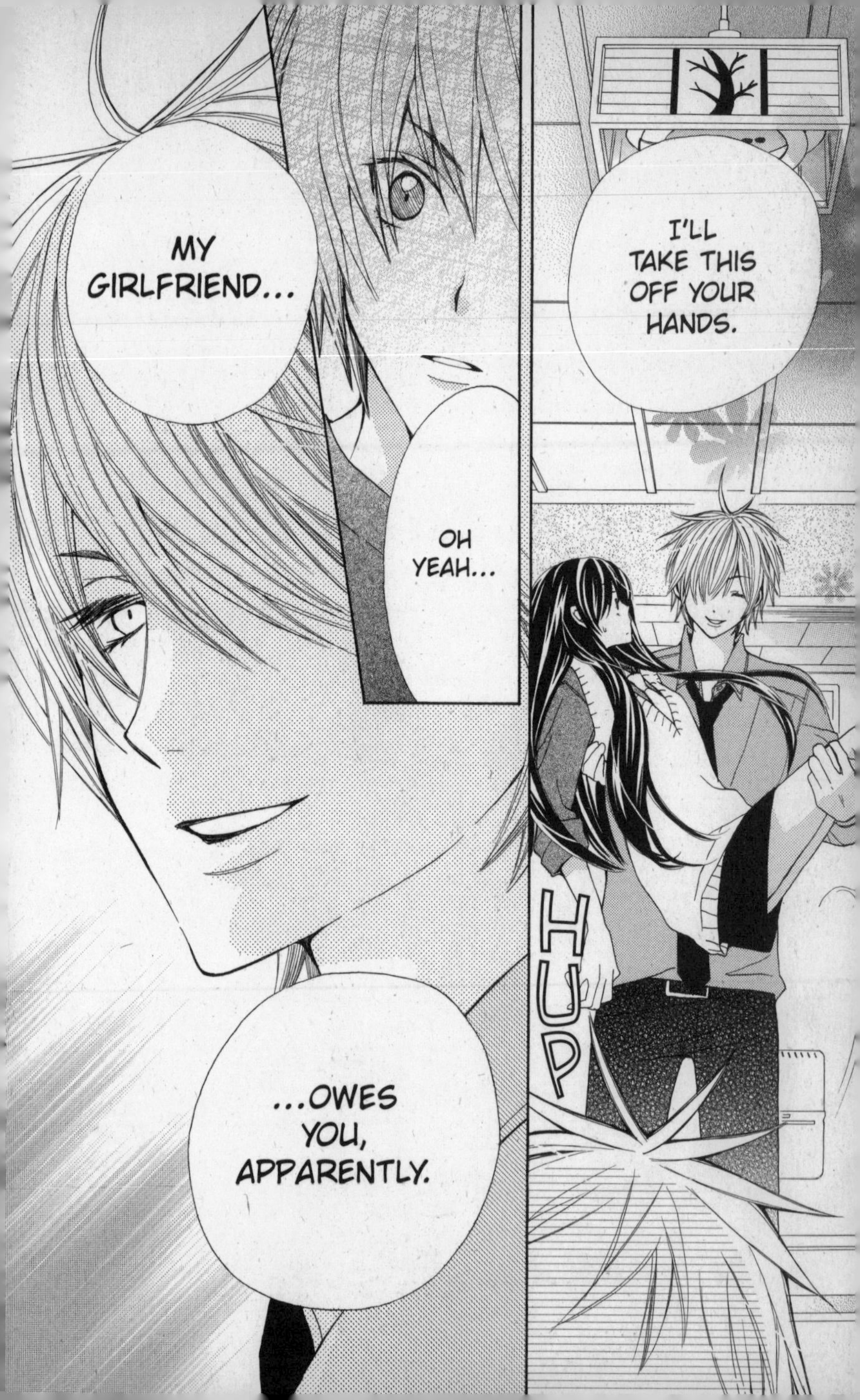
I'LL TAKE THIS OFF YOUR HANDS.
HUP
OH YEAH...
MY GIRLFRIEND...
...OWES YOU, APPARENTLY.

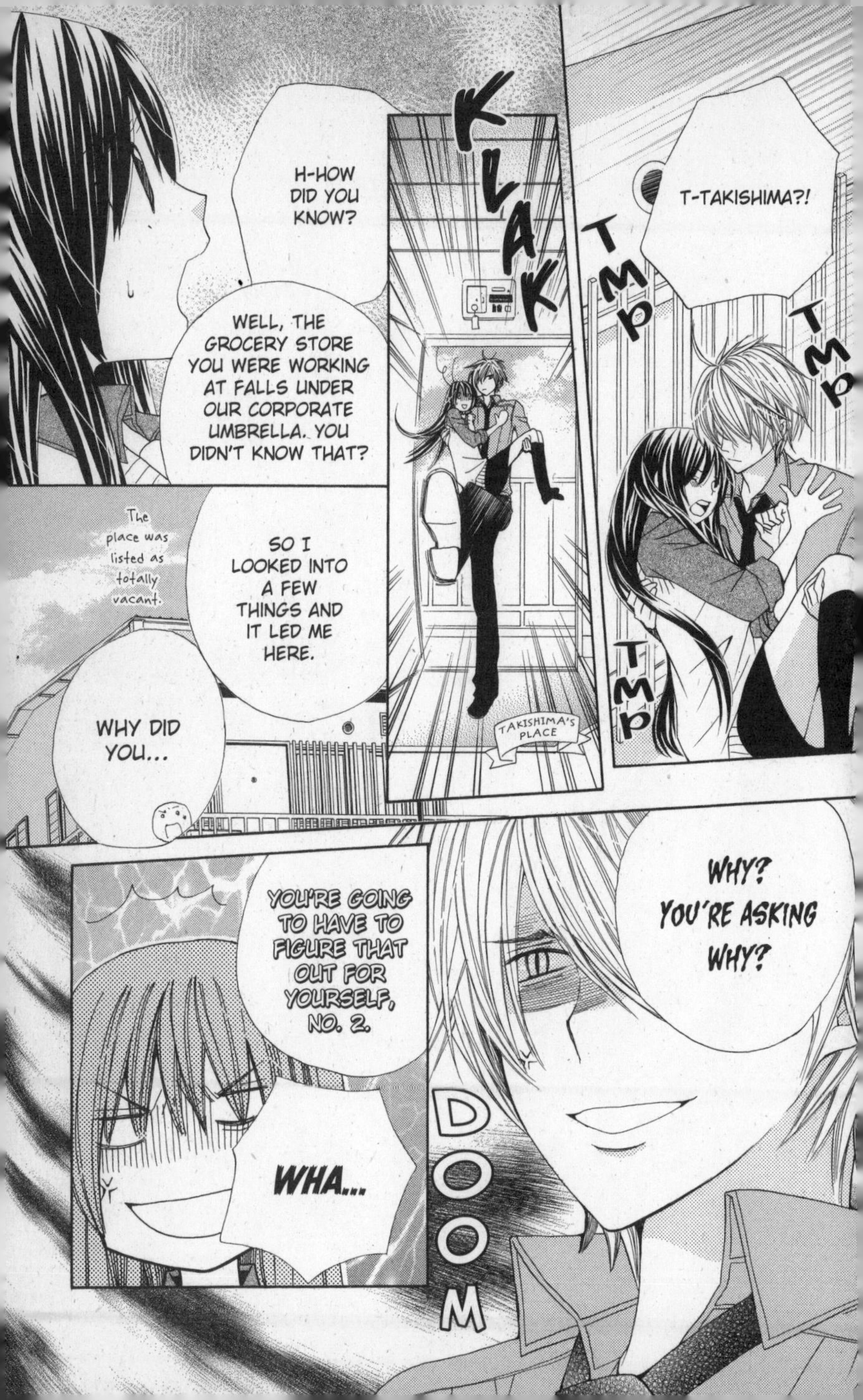
T-TAKISHIMA?!
TMP
TMP
TMP
KLAK
TAKISHIMA'S PLACE
H-HOW DID YOU KNOW?
WELL, THE GROCERY STORE YOU WERE WORKING AT FALLS UNDER OUR CORPORATE UMBRELLA. YOU DIDN'T KNOW THAT?
SO I LOOKED INTO A FEW THINGS AND IT LED ME HERE.
The place was listed as totally vacant.
WHY DID YOU...
WHY? YOU'RE ASKING WHY?
DOOM
YOU'RE GOING TO HAVE TO FIGURE THAT OUT FOR YOURSELF, NO. 2.
WHA...

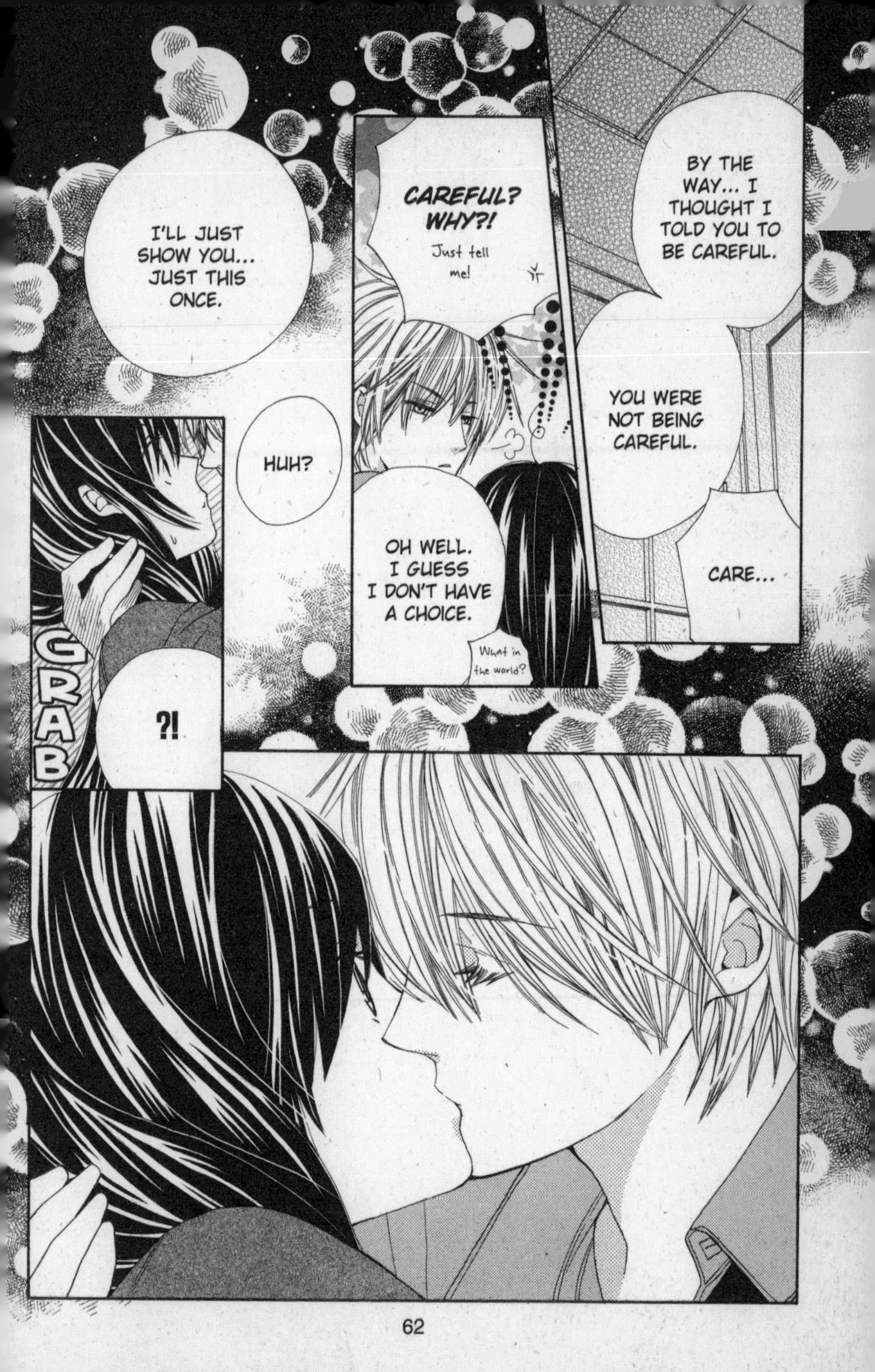
BY THE WAY... I THOUGHT I TOLD YOU TO BE CAREFUL.
YOU WERE NOT BEING CAREFUL.
CARE...
CAREFUL? WHY?!
Just tell me!
OH WELL. I GUESS I DON'T HAVE A CHOICE.
What in the world?
I'LL JUST SHOW YOU... JUST THIS ONCE.
HUH?
GRAB
?!

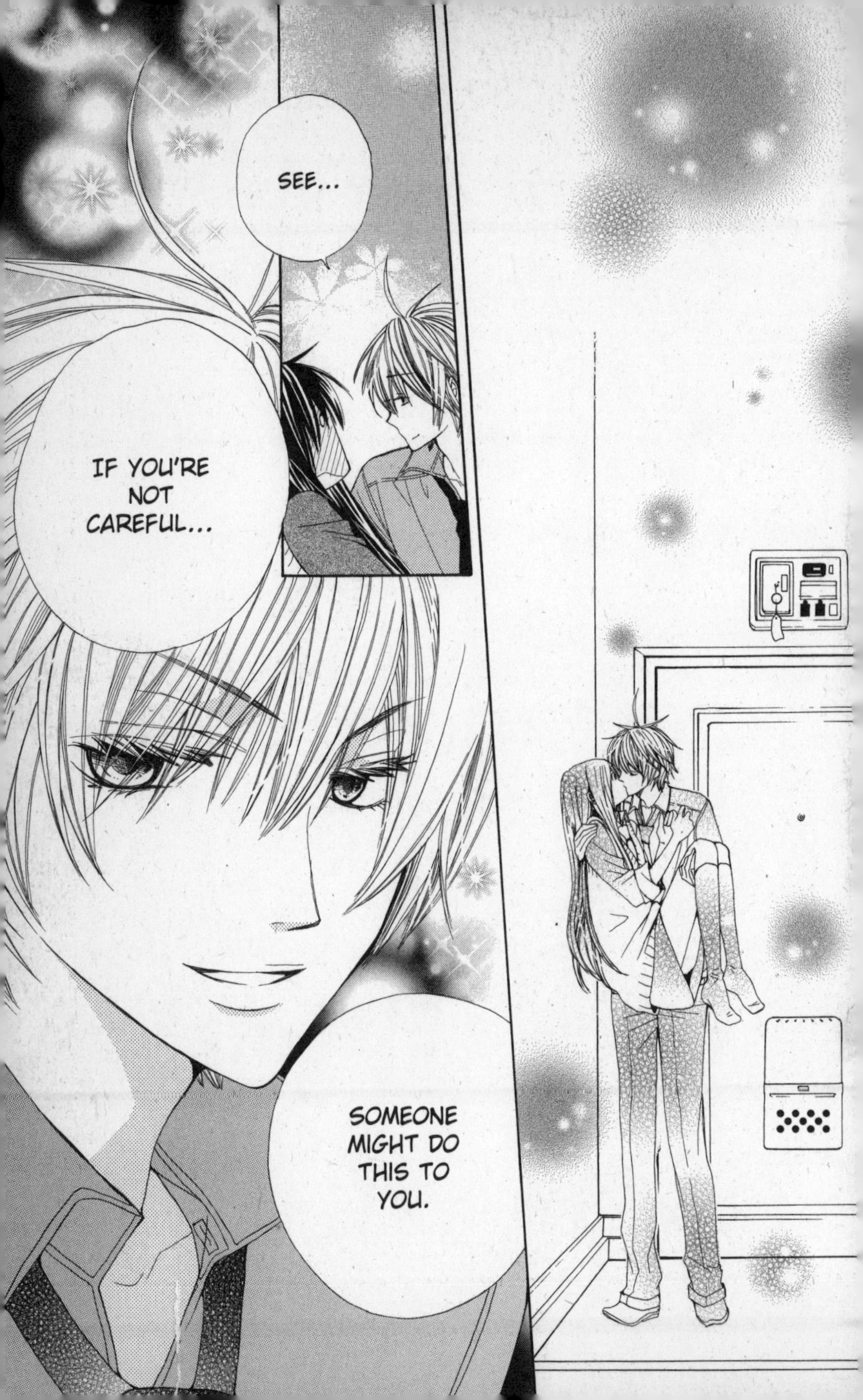
SEE...
IF YOU'RE NOT CAREFUL...
SOMEONE MIGHT DO THIS TO YOU.

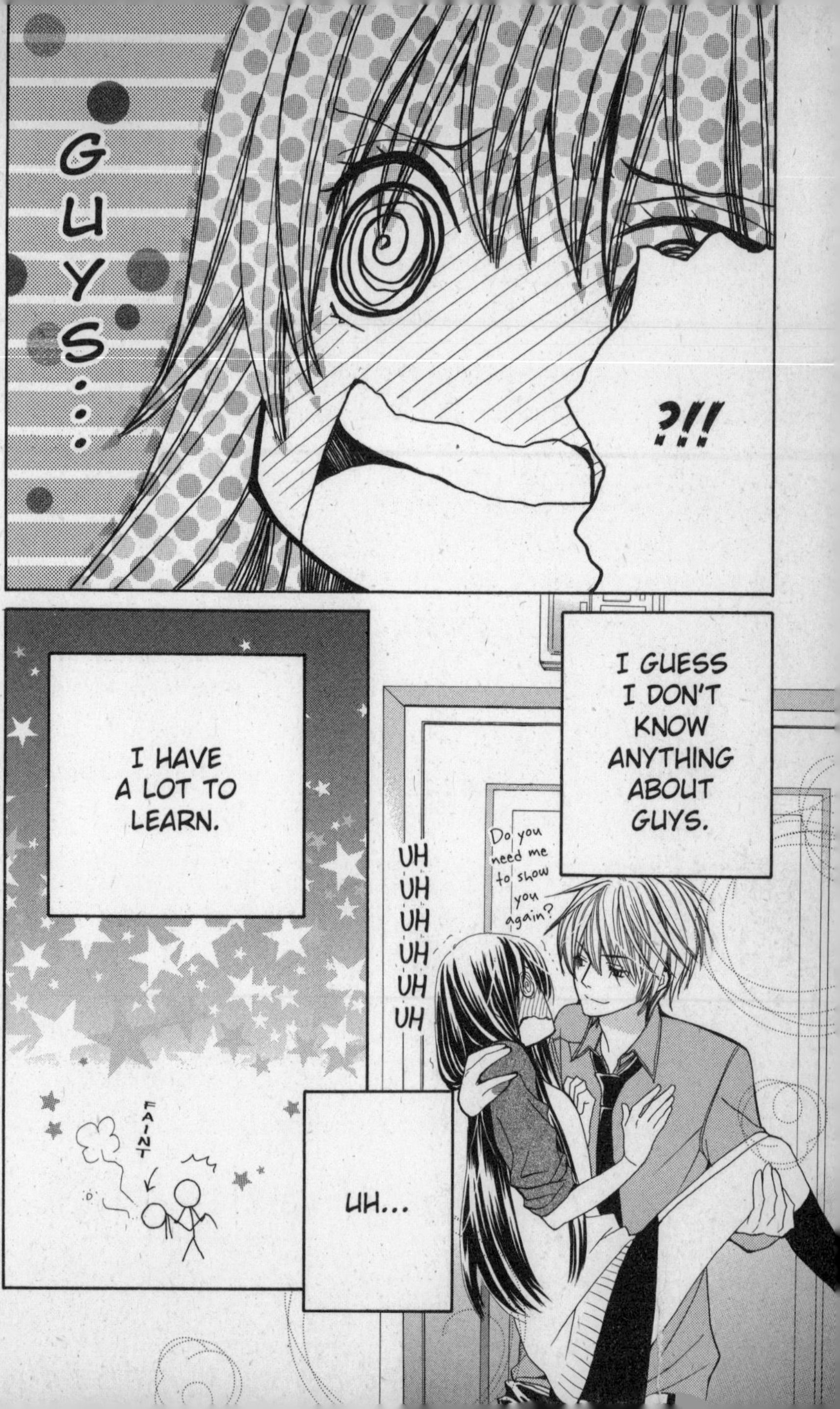
GUYS...
?!!
I GUESS I DON'T KNOW ANYTHING ABOUT GUYS.
Do you need me to show you again?
UH UH UH UH UH UH
UH...
I HAVE A LOT TO LEARN.
FAINT

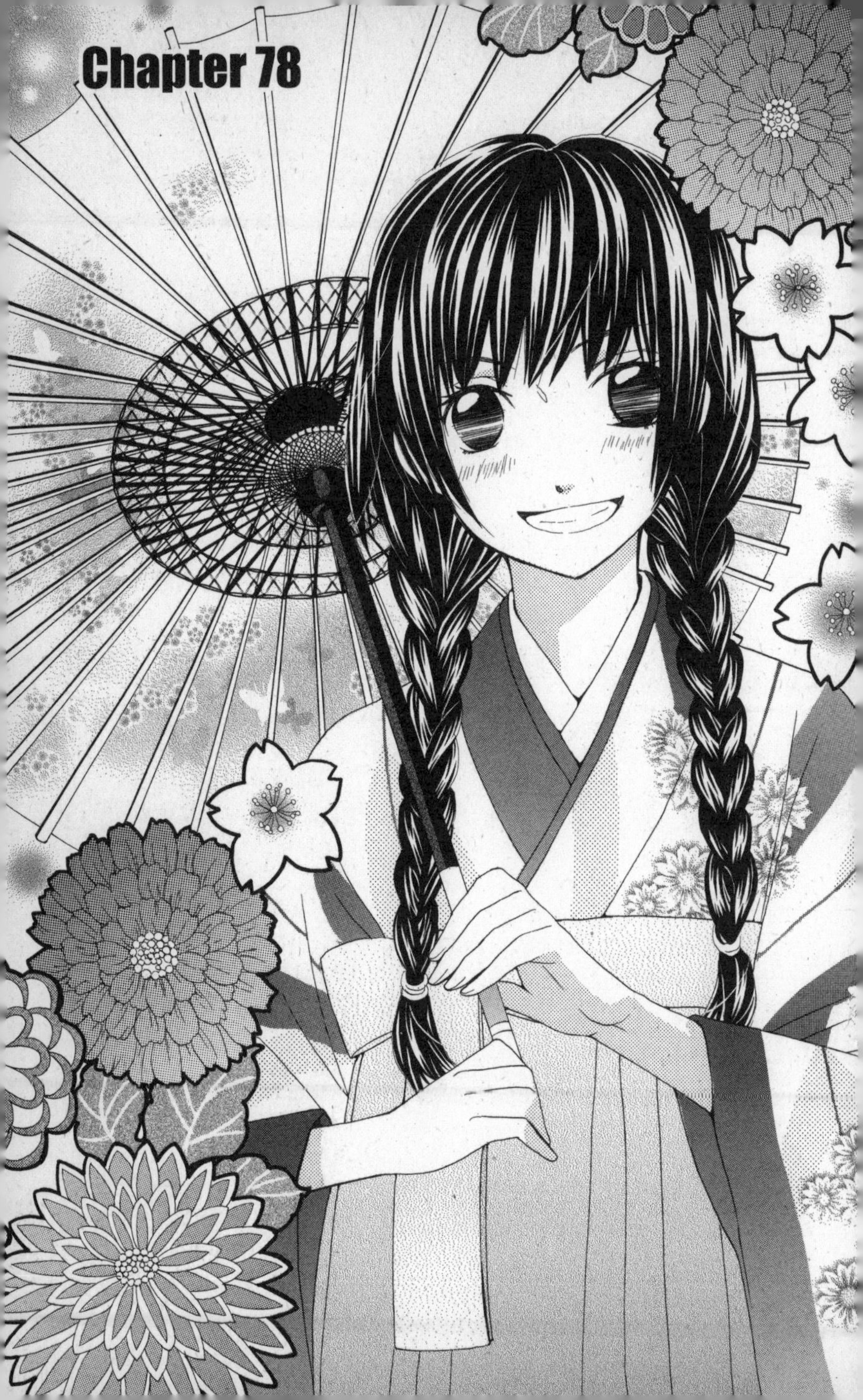
Chapter 78

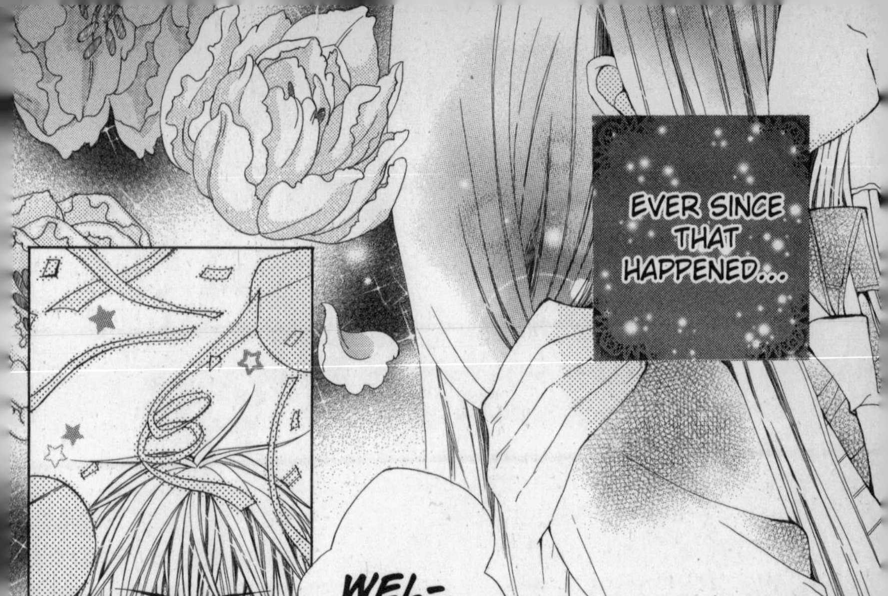
EVER SINCE THAT HAPPENED...
SOME-THING'S BEEN OFF.
WEL-COME HOME!
...

· POPULARITY CONTEST ·

THIS WAS THE VERY FIRST TIME ANYONE HAD DONE A POPULARITY CONTEST FOR ANY OF MY CHARACTERS. I WAS SO WORRIED THAT NO ONE WOULD DO IT, BUT WE ENDED UP GETTING SO MANY VOTES THAT IT ALMOST MADE ME CRY!
ANYWAY, THE RESULTS OF *S.A*'S POPULARITY CONTEST WERE: 1ST HIKARI, 2ND KEI, 3RD TADASHI, 4TH RYU, 5TH MEGUMI, 6TH AKIRA, 7TH JUN! HIKARI ACTUALLY BEAT KEI! SHE'S FINALLY NO. 1! THE SHOCKER WAS THAT SAKURA LOST TO YAPPI... WELL... AND THAT YAHIRO LOST TO THE TADASHI DOLL.♡

FIGHT!!

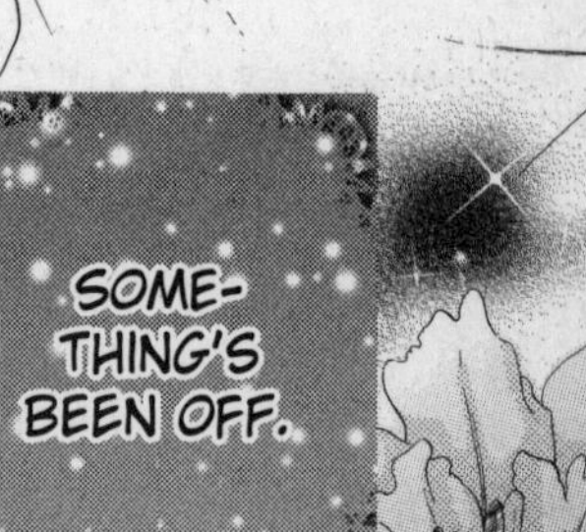
What?!
How in the world?!!

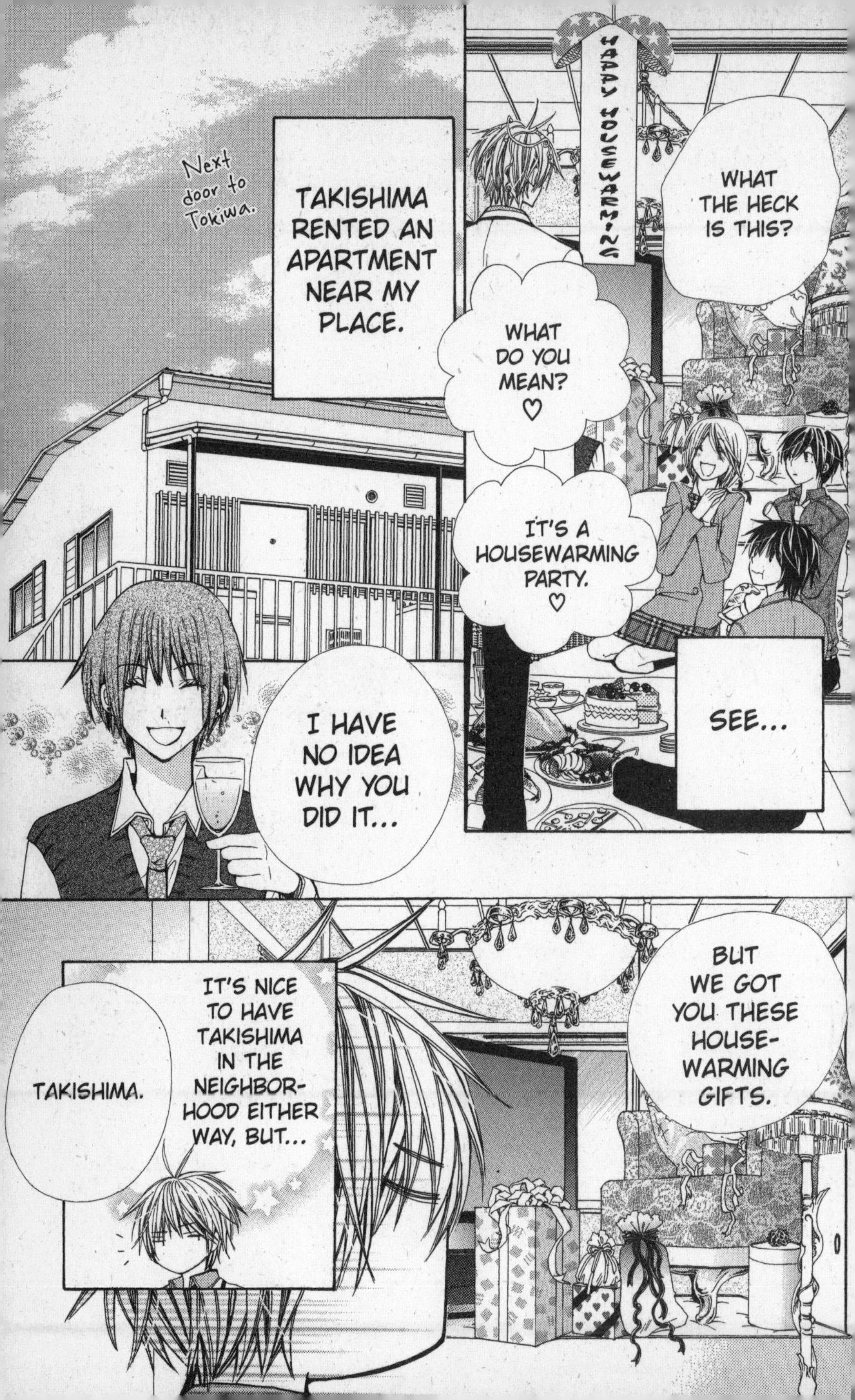
HAPPY HOUSEWARMING
WHAT THE HECK IS THIS?
WHAT DO YOU MEAN? ♡
IT'S A HOUSEWARMING PARTY. ♡
SEE...
TAKISHIMA RENTED AN APARTMENT NEAR MY PLACE.
Next door to Tokiwa.
I HAVE NO IDEA WHY YOU DID IT...
BUT WE GOT YOU THESE HOUSE-WARMING GIFTS.
IT'S NICE TO HAVE TAKISHIMA IN THE NEIGHBOR-HOOD EITHER WAY, BUT...
TAKISHIMA.

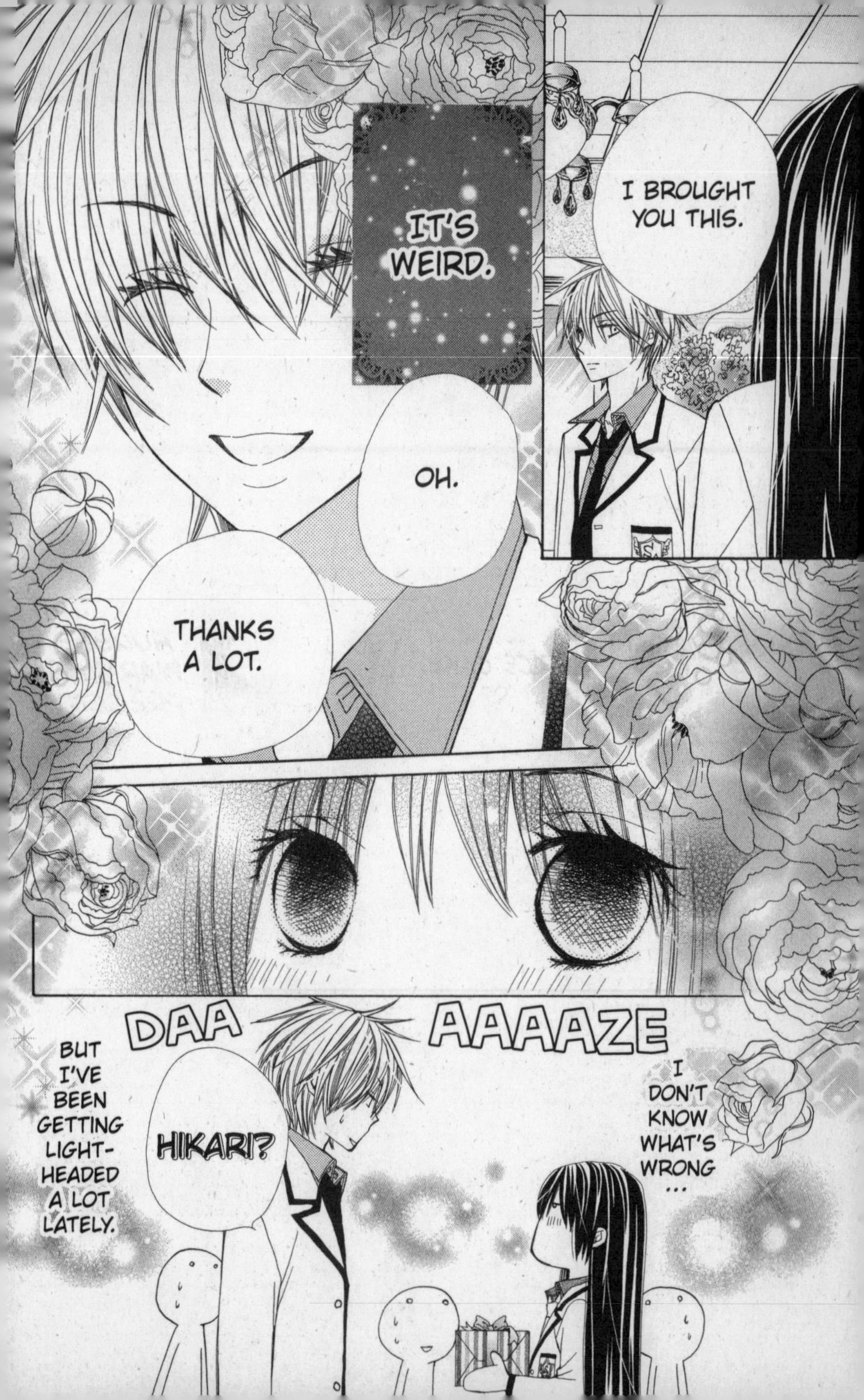
I BROUGHT YOU THIS.
IT'S WEIRD.
OH.
THANKS A LOT.
DAA AAAAAZE
I DON'T KNOW WHAT'S WRONG...
BUT I'VE BEEN GETTING LIGHT-HEADED A LOT LATELY.
HIKARI?

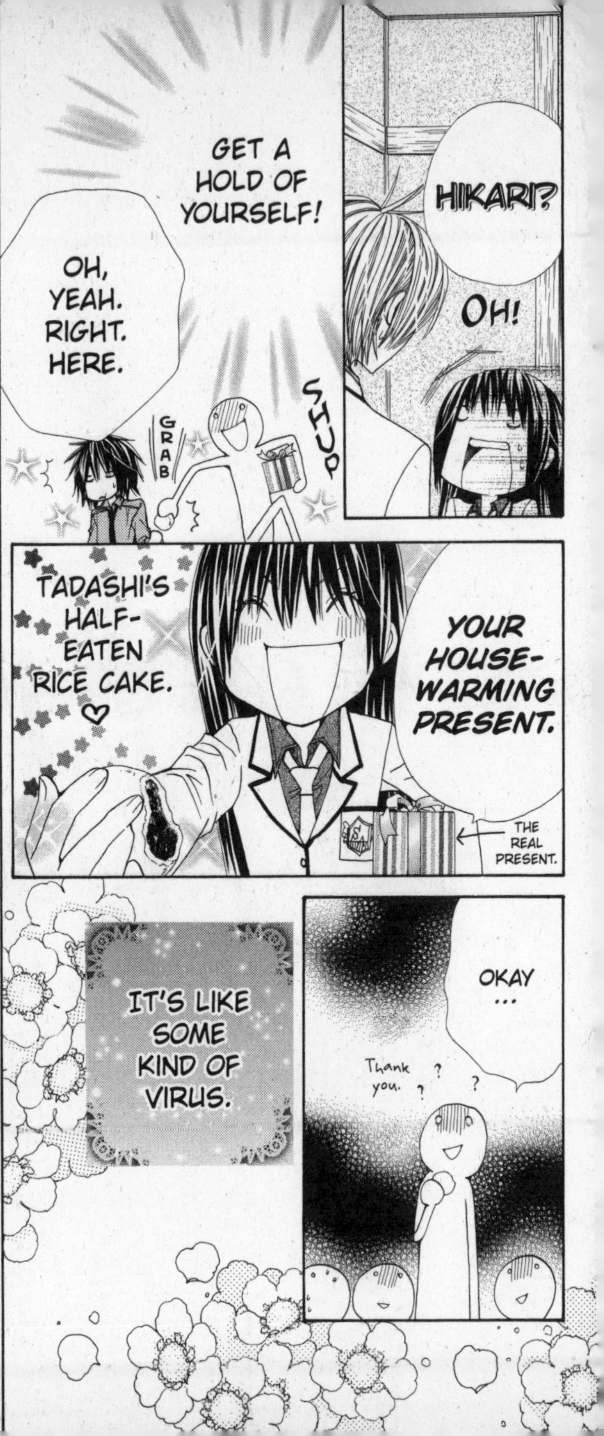
HIKARI?
OH!
GET A HOLD OF YOURSELF!
OH, YEAH. RIGHT. HERE.
SHUP
GRAB
YOUR HOUSE-WARMING PRESENT.
TADASHI'S HALF-EATEN RICE CAKE. ♡
THE REAL PRESENT.
OKAY...
Thank you.
IT'S LIKE SOME KIND OF VIRUS.

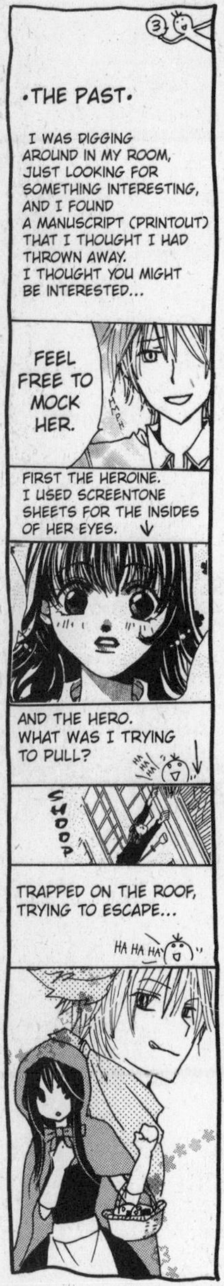
③
•THE PAST•
I WAS DIGGING AROUND IN MY ROOM, JUST LOOKING FOR SOMETHING INTERESTING, AND I FOUND A MANUSCRIPT (PRINTOUT) THAT I THOUGHT I HAD THROWN AWAY. I THOUGHT YOU MIGHT BE INTERESTED...
FEEL FREE TO MOCK HER.
HMPH
FIRST THE HEROINE. I USED SCREENTONE SHEETS FOR THE INSIDES OF HER EYES.
AND THE HERO. WHAT WAS I TRYING TO PULL?
SHOOP
TRAPPED ON THE ROOF, TRYING TO ESCAPE...
HA HA HA

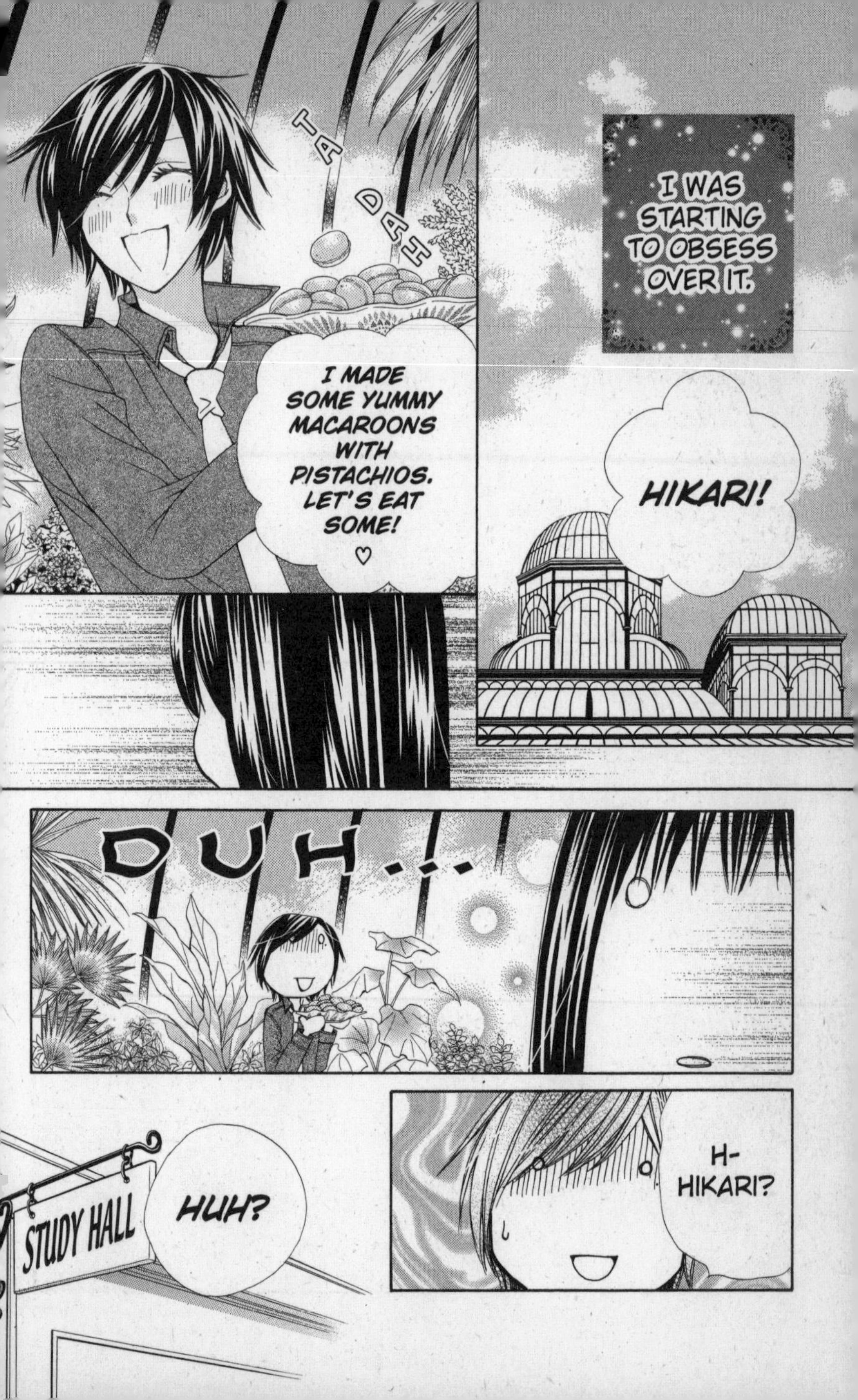
I WAS STARTING TO OBSESS OVER IT.
HIKARI!
TA DAH
I MADE SOME YUMMY MACAROONS WITH PISTACHIOS. LET'S EAT SOME! ♡
DUH...
H- HIKARI?
STUDY HALL
HUH?

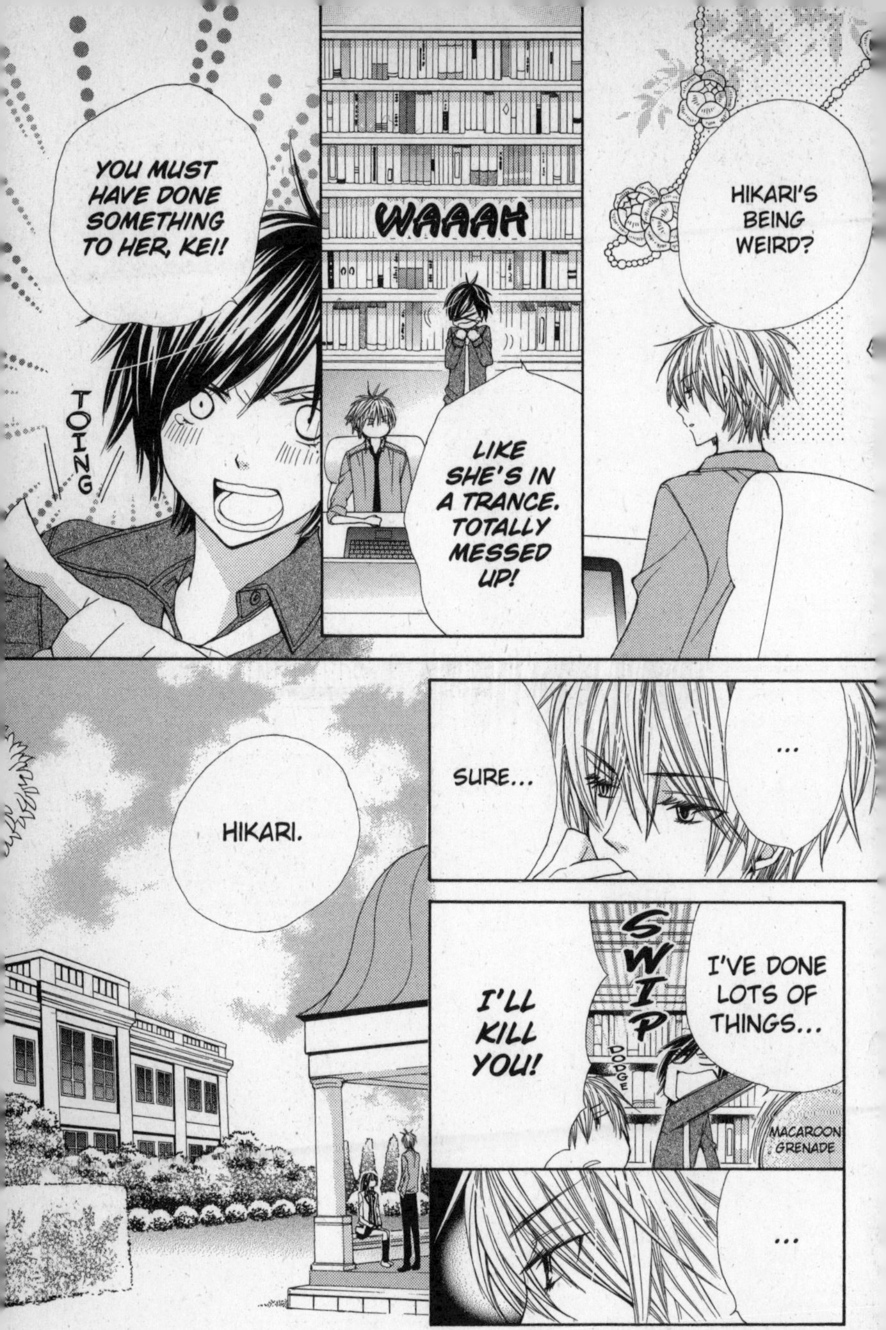
HIKARI'S BEING WEIRD?
WAAAH
LIKE SHE'S IN A TRANCE. TOTALLY MESSED UP!
YOU MUST HAVE DONE SOMETHING TO HER, KEI!
TOING
...
SURE...
I'VE DONE LOTS OF THINGS...
SWIP
I'LL KILL YOU!
DODGE
MACAROON GRENADE
...
HIKARI.

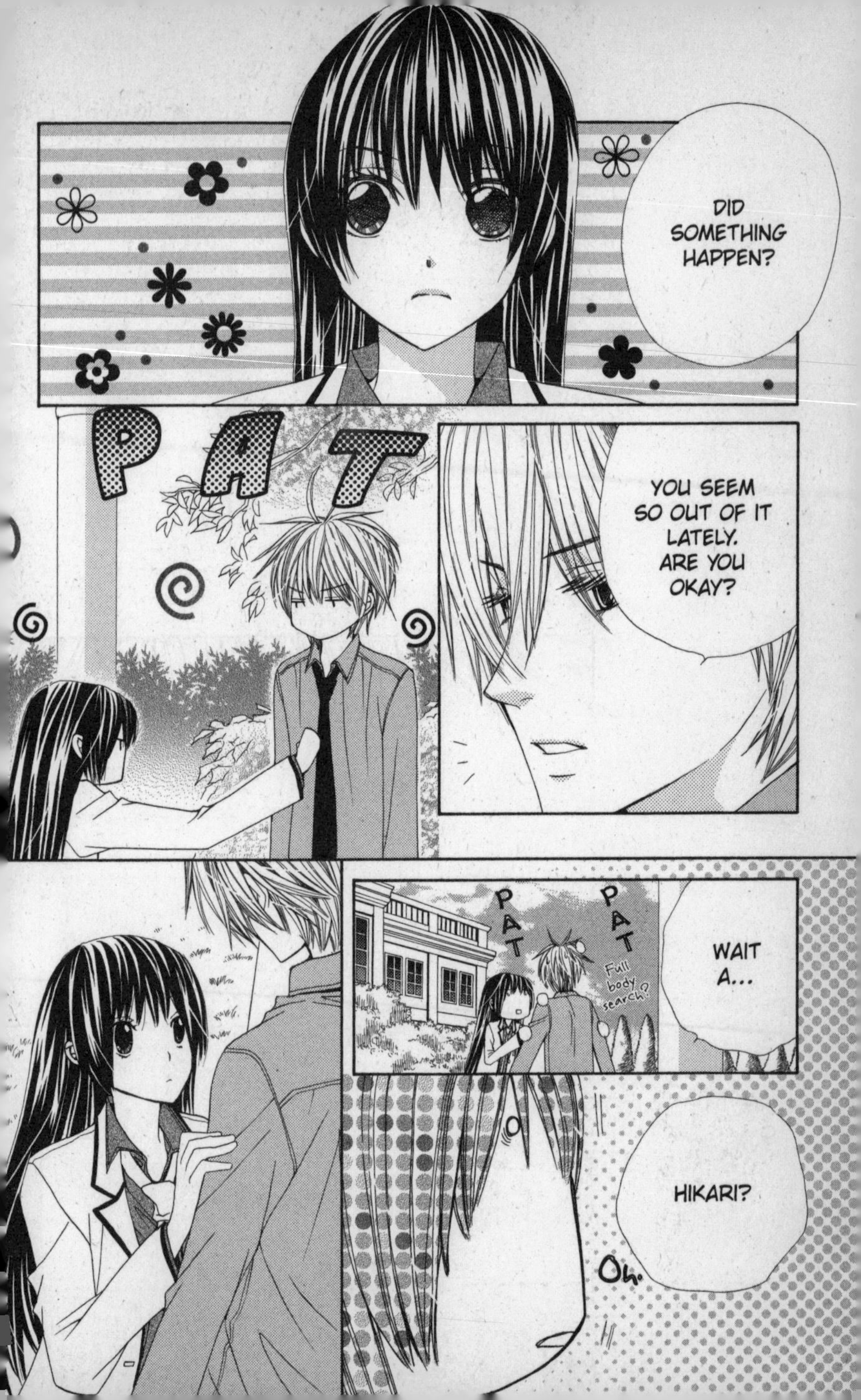
DID SOMETHING HAPPEN?
YOU SEEM SO OUT OF IT LATELY. ARE YOU OKAY?
PAT
WAIT A...
PAT
PAT
Full body search?
HIKARI?
Oh.

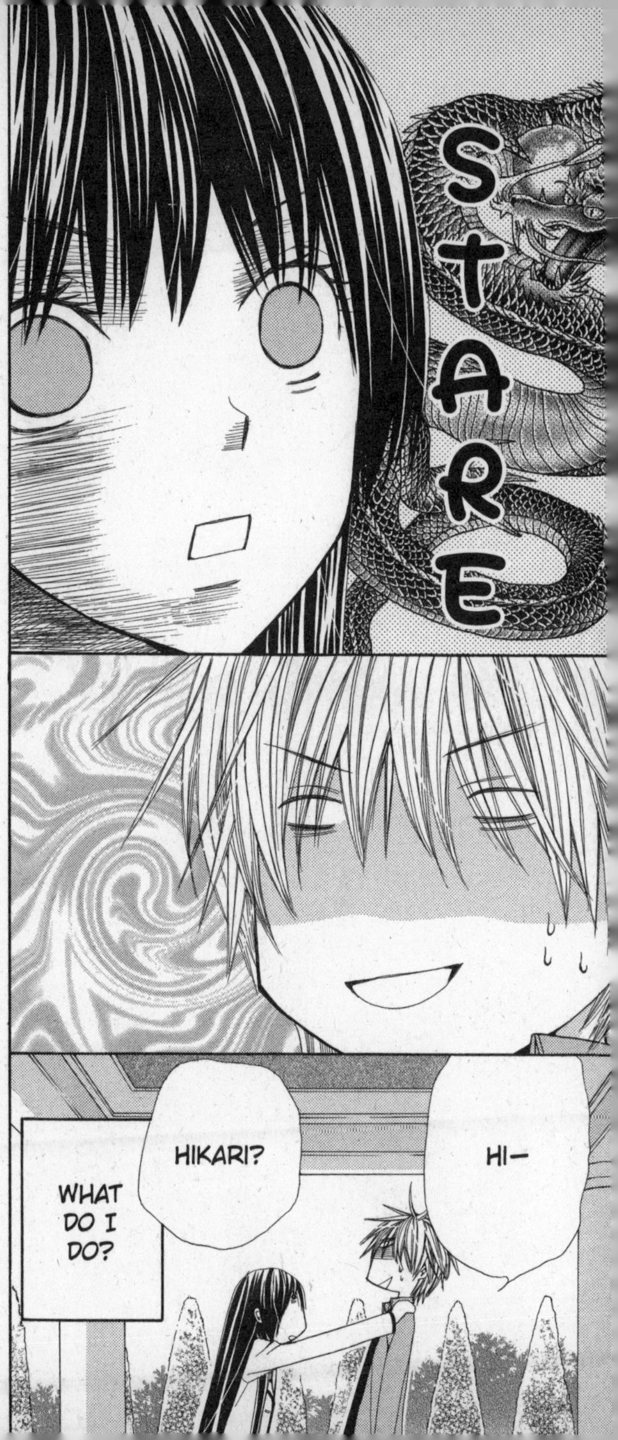
STARE
HI—
HIKARI?
WHAT DO I DO?
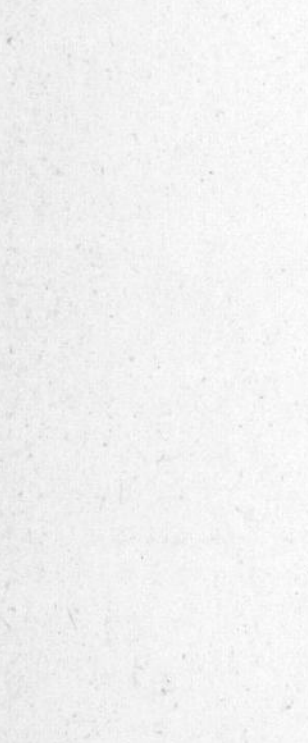

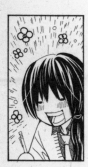

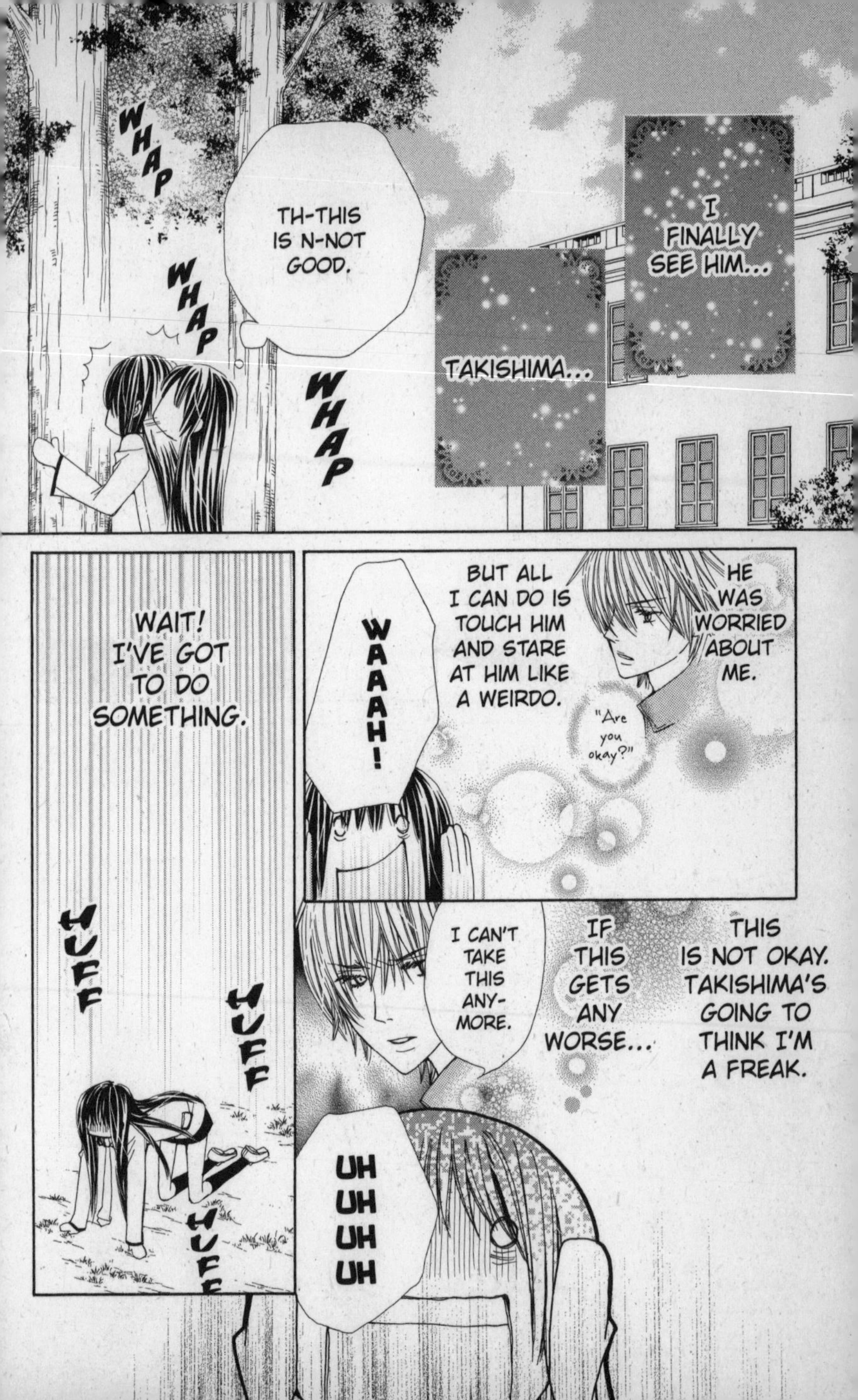
I FINALLY SEE HIM...
TAKISHIMA...
TH-THIS IS N-NOT GOOD.
WHAP
WHAP
WHAP
HE WAS WORRIED ABOUT ME.
"Are you okay?"
BUT ALL I CAN DO IS TOUCH HIM AND STARE AT HIM LIKE A WEIRDO.
WAAAAH!
THIS IS NOT OKAY. TAKISHIMA'S GOING TO THINK I'M A FREAK.
IF THIS GETS ANY WORSE...
I CAN'T TAKE THIS ANY-MORE.
UH UH UH UH
WAIT! I'VE GOT TO DO SOMETHING.
HUFF
HUFF
HUFF

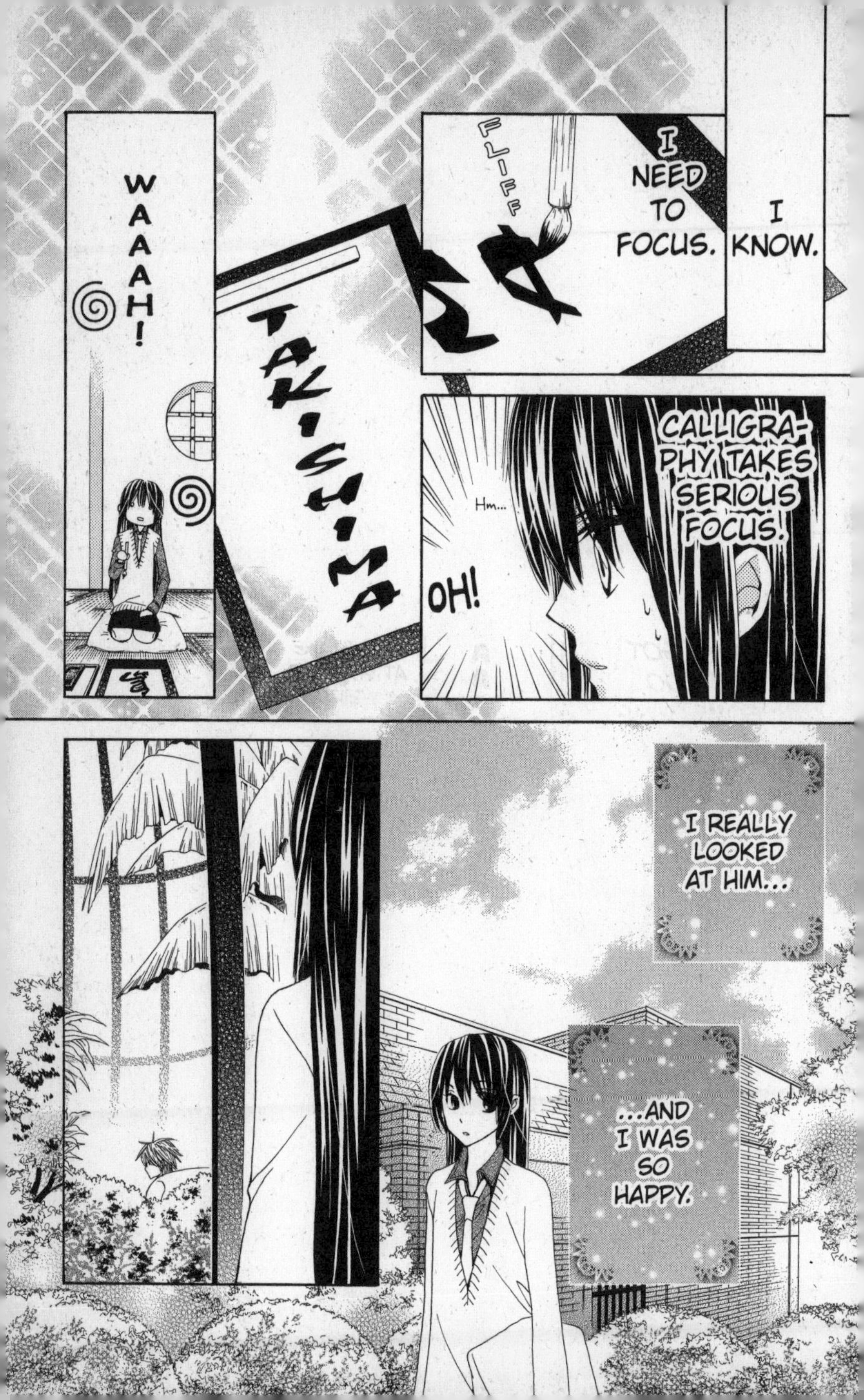
I KNOW.
I NEED TO FOCUS.
FLIFF
CALLIGRA-PHY TAKES SERIOUS FOCUS.
Hm...
OH!
TAKISHIMA
WAAAAH!
I REALLY LOOKED AT HIM...
...AND I WAS SO HAPPY.

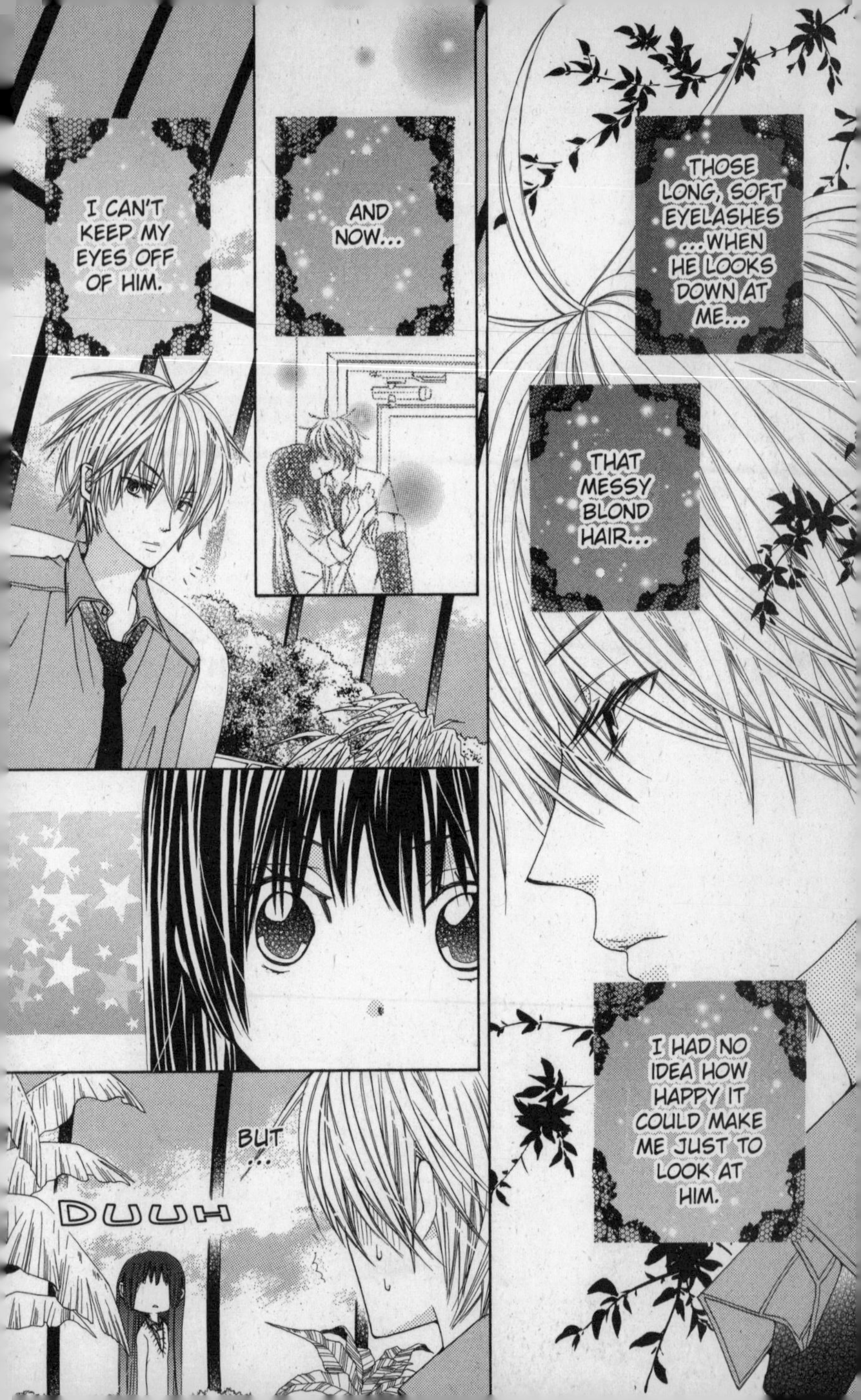
THOSE LONG, SOFT EYELASHES ...WHEN HE LOOKS DOWN AT ME...
THAT MESSY BLOND HAIR...
I HAD NO IDEA HOW HAPPY IT COULD MAKE ME JUST TO LOOK AT HIM.
AND NOW...
I CAN'T KEEP MY EYES OFF OF HIM.
BUT...
DUUH

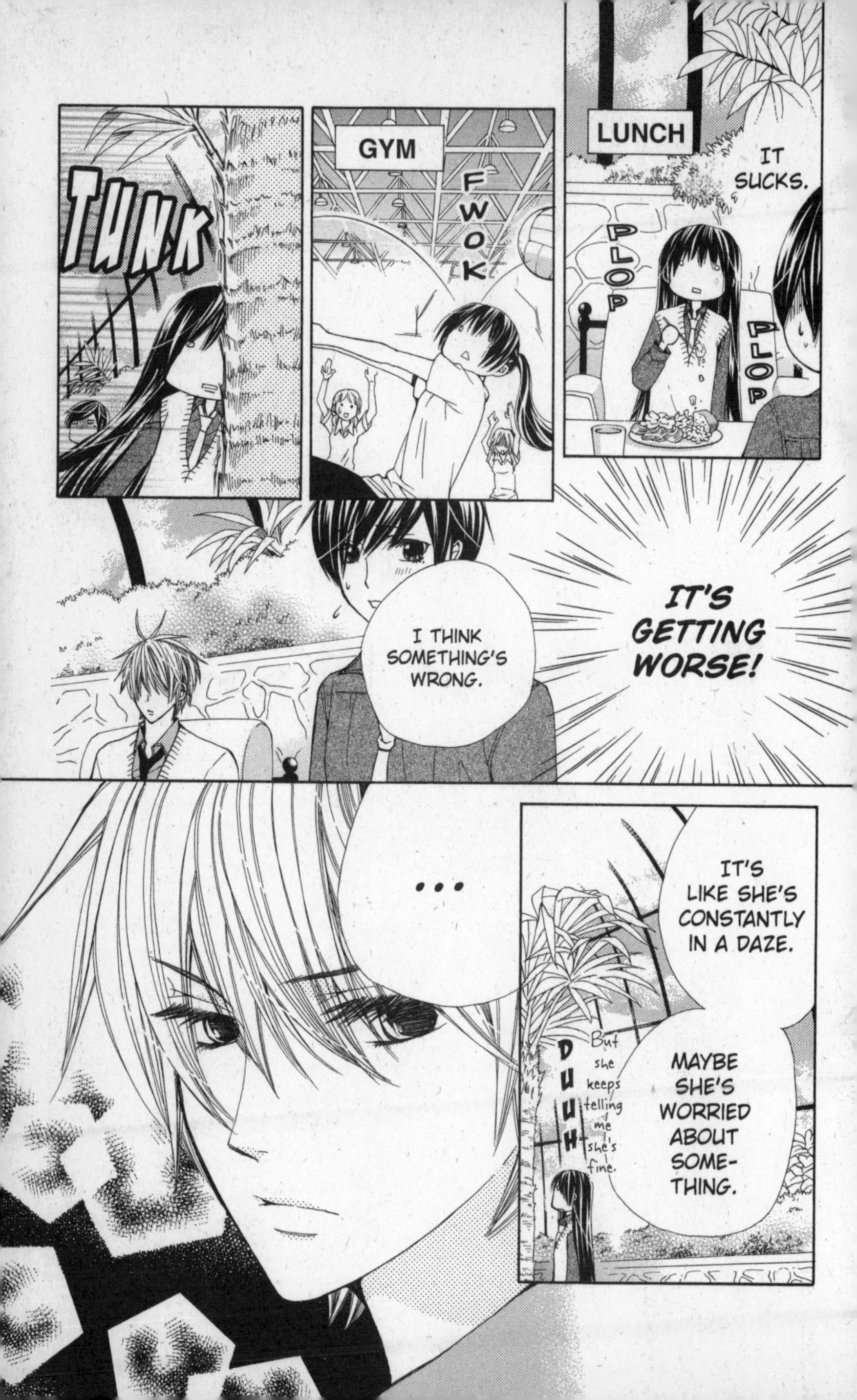
LUNCH
IT SUCKS.
PLOP
PLOP
GYM
FWOK
TUNK
IT'S GETTING WORSE!
I THINK SOMETHING'S WRONG.
IT'S LIKE SHE'S CONSTANTLY IN A DAZE.
MAYBE SHE'S WORRIED ABOUT SOME-THING.
But she keeps telling me she's fine.
DUUH
...

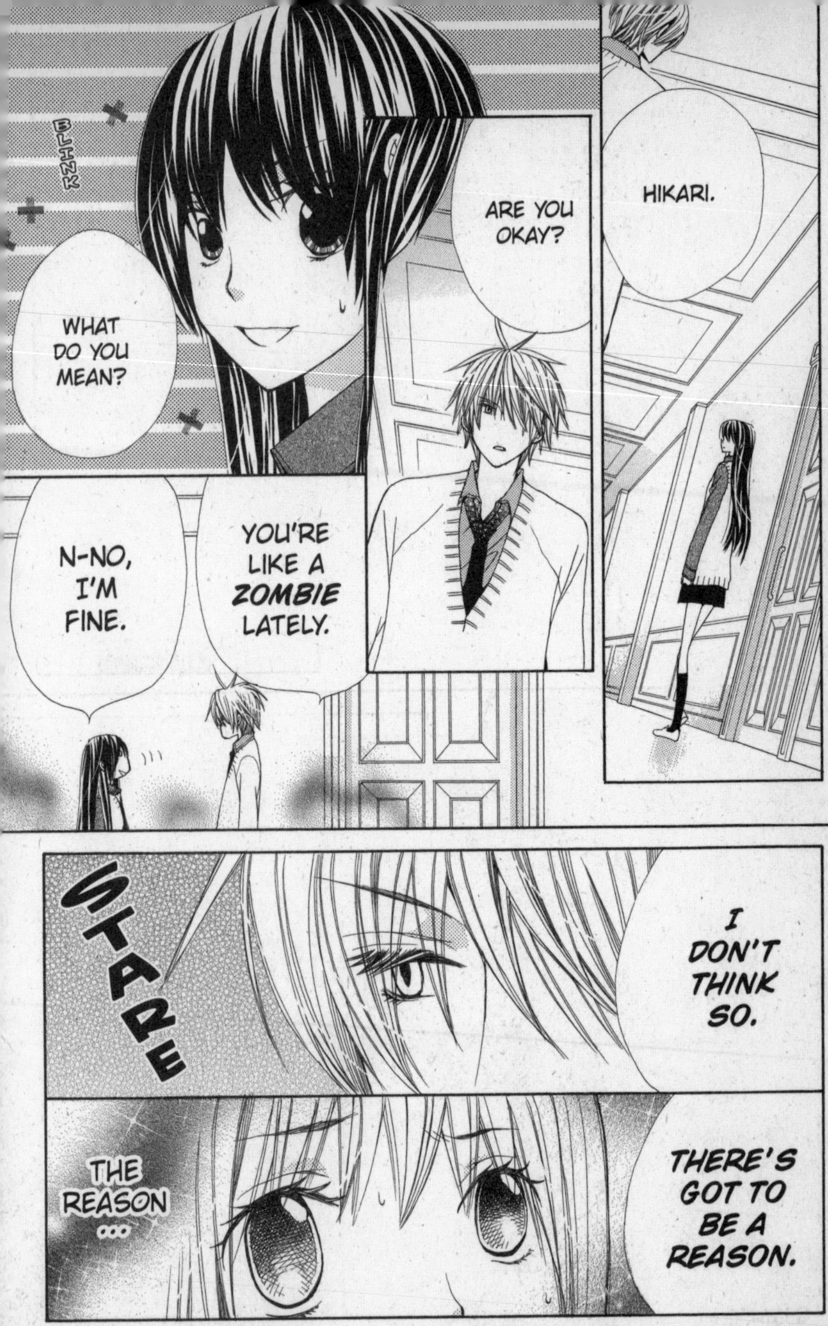
HIKARI.
ARE YOU OKAY?
BLINK
WHAT DO YOU MEAN?
YOU'RE LIKE A *ZOMBIE* LATELY.
N-NO, I'M FINE.
I DON'T THINK SO.
STARE
THERE'S GOT TO BE A REASON.
THE REASON...

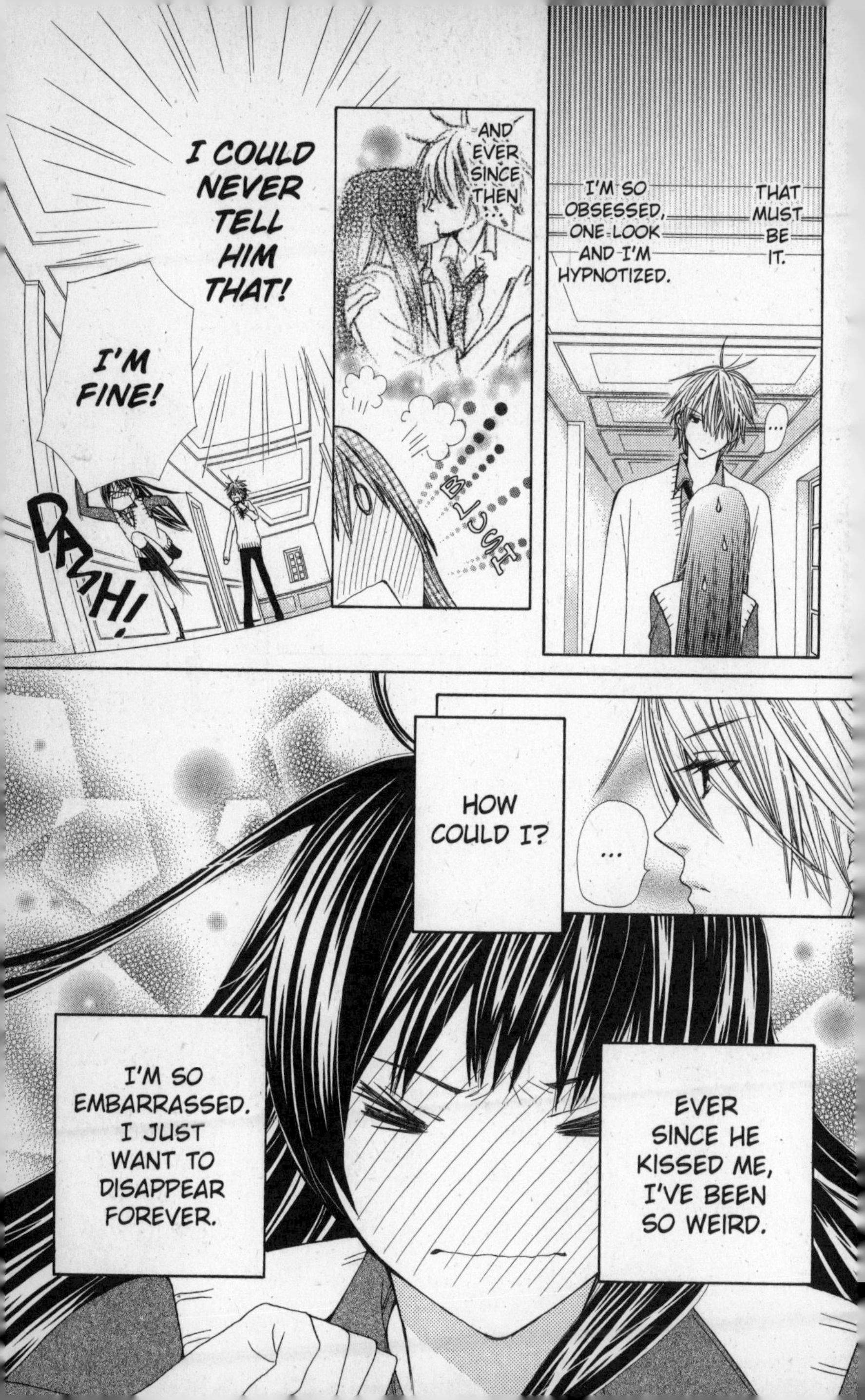
THAT MUST BE IT.
I'M SO OBSESSED, ONE LOOK AND I'M HYPNOTIZED.
...
AND EVER SINCE THEN
BLUSH
I COULD NEVER TELL HIM THAT!
I'M FINE!
DASH!
HOW COULD I?
...
EVER SINCE HE KISSED ME, I'VE BEEN SO WEIRD.
I'M SO EMBARRASSED. I JUST WANT TO DISAPPEAR FOREVER.

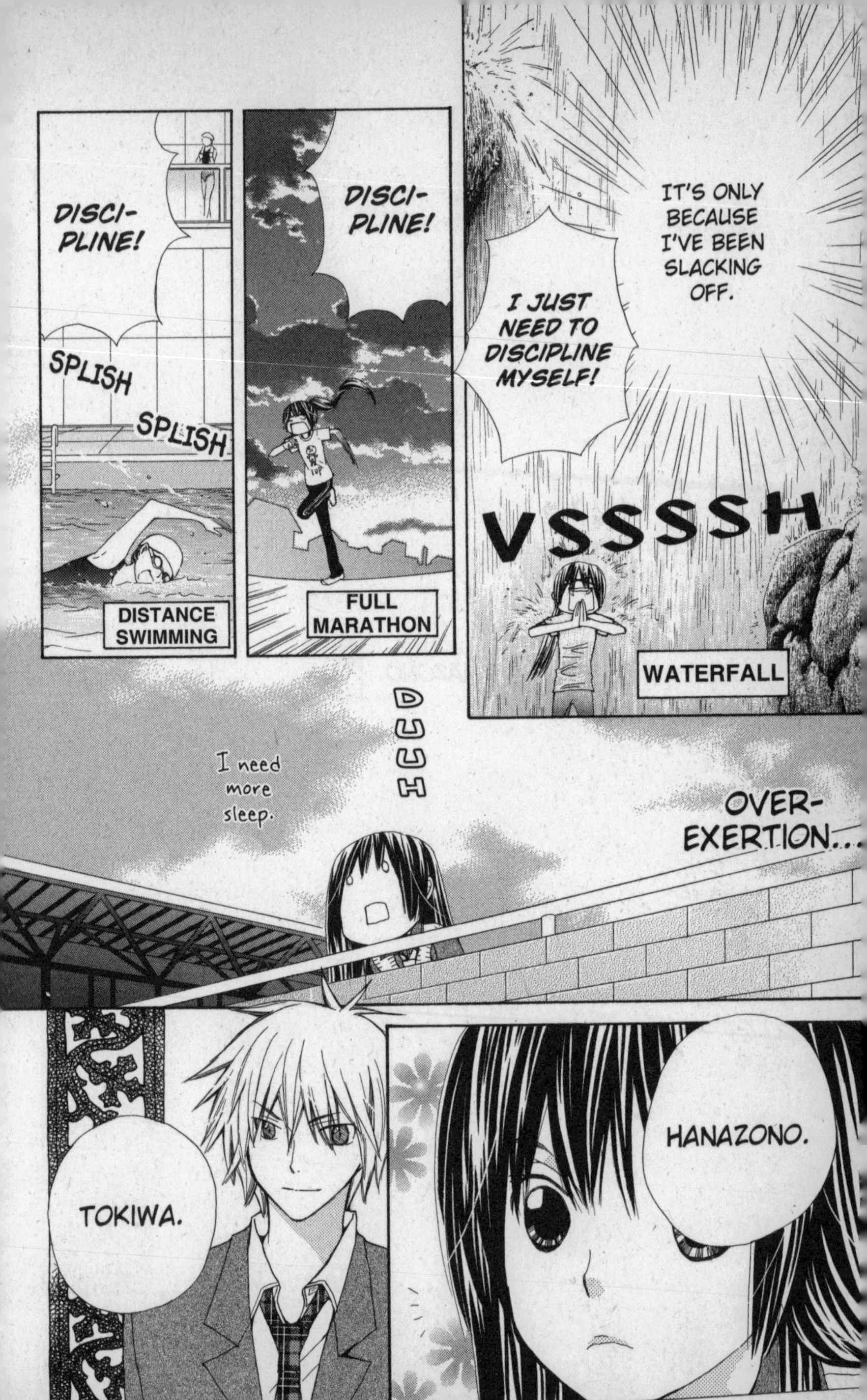
IT'S ONLY BECAUSE I'VE BEEN SLACKING OFF.
I JUST NEED TO DISCIPLINE MYSELF!
VSSSSH
WATERFALL
DISCI-PLINE!
FULL MARATHON
DISCI-PLINE!
SPLISH
SPLISH
DISTANCE SWIMMING
OVER-EXERTION...
DUUH
I need more sleep.
HANAZONO.
TOKIWA.

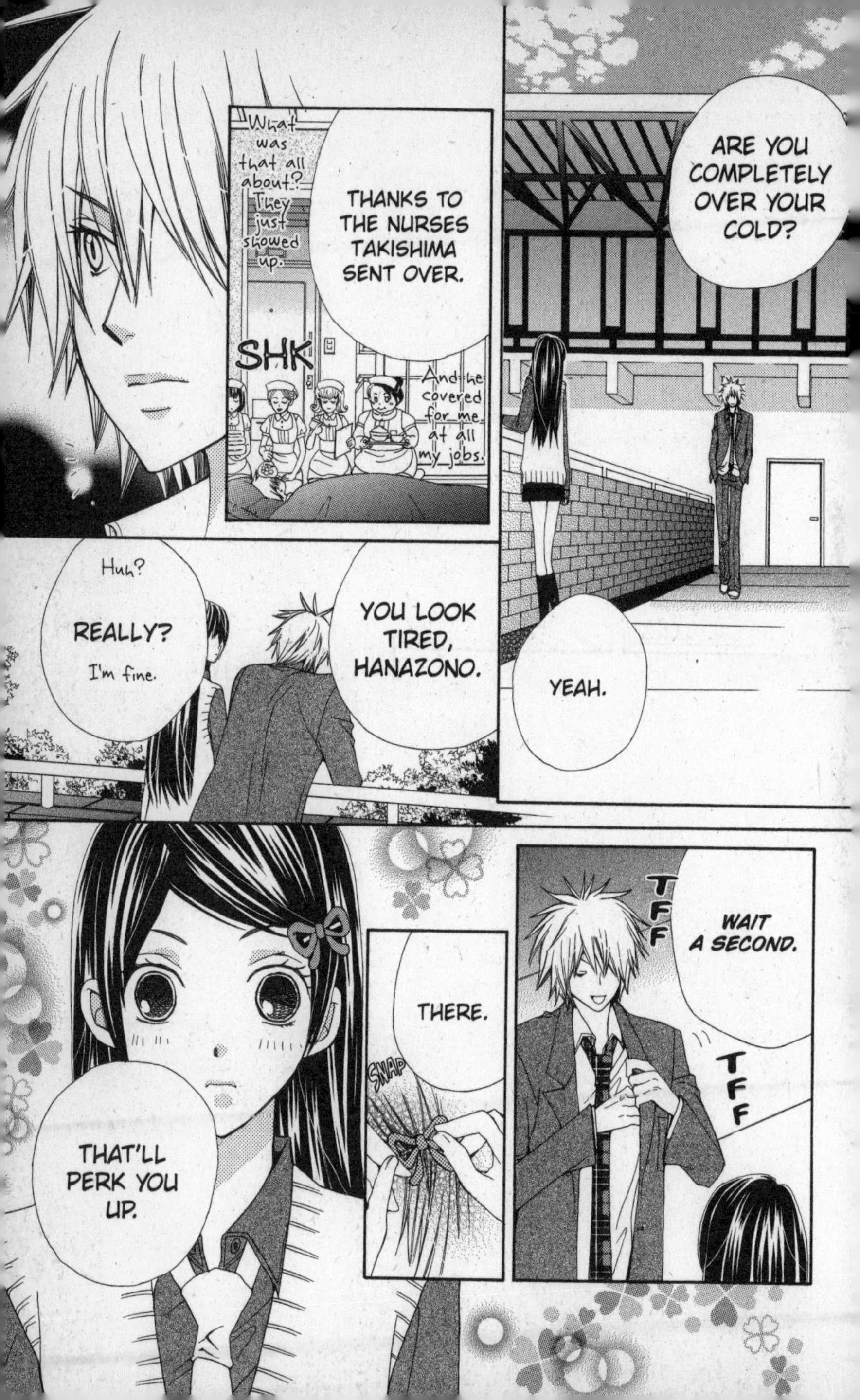
ARE YOU COMPLETELY OVER YOUR COLD?
YEAH.
THANKS TO THE NURSES TAKISHIMA SENT OVER.
What was that all about? They just showed up.
SHK
And he covered for me at all my jobs.
YOU LOOK TIRED, HANAZONO.
Huh?
REALLY?
I'm fine.
WAIT A SECOND.
TFF
TFF
THERE.
SNAP
THAT'LL PERK YOU UP.

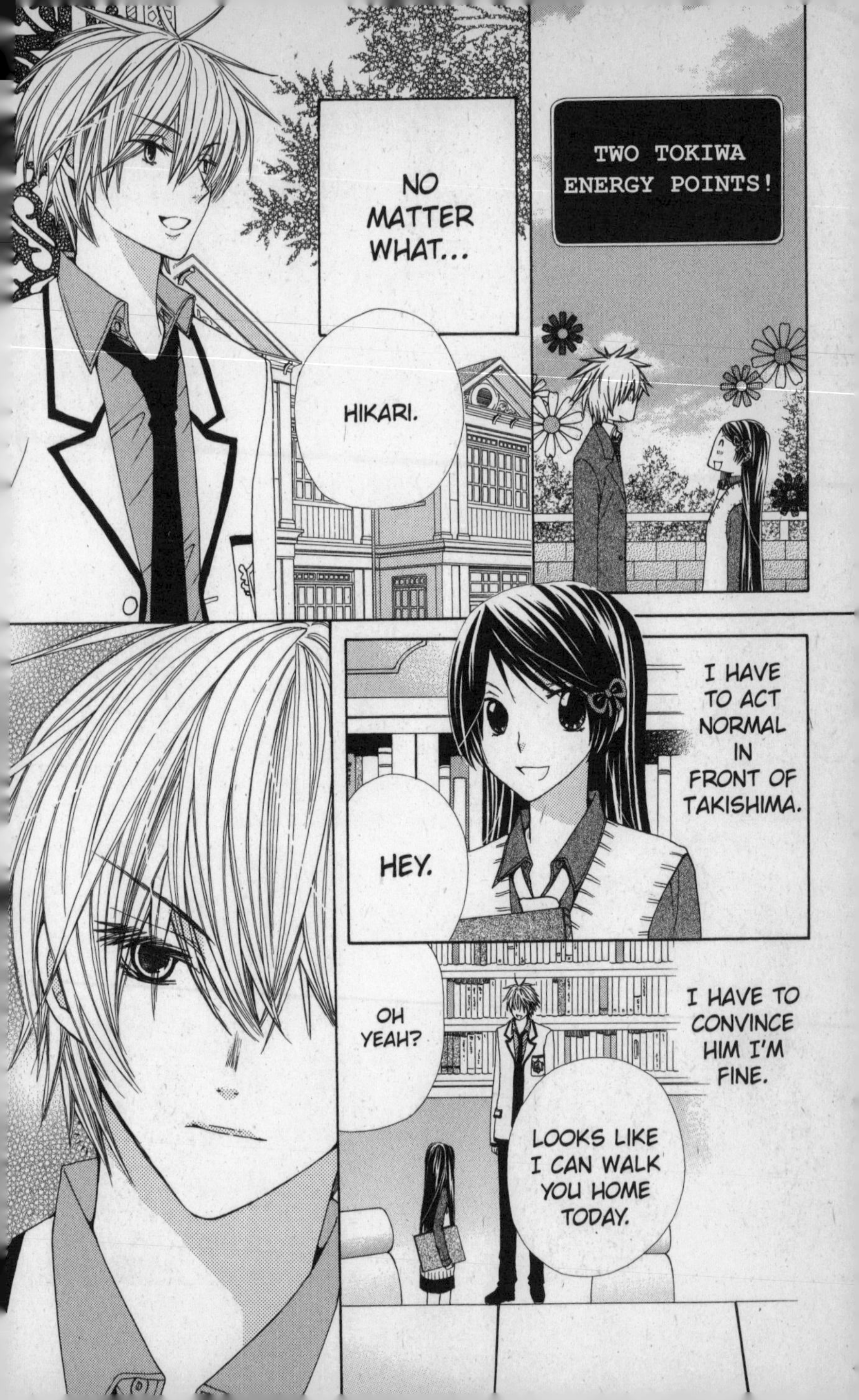
TWO TOKIWA ENERGY POINTS!
NO MATTER WHAT...
HIKARI.
I HAVE TO ACT NORMAL IN FRONT OF TAKISHIMA.
HEY.
I HAVE TO CONVINCE HIM I'M FINE.
LOOKS LIKE I CAN WALK YOU HOME TODAY.
OH YEAH?

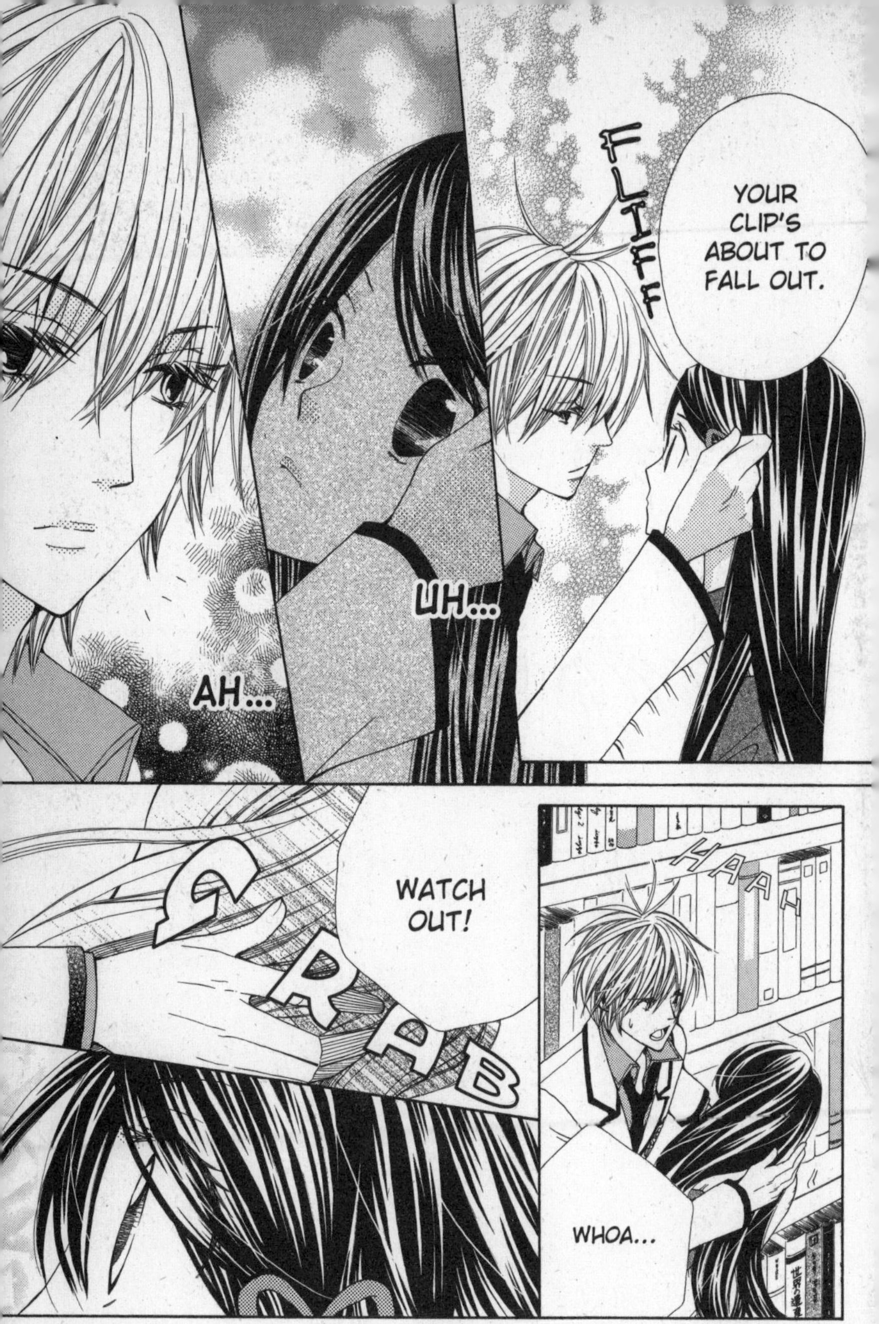
FLIFFF
YOUR CLIP'S ABOUT TO FALL OUT.
UH...
AH...
HAAAH
WHOA...
WATCH OUT!
GRAB

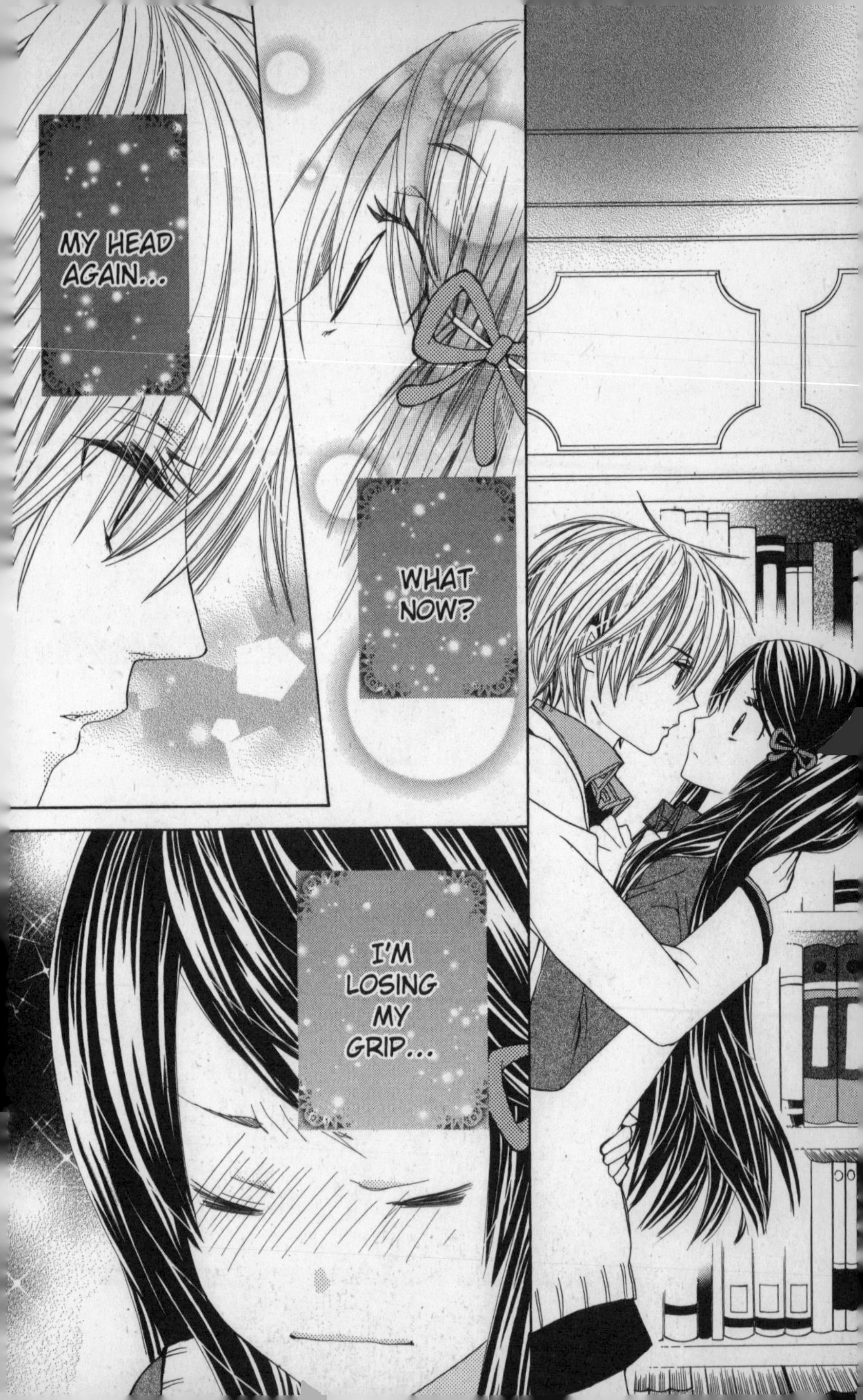
WHAT NOW?
MY HEAD AGAIN...
I'M LOSING MY GRIP...

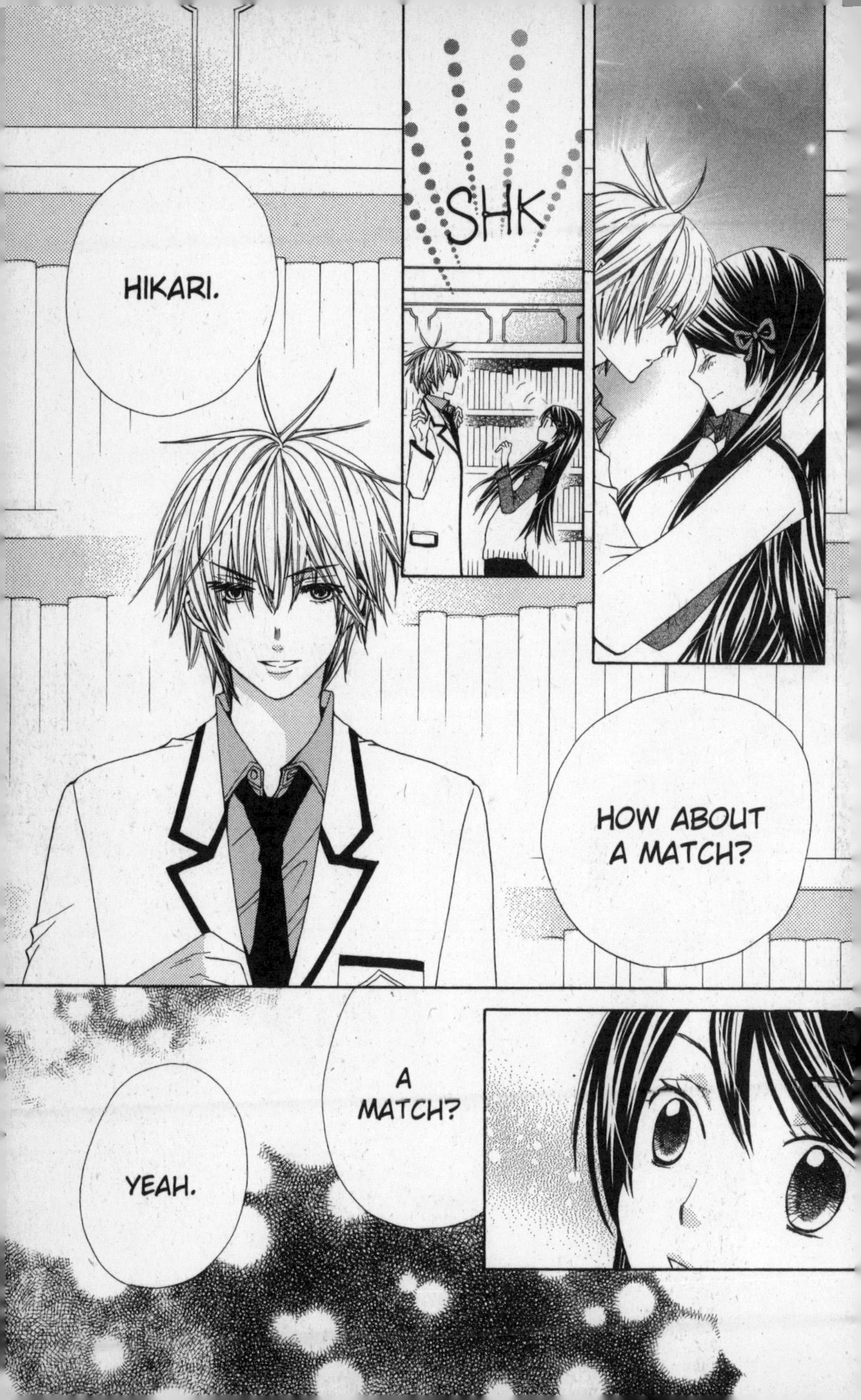
SHK
HIKARI.
HOW ABOUT A MATCH?
A MATCH?
YEAH.

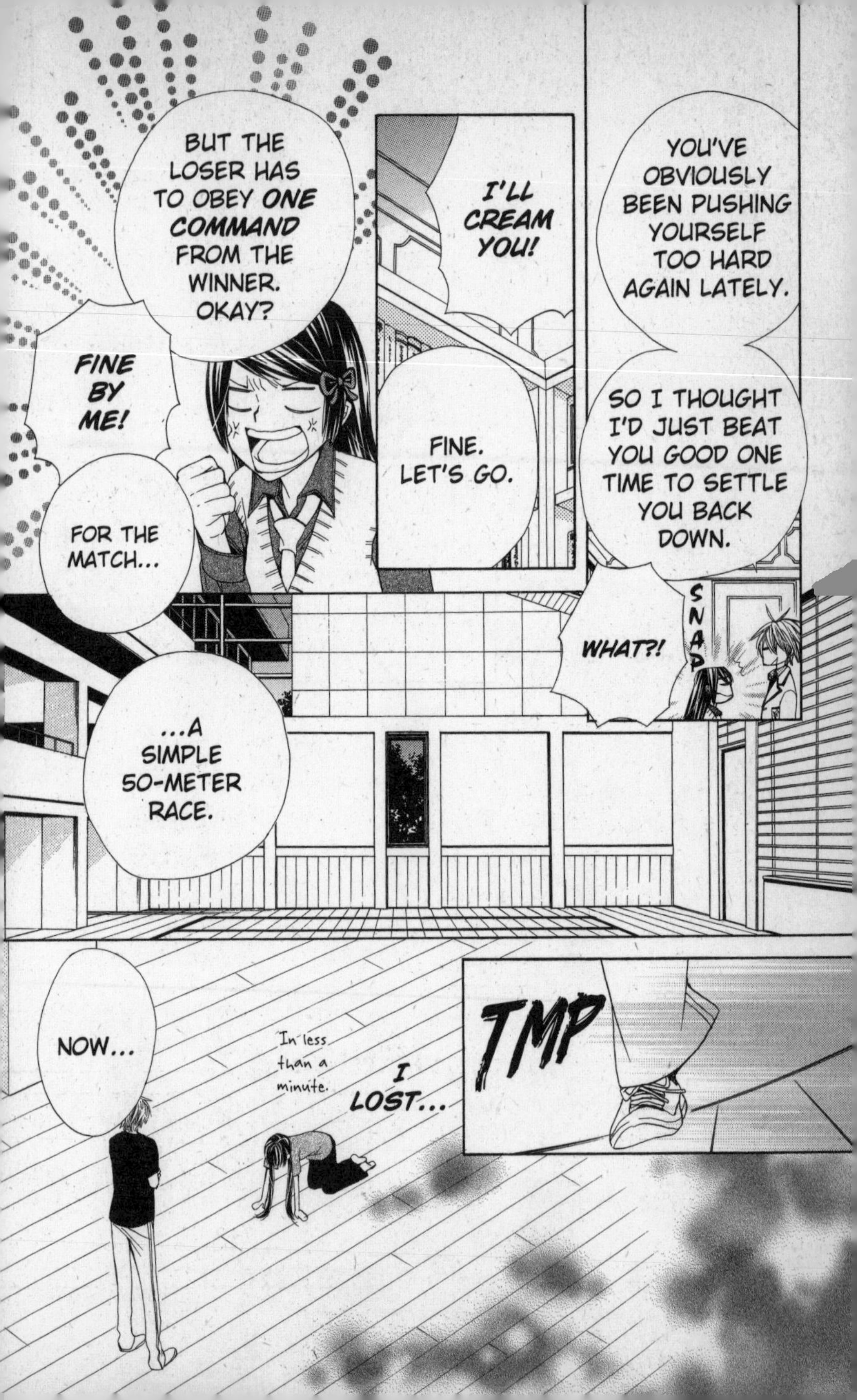

YOU'VE OBVIOUSLY BEEN PUSHING YOURSELF TOO HARD AGAIN LATELY.
SO I THOUGHT I'D JUST BEAT YOU GOOD ONE TIME TO SETTLE YOU BACK DOWN.
WHAT?!
SNAP
I'LL CREAM YOU!
FINE. LET'S GO.
BUT THE LOSER HAS TO OBEY ONE COMMAND FROM THE WINNER. OKAY?
FINE BY ME!
FOR THE MATCH...
...A SIMPLE 50-METER RACE.
TMP
NOW...
I LOST...
In less than a minute.

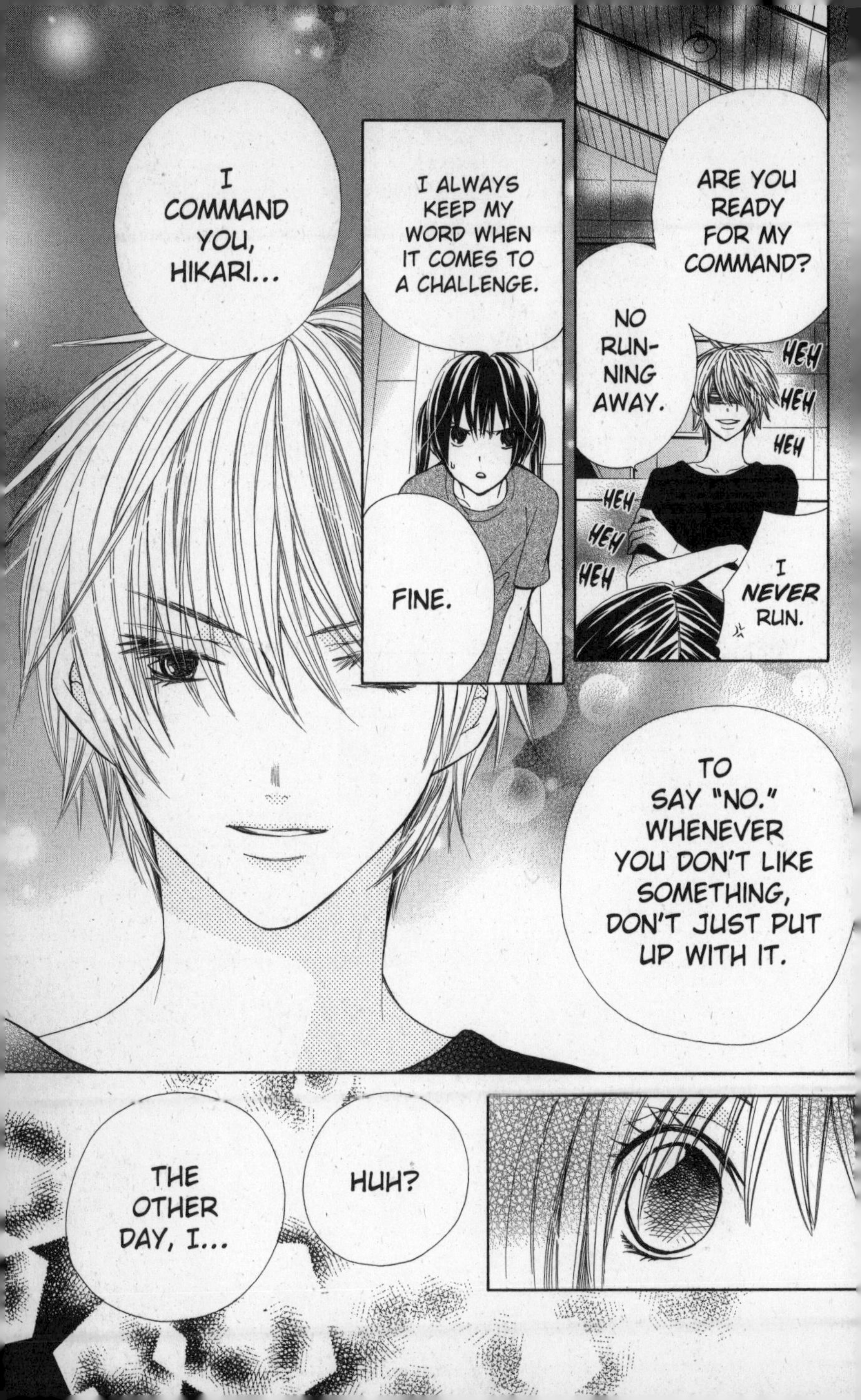
ARE YOU READY FOR MY COMMAND?
NO RUN-NING AWAY.
HEH HEH HEH
HEH HEH HEH
I NEVER RUN.
I ALWAYS KEEP MY WORD WHEN IT COMES TO A CHALLENGE.
FINE.
I COMMAND YOU, HIKARI...
TO SAY "NO." WHENEVER YOU DON'T LIKE SOMETHING, DON'T JUST PUT UP WITH IT.
HUH?
THE OTHER DAY, I...

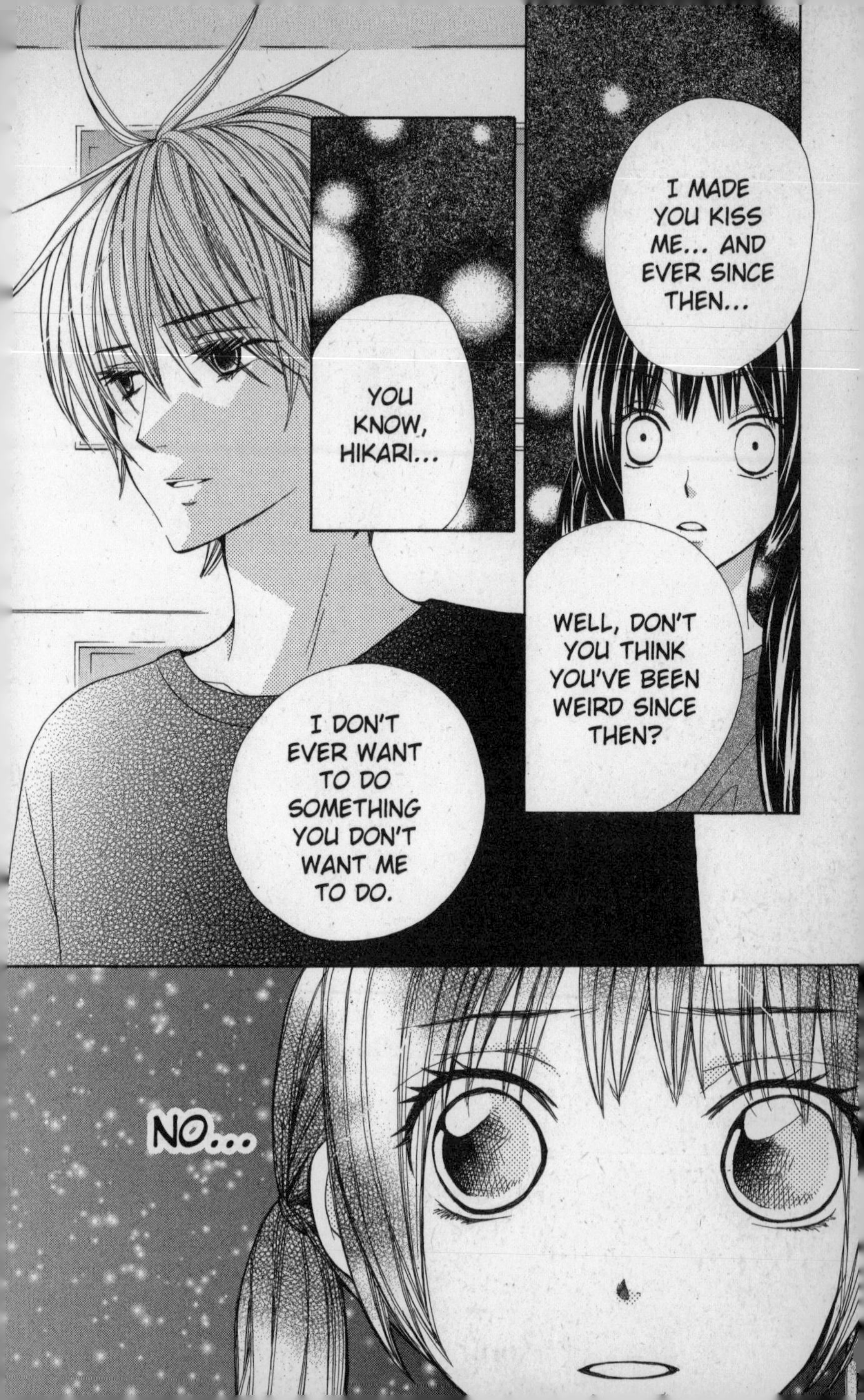
I MADE YOU KISS ME... AND EVER SINCE THEN...
WELL, DON'T YOU THINK YOU'VE BEEN WEIRD SINCE THEN?
YOU KNOW, HIKARI...
I DON'T EVER WANT TO DO SOMETHING YOU DON'T WANT ME TO DO.
NO...

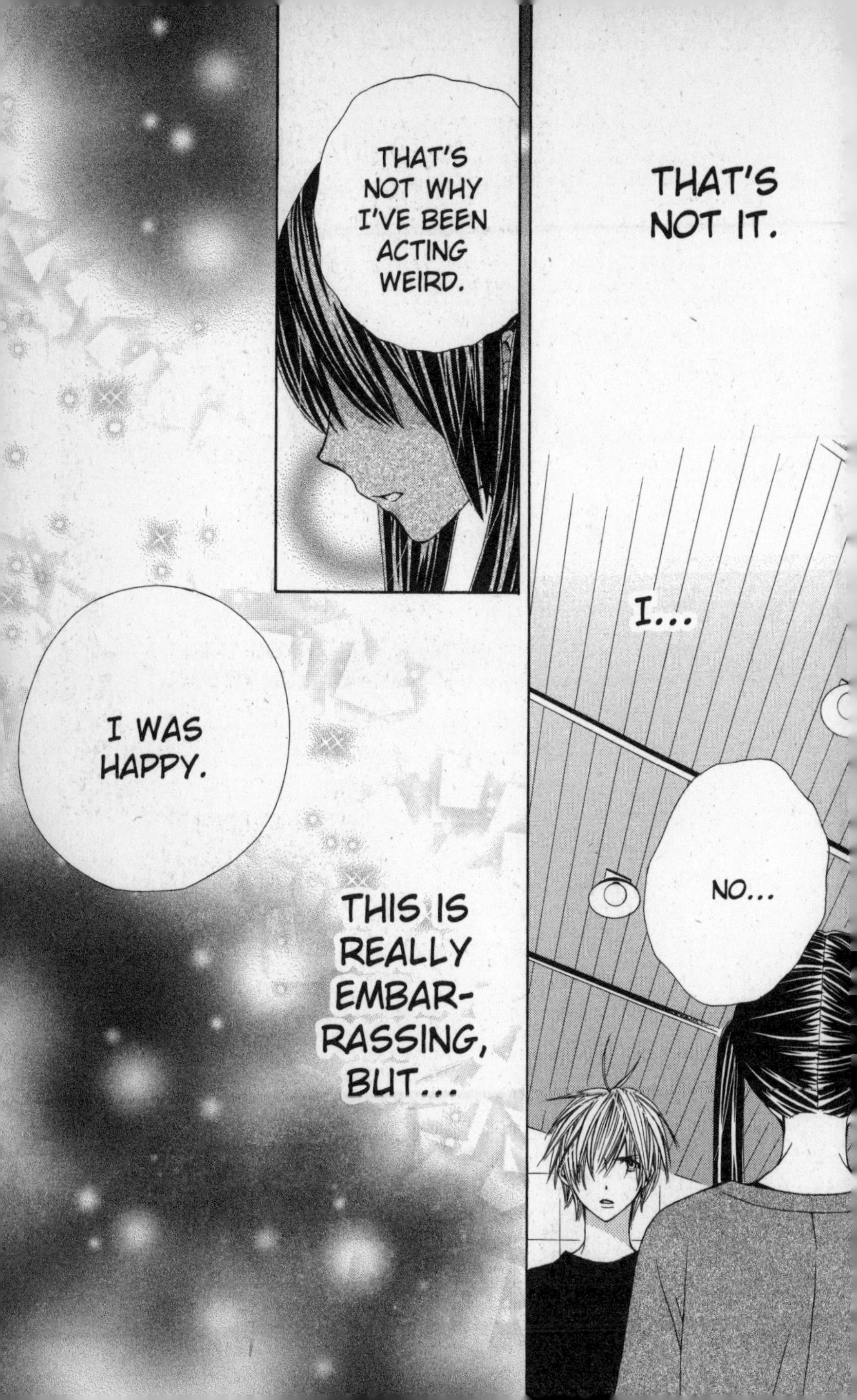
THAT'S NOT IT.
I...
NO...
THAT'S NOT WHY I'VE BEEN ACTING WEIRD.
THIS IS REALLY EMBARRASSING, BUT...
I WAS HAPPY.

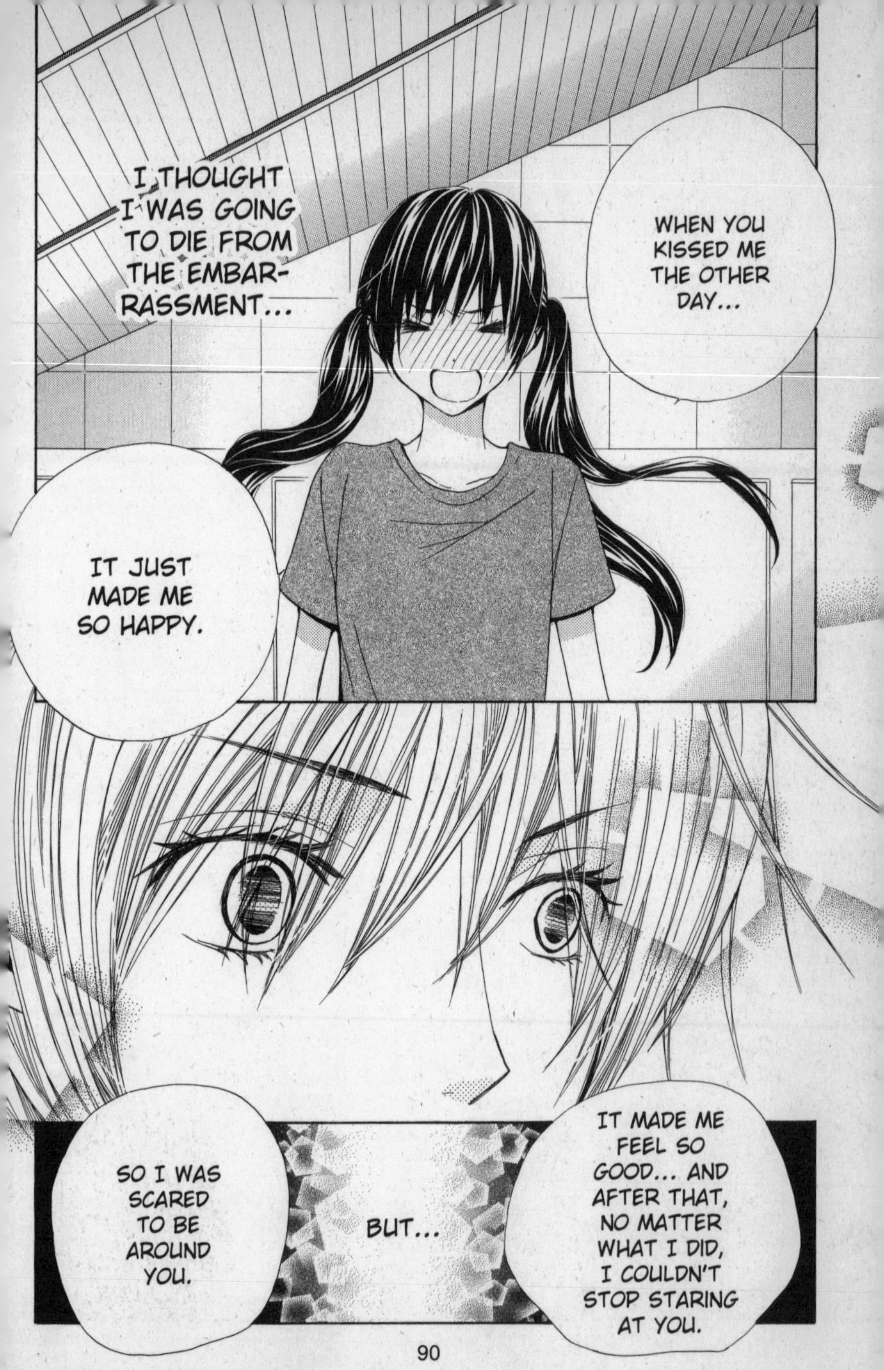
WHEN YOU KISSED ME THE OTHER DAY...
I THOUGHT I WAS GOING TO DIE FROM THE EMBAR-RASSMENT...
IT JUST MADE ME SO HAPPY.
IT MADE ME FEEL SO GOOD... AND AFTER THAT, NO MATTER WHAT I DID, I COULDN'T STOP STARING AT YOU.
BUT...
SO I WAS SCARED TO BE AROUND YOU.

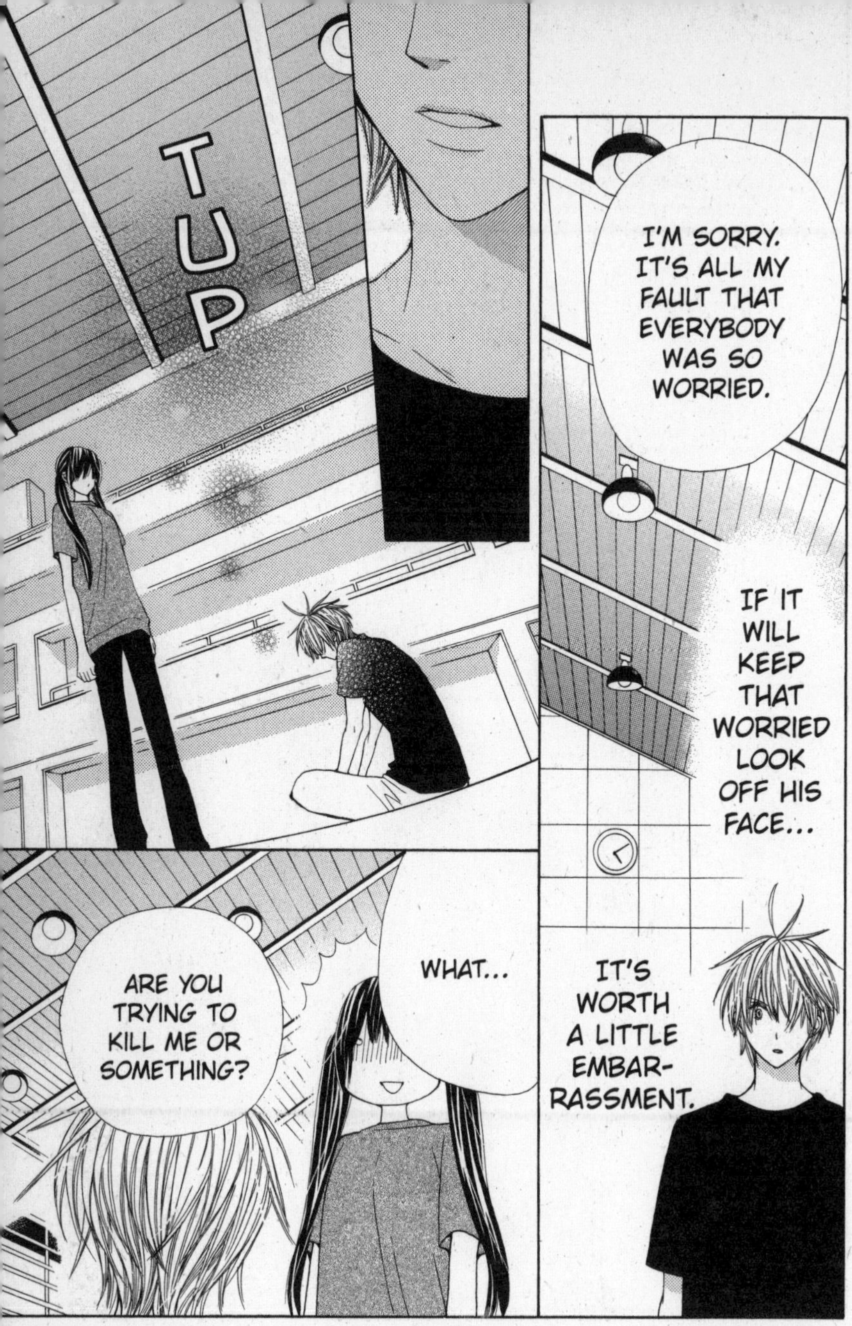
I'M SORRY. IT'S ALL MY FAULT THAT EVERYBODY WAS SO WORRIED.
IF IT WILL KEEP THAT WORRIED LOOK OFF HIS FACE...
IT'S WORTH A LITTLE EMBAR-RASSMENT.
TUP
WHAT...
ARE YOU TRYING TO KILL ME OR SOMETHING?

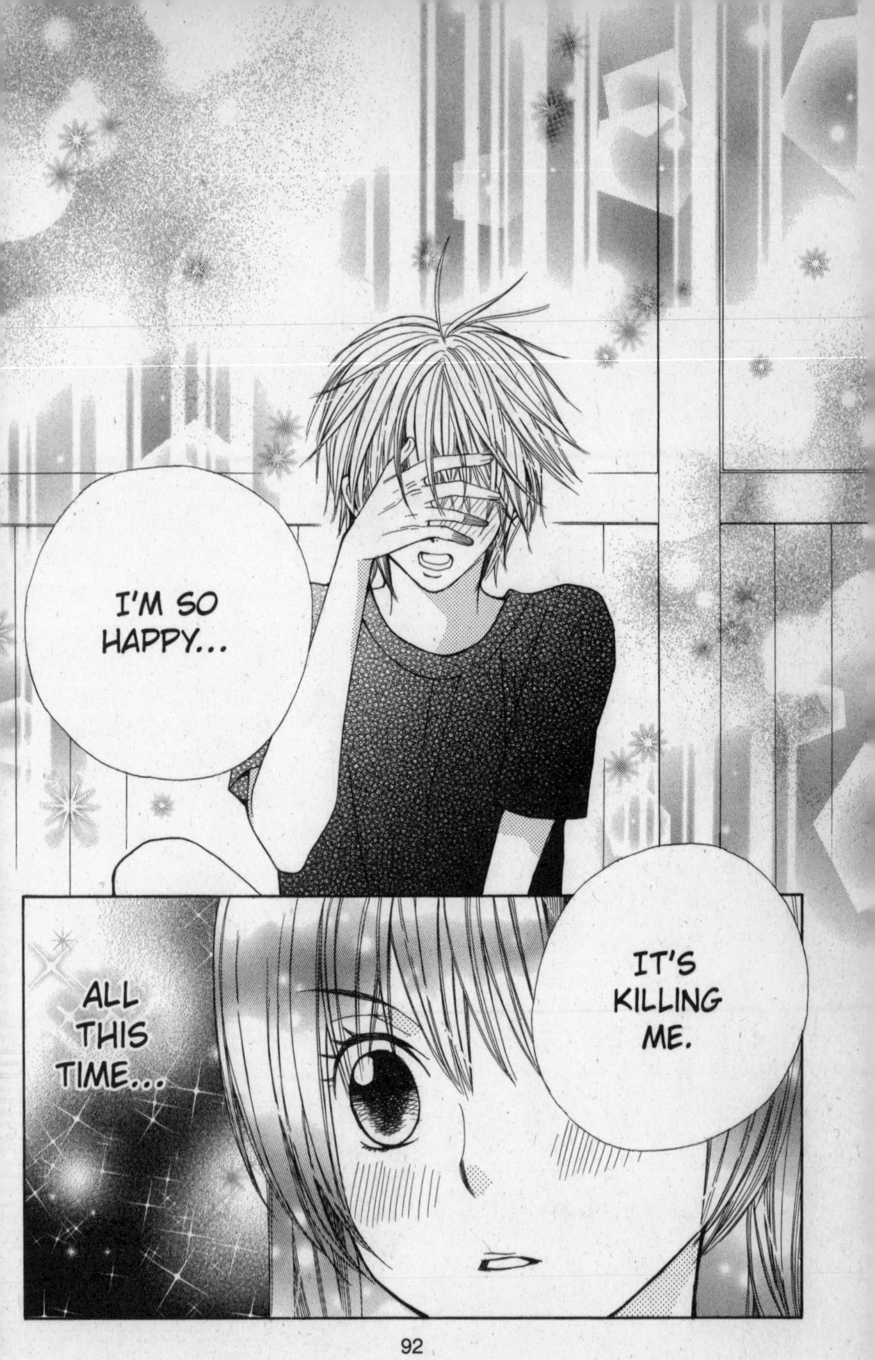
I'M SO HAPPY...
IT'S KILLING ME.
ALL THIS TIME...

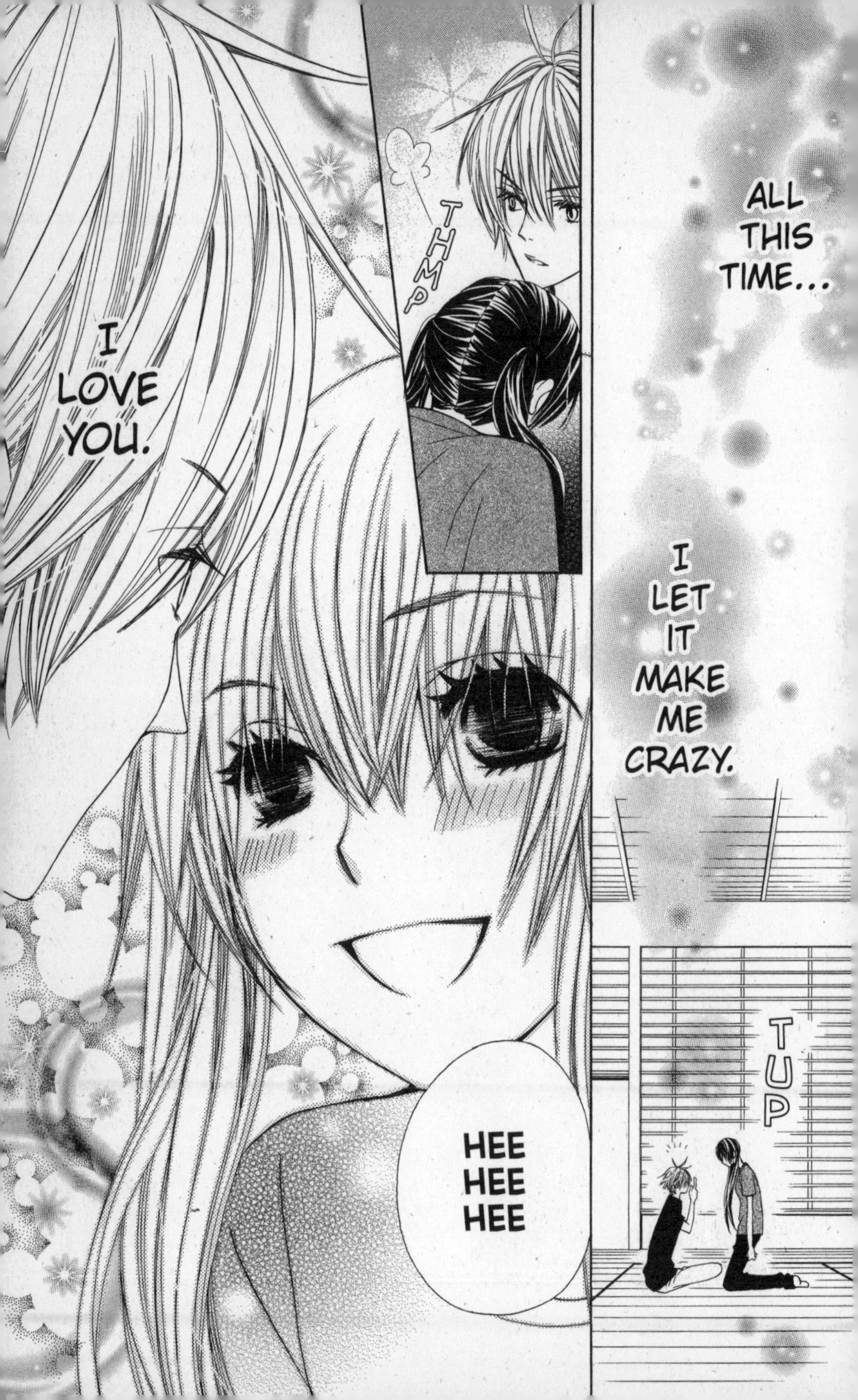
ALL THIS TIME...
I LET IT MAKE ME CRAZY.
TUP
THMP
I LOVE YOU.
HEE HEE HEE

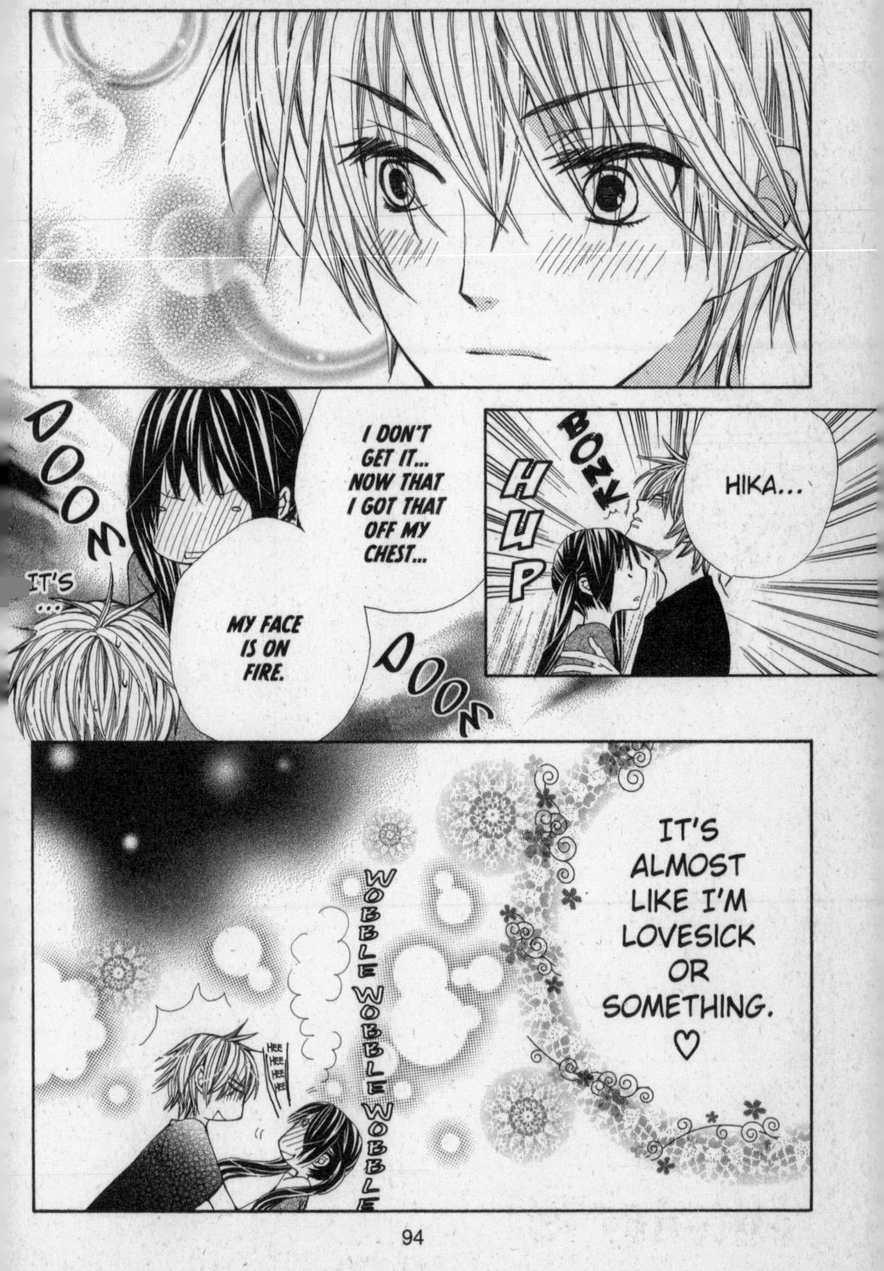
BONK
HUP
HIKA...
DOOOM
I DON'T GET IT... NOW THAT I GOT THAT OFF MY CHEST...
MY FACE IS ON FIRE.
IT'S...
DOOM
IT'S ALMOST LIKE I'M LOVESICK OR SOMETHING. ♡
WOBBLE WOBBLE WOBBLE
HEE HEE HEE HEE

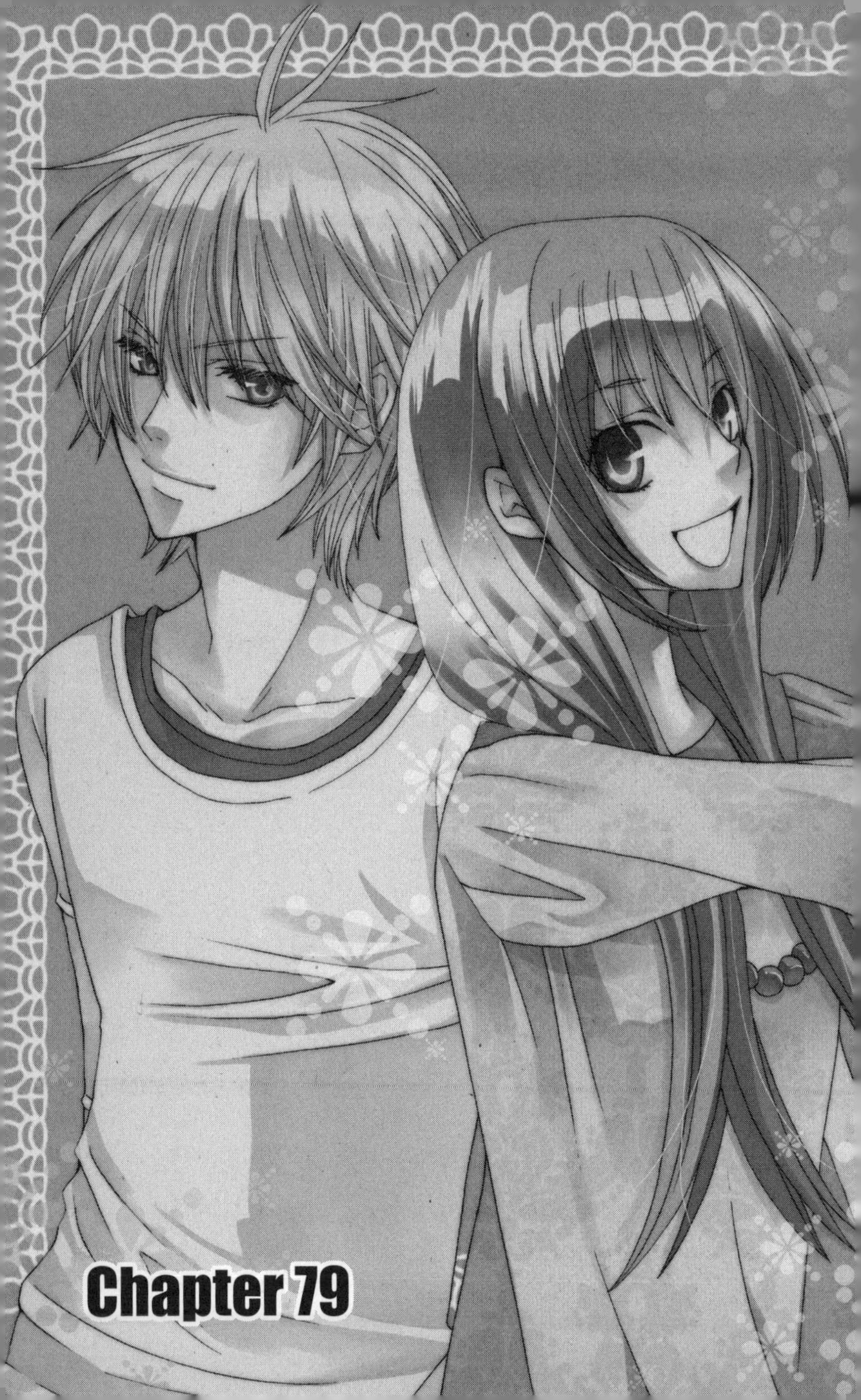
Chapter 79

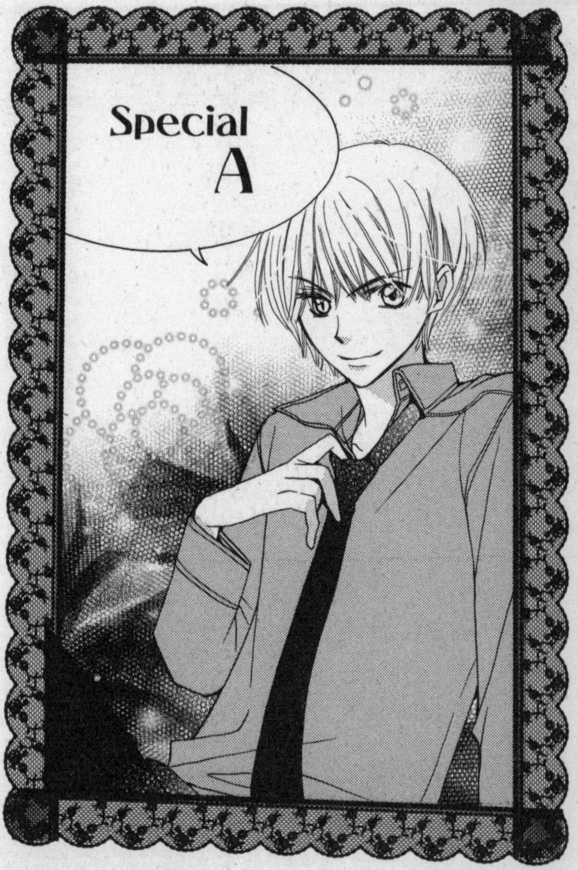
Special A

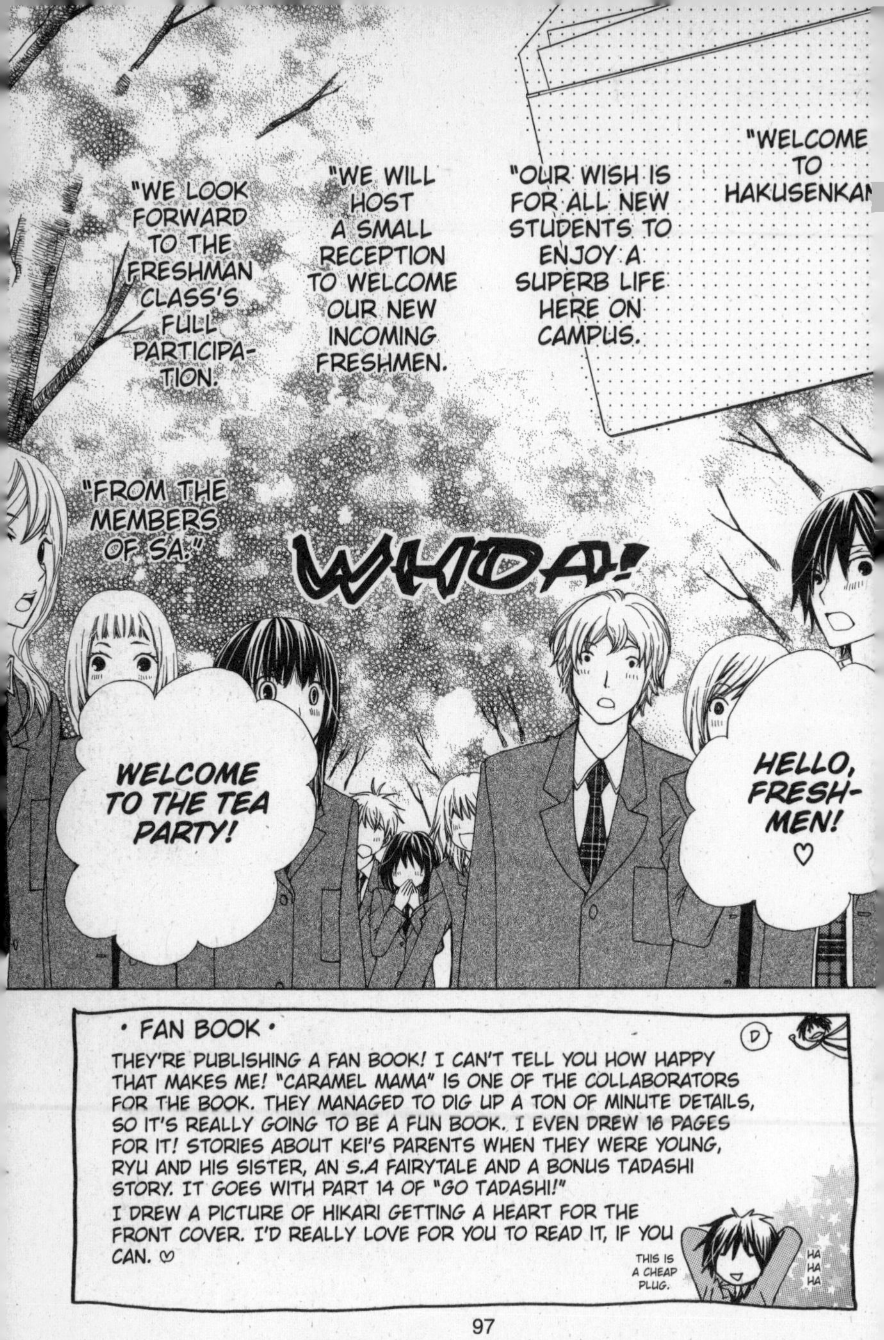
"WELCOME TO HAKUSENKAN
"OUR WISH IS FOR ALL NEW STUDENTS TO ENJOY A SUPERB LIFE HERE ON CAMPUS.
"WE WILL HOST A SMALL RECEPTION TO WELCOME OUR NEW INCOMING FRESHMEN.
"WE LOOK FORWARD TO THE FRESHMAN CLASS'S FULL PARTICIPA-TION.
"FROM THE MEMBERS OF SA."
WHOA!
HELLO, FRESH-MEN! ♡
WELCOME TO THE TEA PARTY!

• FAN BOOK •

THEY'RE PUBLISHING A FAN BOOK! I CAN'T TELL YOU HOW HAPPY THAT MAKES ME! "CARAMEL MAMA" IS ONE OF THE COLLABORATORS FOR THE BOOK. THEY MANAGED TO DIG UP A TON OF MINUTE DETAILS, SO IT'S REALLY GOING TO BE A FUN BOOK. I EVEN DREW 16 PAGES FOR IT! STORIES ABOUT KEI'S PARENTS WHEN THEY WERE YOUNG, RYU AND HIS SISTER, AN *S.A* FAIRYTALE AND A BONUS TADASHI STORY. IT GOES WITH PART 14 OF "GO TADASHI!"

I DREW A PICTURE OF HIKARI GETTING A HEART FOR THE FRONT COVER. I'D REALLY LOVE FOR YOU TO READ IT, IF YOU CAN. ♡

THIS IS A CHEAP PLUG.

HA HA HA

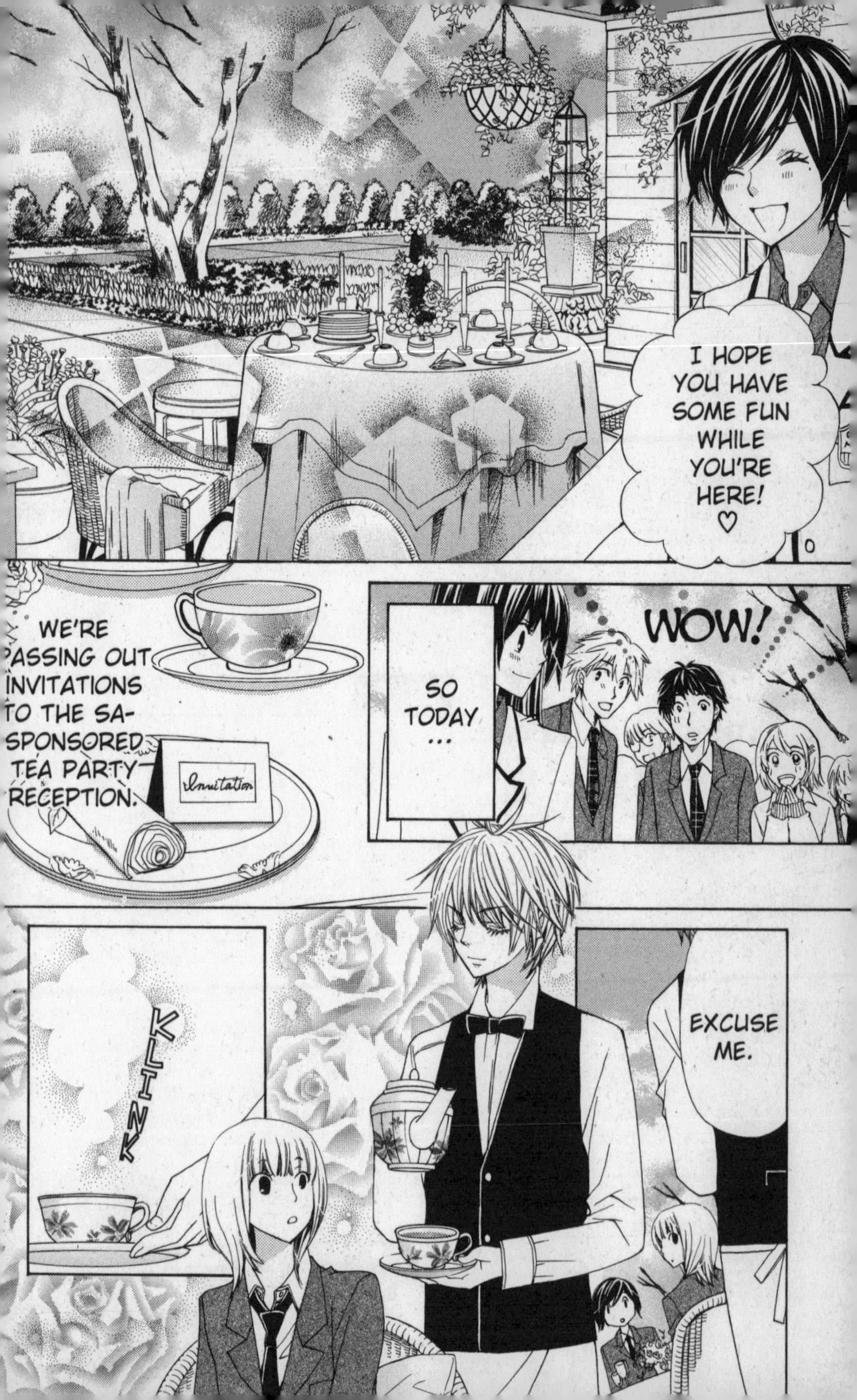
I HOPE YOU HAVE SOME FUN WHILE YOU'RE HERE! ♡
SO TODAY...
WOW!
WE'RE PASSING OUT INVITATIONS TO THE SA-SPONSORED TEA PARTY RECEPTION.
Invitation
EXCUSE ME.
KLINK

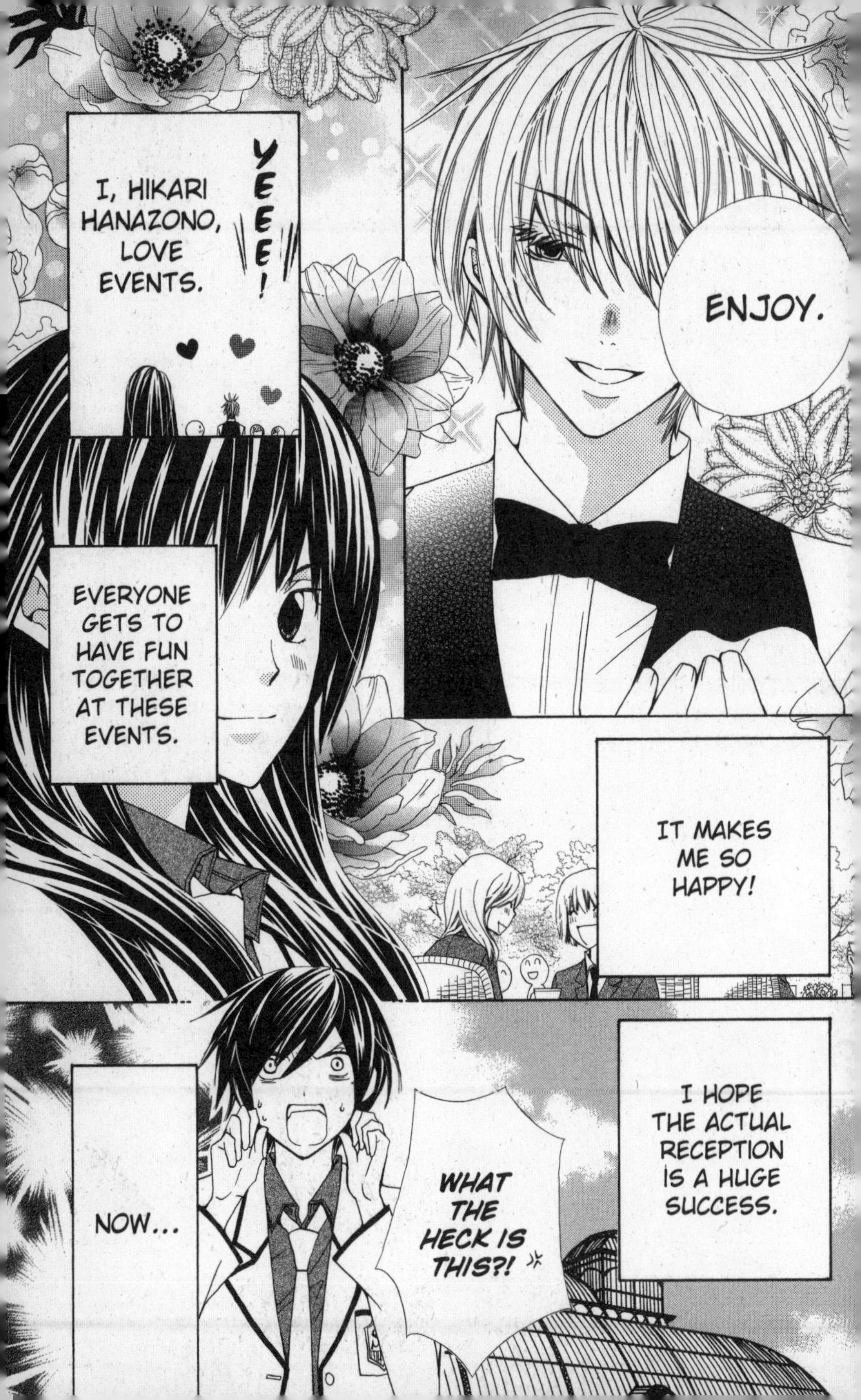

ENJOY.
I, HIKARI HANAZONO, LOVE EVENTS.
YEEE!
EVERYONE GETS TO HAVE FUN TOGETHER AT THESE EVENTS.
IT MAKES ME SO HAPPY!
I HOPE THE ACTUAL RECEPTION IS A HUGE SUCCESS.
NOW...
WHAT THE HECK IS THIS?!

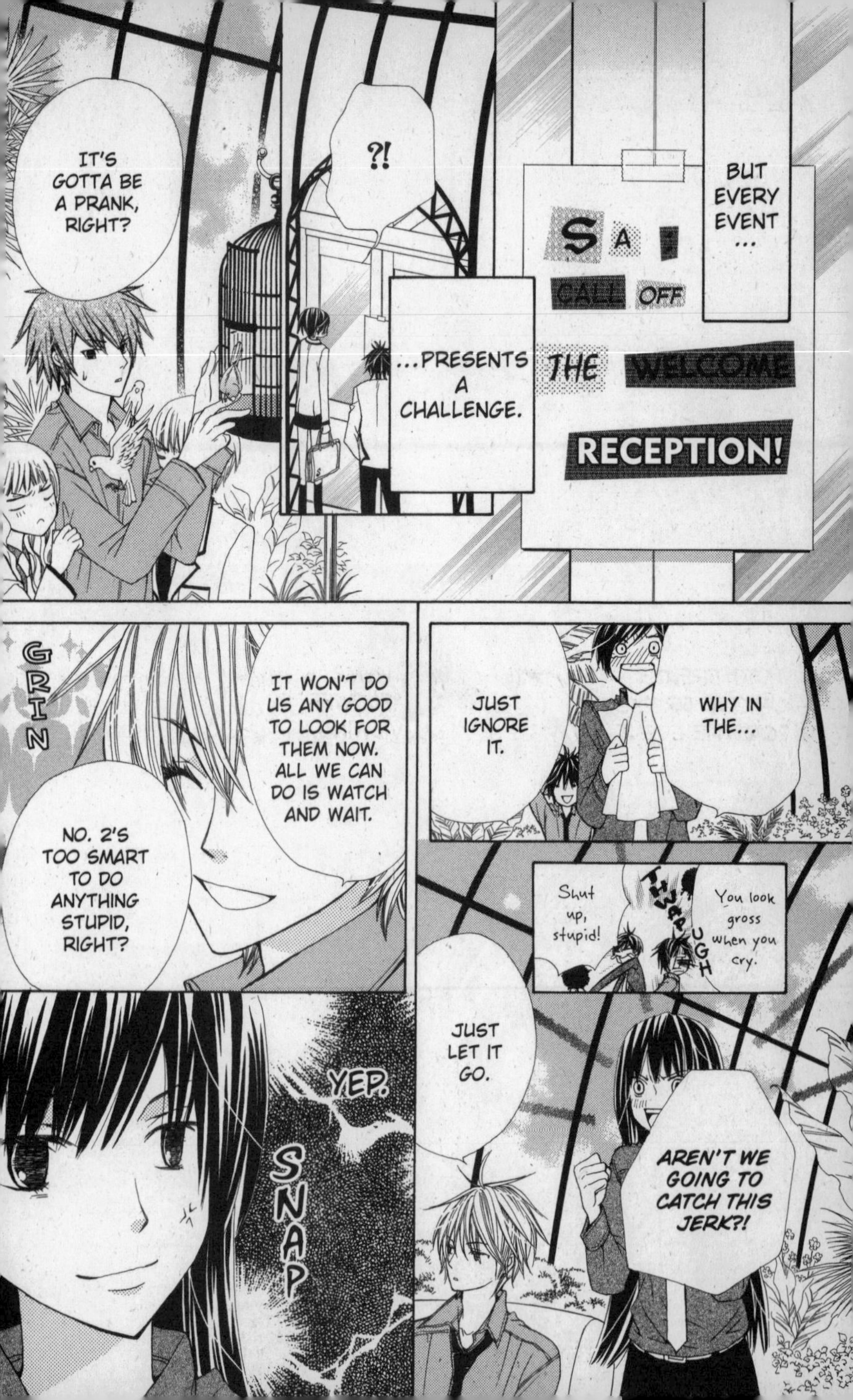
BUT EVERY EVENT...
S A : CALL OFF THE WELCOME RECEPTION!
?!
...PRESENTS A CHALLENGE.
IT'S GOTTA BE A PRANK, RIGHT?
WHY IN THE...
JUST IGNORE IT.
You look gross when you cry.
THWAP
UGH
Shut up, stupid!
AREN'T WE GOING TO CATCH THIS JERK?!
JUST LET IT GO.
GRIN
IT WON'T DO US ANY GOOD TO LOOK FOR THEM NOW. ALL WE CAN DO IS WATCH AND WAIT.
NO. 2'S TOO SMART TO DO ANYTHING STUPID, RIGHT?
YEP.
SNAP

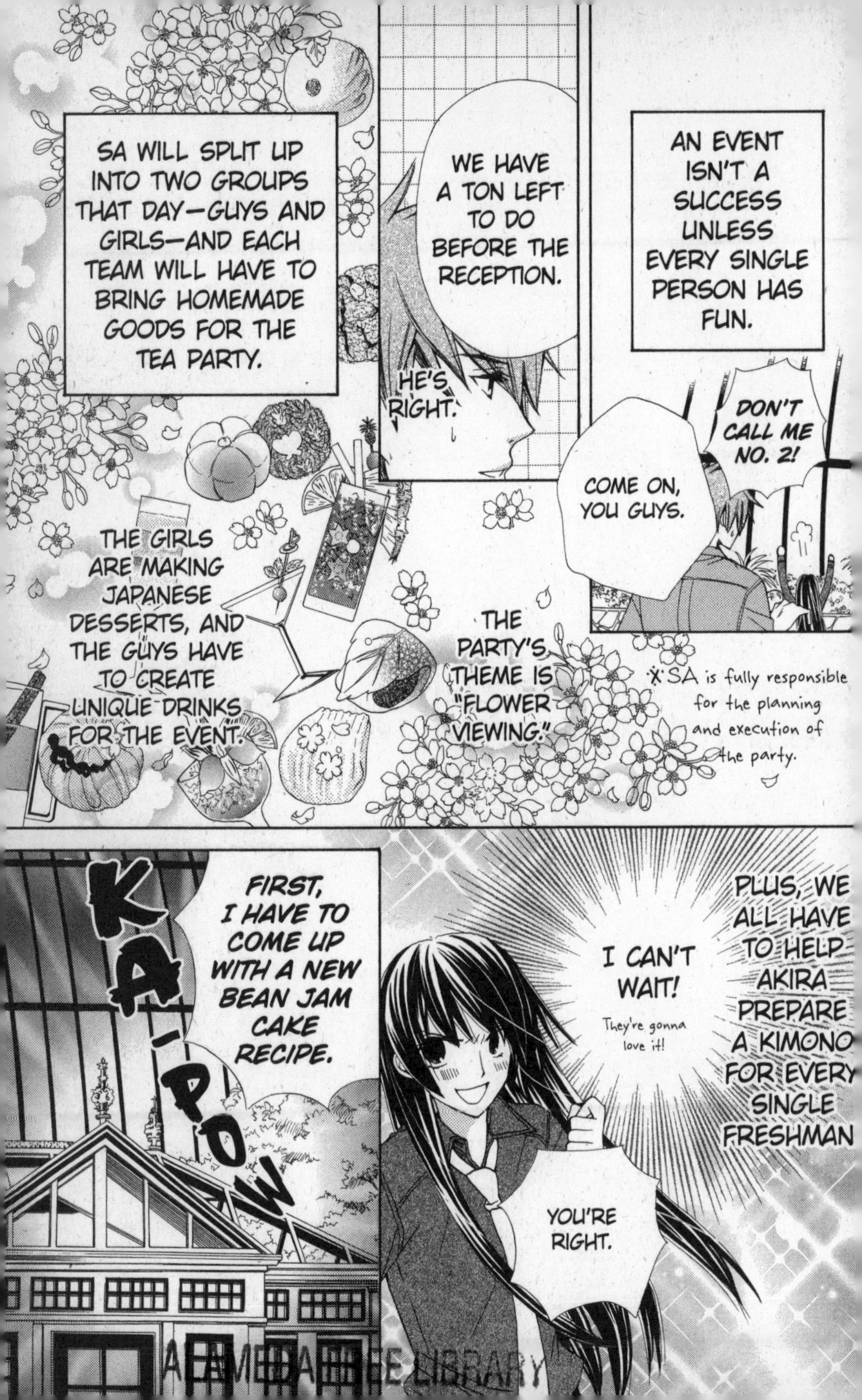
AN EVENT ISN'T A SUCCESS UNLESS EVERY SINGLE PERSON HAS FUN.
DON'T CALL ME NO. 2!
COME ON, YOU GUYS.
WE HAVE A TON LEFT TO DO BEFORE THE RECEPTION.
HE'S RIGHT.
SA WILL SPLIT UP INTO TWO GROUPS THAT DAY—GUYS AND GIRLS—AND EACH TEAM WILL HAVE TO BRING HOMEMADE GOODS FOR THE TEA PARTY.
THE PARTY'S THEME IS "FLOWER VIEWING."
※SA is fully responsible for the planning and execution of the party.
THE GIRLS ARE MAKING JAPANESE DESSERTS, AND THE GUYS HAVE TO CREATE UNIQUE DRINKS FOR THE EVENT.
PLUS, WE ALL HAVE TO HELP AKIRA PREPARE A KIMONO FOR EVERY SINGLE FRESHMAN
I CAN'T WAIT!
They're gonna love it!
YOU'RE RIGHT.
FIRST, I HAVE TO COME UP WITH A NEW BEAN JAM CAKE RECIPE.
KA-POW

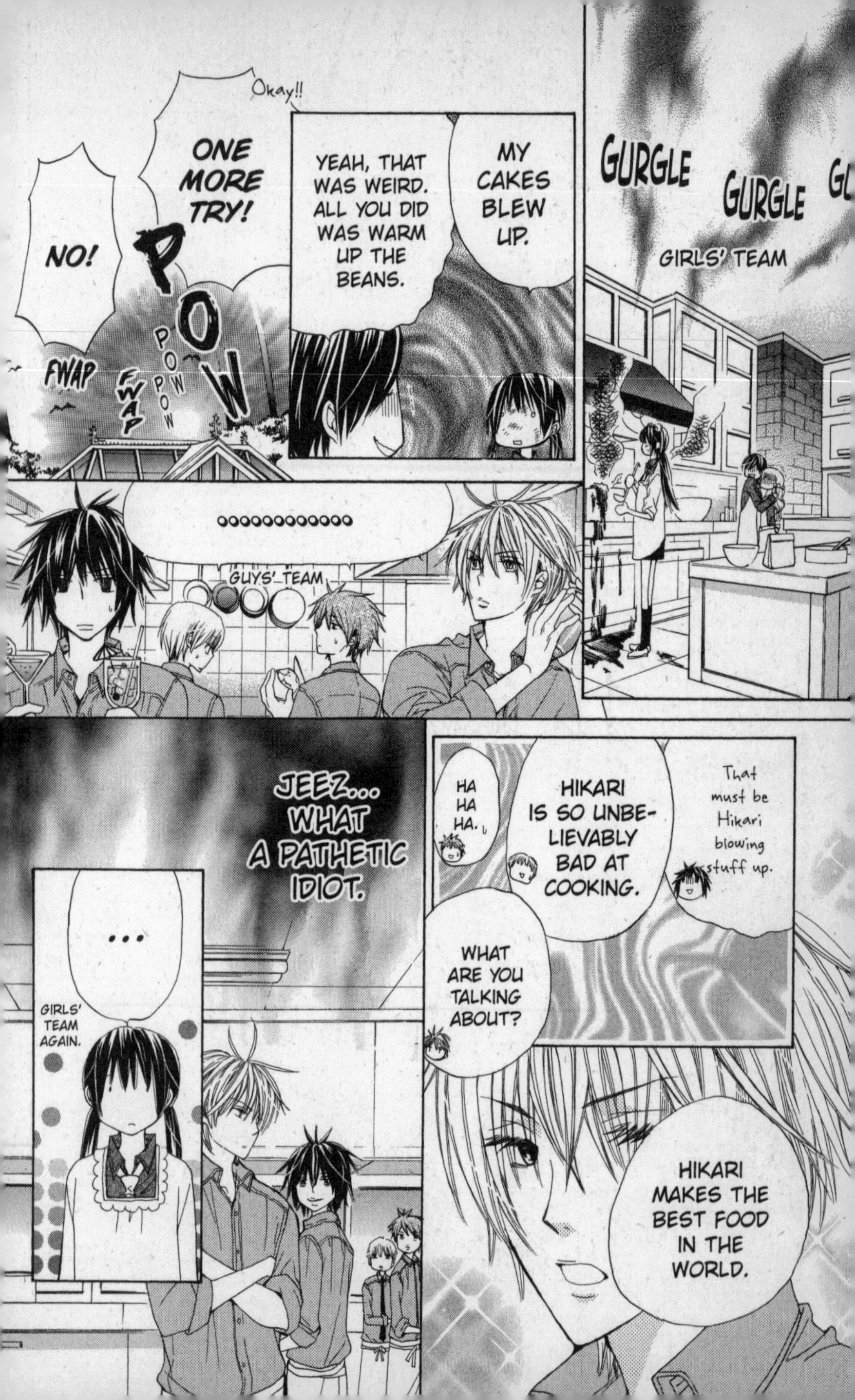
GURGLE
GURGLE
GIRLS' TEAM
MY CAKES BLEW UP.
YEAH, THAT WAS WEIRD. ALL YOU DID WAS WARM UP THE BEANS.
Okay!!
ONE MORE TRY!
NO!
POW
POW POW
FWAP
FWAP
FWAP
GUYS' TEAM
....
That must be Hikari blowing stuff up.
HIKARI IS SO UNBE-LIEVABLY BAD AT COOKING.
HA HA HA.
WHAT ARE YOU TALKING ABOUT?
HIKARI MAKES THE BEST FOOD IN THE WORLD.
JEEZ... WHAT A PATHETIC IDIOT.
...
GIRLS' TEAM AGAIN.

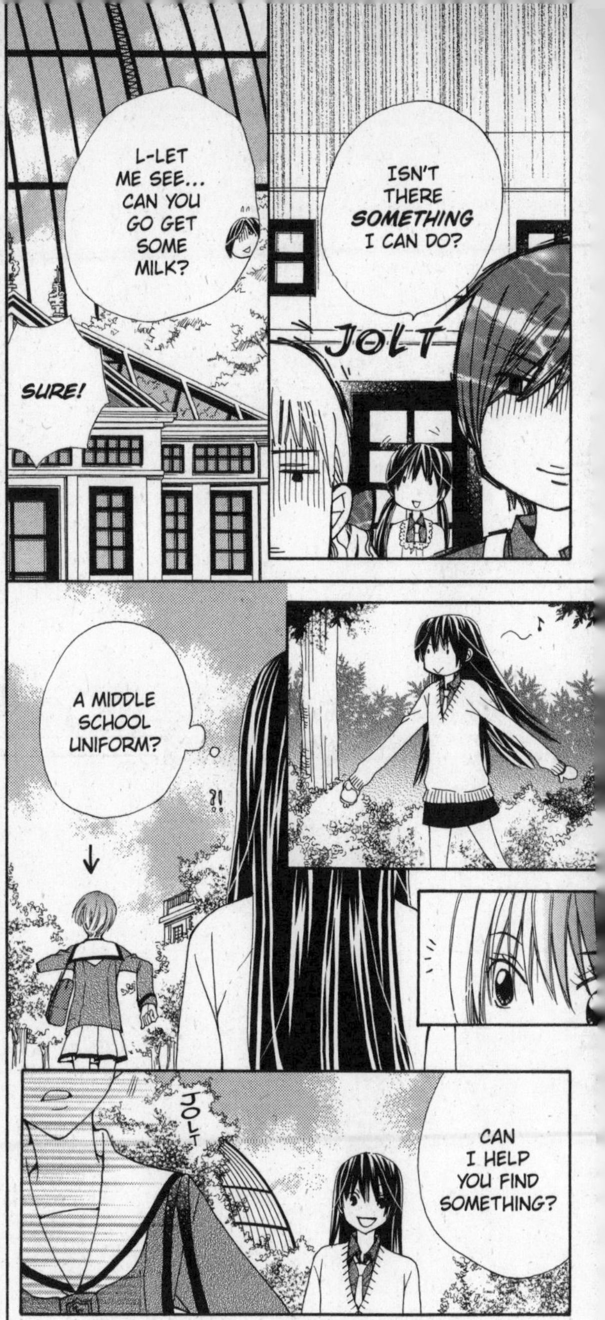
ISN'T THERE SOMETHING I CAN DO?
JOLT
L-LET ME SEE... CAN YOU GO GET SOME MILK?
SURE!
A MIDDLE SCHOOL UNIFORM?
?!
CAN I HELP YOU FIND SOMETHING?
JOLT

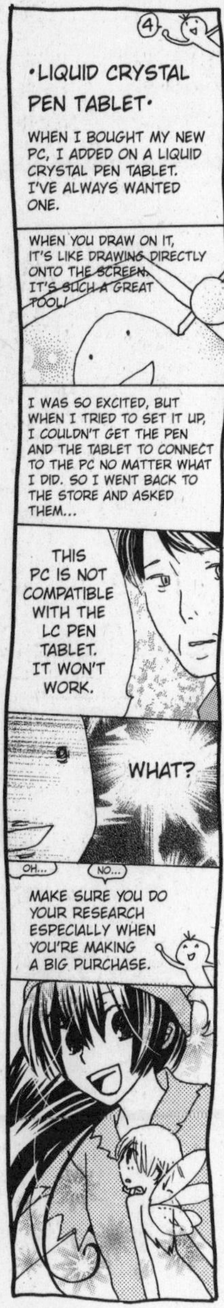
4
•LIQUID CRYSTAL PEN TABLET•
WHEN I BOUGHT MY NEW PC, I ADDED ON A LIQUID CRYSTAL PEN TABLET. I'VE ALWAYS WANTED ONE.
WHEN YOU DRAW ON IT, IT'S LIKE DRAWING DIRECTLY ONTO THE SCREEN. IT'S SUCH A GREAT TOOL!
I WAS SO EXCITED, BUT WHEN I TRIED TO SET IT UP, I COULDN'T GET THE PEN AND THE TABLET TO CONNECT TO THE PC NO MATTER WHAT I DID. SO I WENT BACK TO THE STORE AND ASKED THEM...
THIS PC IS NOT COMPATIBLE WITH THE LC PEN TABLET. IT WON'T WORK.
WHAT?
OH...
NO...
MAKE SURE YOU DO YOUR RESEARCH ESPECIALLY WHEN YOU'RE MAKING A BIG PURCHASE.

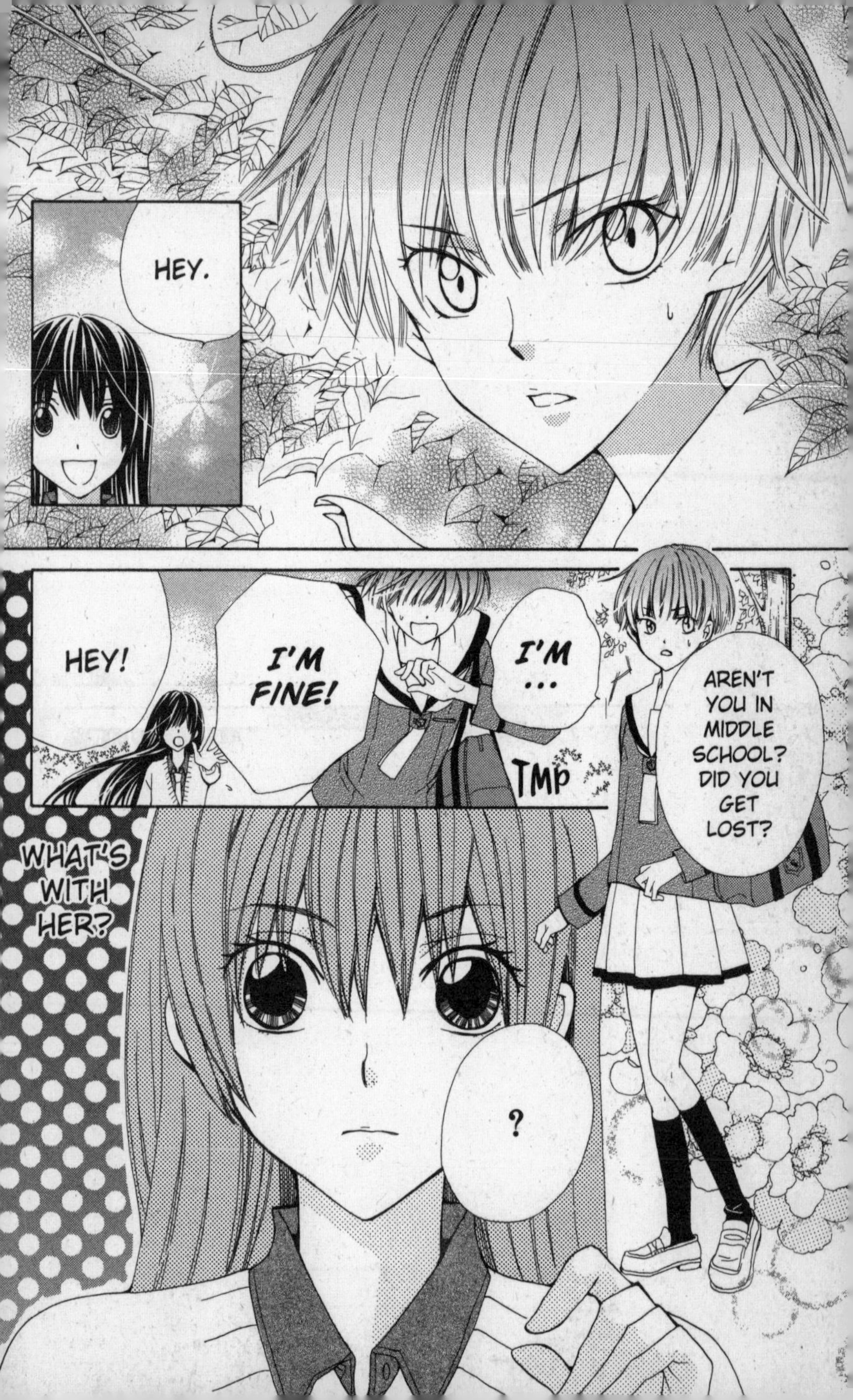
HEY.
I'M ...
I'M FINE!
HEY!
TMp
AREN'T YOU IN MIDDLE SCHOOL? DID YOU GET LOST?
?
WHAT'S WITH HER?

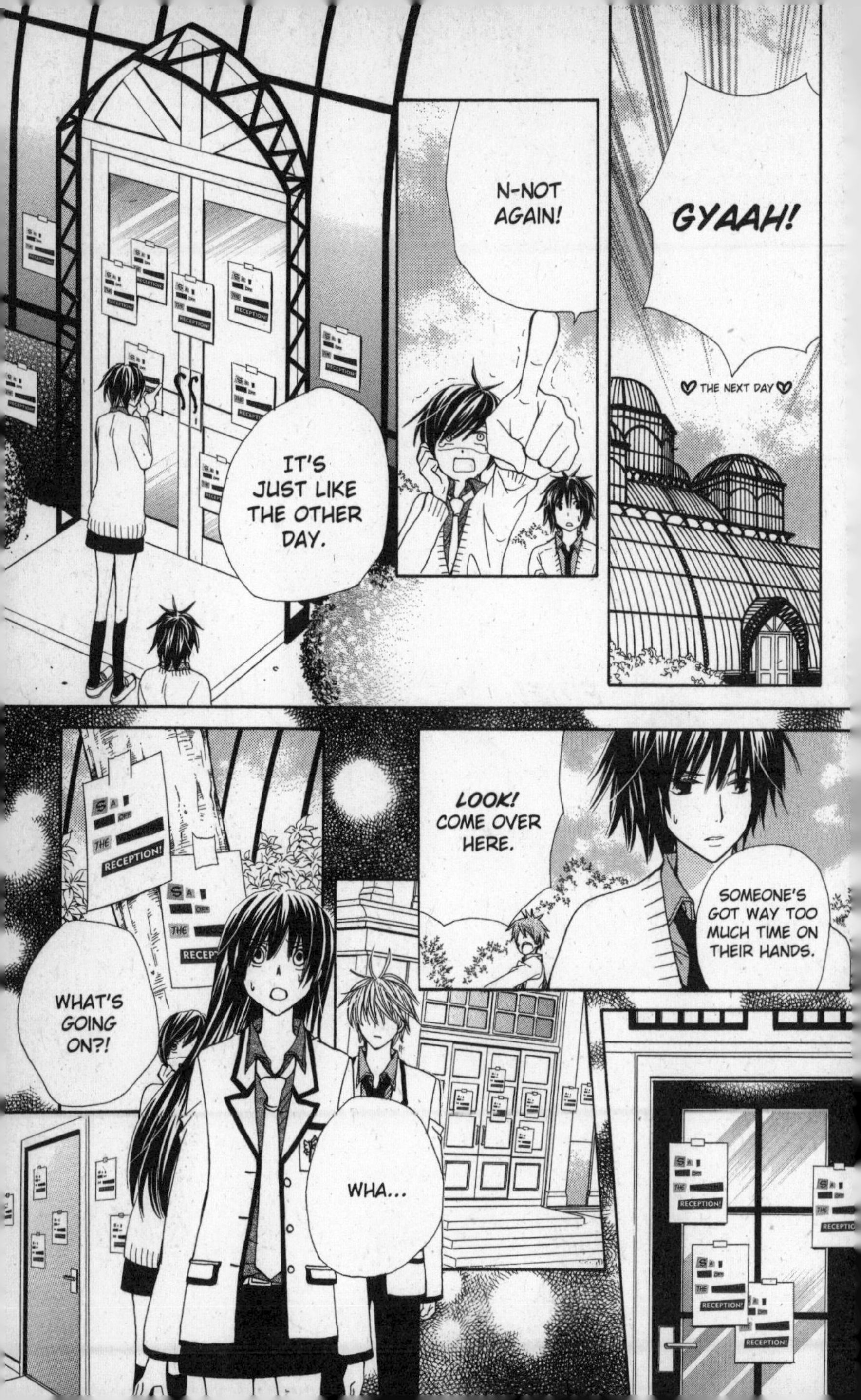
GYAAH!
THE NEXT DAY
N-NOT AGAIN!
IT'S JUST LIKE THE OTHER DAY.
LOOK! COME OVER HERE.
SOMEONE'S GOT WAY TOO MUCH TIME ON THEIR HANDS.
WHAT'S GOING ON?!
WHA...

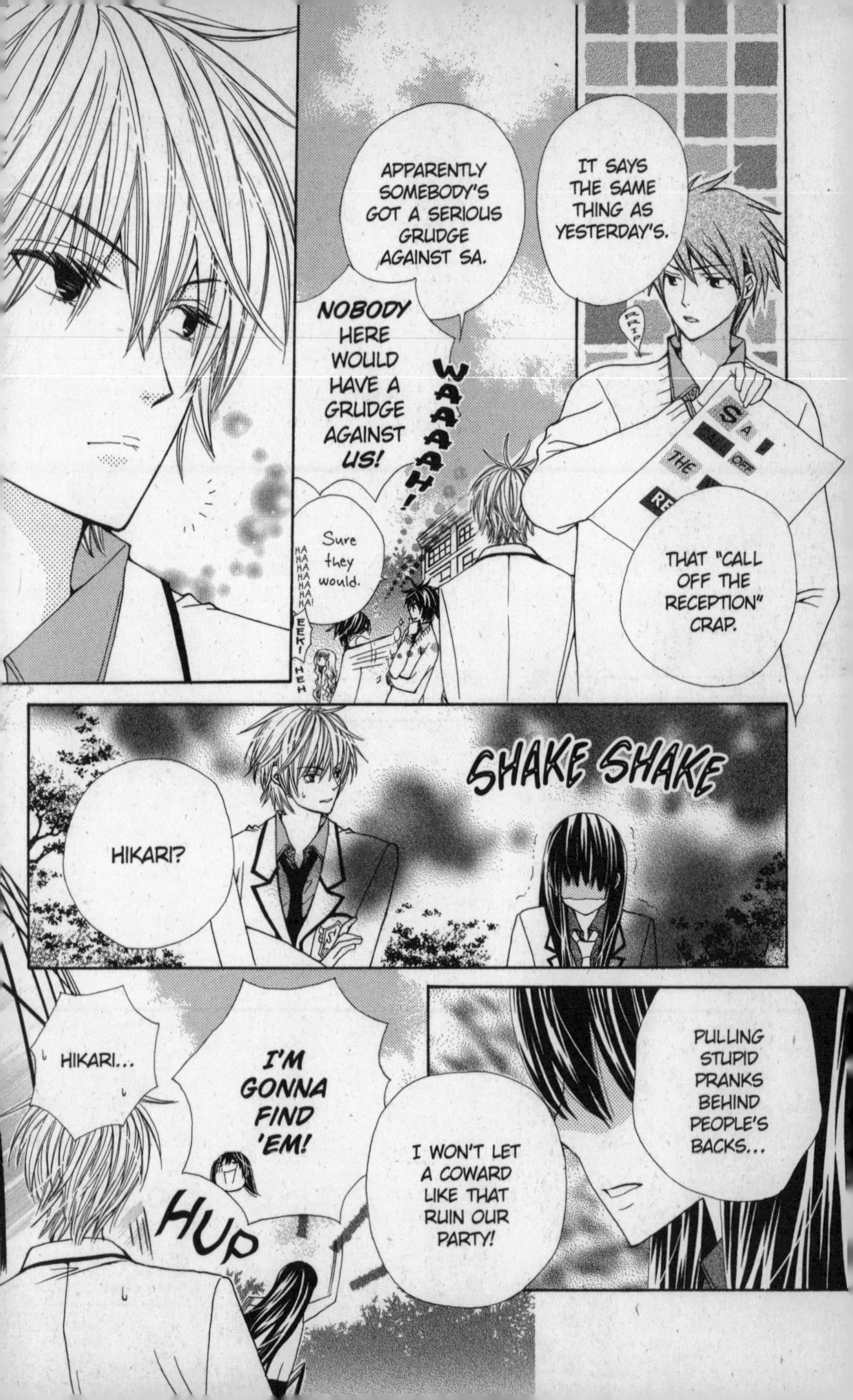
RRIP
IT SAYS THE SAME THING AS YESTERDAY'S.
THAT "CALL OFF THE RECEPTION" CRAP.
APPARENTLY SOMEBODY'S GOT A SERIOUS GRUDGE AGAINST SA.
NOBODY HERE WOULD HAVE A GRUDGE AGAINST US!
WAAAAAH!
Sure they would.
HA HA HA HA HA HA HA!
EEK!
HEH
SHAKE SHAKE
HIKARI?
PULLING STUPID PRANKS BEHIND PEOPLE'S BACKS...
I WON'T LET A COWARD LIKE THAT RUIN OUR PARTY!
I'M GONNA FIND 'EM!
HUP
HIKARI...

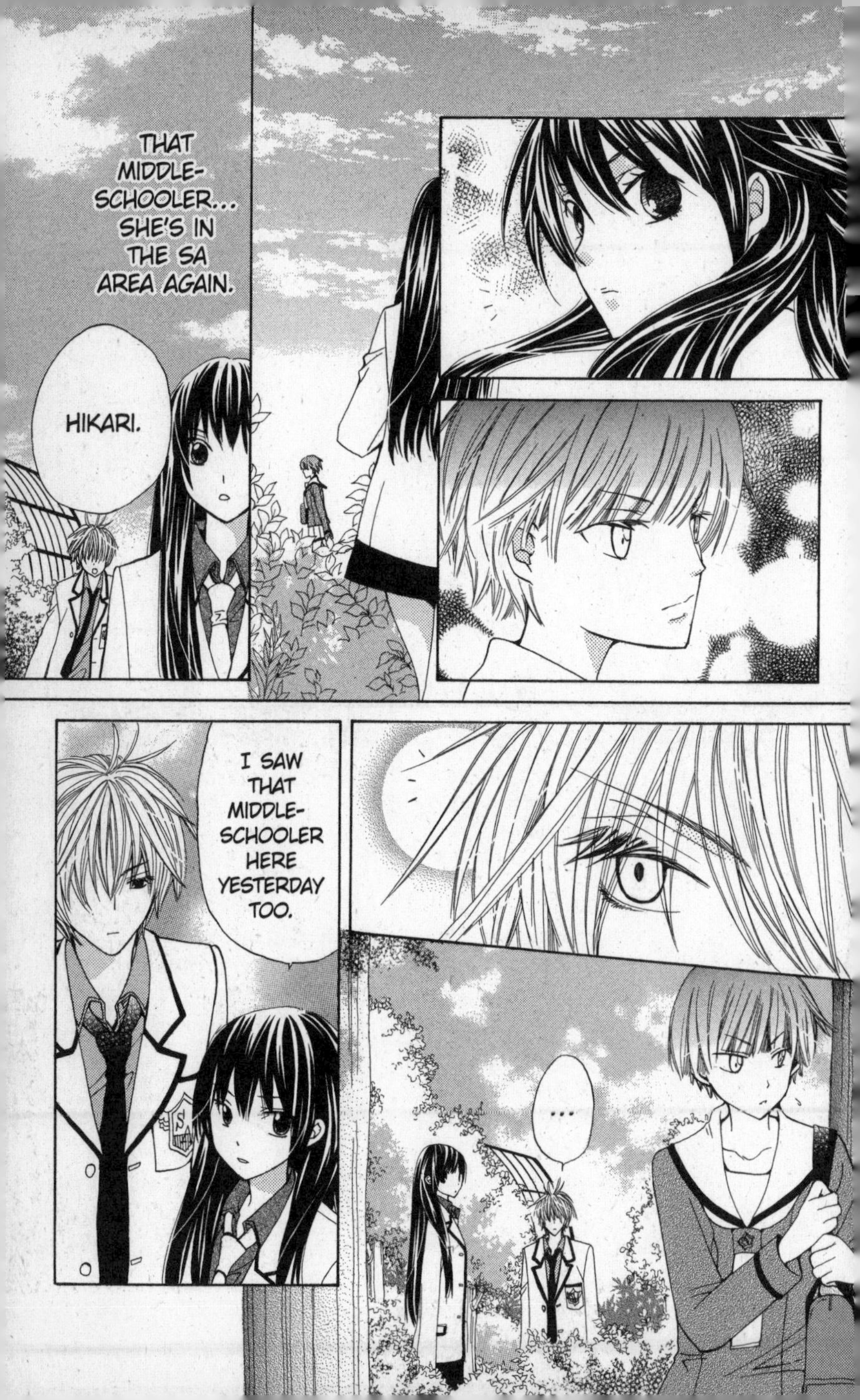
THAT MIDDLE-SCHOOLER... SHE'S IN THE SA AREA AGAIN.
HIKARI.
...
I SAW THAT MIDDLE-SCHOOLER HERE YESTERDAY TOO.

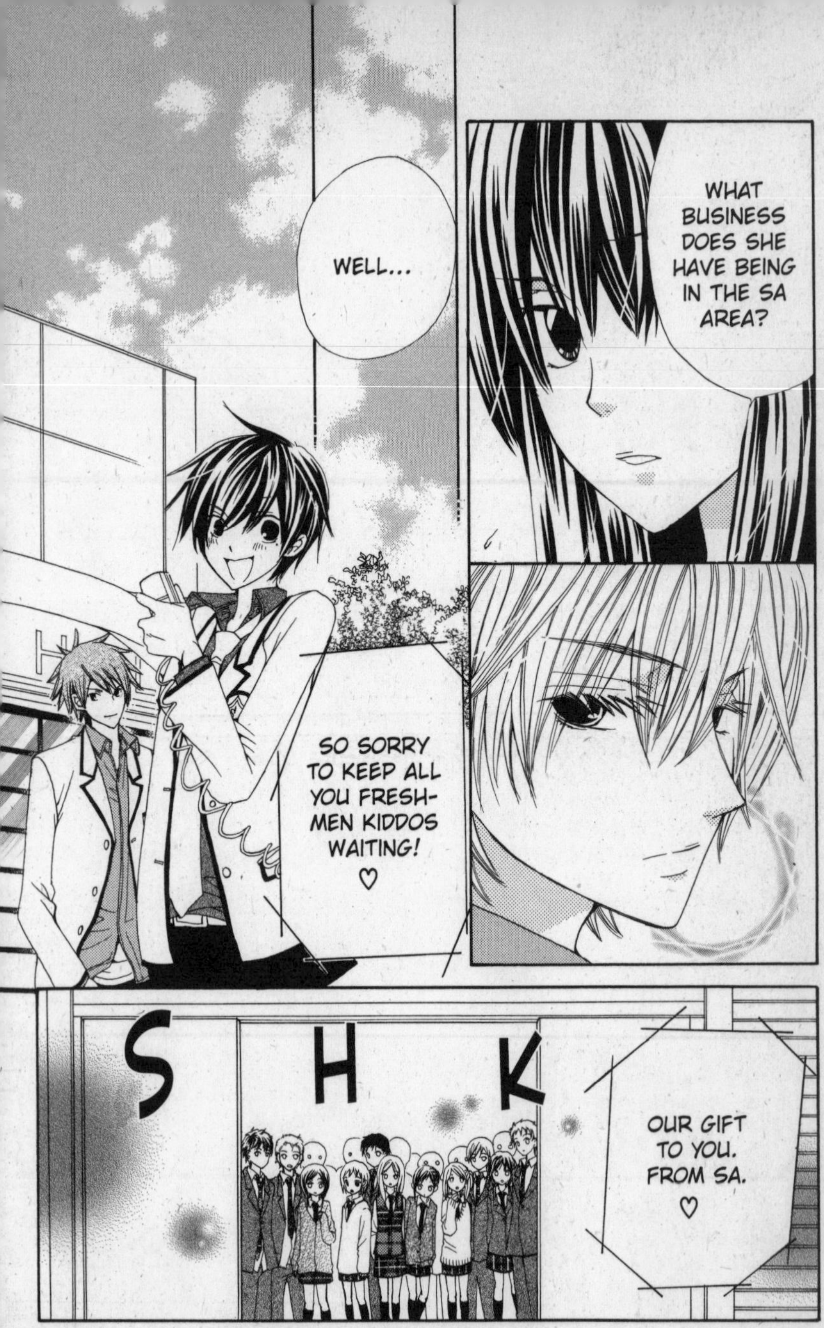
WHAT BUSINESS DOES SHE HAVE BEING IN THE SA AREA?
WELL...
SO SORRY TO KEEP ALL YOU FRESH-MEN KIDDOS WAITING! ♡
OUR GIFT TO YOU. FROM SA. ♡
S H K

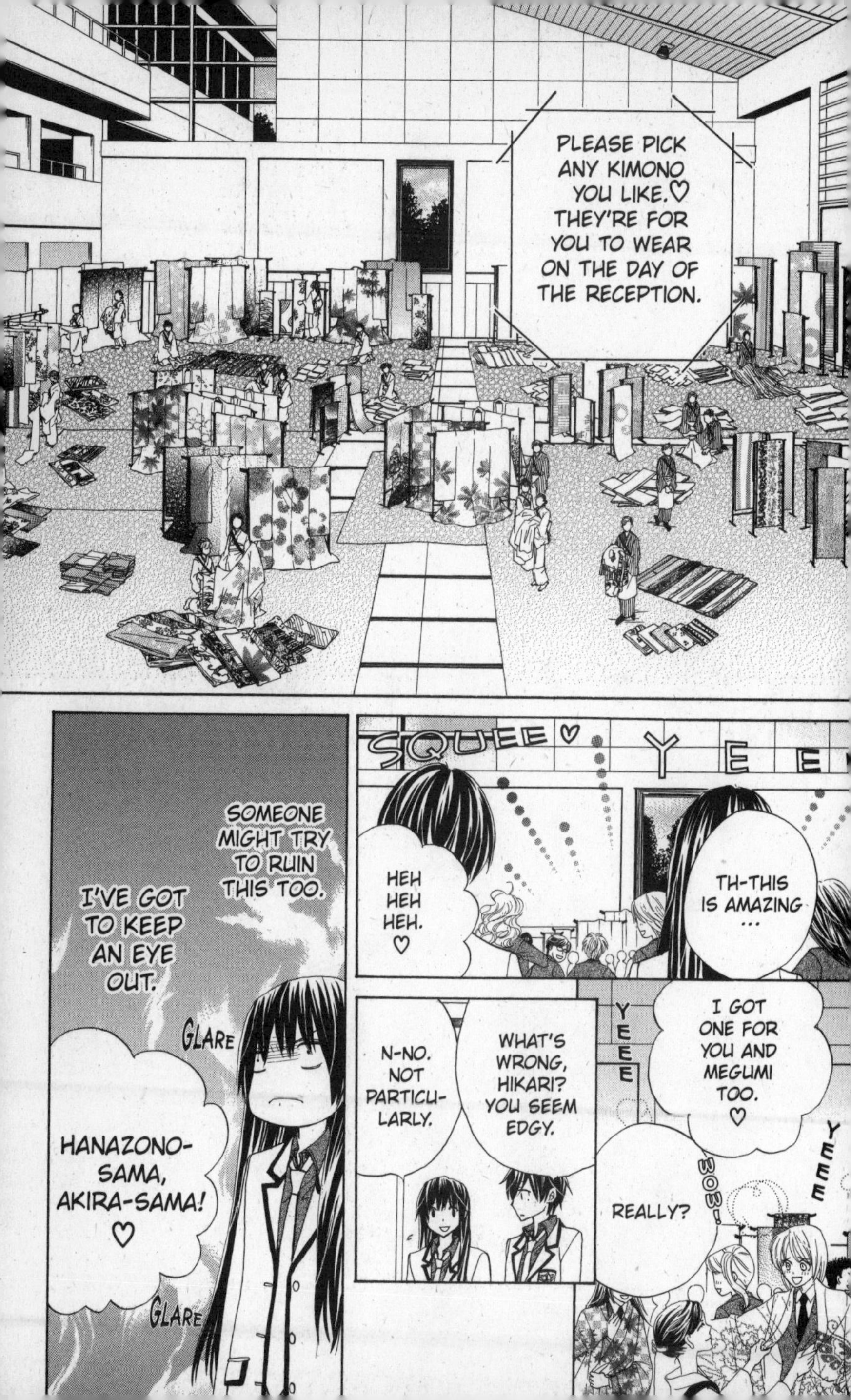
PLEASE PICK ANY KIMONO YOU LIKE.♡ THEY'RE FOR YOU TO WEAR ON THE DAY OF THE RECEPTION.
Y E E
SQUEEE♡
TH-THIS IS AMAZING...
HEH HEH HEH.♡
I GOT ONE FOR YOU AND MEGUMI TOO.♡
YEEE
YEEE
YEEE
BOW!
REALLY?
WHAT'S WRONG, HIKARI? YOU SEEM EDGY.
N-NO. NOT PARTICU-LARLY.
SOMEONE MIGHT TRY TO RUIN THIS TOO.
I'VE GOT TO KEEP AN EYE OUT.
GLARE
HANAZONO-SAMA, AKIRA-SAMA!♡
GLARE

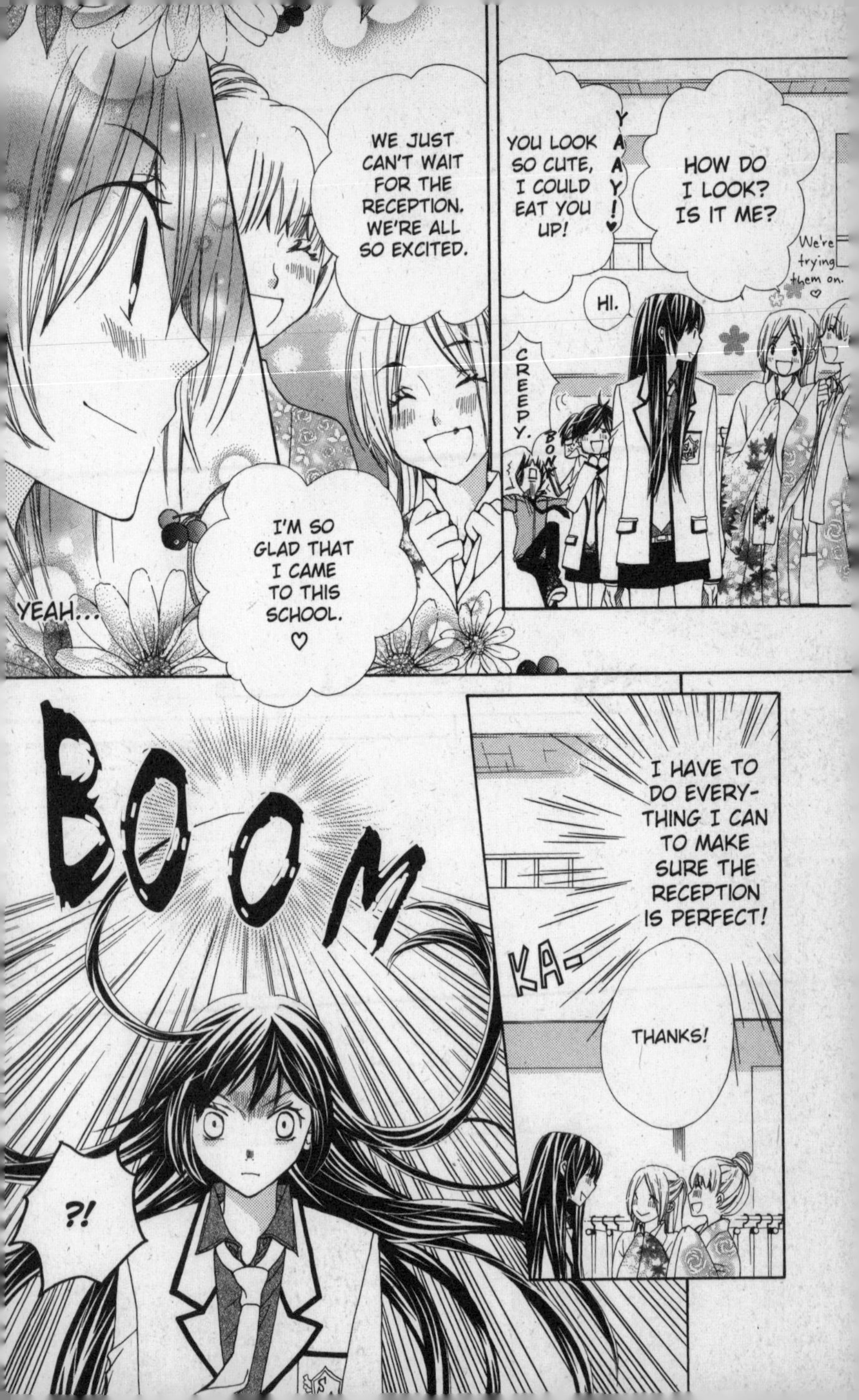
HOW DO I LOOK? IS IT ME?
We're trying them on. ♡
YAAY! ♥
YOU LOOK SO CUTE, I COULD EAT YOU UP!
HI.
CREEPY.
BONK
WE JUST CAN'T WAIT FOR THE RECEPTION. WE'RE ALL SO EXCITED.
I'M SO GLAD THAT I CAME TO THIS SCHOOL. ♡
YEAH...
I HAVE TO DO EVERY-THING I CAN TO MAKE SURE THE RECEPTION IS PERFECT!
THANKS!
KA-
BOOM
?!

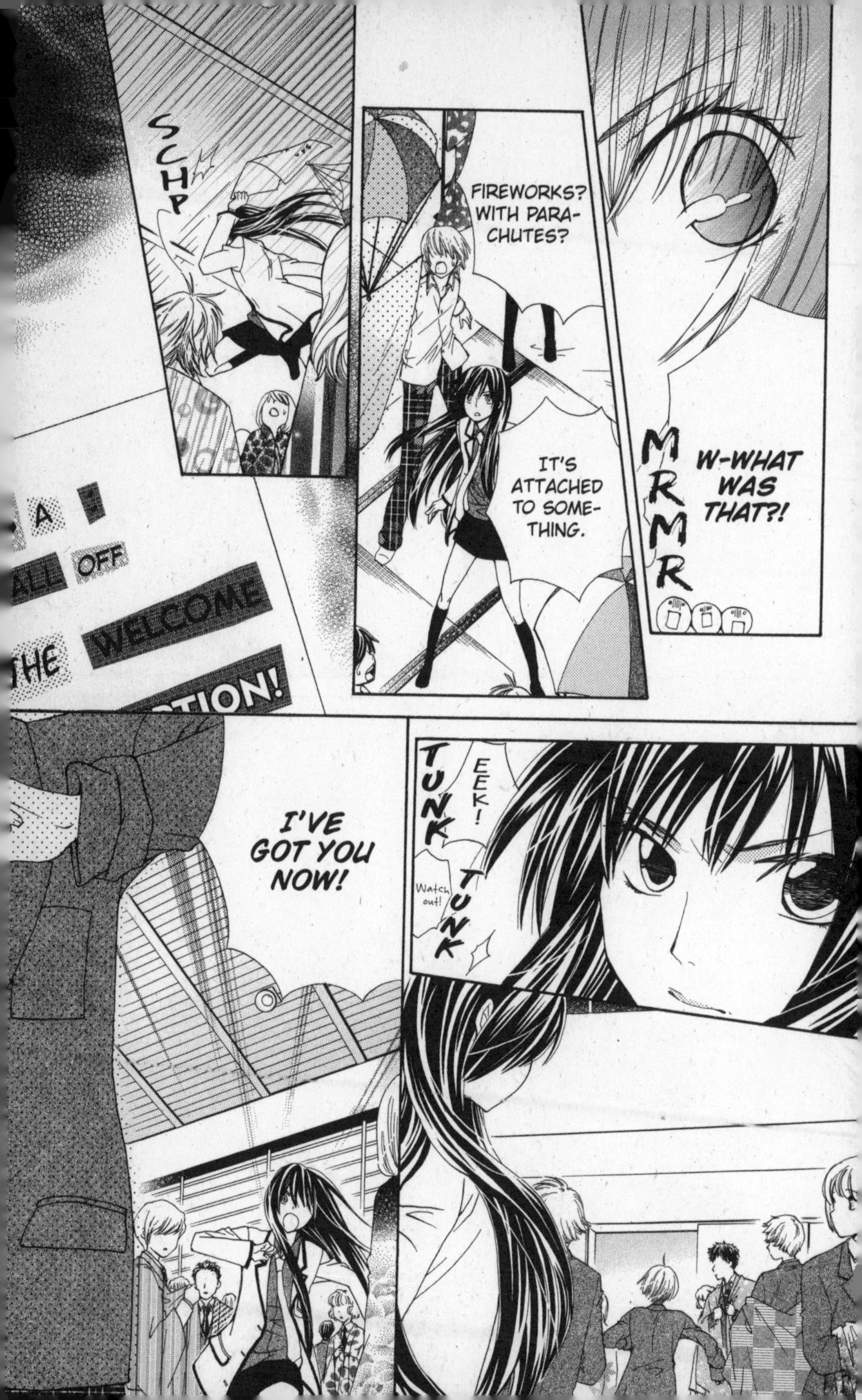
MRMR
W-WHAT WAS THAT?!
FIREWORKS? WITH PARA-CHUTES?
IT'S ATTACHED TO SOME-THING.
SCHP
A
ALL OFF
HE WELCOME
TION!
EEK!
TUNK
Watch out!
TUNK
I'VE GOT YOU NOW!

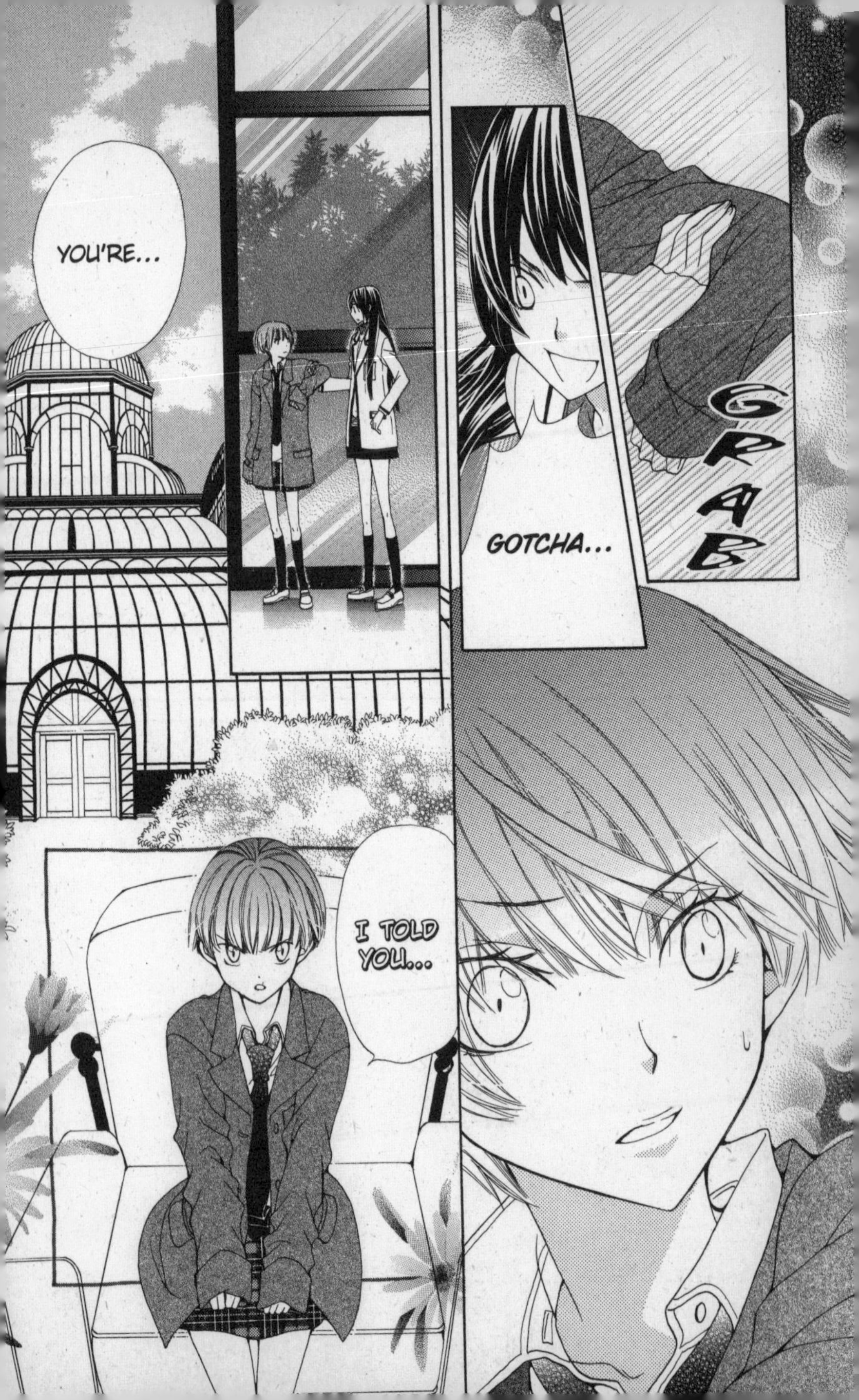
GRAB
GOTCHA...
YOU'RE...
I TOLD YOU...

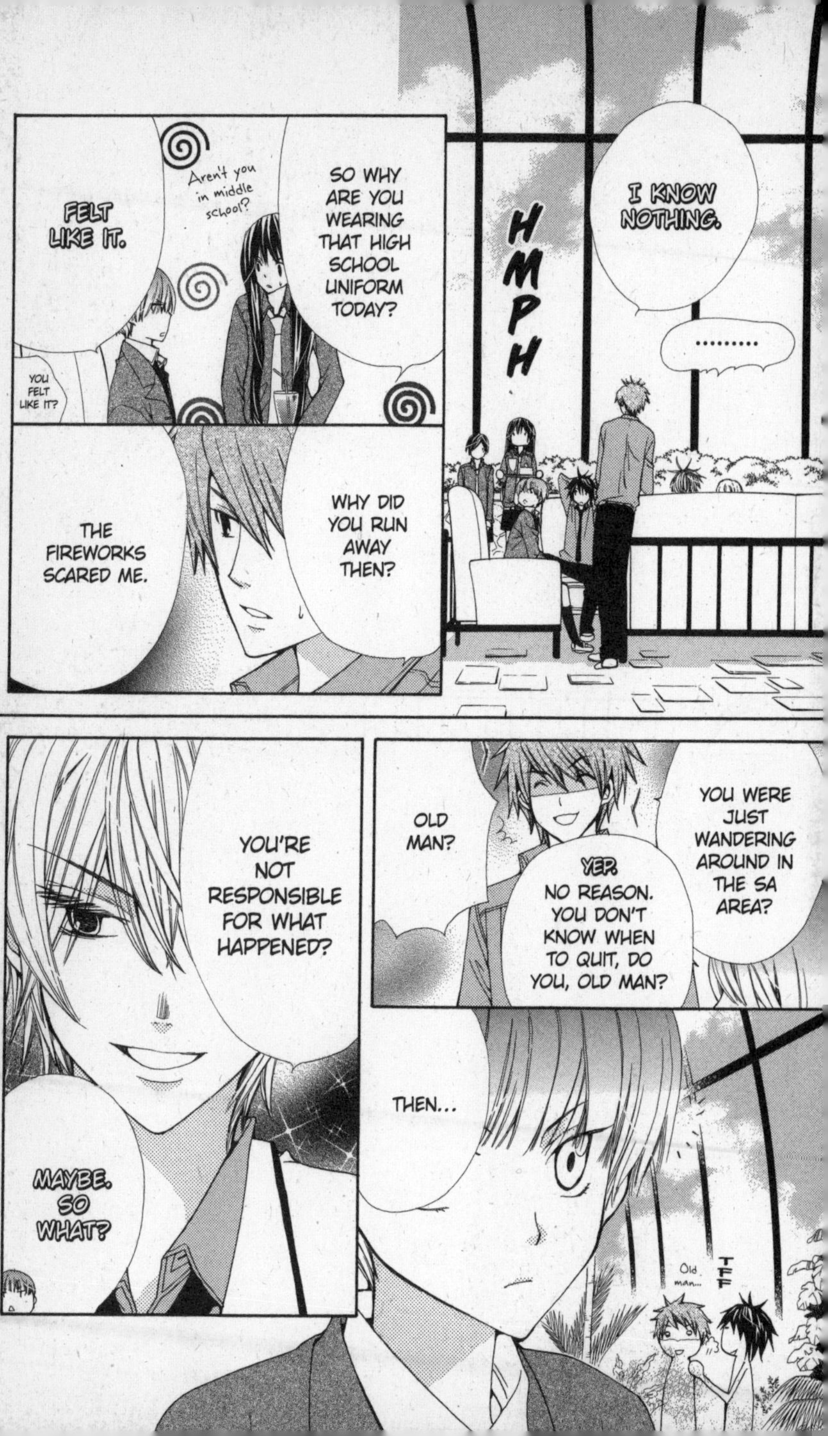
I KNOW NOTHING.
HMPH
....
SO WHY ARE YOU WEARING THAT HIGH SCHOOL UNIFORM TODAY?
Aren't you in middle school?
FELT LIKE IT.
YOU FELT LIKE IT?
WHY DID YOU RUN AWAY THEN?
THE FIREWORKS SCARED ME.
YOU WERE JUST WANDERING AROUND IN THE SA AREA?
YEP. NO REASON. YOU DON'T KNOW WHEN TO QUIT, DO YOU, OLD MAN?
OLD MAN?
THEN...
Old man...
TFF
YOU'RE NOT RESPONSIBLE FOR WHAT HAPPENED?
MAYBE. SO WHAT?

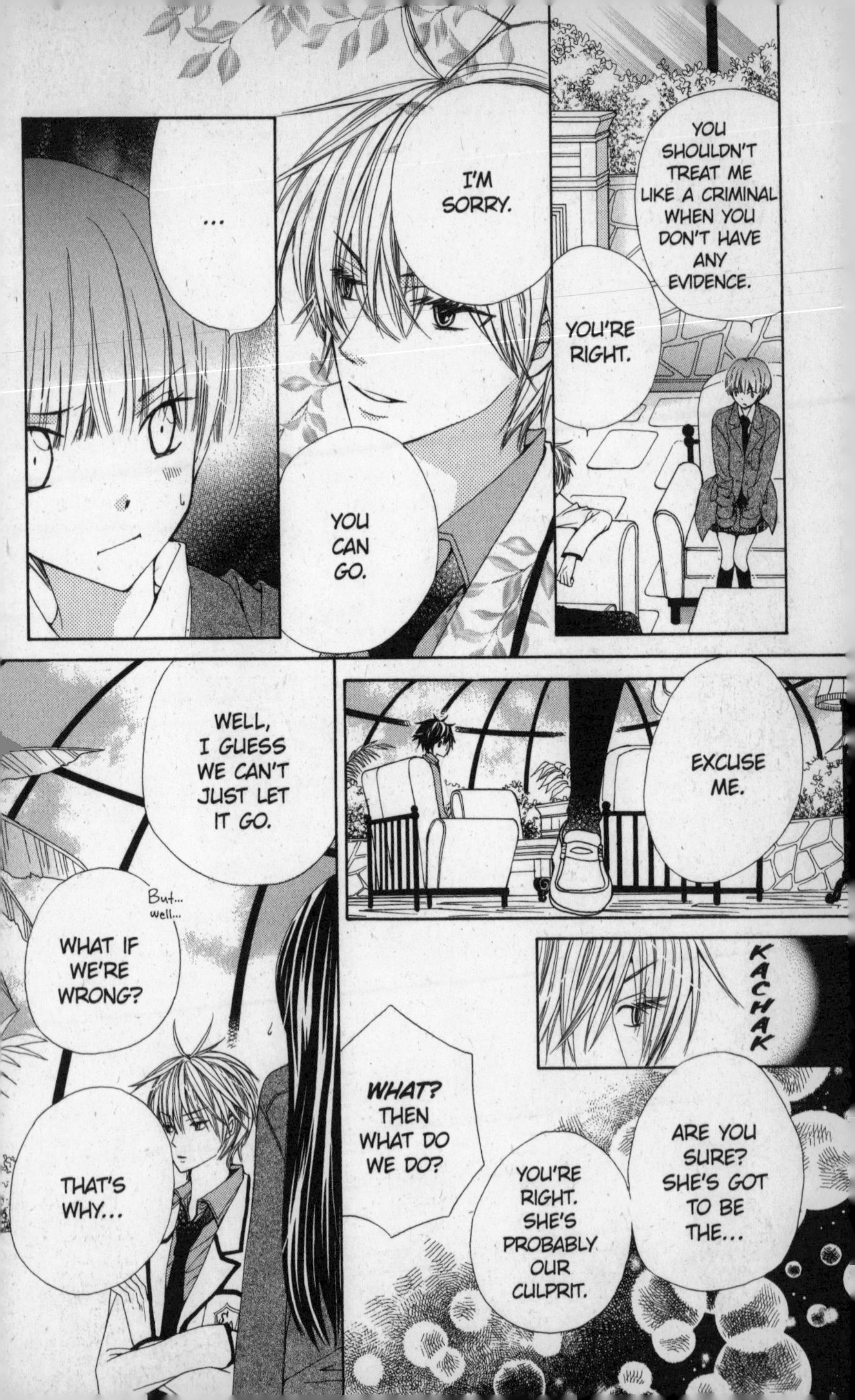

YOU SHOULDN'T TREAT ME LIKE A CRIMINAL WHEN YOU DON'T HAVE ANY EVIDENCE.
YOU'RE RIGHT.
I'M SORRY.
YOU CAN GO.
...
EXCUSE ME.
KACHAK
ARE YOU SURE? SHE'S GOT TO BE THE...
YOU'RE RIGHT. SHE'S PROBABLY OUR CULPRIT.
WHAT? THEN WHAT DO WE DO?
WELL, I GUESS WE CAN'T JUST LET IT GO.
But... well...
WHAT IF WE'RE WRONG?
THAT'S WHY...

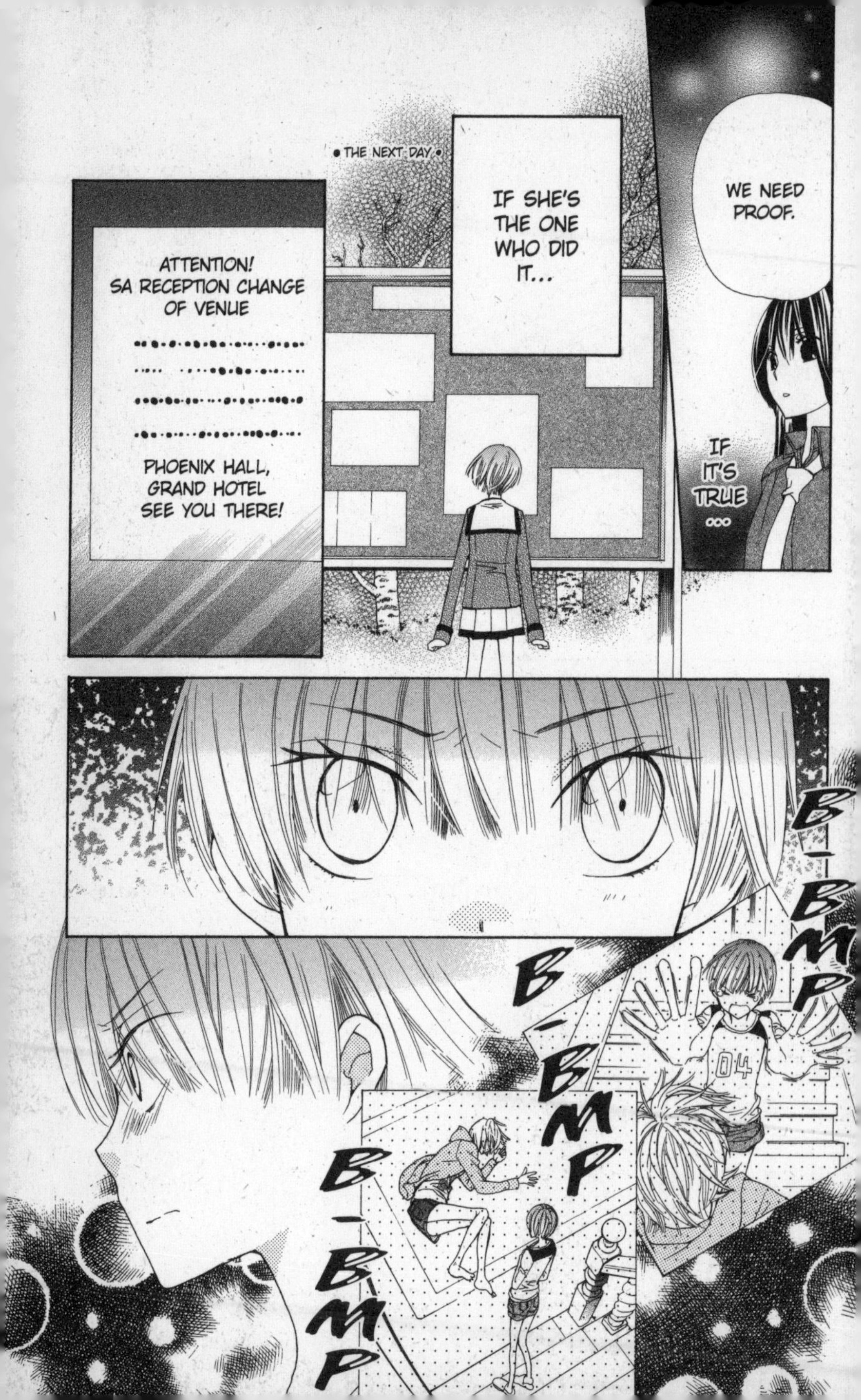
WE NEED PROOF.
IF IT'S TRUE...
IF SHE'S THE ONE WHO DID IT...
THE NEXT DAY
ATTENTION! SA RECEPTION CHANGE OF VENUE
PHOENIX HALL, GRAND HOTEL SEE YOU THERE!
B-BMP
B-BMP
B-BMP
04

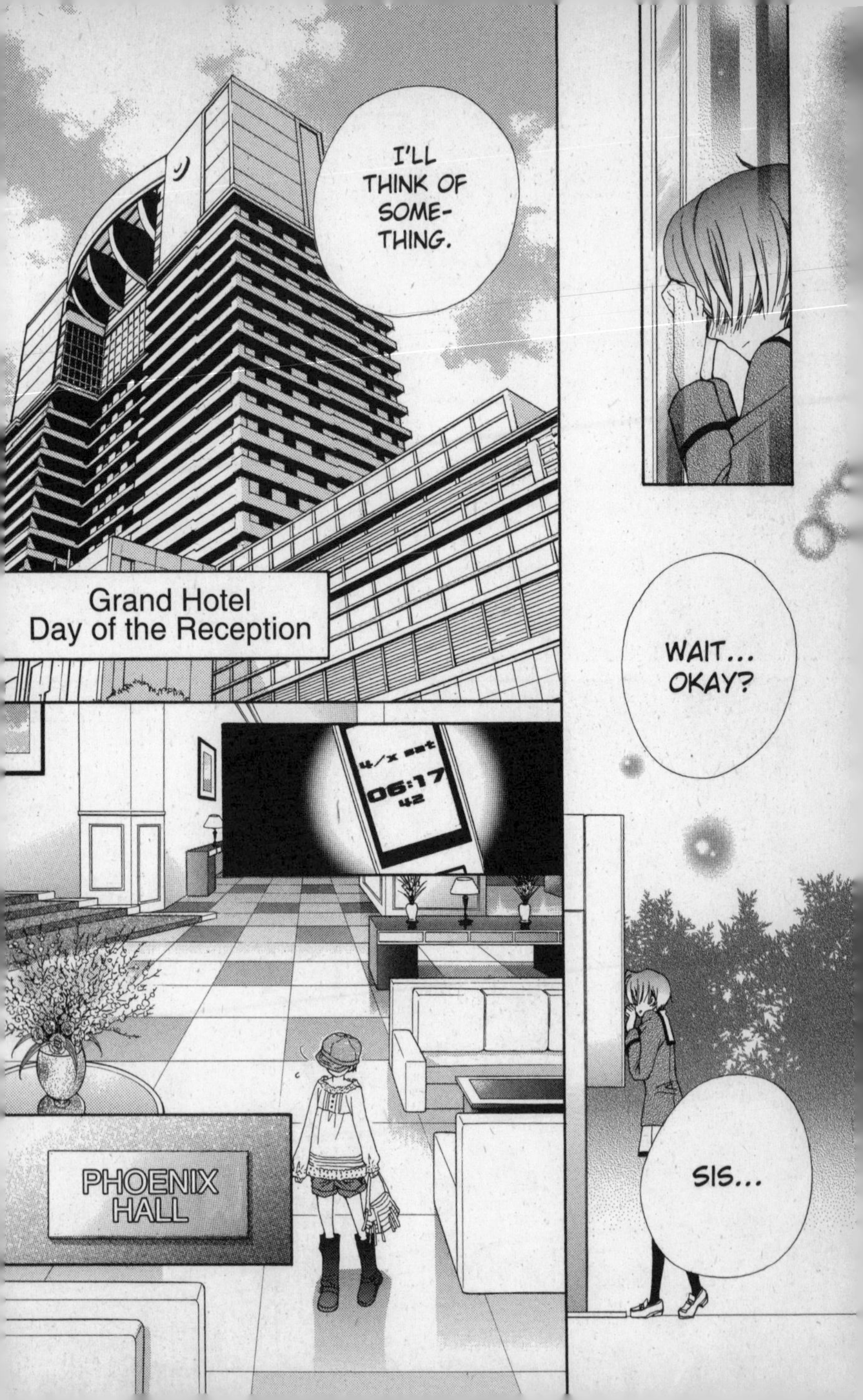
I'LL THINK OF SOME-THING.
WAIT... OKAY?
Grand Hotel
Day of the Reception
4/x sat
06:17
42
PHOENIX HALL
SIS...

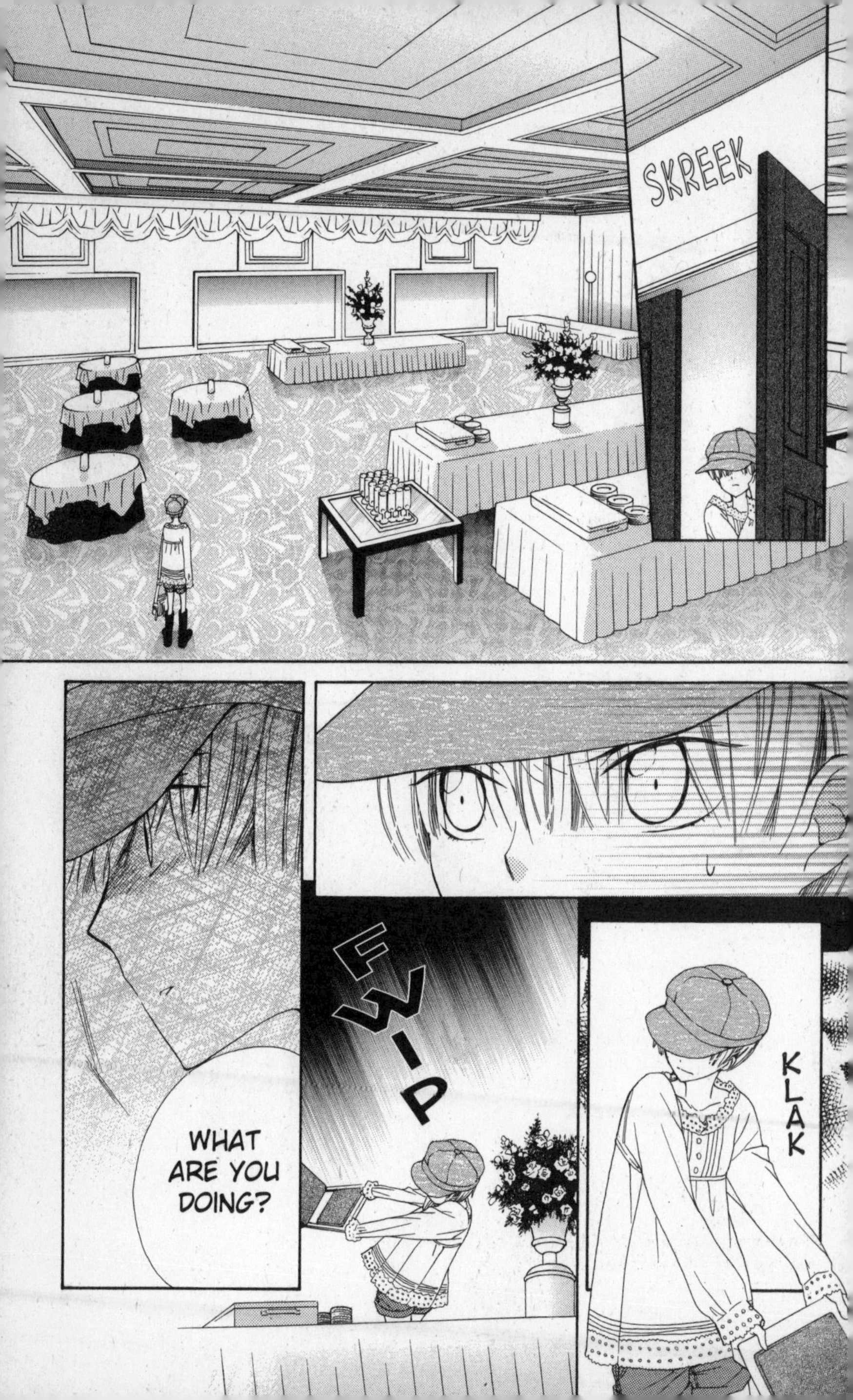
SKREEK
KLAK
FWIP
WHAT ARE YOU DOING?

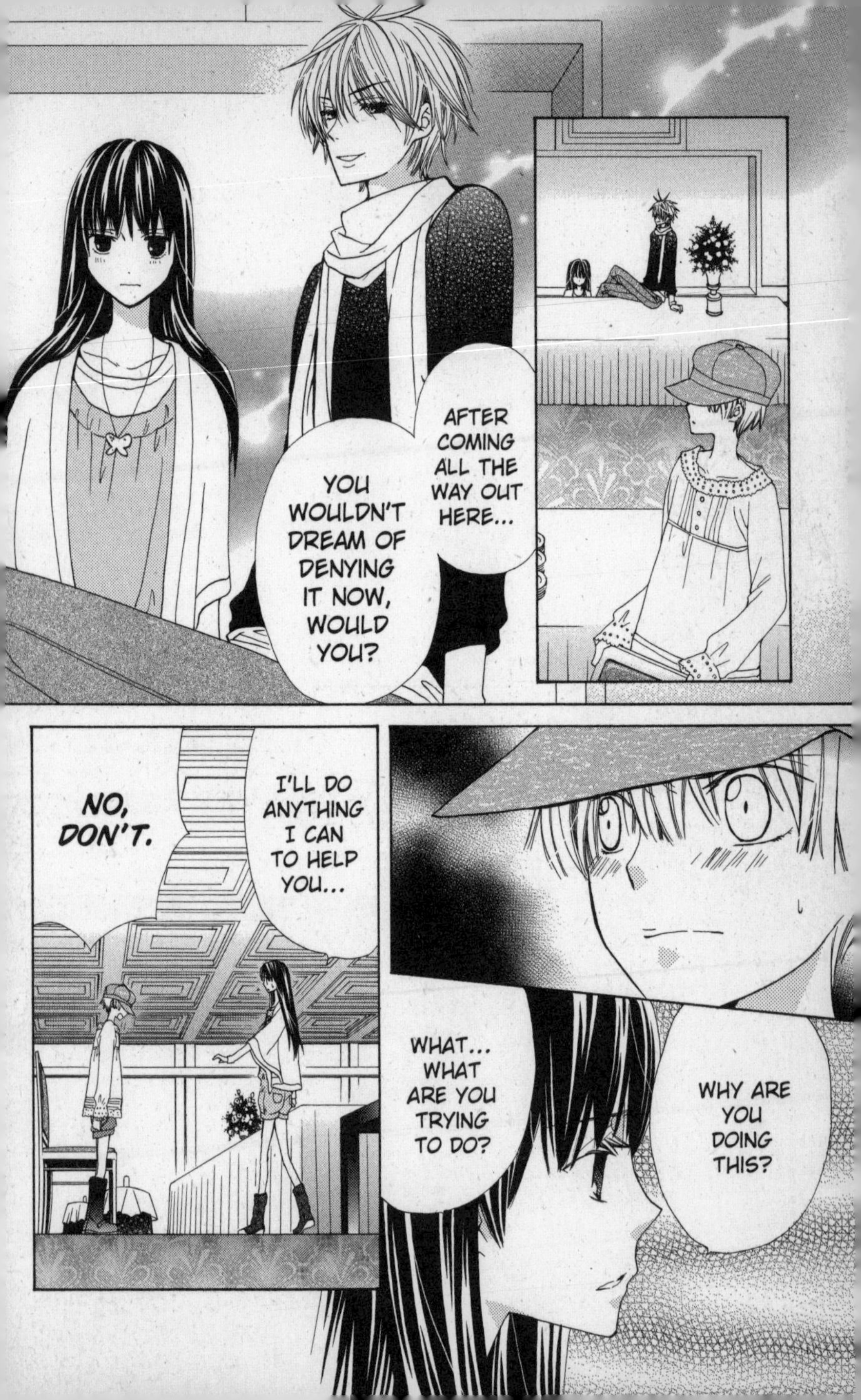
AFTER COMING ALL THE WAY OUT HERE...
YOU WOULDN'T DREAM OF DENYING IT NOW, WOULD YOU?
WHY ARE YOU DOING THIS?
WHAT... WHAT ARE YOU TRYING TO DO?
I'LL DO ANYTHING I CAN TO HELP YOU...
NO, DON'T.

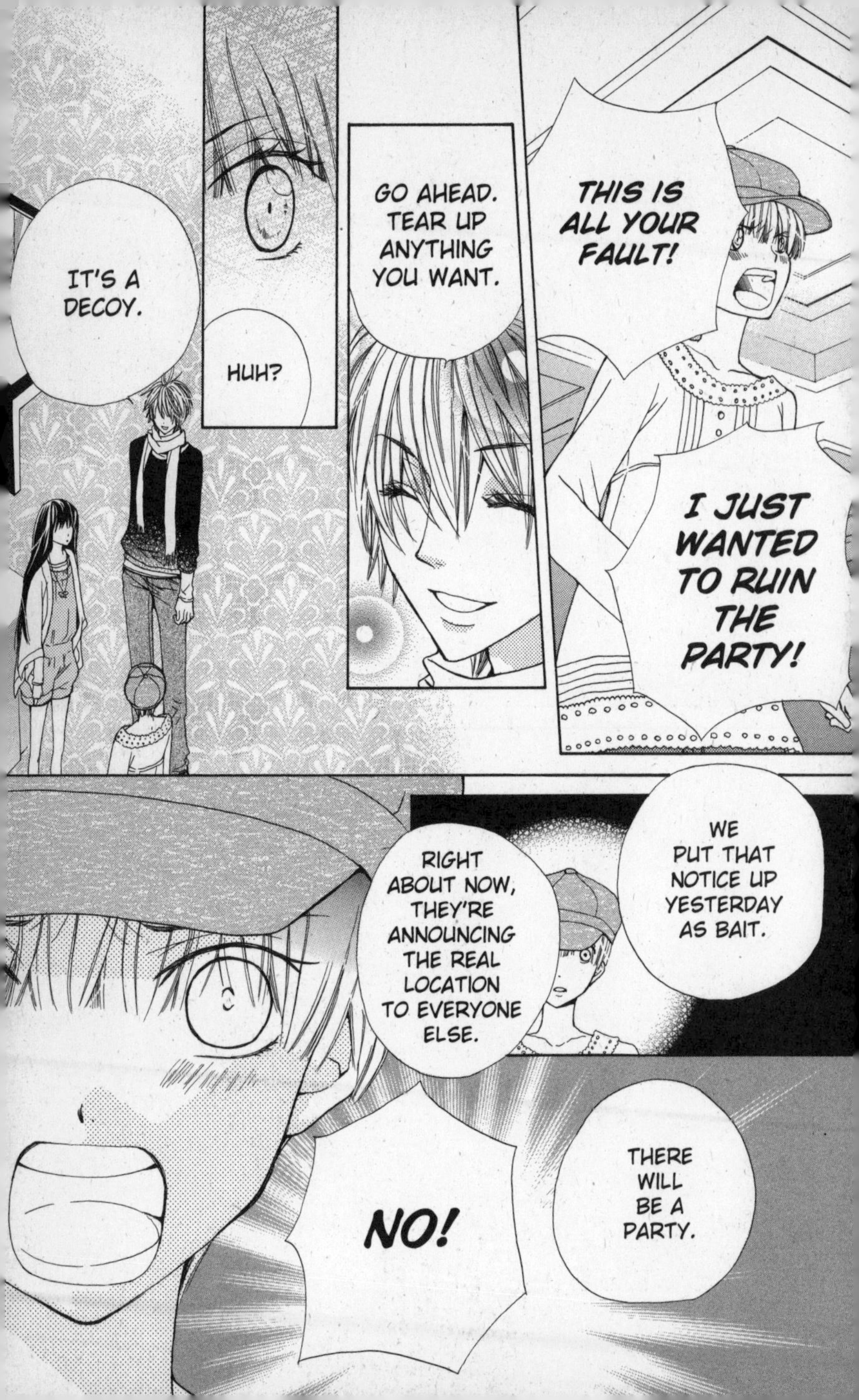
THIS IS ALL YOUR FAULT!
I JUST WANTED TO RUIN THE PARTY!
GO AHEAD. TEAR UP ANYTHING YOU WANT.
HUH?
IT'S A DECOY.
WE PUT THAT NOTICE UP YESTERDAY AS BAIT.
RIGHT ABOUT NOW, THEY'RE ANNOUNCING THE REAL LOCATION TO EVERYONE ELSE.
THERE WILL BE A PARTY.
NO!

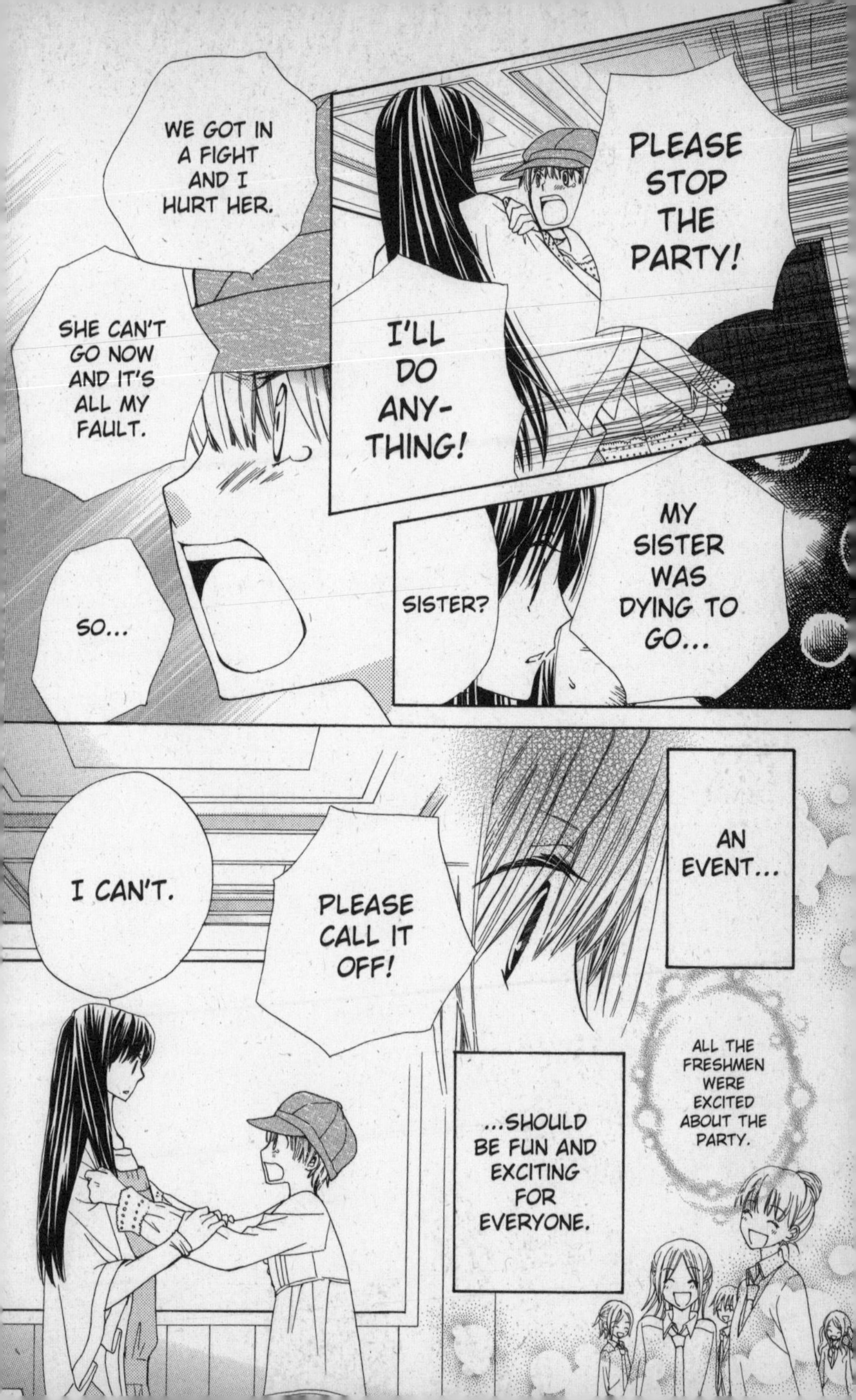
PLEASE STOP THE PARTY!
I'LL DO ANY-THING!
MY SISTER WAS DYING TO GO...
SISTER?
WE GOT IN A FIGHT AND I HURT HER.
SHE CAN'T GO NOW AND IT'S ALL MY FAULT.
SO...
AN EVENT...
...SHOULD BE FUN AND EXCITING FOR EVERYONE.
ALL THE FRESHMEN WERE EXCITED ABOUT THE PARTY.
PLEASE CALL IT OFF!
I CAN'T.

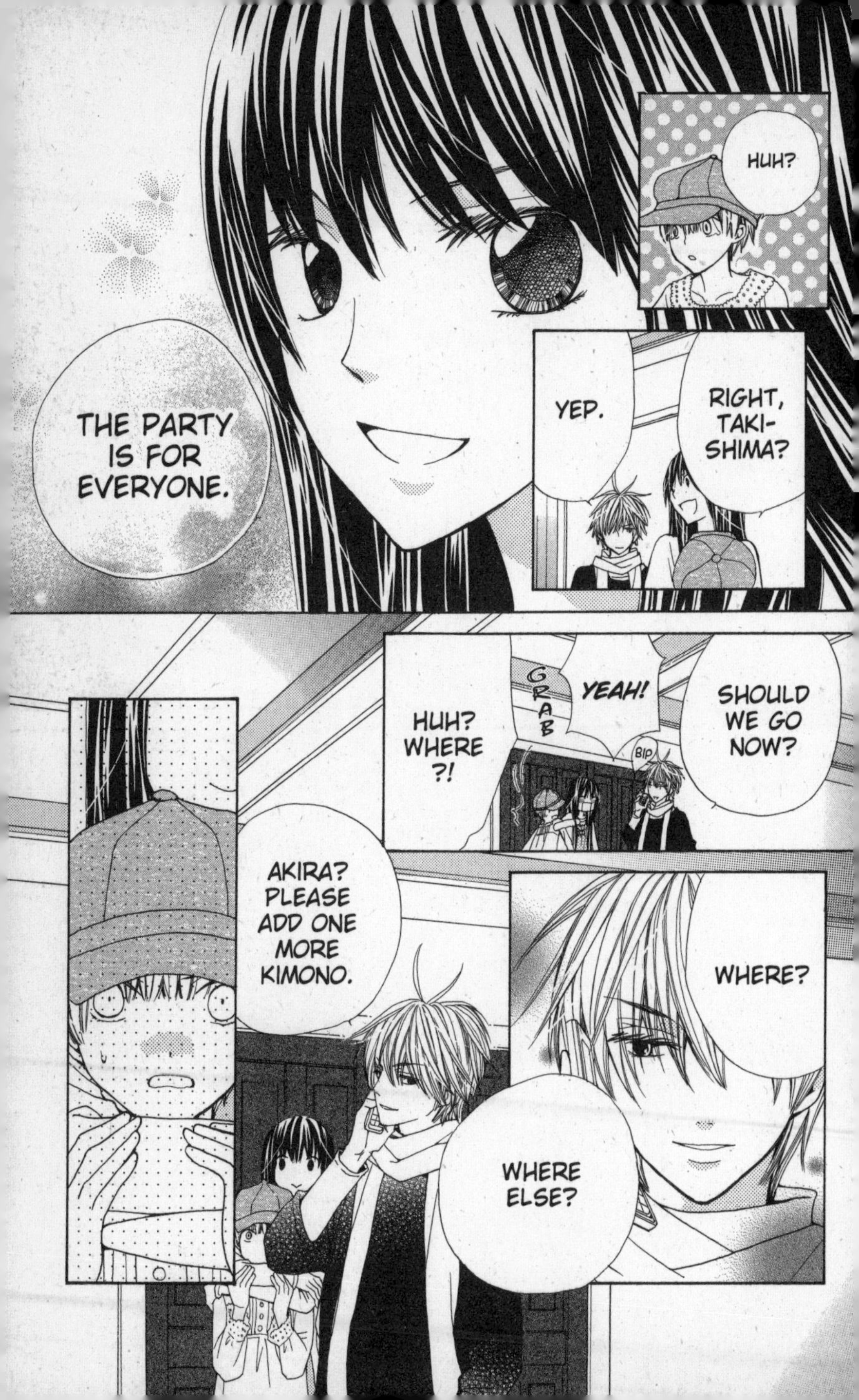
THE PARTY IS FOR EVERYONE.
HUH?
RIGHT, TAKI-SHIMA?
YEP.
SHOULD WE GO NOW?
YEAH!
GRAB
BIP
HUH? WHERE ?!
WHERE?
WHERE ELSE?
AKIRA? PLEASE ADD ONE MORE KIMONO.

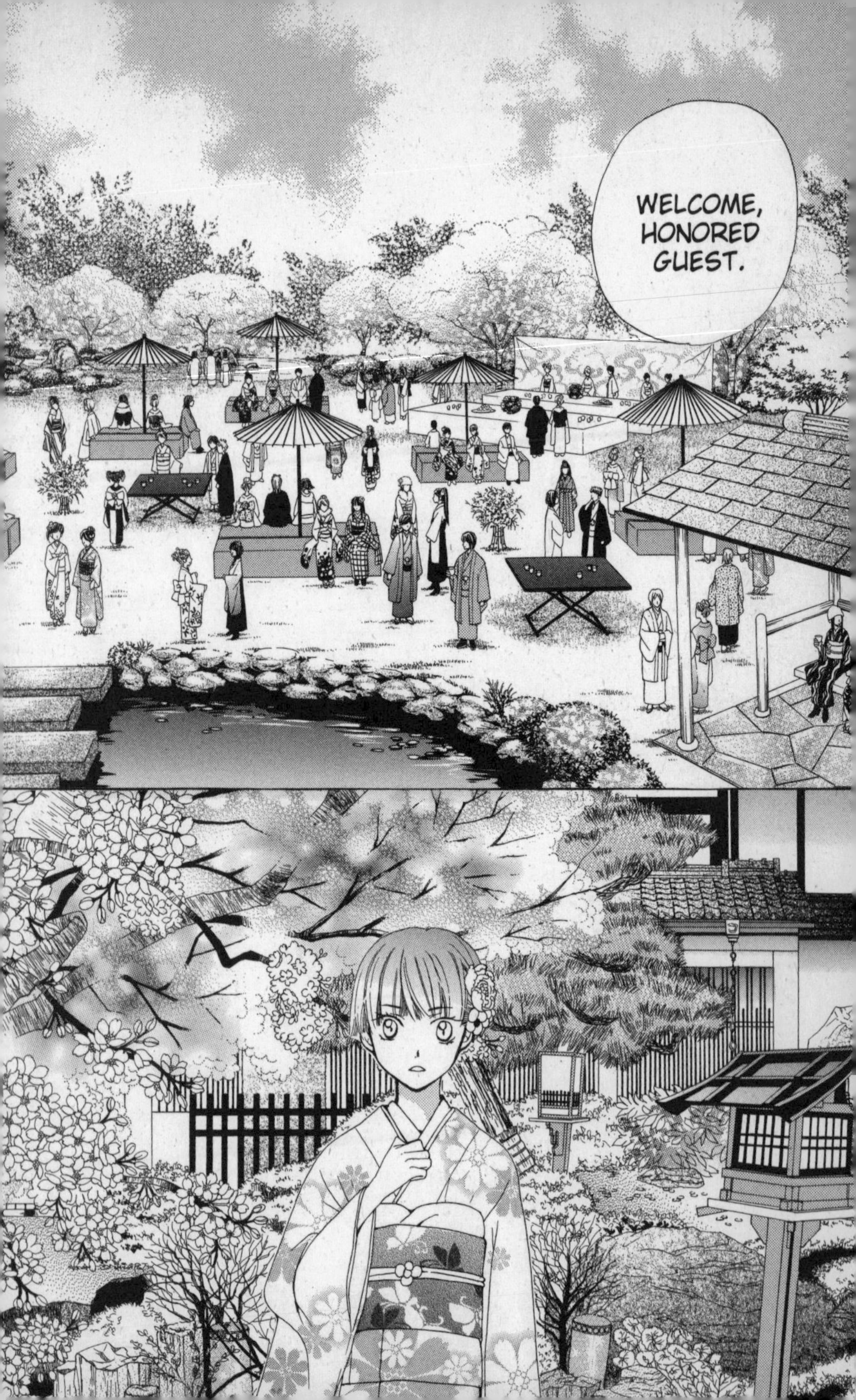
WELCOME, HONORED GUEST.

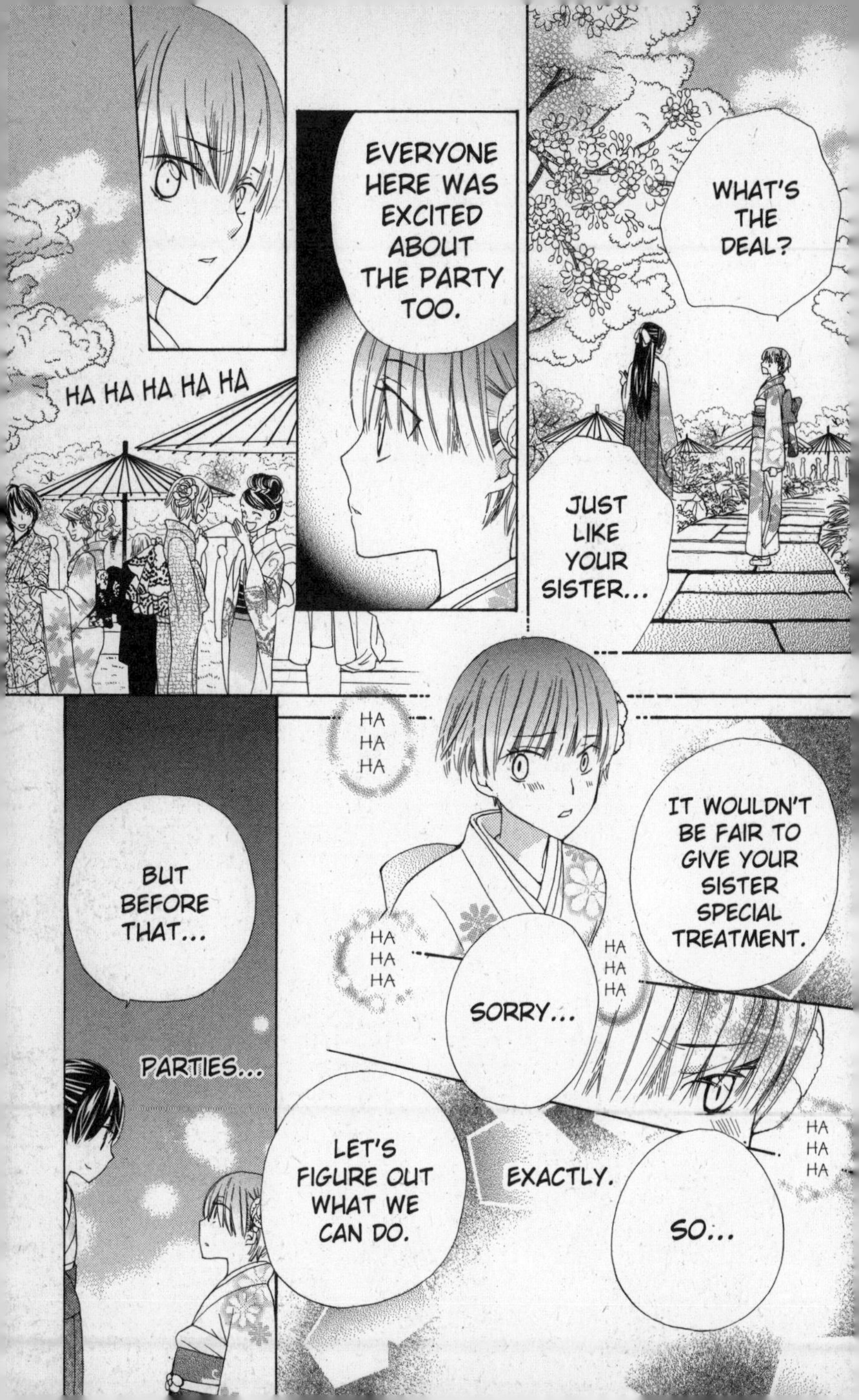
WHAT'S THE DEAL?
JUST LIKE YOUR SISTER...
EVERYONE HERE WAS EXCITED ABOUT THE PARTY TOO.
HA HA HA HA HA
HA HA HA
IT WOULDN'T BE FAIR TO GIVE YOUR SISTER SPECIAL TREATMENT.
HA HA HA
HA HA HA
SORRY...
HA HA HA
SO...
EXACTLY.
LET'S FIGURE OUT WHAT WE CAN DO.
BUT BEFORE THAT...
PARTIES...

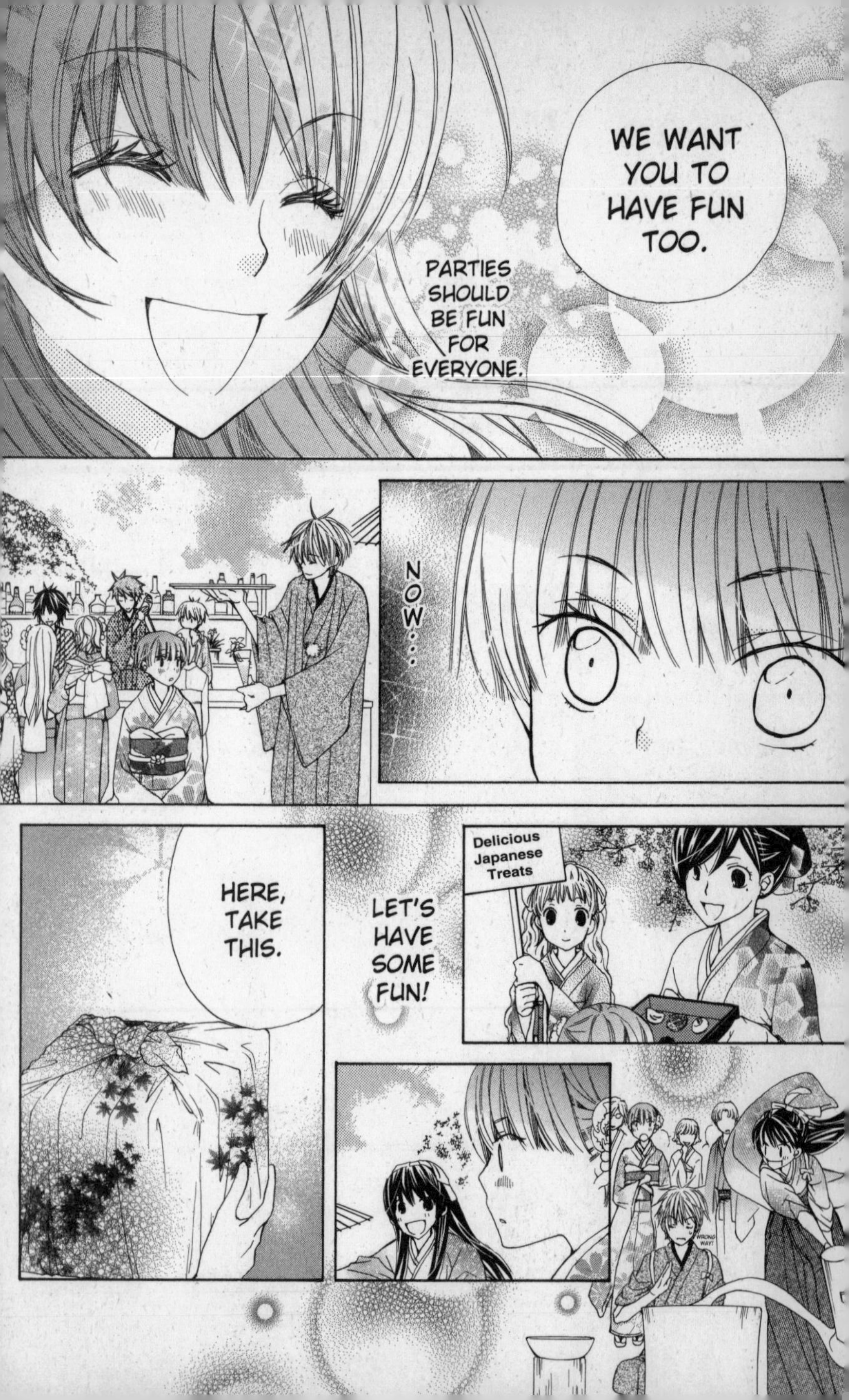

WE WANT YOU TO HAVE FUN TOO.
PARTIES SHOULD BE FUN FOR EVERYONE.
NOW...
Delicious Japanese Treats
LET'S HAVE SOME FUN!
WRONG WAY!
HERE, TAKE THIS.

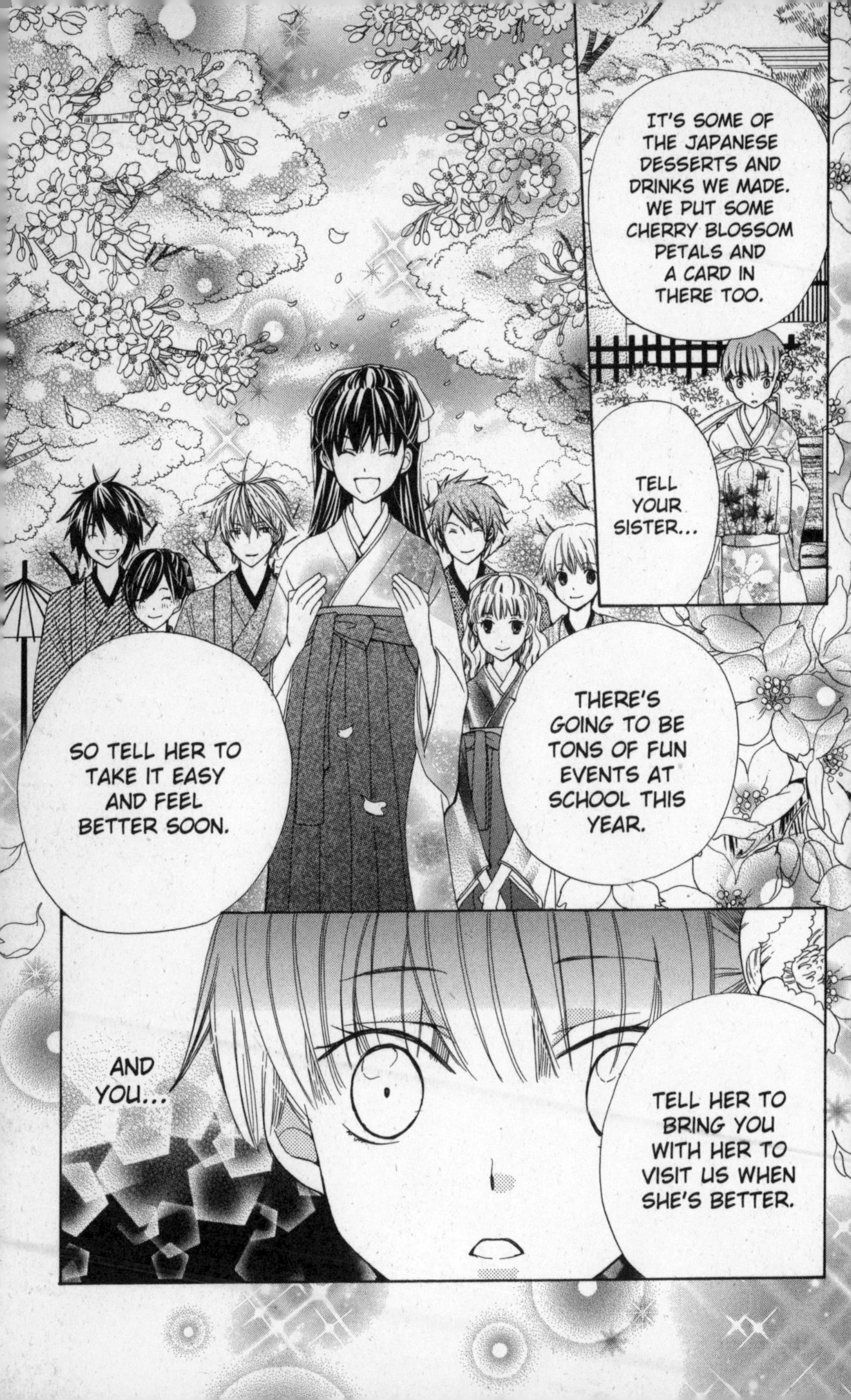
IT'S SOME OF THE JAPANESE DESSERTS AND DRINKS WE MADE. WE PUT SOME CHERRY BLOSSOM PETALS AND A CARD IN THERE TOO.
TELL YOUR SISTER...
THERE'S GOING TO BE TONS OF FUN EVENTS AT SCHOOL THIS YEAR.
SO TELL HER TO TAKE IT EASY AND FEEL BETTER SOON.
AND YOU...
TELL HER TO BRING YOU WITH HER TO VISIT US WHEN SHE'S BETTER.

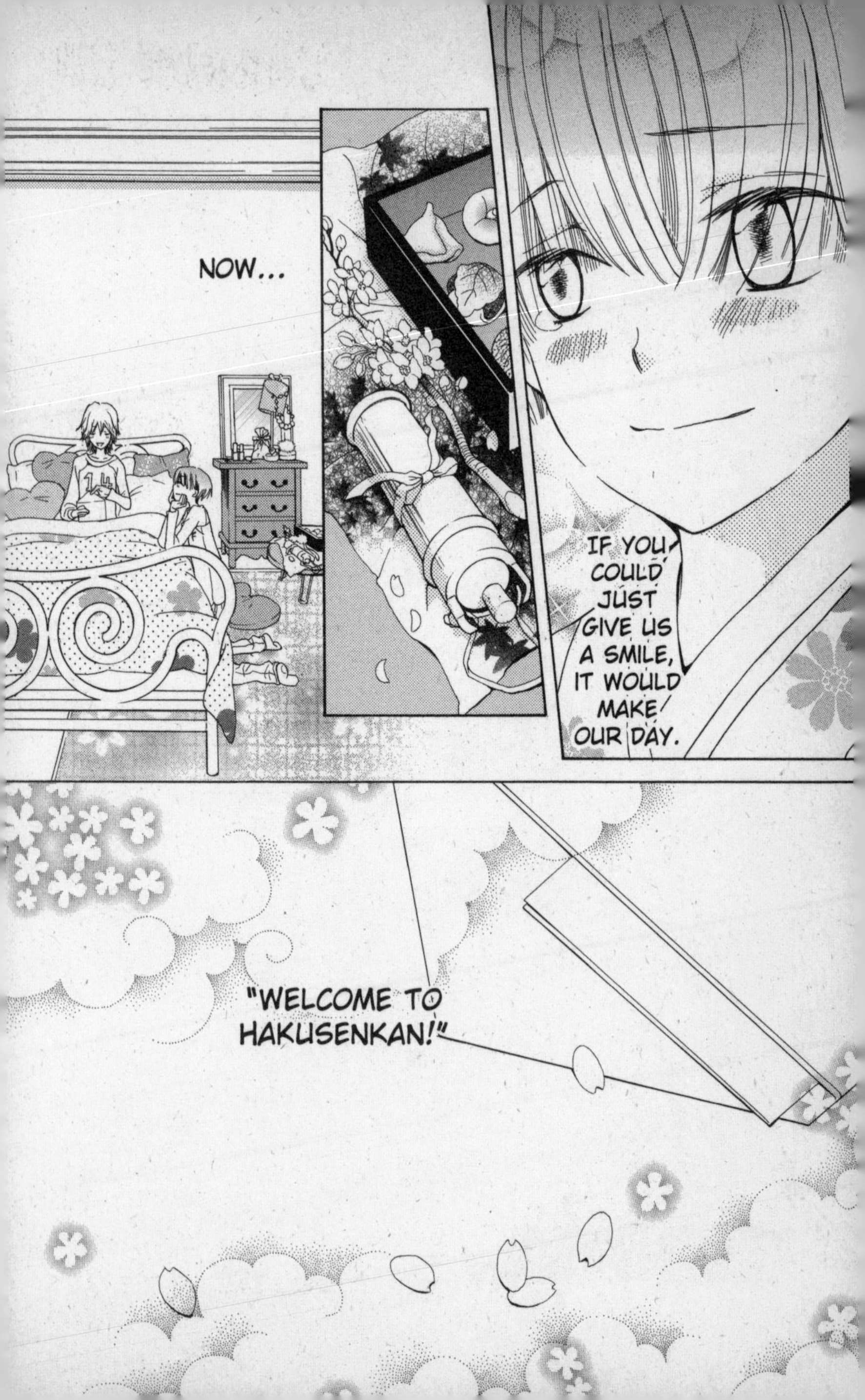
IF YOU COULD JUST GIVE US A SMILE, IT WOULD MAKE OUR DAY.
NOW...
"WELCOME TO HAKUSENKAN!"

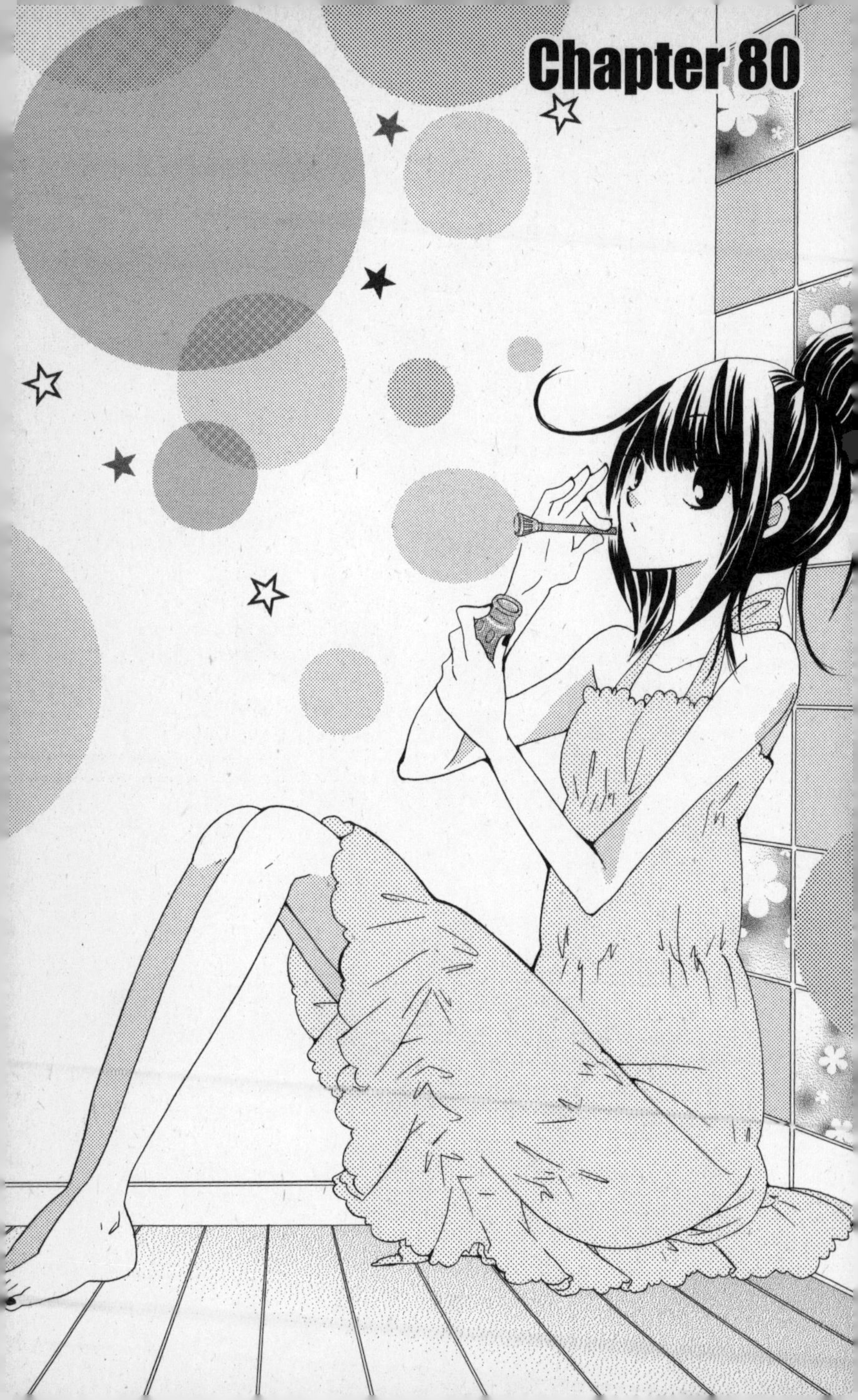
Chapter 80

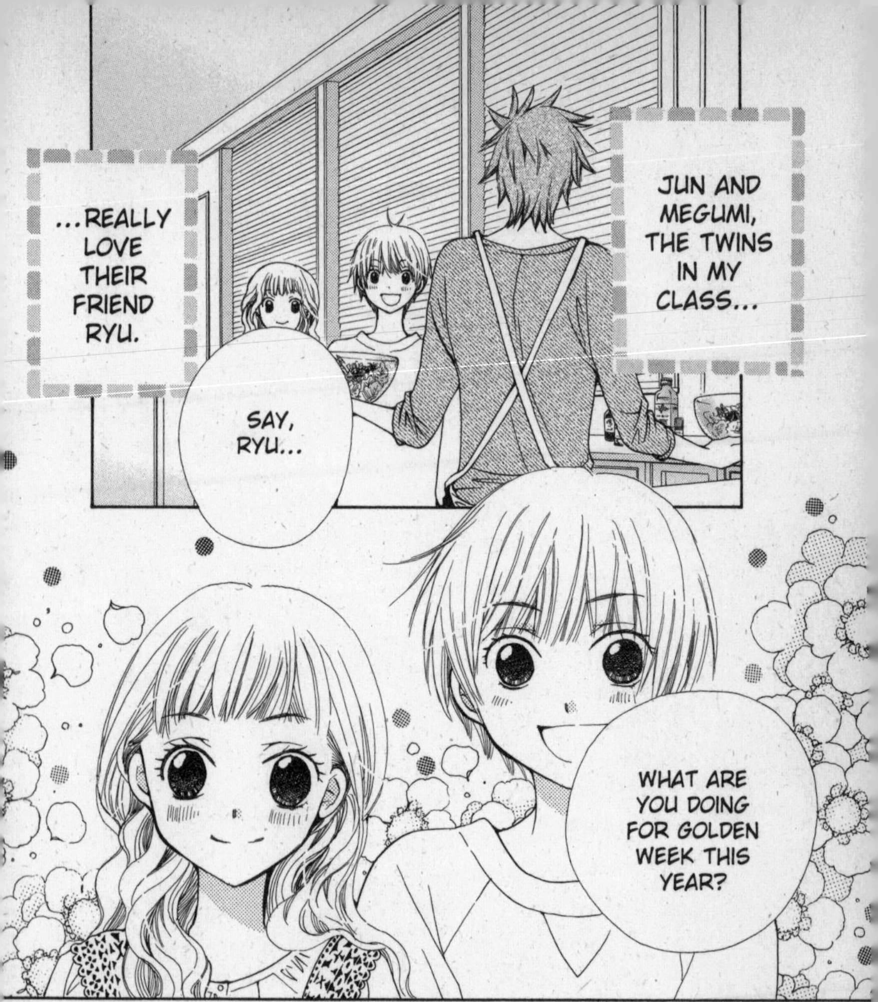
JUN AND MEGUMI, THE TWINS IN MY CLASS...
...REALLY LOVE THEIR FRIEND RYU.
SAY, RYU...
WHAT ARE YOU DOING FOR GOLDEN WEEK THIS YEAR?

· ANIME ·

I LOVE WATCHING THE *S.A* ANIME! HAVE YOU SEEN IT? I'M SO SORRY IF YOU CAN'T GET THE SHOW WHERE YOU LIVE!

I LOVE WATCHING EACH EPISODE FOR THE ACTORS' AD LIBS AND ALL THE FUN SCENES. THANK YOU SO MUCH FOR DOING SUCH A GREAT JOB WITH SO MANY EMBARRASSING LINES!

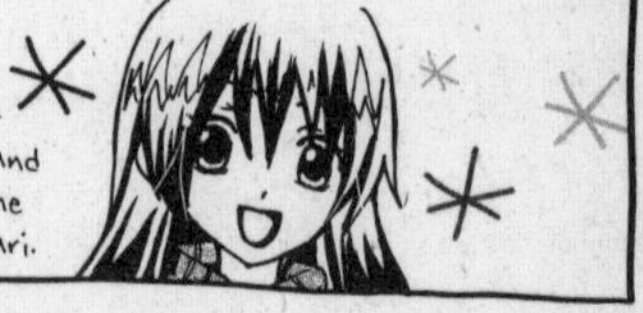

I'm just so happy! I got carried away and drew the anime version of Hikari.

Please forgive me.

You can't see anyone's eyebrows through their hair in the anime.

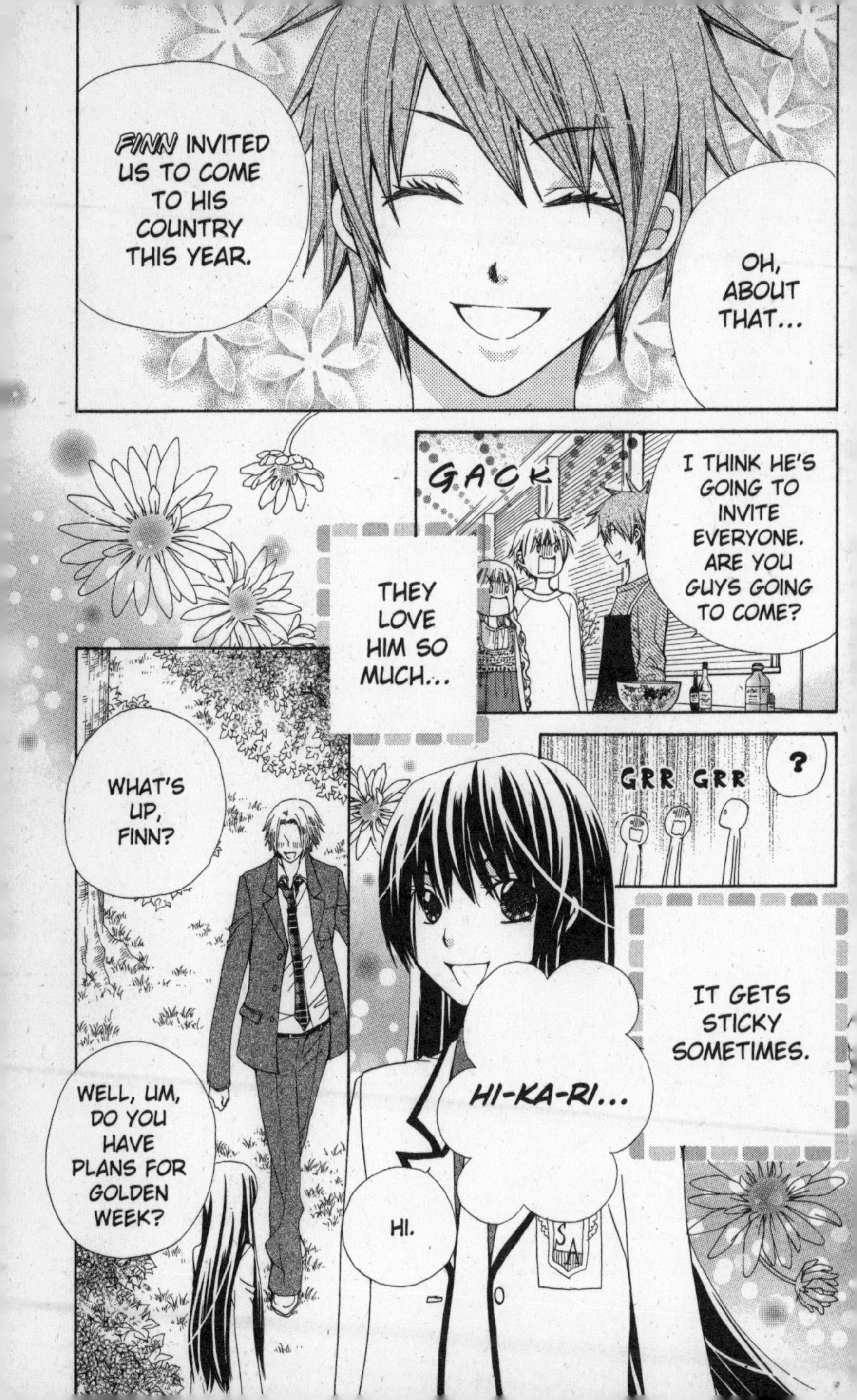
OH, ABOUT THAT...
FINN INVITED US TO COME TO HIS COUNTRY THIS YEAR.
I THINK HE'S GOING TO INVITE EVERYONE. ARE YOU GUYS GOING TO COME?
GACK
THEY LOVE HIM SO MUCH...
?
GRR GRR
IT GETS STICKY SOMETIMES.
HI-KA-RI...
HI.
WHAT'S UP, FINN?
WELL, UM, DO YOU HAVE PLANS FOR GOLDEN WEEK?

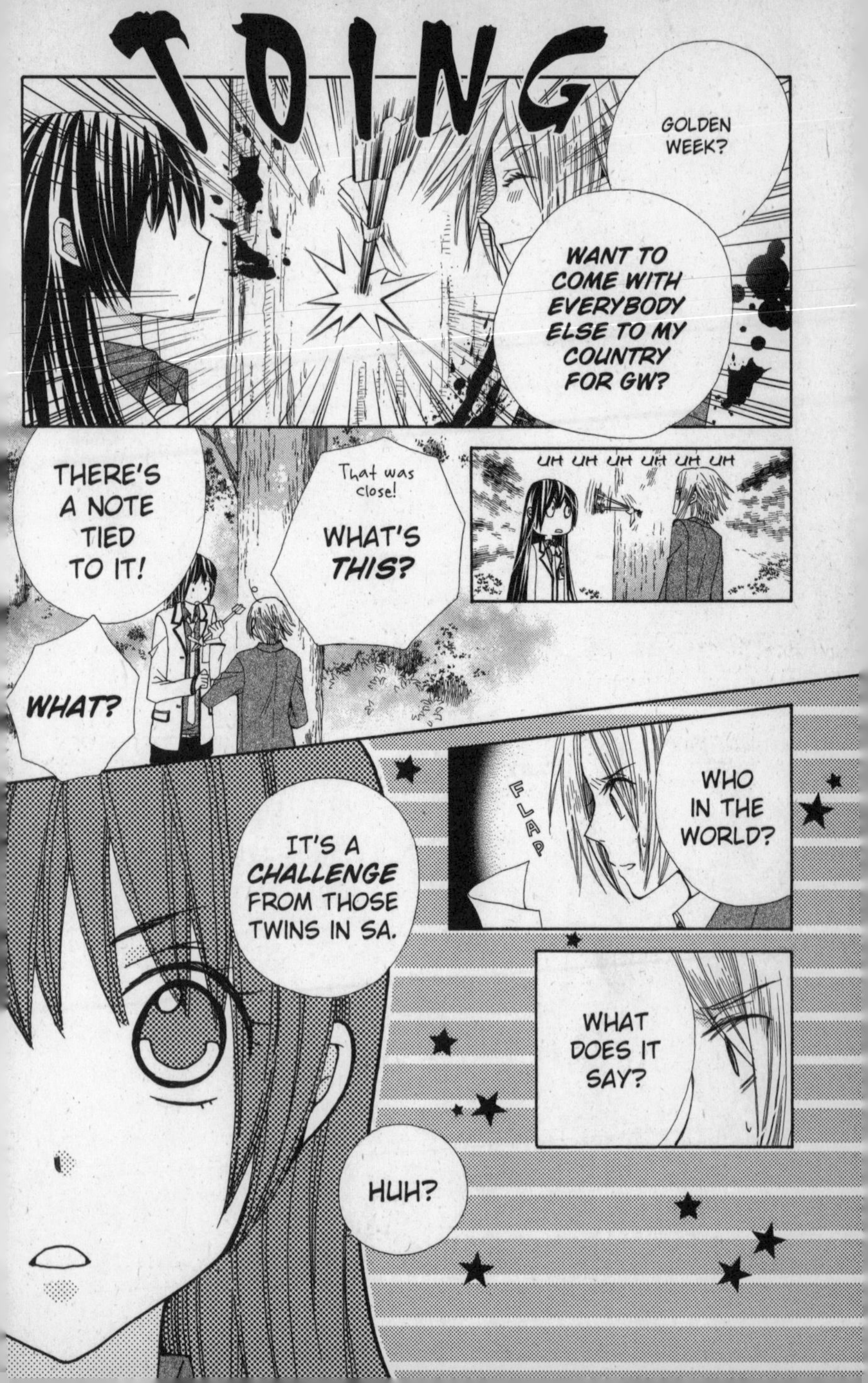
GOLDEN WEEK?
WANT TO COME WITH EVERYBODY ELSE TO MY COUNTRY FOR GW?
TOING
UH UH UH UH UH UH
That was close!
WHAT'S THIS?
THERE'S A NOTE TIED TO IT!
WHAT?
WHO IN THE WORLD?
FLAP
WHAT DOES IT SAY?
IT'S A CHALLENGE FROM THOSE TWINS IN SA.
HUH?

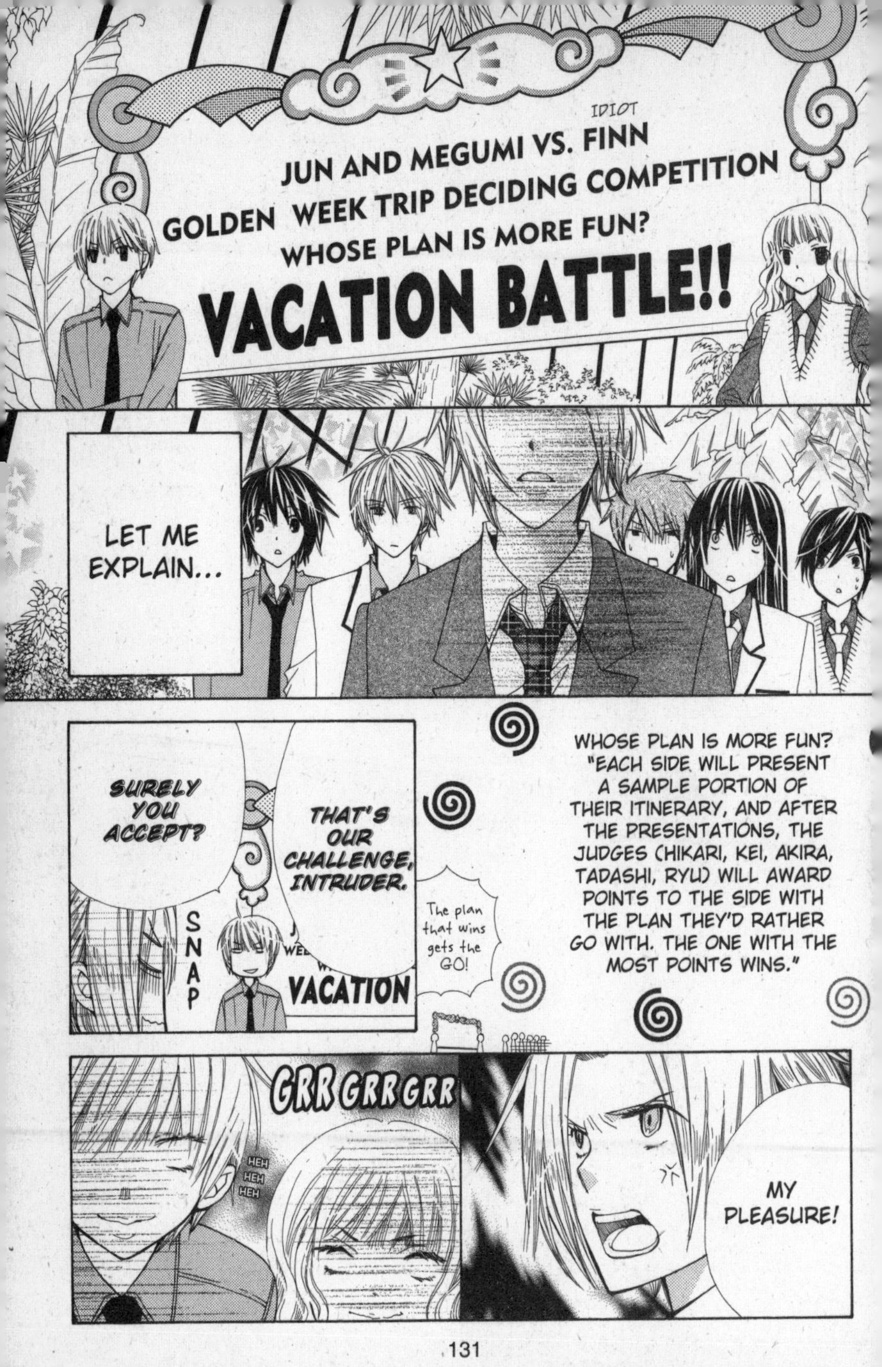
IDIOT
JUN AND MEGUMI VS. FINN
GOLDEN WEEK TRIP DECIDING COMPETITION
WHOSE PLAN IS MORE FUN?
VACATION BATTLE!!
LET ME EXPLAIN...
WHOSE PLAN IS MORE FUN? "EACH SIDE WILL PRESENT A SAMPLE PORTION OF THEIR ITINERARY, AND AFTER THE PRESENTATIONS, THE JUDGES (HIKARI, KEI, AKIRA, TADASHI, RYU) WILL AWARD POINTS TO THE SIDE WITH THE PLAN THEY'D RATHER GO WITH. THE ONE WITH THE MOST POINTS WINS."
The plan that wins gets the GO!
THAT'S OUR CHALLENGE, INTRUDER.
SURELY YOU ACCEPT?
SNAP
VACATION
MY PLEASURE!
GRR GRR GRR
HEH HEH HEH

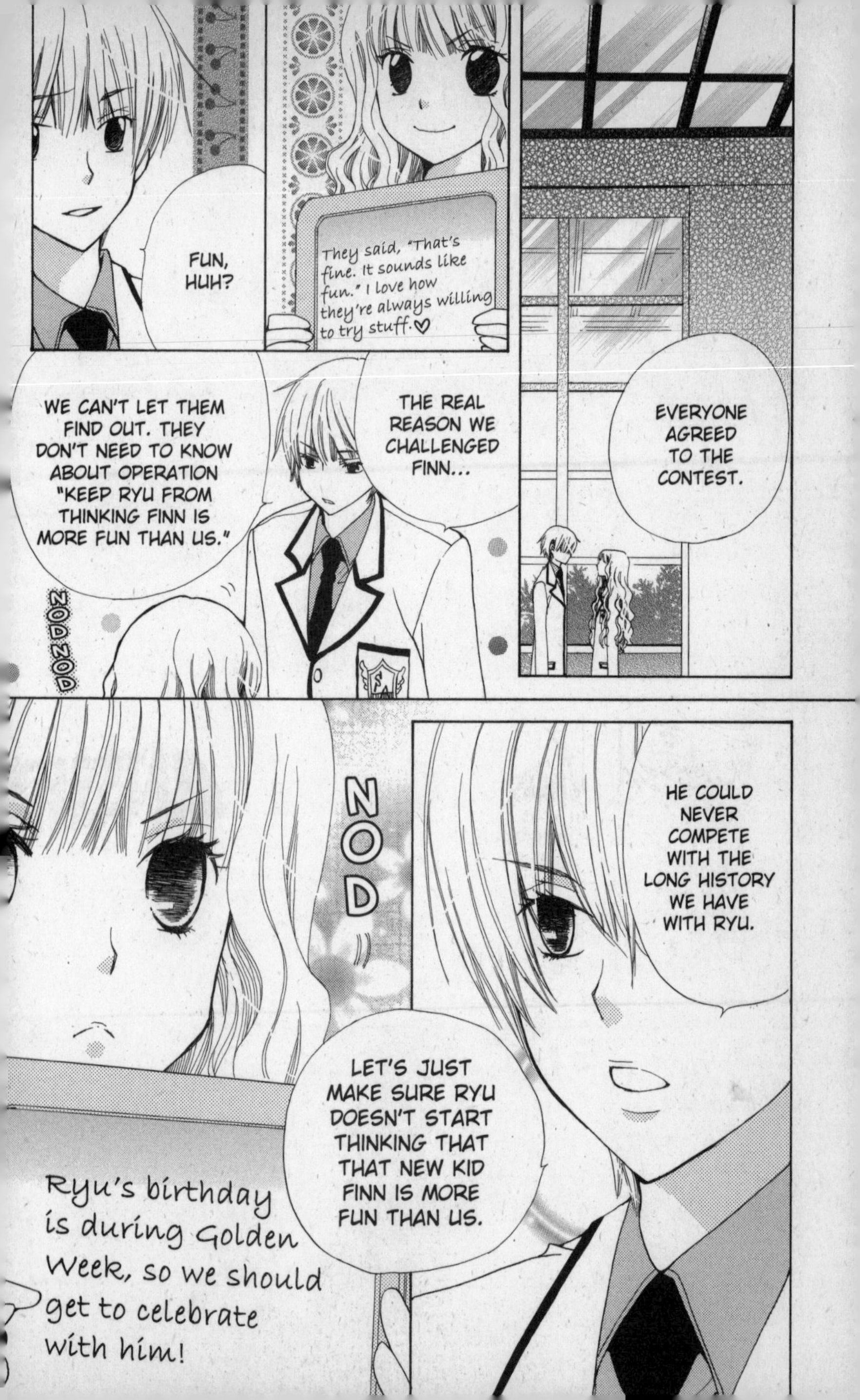
EVERYONE AGREED TO THE CONTEST.
They said, "That's fine. It sounds like fun." I love how they're always willing to try stuff.♡
FUN, HUH?
THE REAL REASON WE CHALLENGED FINN...
WE CAN'T LET THEM FIND OUT. THEY DON'T NEED TO KNOW ABOUT OPERATION "KEEP RYU FROM THINKING FINN IS MORE FUN THAN US."
NOD NOD
HE COULD NEVER COMPETE WITH THE LONG HISTORY WE HAVE WITH RYU.
NOD
LET'S JUST MAKE SURE RYU DOESN'T START THINKING THAT THAT NEW KID FINN IS MORE FUN THAN US.
Ryu's birthday is during Golden Week, so we should get to celebrate with him!

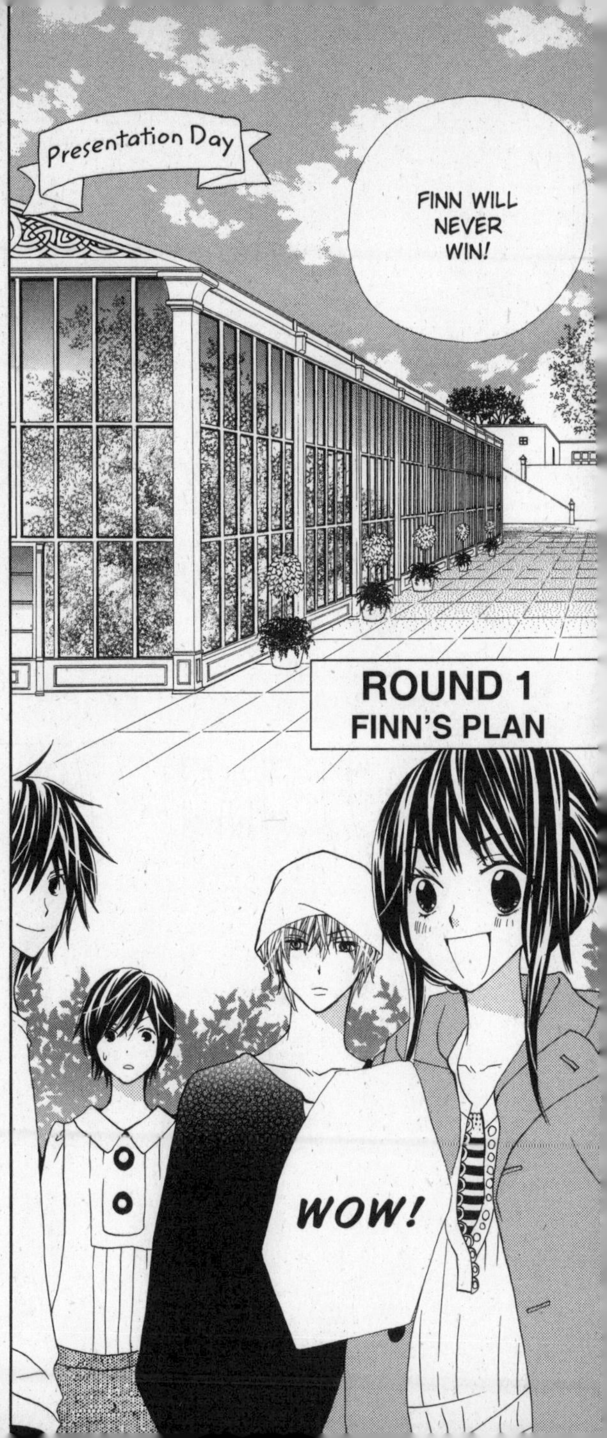
FINN WILL NEVER WIN!
Presentation Day
ROUND 1
FINN'S PLAN
WOW!

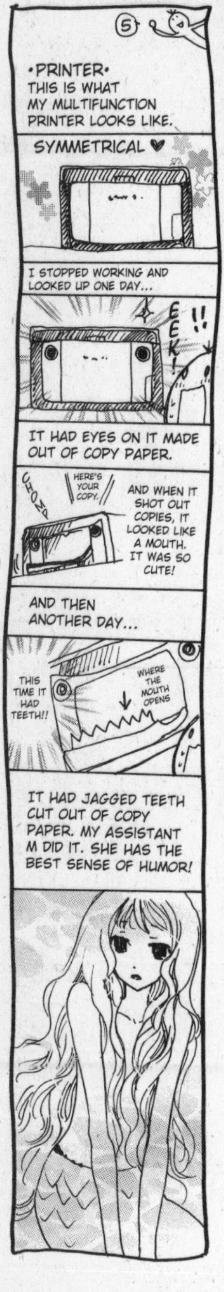
5
•PRINTER•
THIS IS WHAT MY MULTIFUNCTION PRINTER LOOKS LIKE.
SYMMETRICAL ♥
I STOPPED WORKING AND LOOKED UP ONE DAY...
EEEK!
!!
IT HAD EYES ON IT MADE OUT OF COPY PAPER.
CHOMP
HERE'S YOUR COPY.
AND WHEN IT SHOT OUT COPIES, IT LOOKED LIKE A MOUTH. IT WAS SO CUTE!
AND THEN ANOTHER DAY...
THIS TIME IT HAD TEETH!!
WHERE THE MOUTH OPENS
IT HAD JAGGED TEETH CUT OUT OF COPY PAPER. MY ASSISTANT M DID IT. SHE HAS THE BEST SENSE OF HUMOR!

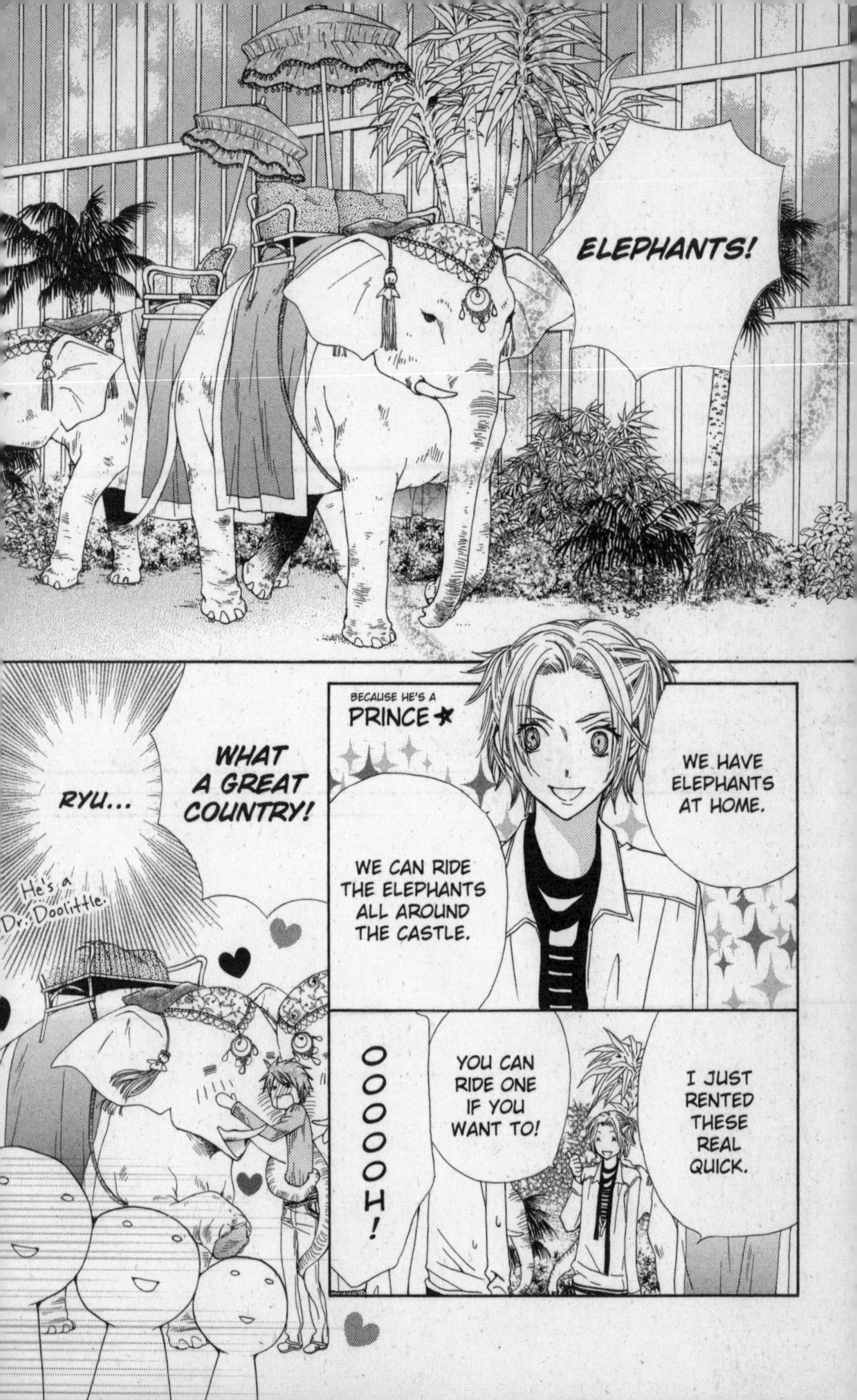
ELEPHANTS!
BECAUSE HE'S A PRINCE ★
WE HAVE ELEPHANTS AT HOME.
WE CAN RIDE THE ELEPHANTS ALL AROUND THE CASTLE.
I JUST RENTED THESE REAL QUICK.
YOU CAN RIDE ONE IF YOU WANT TO!
OOOOOOH!
WHAT A GREAT COUNTRY!
RYU...
He's a Dr. Doolittle.

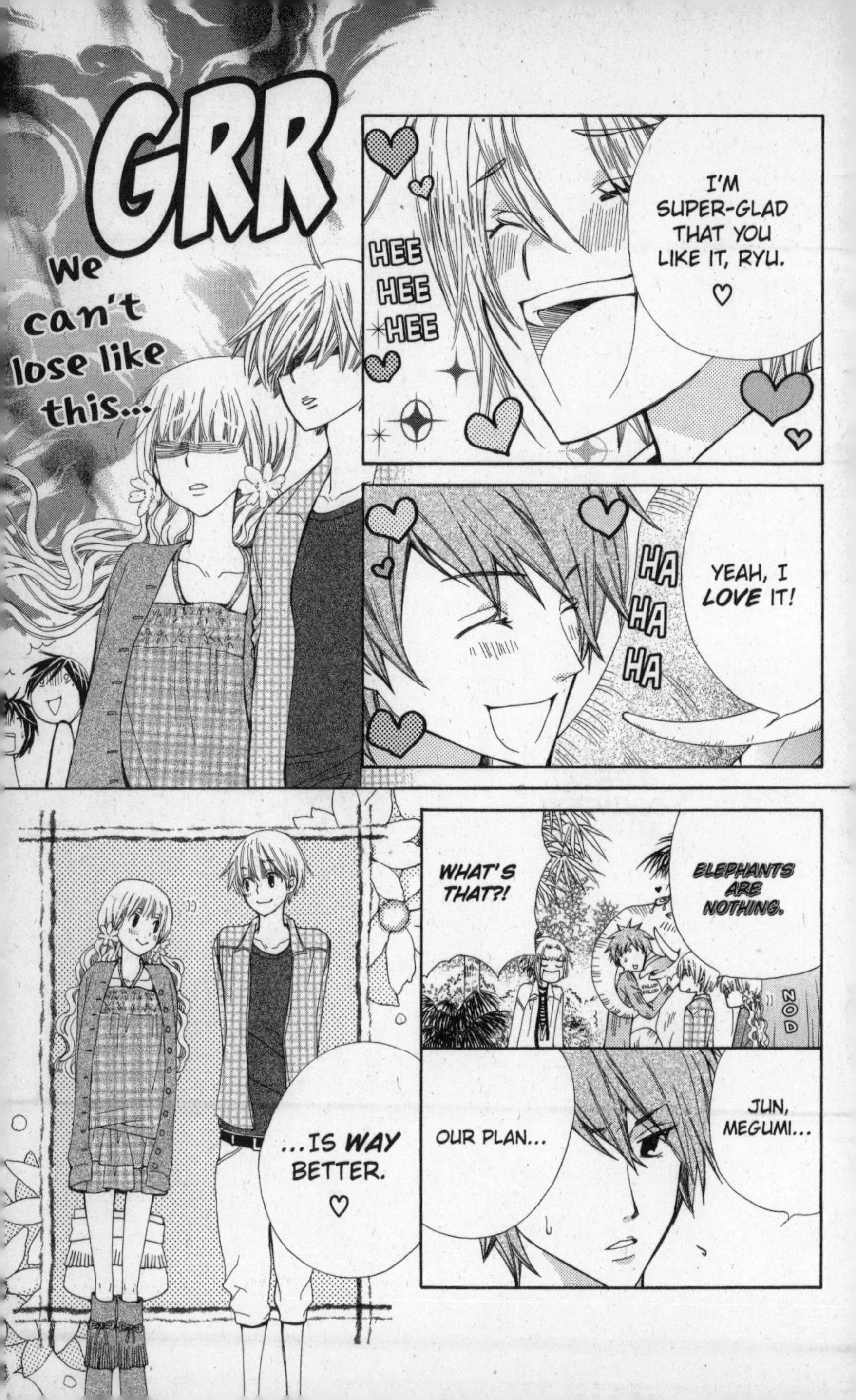
I'M SUPER-GLAD THAT YOU LIKE IT, RYU. ♡
HEE HEE HEE
YEAH, I LOVE IT!
HA HA HA
GRR
We can't lose like this...
ELEPHANTS ARE NOTHING.
WHAT'S THAT?!
NOD
JUN, MEGUMI...
OUR PLAN...
...IS WAY BETTER. ♡

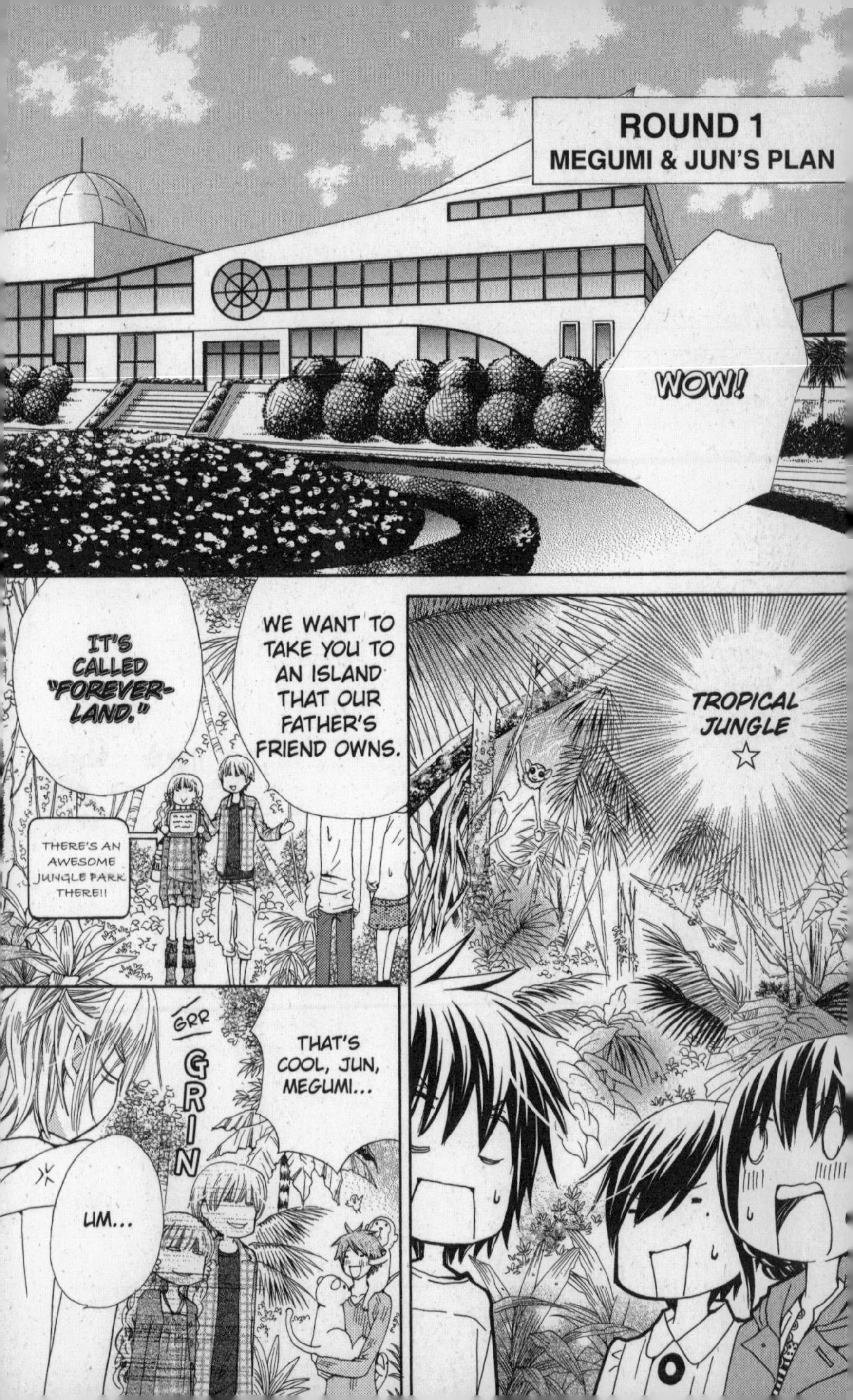
ROUND 1
MEGUMI & JUN'S PLAN
WOW!
TROPICAL JUNGLE ☆
WE WANT TO TAKE YOU TO AN ISLAND THAT OUR FATHER'S FRIEND OWNS.
IT'S CALLED "FOREVER-LAND."
THERE'S AN AWESOME JUNGLE PARK THERE!!
GRR
GRIN
THAT'S COOL, JUN, MEGUMI...
UM...

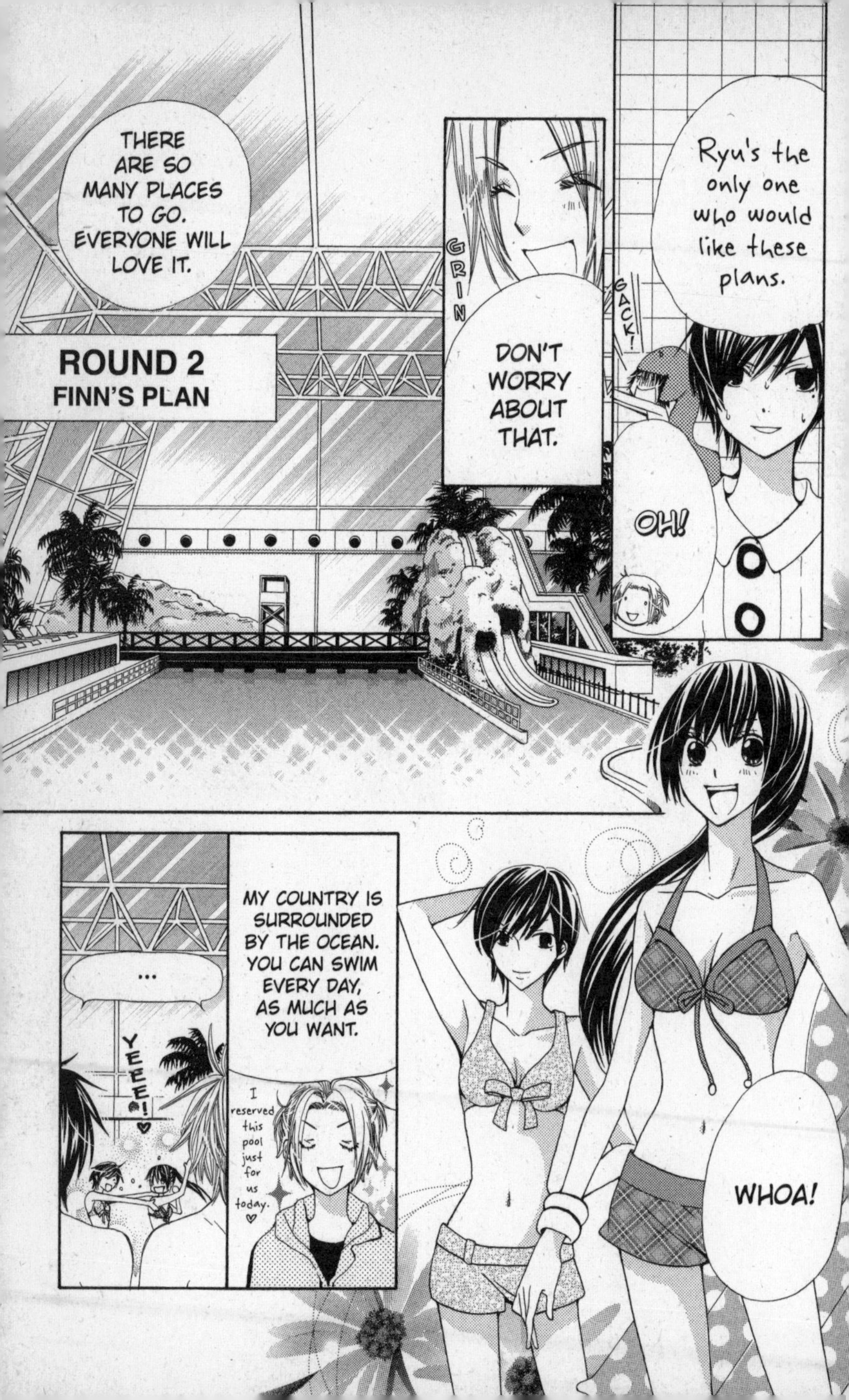
Ryu's the only one who would like these plans.
GACK!
OH!
GRIN
DON'T WORRY ABOUT THAT.
THERE ARE SO MANY PLACES TO GO. EVERYONE WILL LOVE IT.
ROUND 2
FINN'S PLAN
WHOA!
MY COUNTRY IS SURROUNDED BY THE OCEAN. YOU CAN SWIM EVERY DAY, AS MUCH AS YOU WANT.
I reserved this pool just for us today.
...
YEEEE!

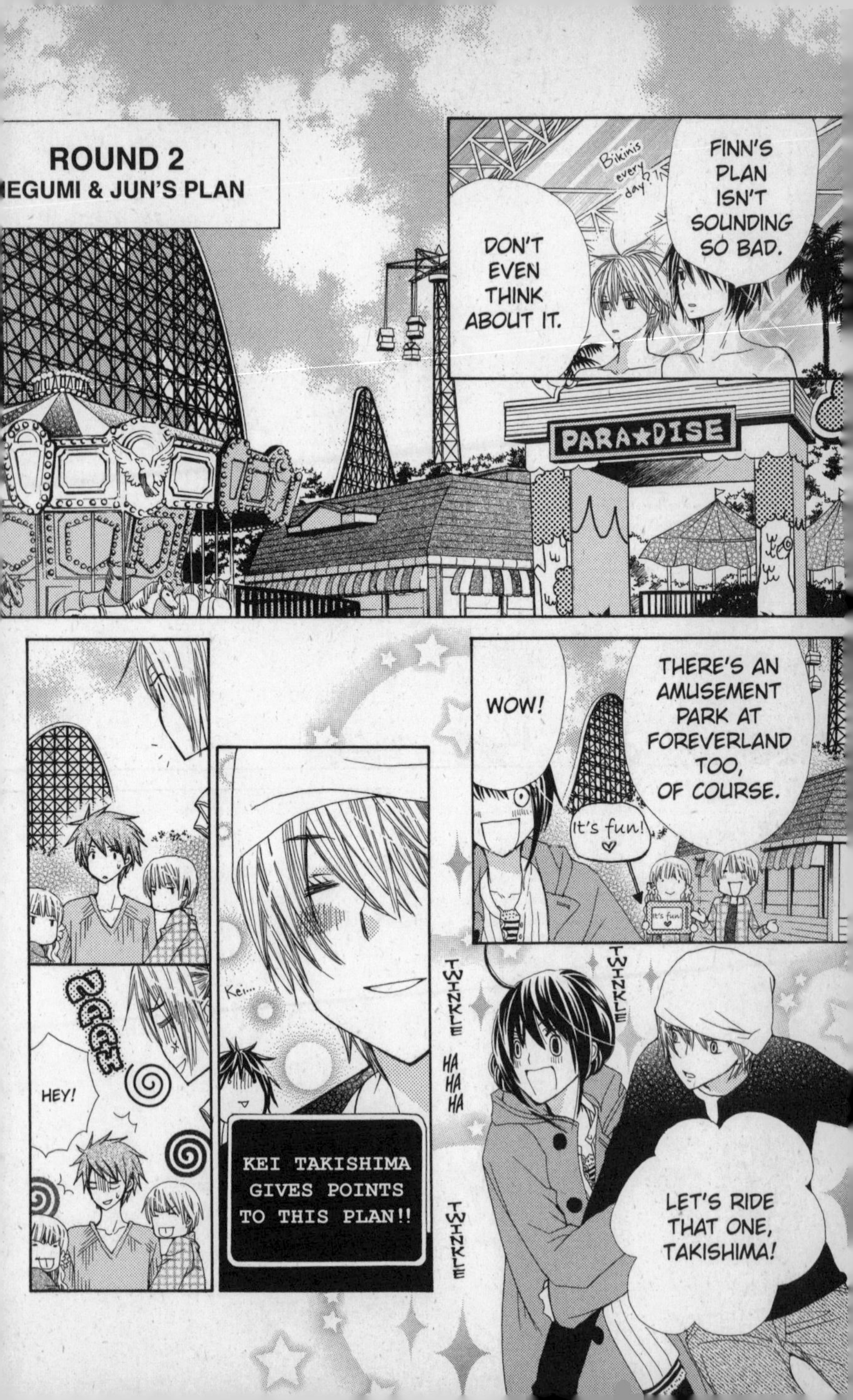
ROUND 2
EGUMI & JUN'S PLAN
FINN'S PLAN ISN'T SOUNDING SO BAD.
Bikinis every day?
DON'T EVEN THINK ABOUT IT.
PARA★DISE
THERE'S AN AMUSEMENT PARK AT FOREVERLAND TOO, OF COURSE.
WOW!
It's fun!
It's fun
TWINKLE
TWINKLE
LET'S RIDE THAT ONE, TAKISHIMA!
HA HA HA
TWINKLE
Kei...
KEI TAKISHIMA GIVES POINTS TO THIS PLAN!!
HEY!

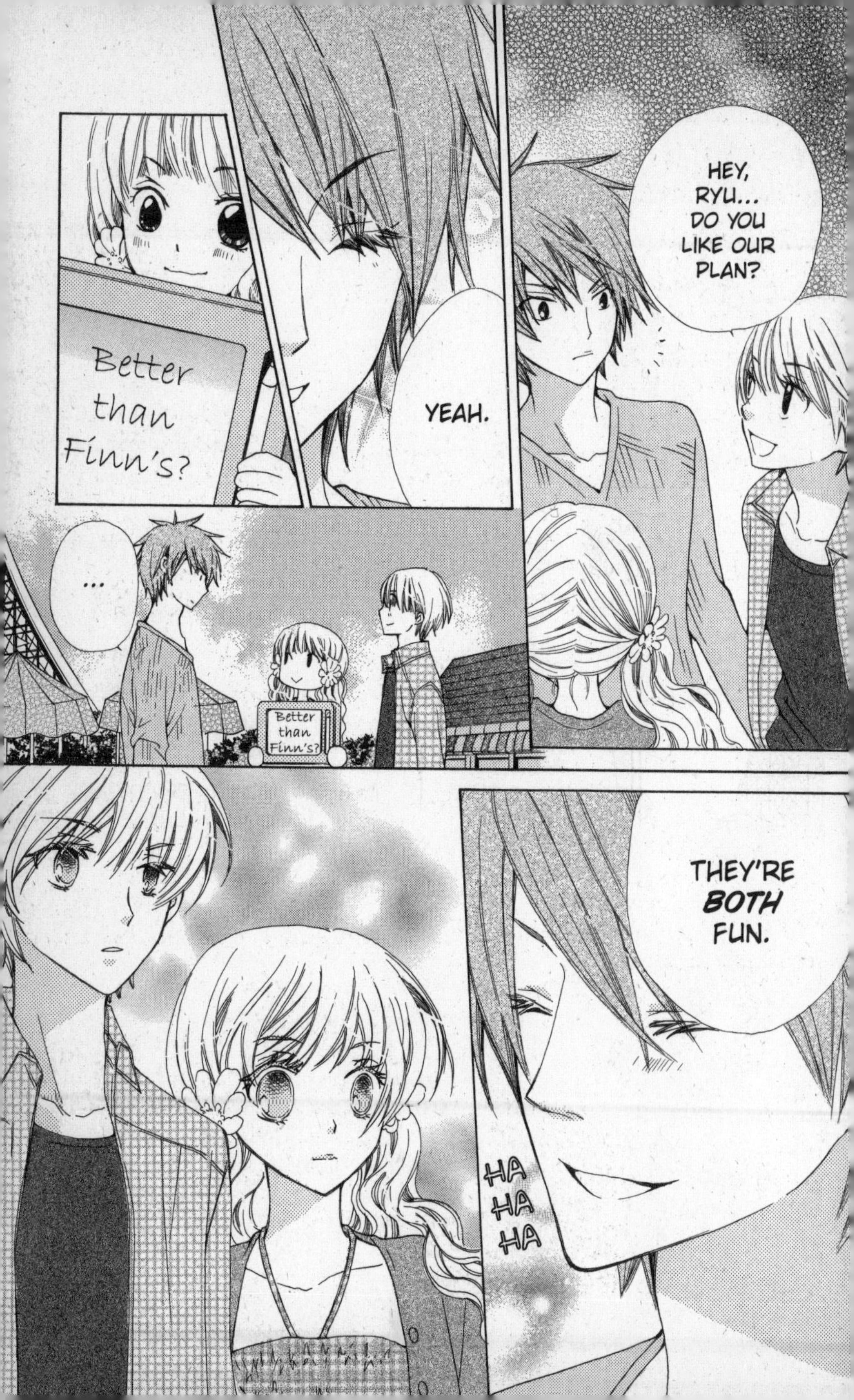
HEY, RYU... DO YOU LIKE OUR PLAN?
YEAH.
Better than Finn's?
...
Better than Finn's?
THEY'RE *BOTH* FUN.
HA HA HA

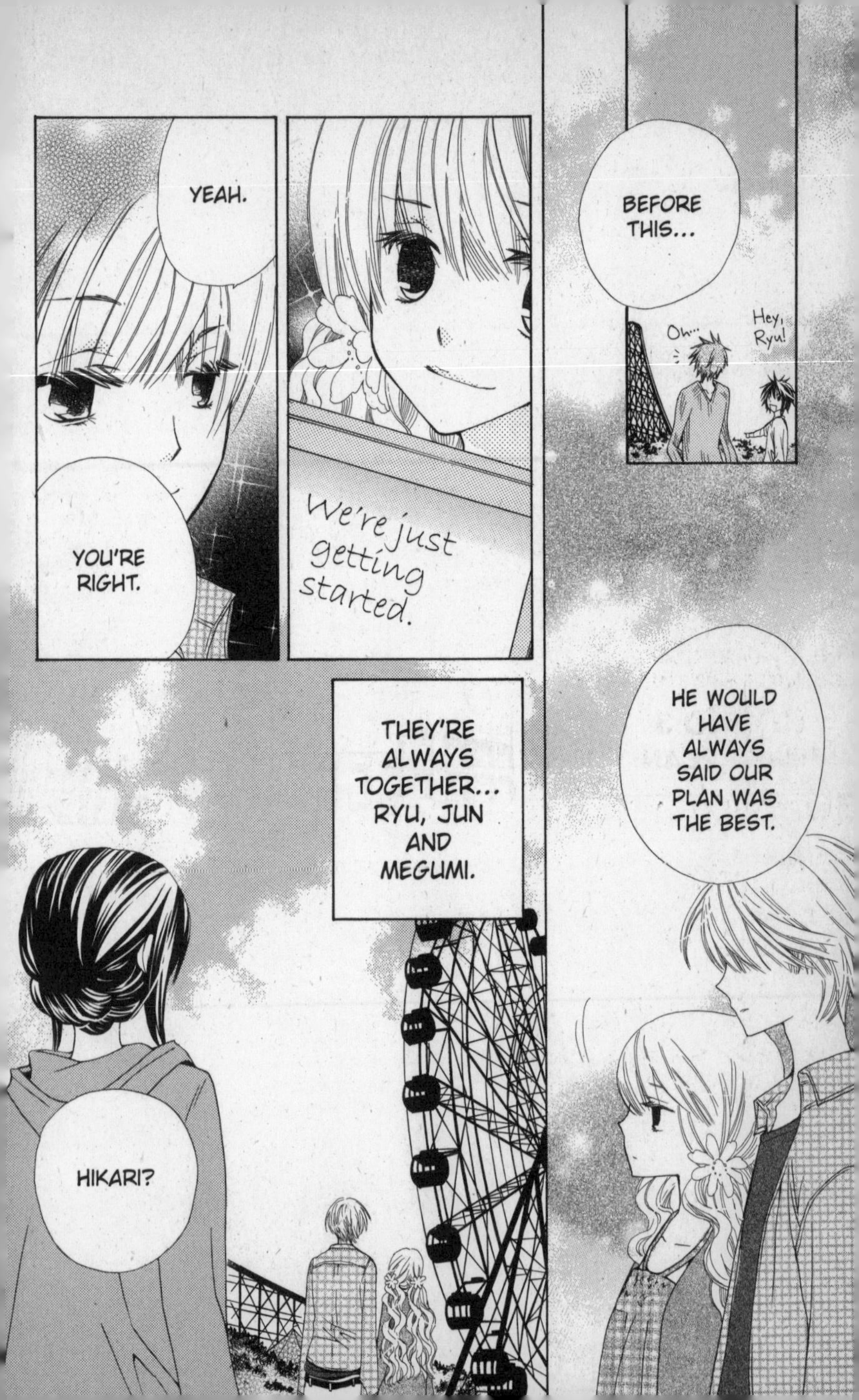
BEFORE THIS...
Hey, Ryu!
Oh...
HE WOULD HAVE ALWAYS SAID OUR PLAN WAS THE BEST.
We're just getting started.
YEAH.
YOU'RE RIGHT.
THEY'RE ALWAYS TOGETHER... RYU, JUN AND MEGUMI.
HIKARI?

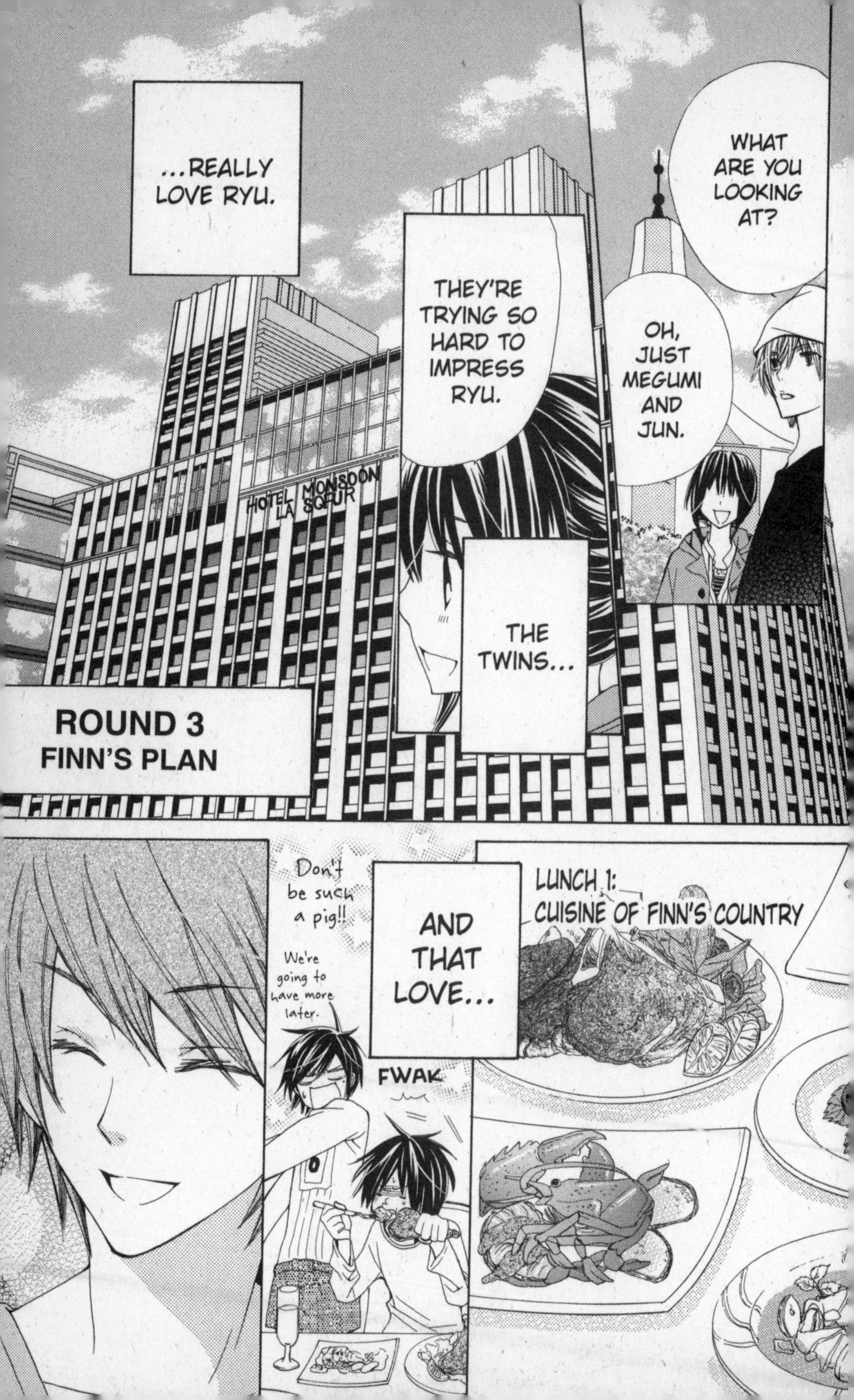
WHAT ARE YOU LOOKING AT?
OH, JUST MEGUMI AND JUN.
THEY'RE TRYING SO HARD TO IMPRESS RYU.
THE TWINS...
...REALLY LOVE RYU.
ROUND 3 FINN'S PLAN
LUNCH 1: CUISINE OF FINN'S COUNTRY
AND THAT LOVE...
Don't be such a pig!!
We're going to have more later.
FWAK

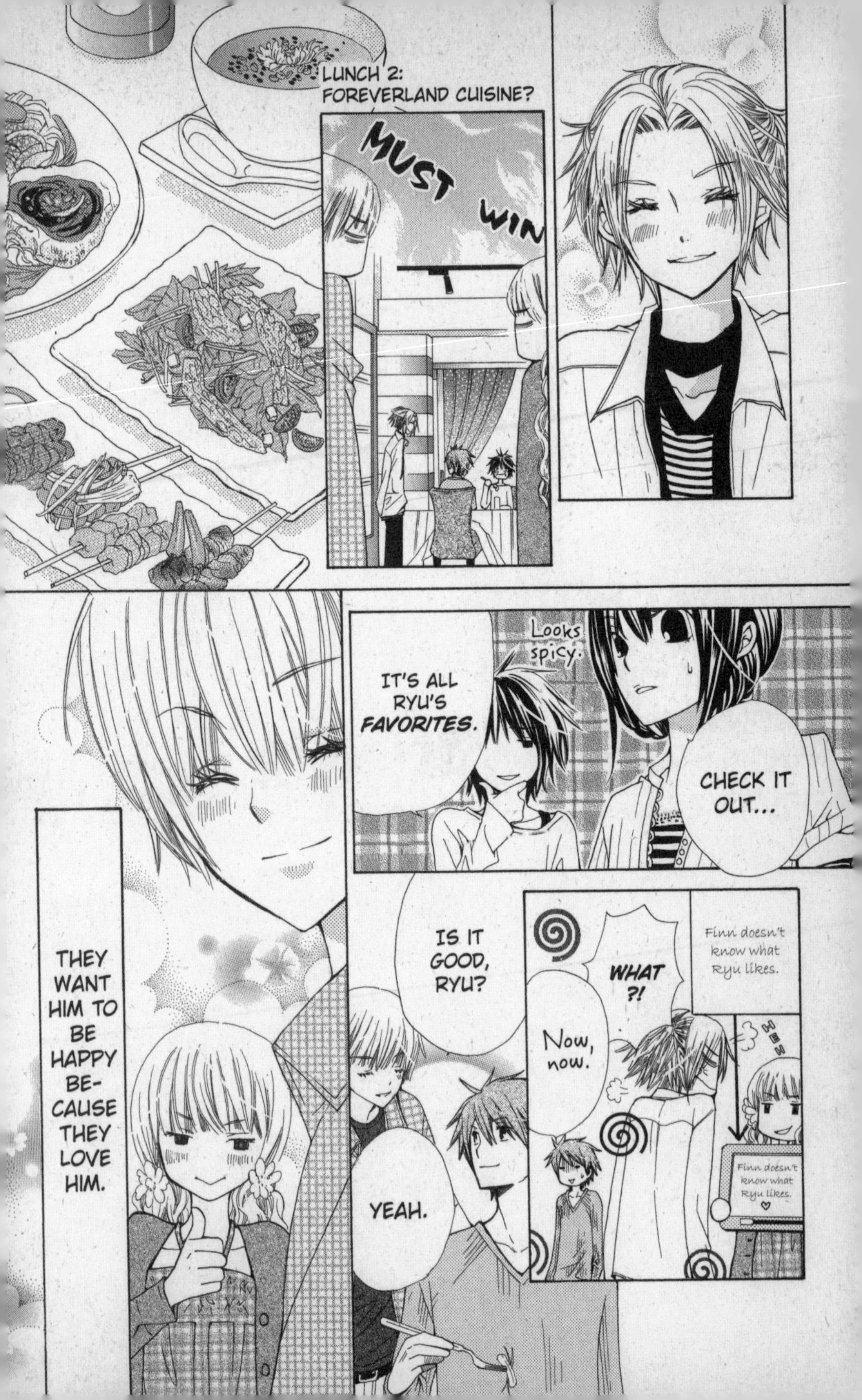
MUST WIN
LUNCH 2: FOREVERLAND CUISINE?
CHECK IT OUT...
Looks spicy.
IT'S ALL RYU'S FAVORITES.
Finn doesn't know what Ryu likes.
WHAT?!
Now, now.
HEH
Finn doesn't know what Ryu likes. ♥
IS IT GOOD, RYU?
YEAH.
THEY WANT HIM TO BE HAPPY BE-CAUSE THEY LOVE HIM.

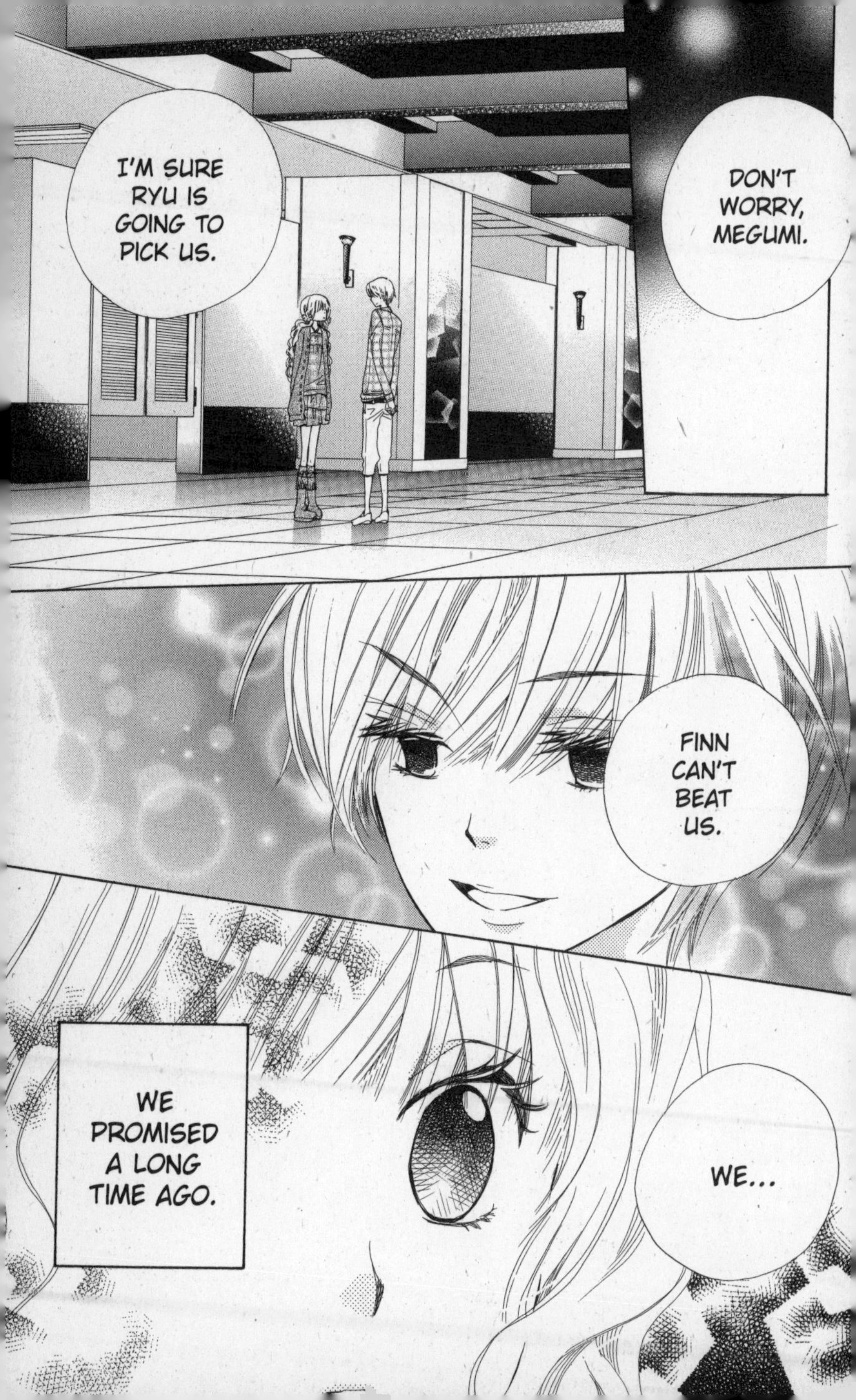
DON'T WORRY, MEGUMI.
I'M SURE RYU IS GOING TO PICK US.
FINN CAN'T BEAT US.
WE...
WE PROMISED A LONG TIME AGO.

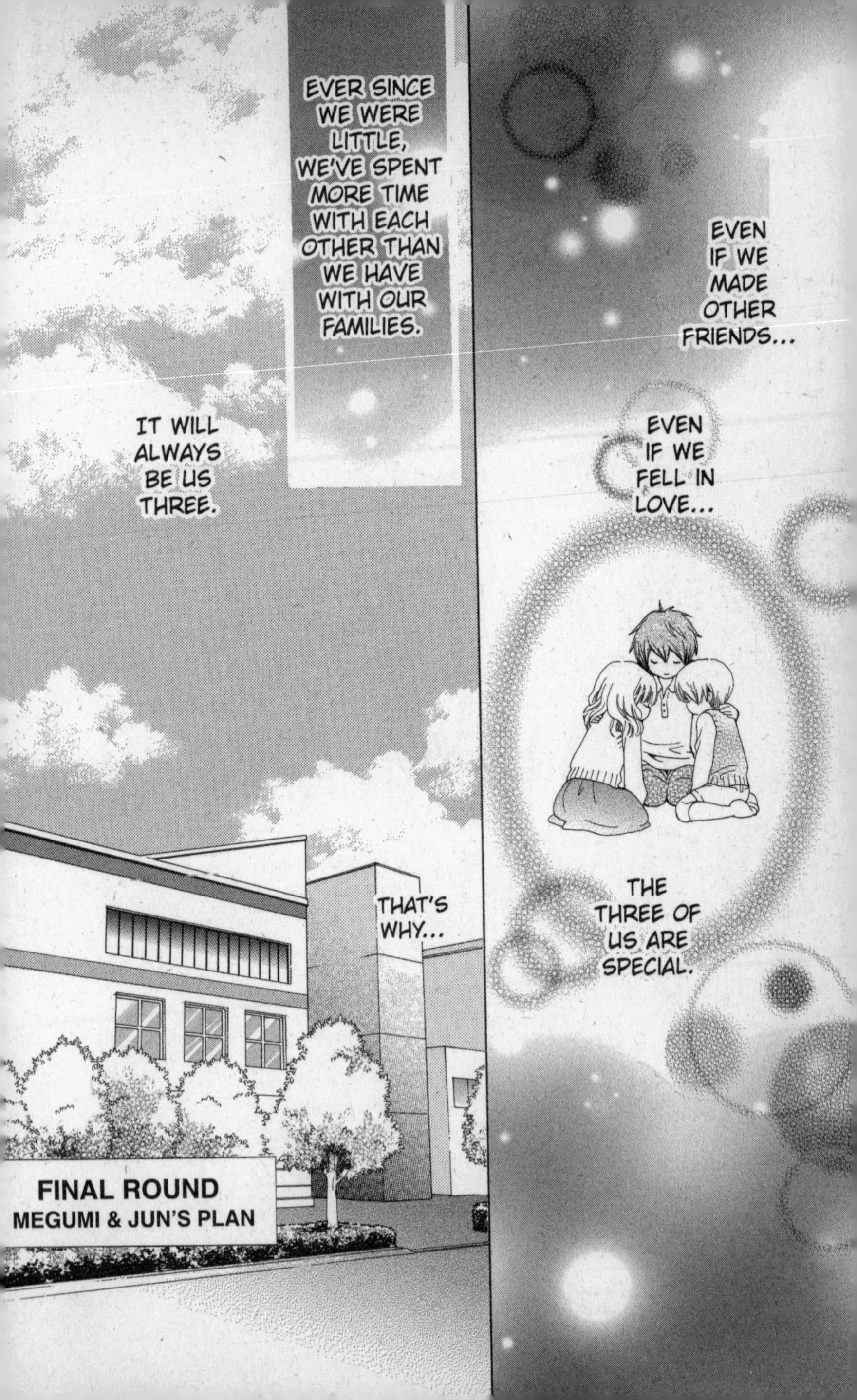
EVEN IF WE MADE OTHER FRIENDS...
EVEN IF WE FELL IN LOVE...
THE THREE OF US ARE SPECIAL.
EVER SINCE WE WERE LITTLE, WE'VE SPENT MORE TIME WITH EACH OTHER THAN WE HAVE WITH OUR FAMILIES.
IT WILL ALWAYS BE US THREE.
THAT'S WHY...
FINAL ROUND
MEGUMI & JUN'S PLAN

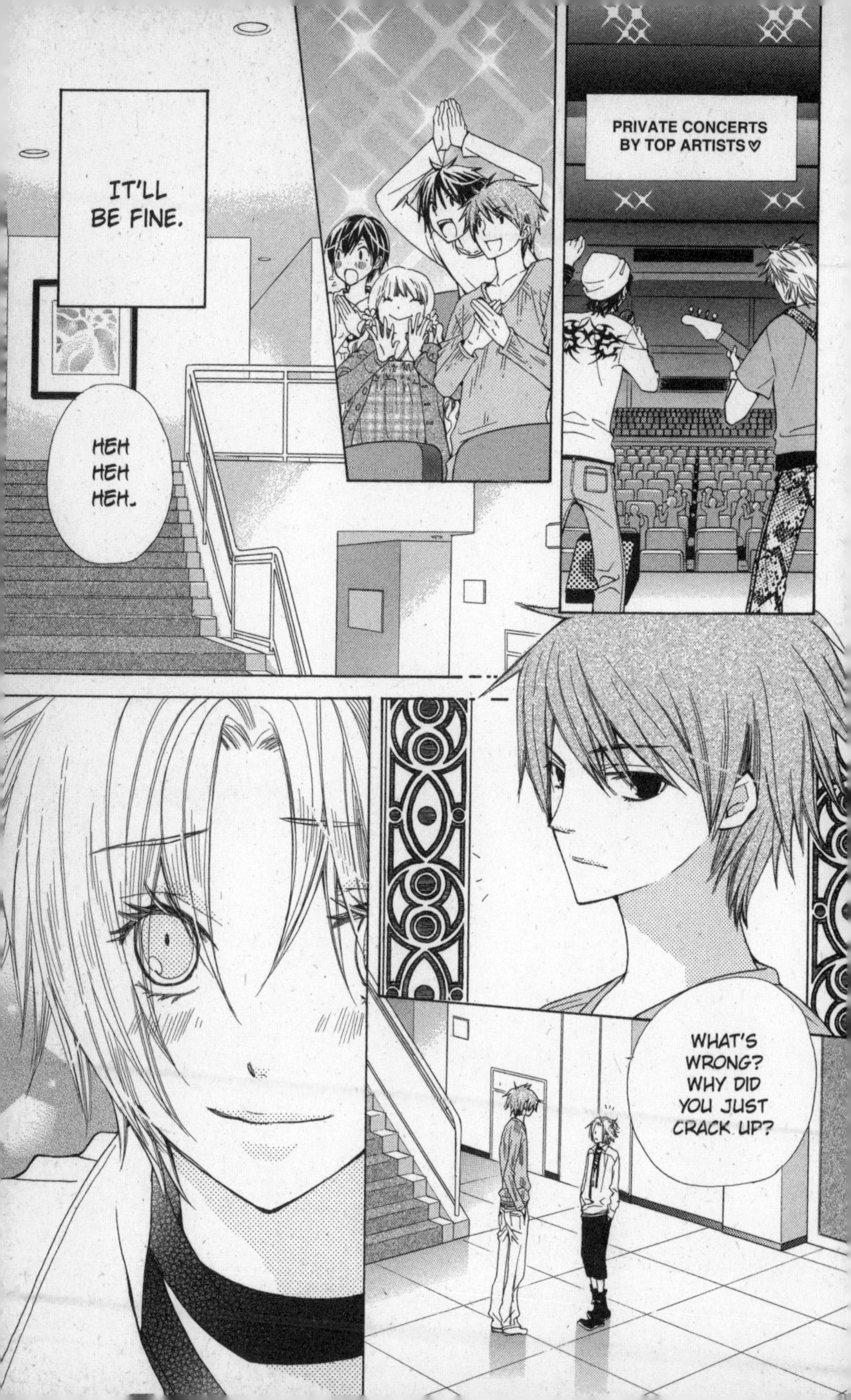
PRIVATE CONCERTS BY TOP ARTISTS♡
IT'LL BE FINE.
HEH HEH HEH.
WHAT'S WRONG? WHY DID YOU JUST CRACK UP?

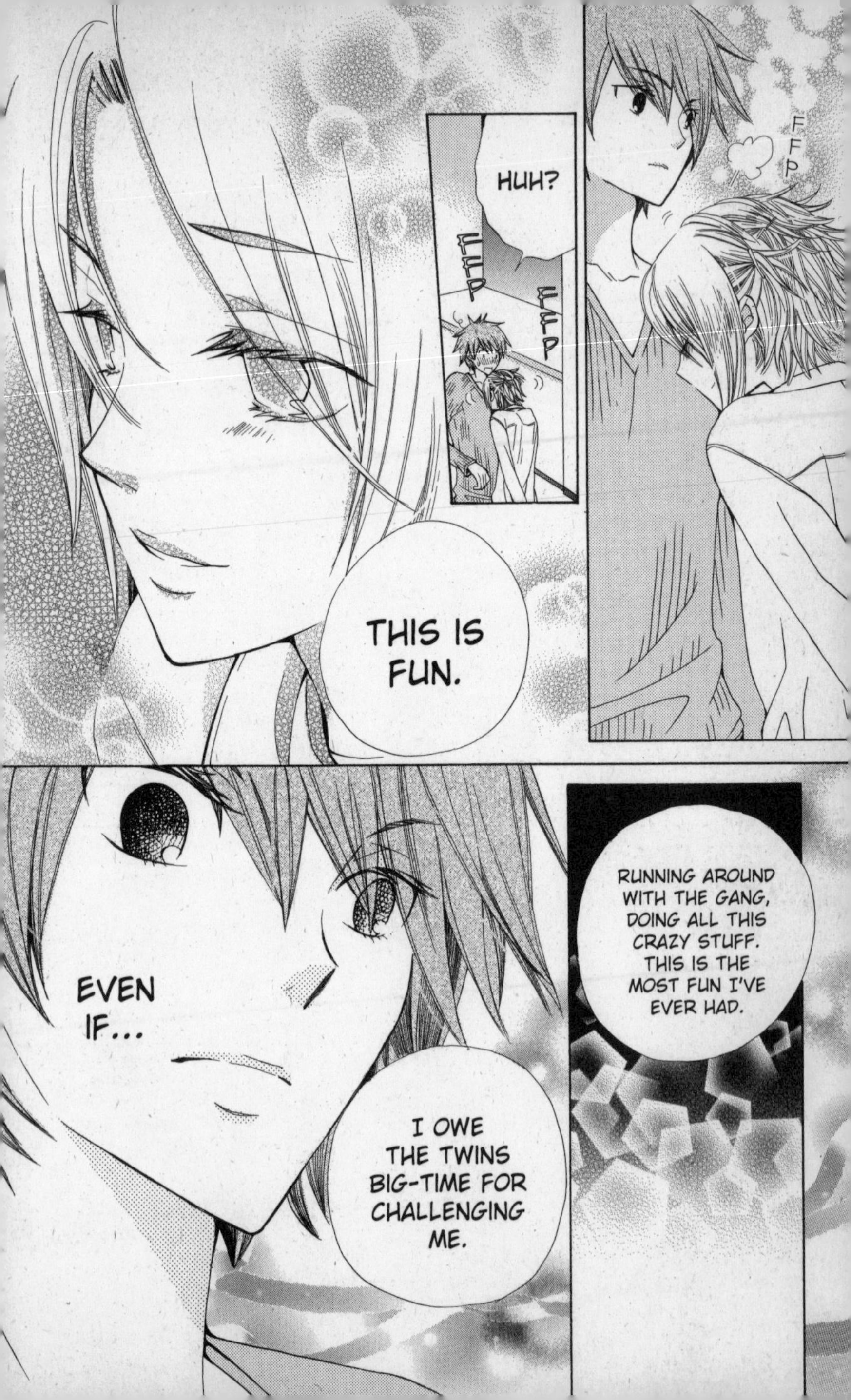
FFP
HUH?
FFP
FFP
THIS IS FUN.
RUNNING AROUND WITH THE GANG, DOING ALL THIS CRAZY STUFF. THIS IS THE MOST FUN I'VE EVER HAD.
EVEN IF...
I OWE THE TWINS BIG-TIME FOR CHALLENGING ME.

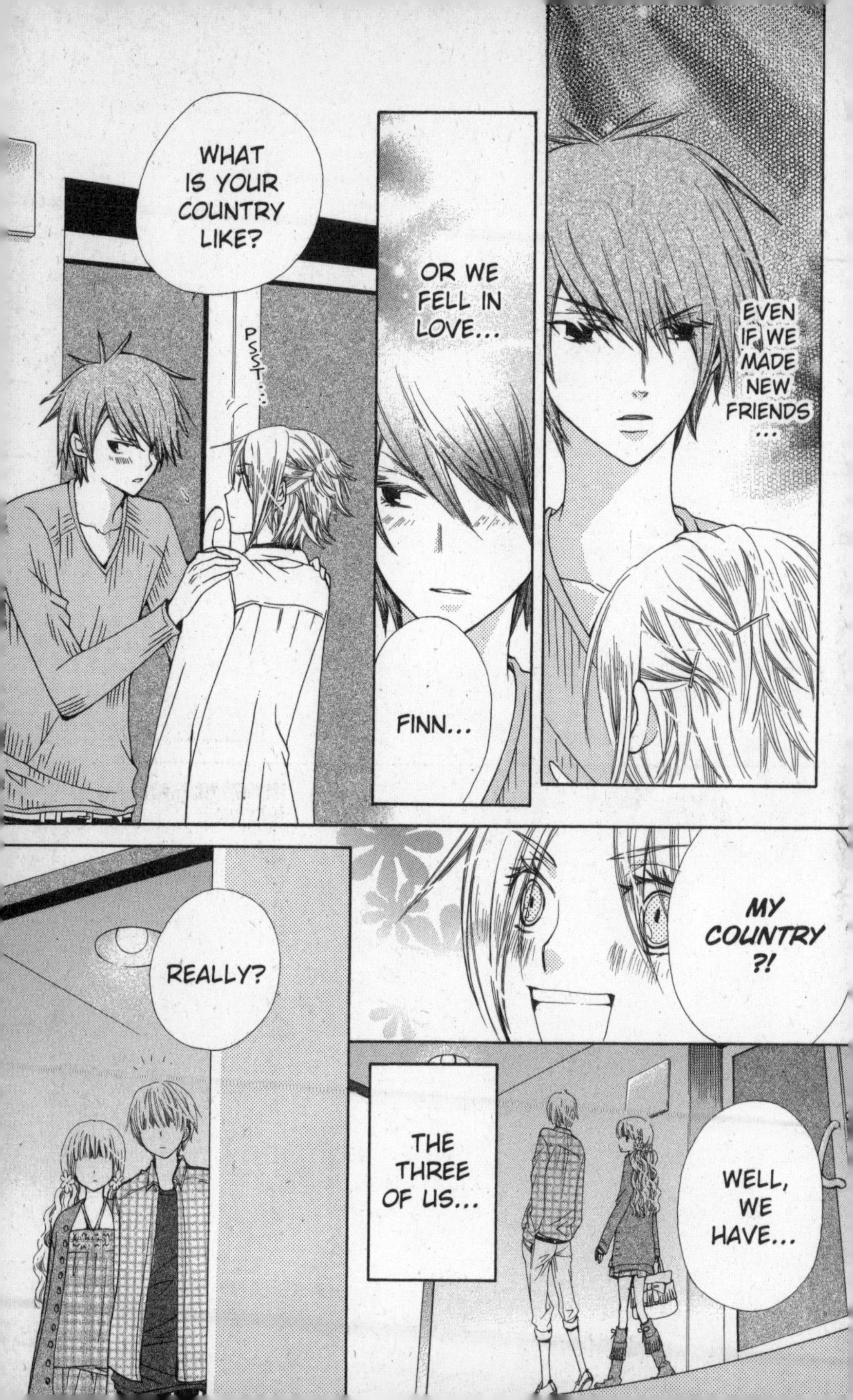
EVEN IF WE MADE NEW FRIENDS...
OR WE FELL IN LOVE...
FINN...
WHAT IS YOUR COUNTRY LIKE?
PSST...
MY COUNTRY?!
WELL, WE HAVE...
THE THREE OF US...
REALLY?

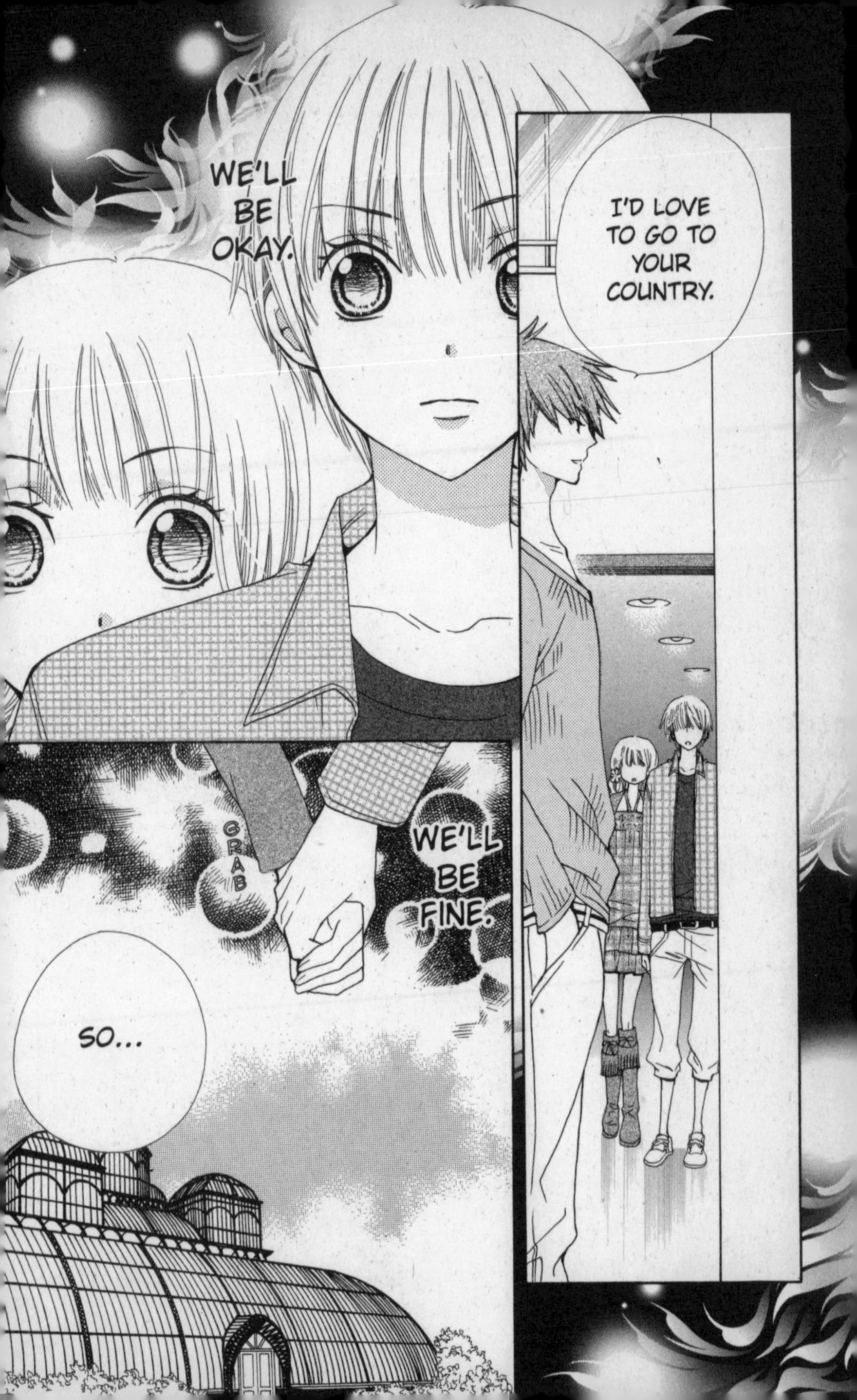
I'D LOVE TO GO TO YOUR COUNTRY.
WE'LL BE OKAY.
WE'LL BE FINE.
GRAB
SO...

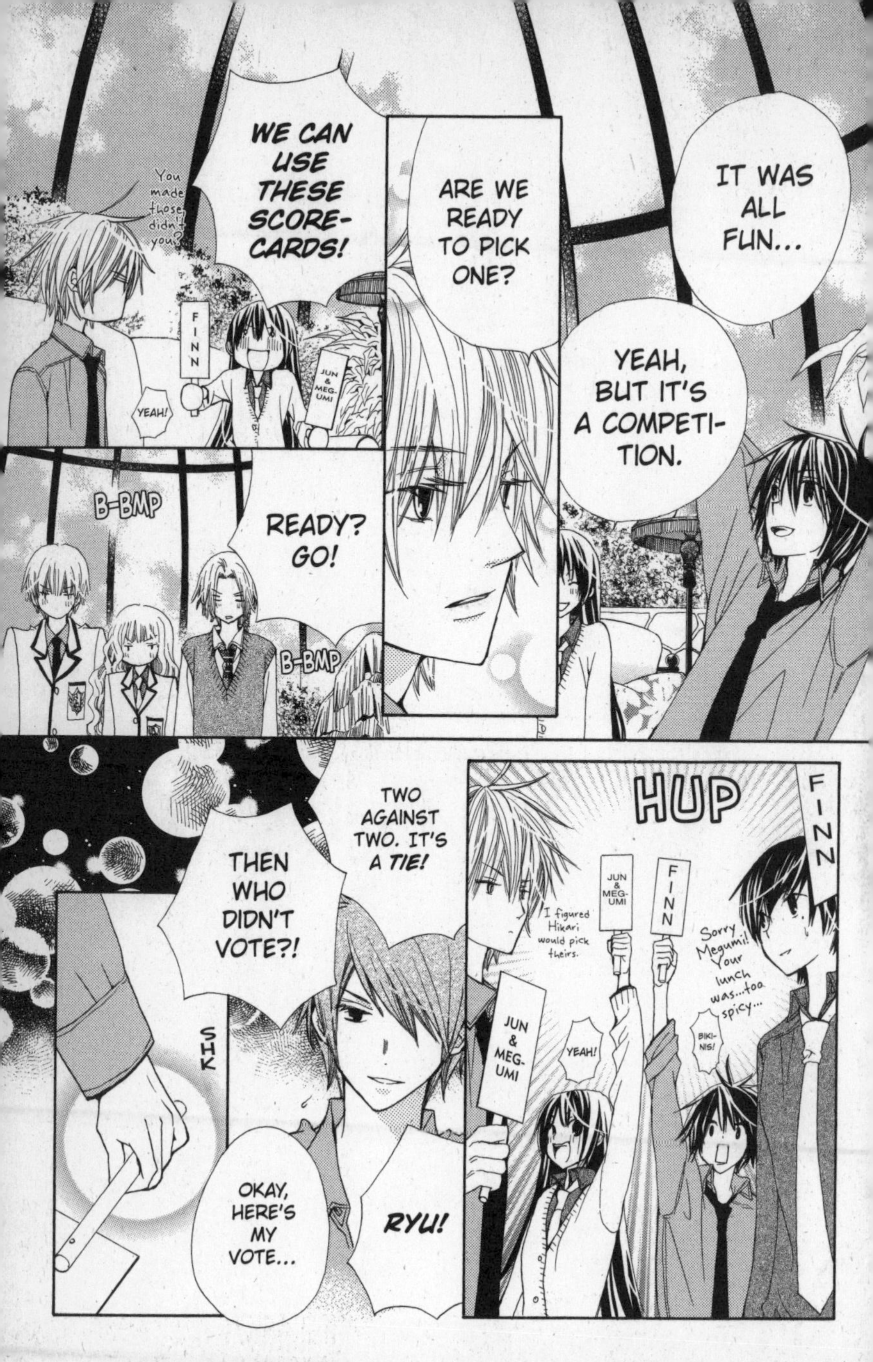
IT WAS ALL FUN...
YEAH, BUT IT'S A COMPETITION.
ARE WE READY TO PICK ONE?
WE CAN USE THESE SCORECARDS!
You made those, didn't you?
FINN
JUN & MEGUMI
YEAH!
B-BMP
READY? GO!
B-BMP
HUP
FINN
FINN
JUN & MEGUMI
I figured Hikari would pick theirs.
Sorry Megumi! Your lunch was...too spicy...
BIKINIS!
JUN & MEGUMI
YEAH!
TWO AGAINST TWO. IT'S A TIE!
THEN WHO DIDN'T VOTE?!
SHK
OKAY, HERE'S MY VOTE...
RYU!

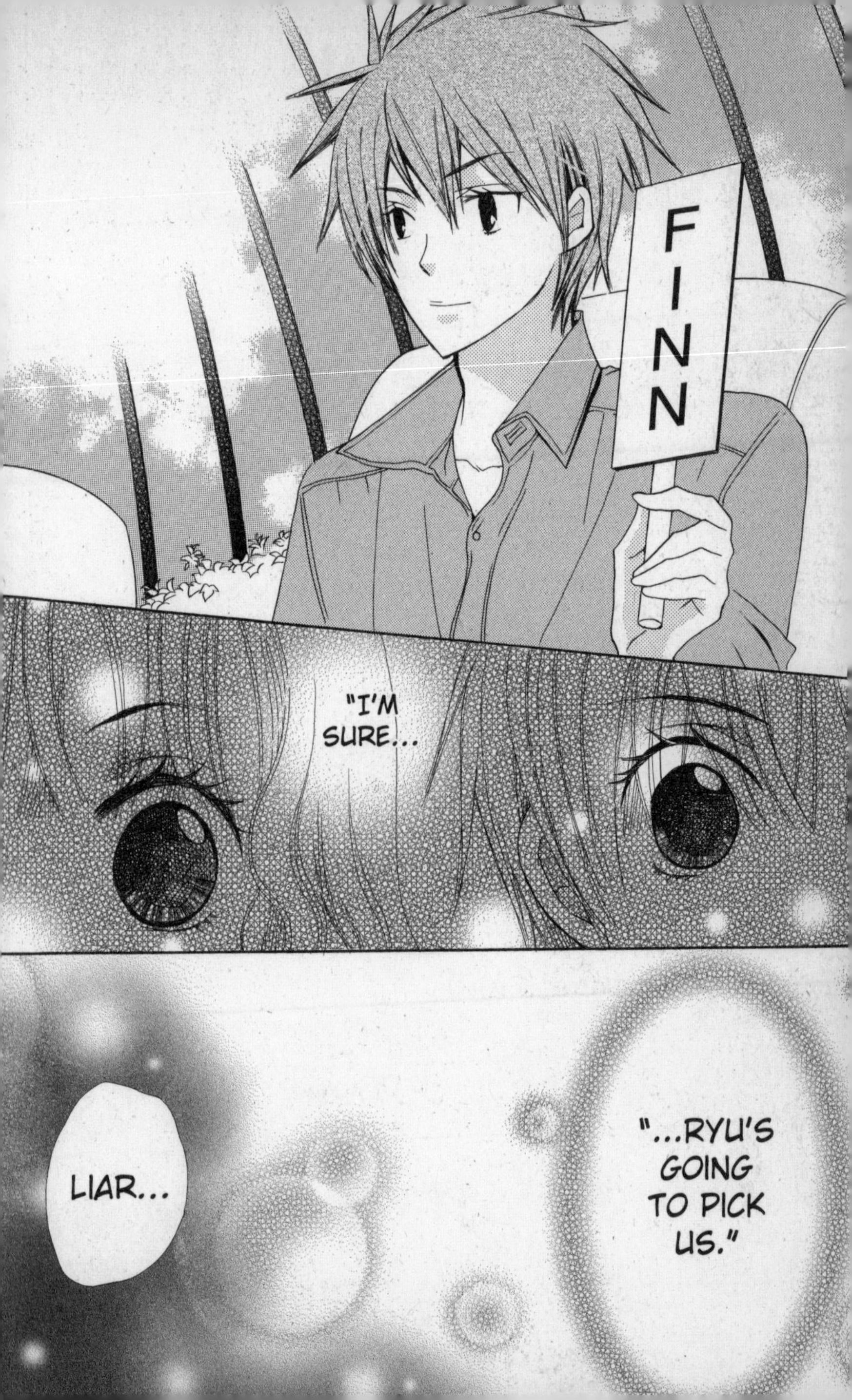
FINN
"I'M SURE...
"...RYU'S GOING TO PICK US."
LIAR...

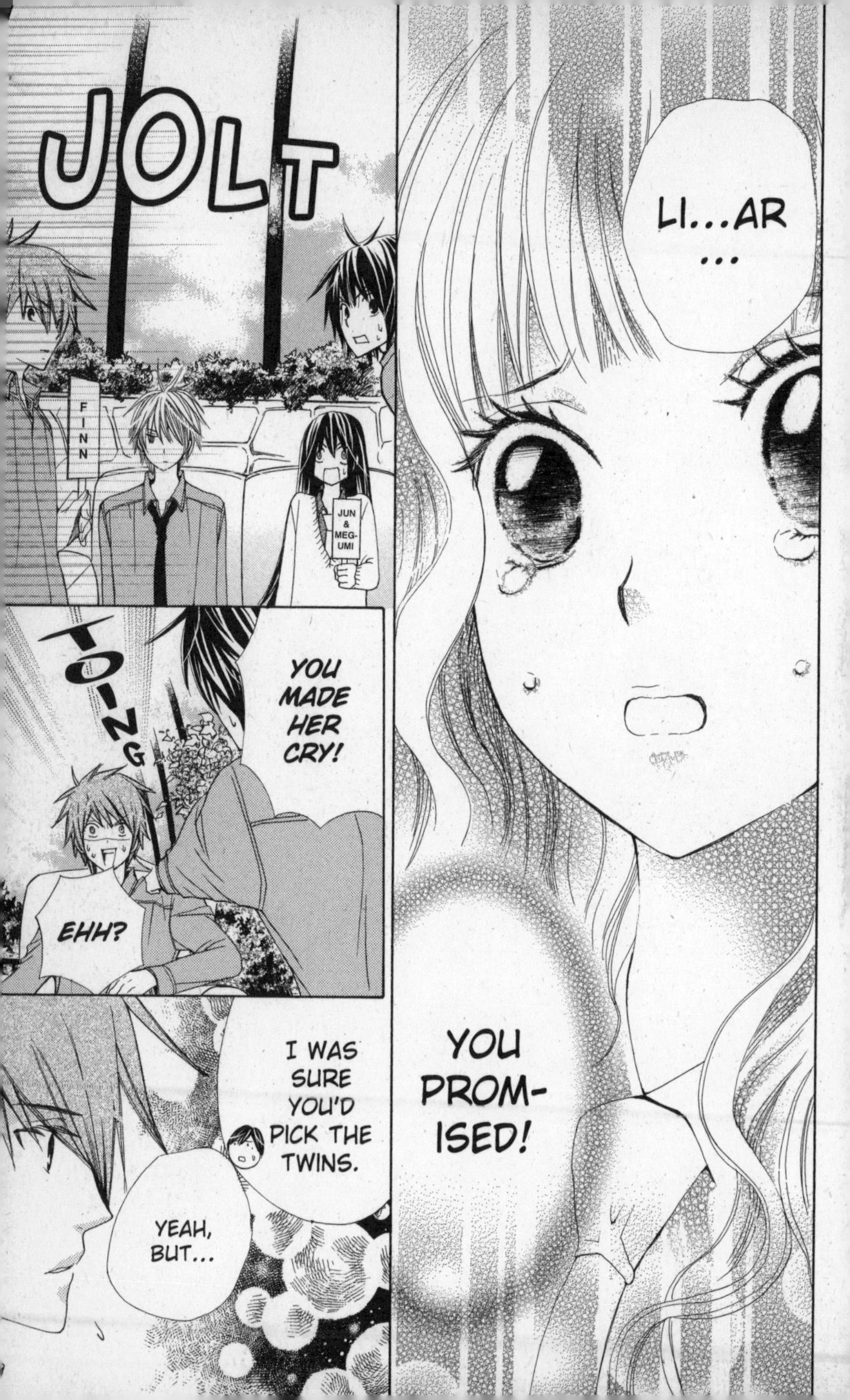
LI...AR ...
YOU PROM-ISED!
JOLT
FINN
JUN & MEG-UMI
TOING
YOU MADE HER CRY!
EHH?
I WAS SURE YOU'D PICK THE TWINS.
YEAH, BUT...

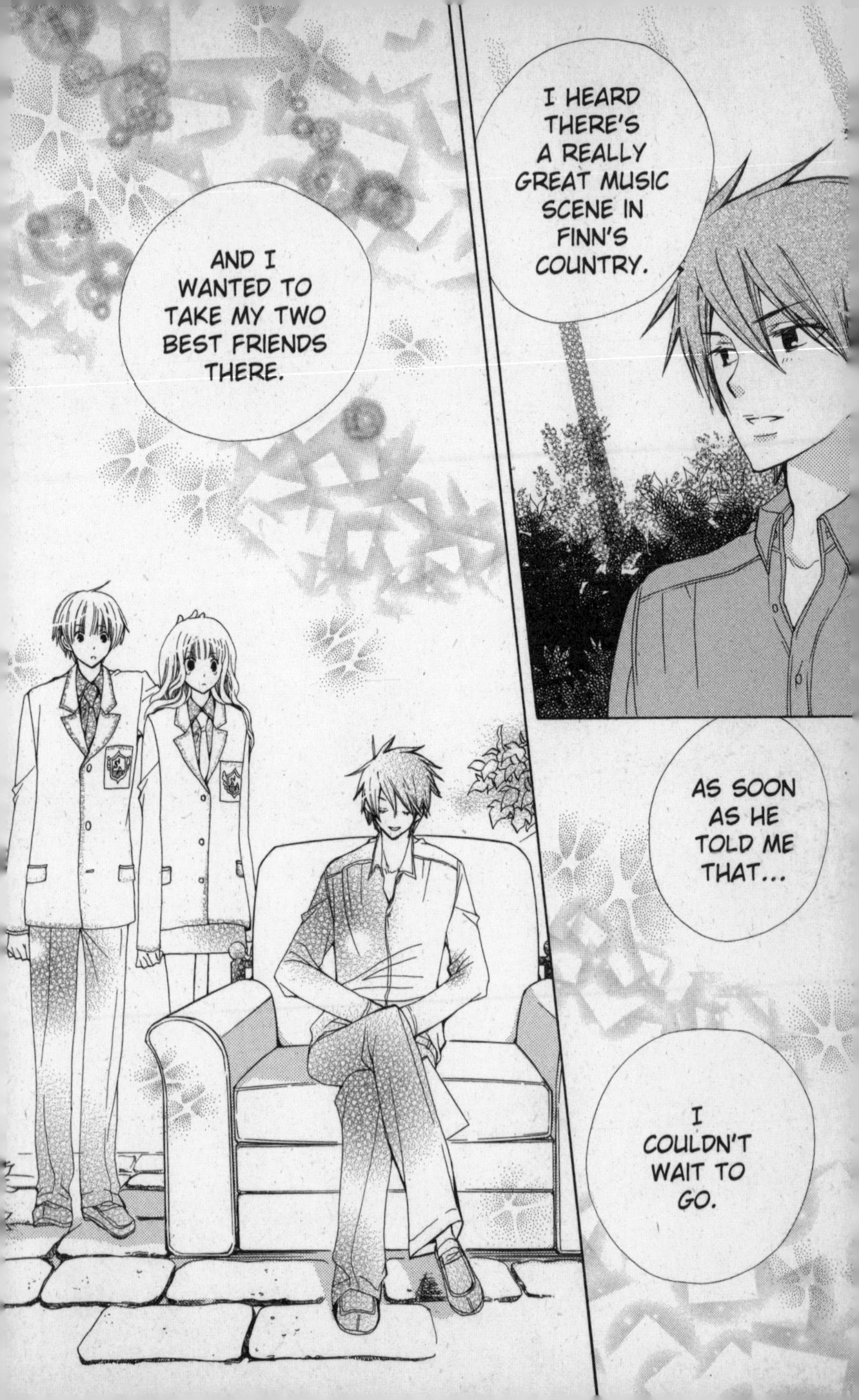
I HEARD THERE'S A REALLY GREAT MUSIC SCENE IN FINN'S COUNTRY.
AS SOON AS HE TOLD ME THAT...
I COULDN'T WAIT TO GO.
AND I WANTED TO TAKE MY TWO BEST FRIENDS THERE.

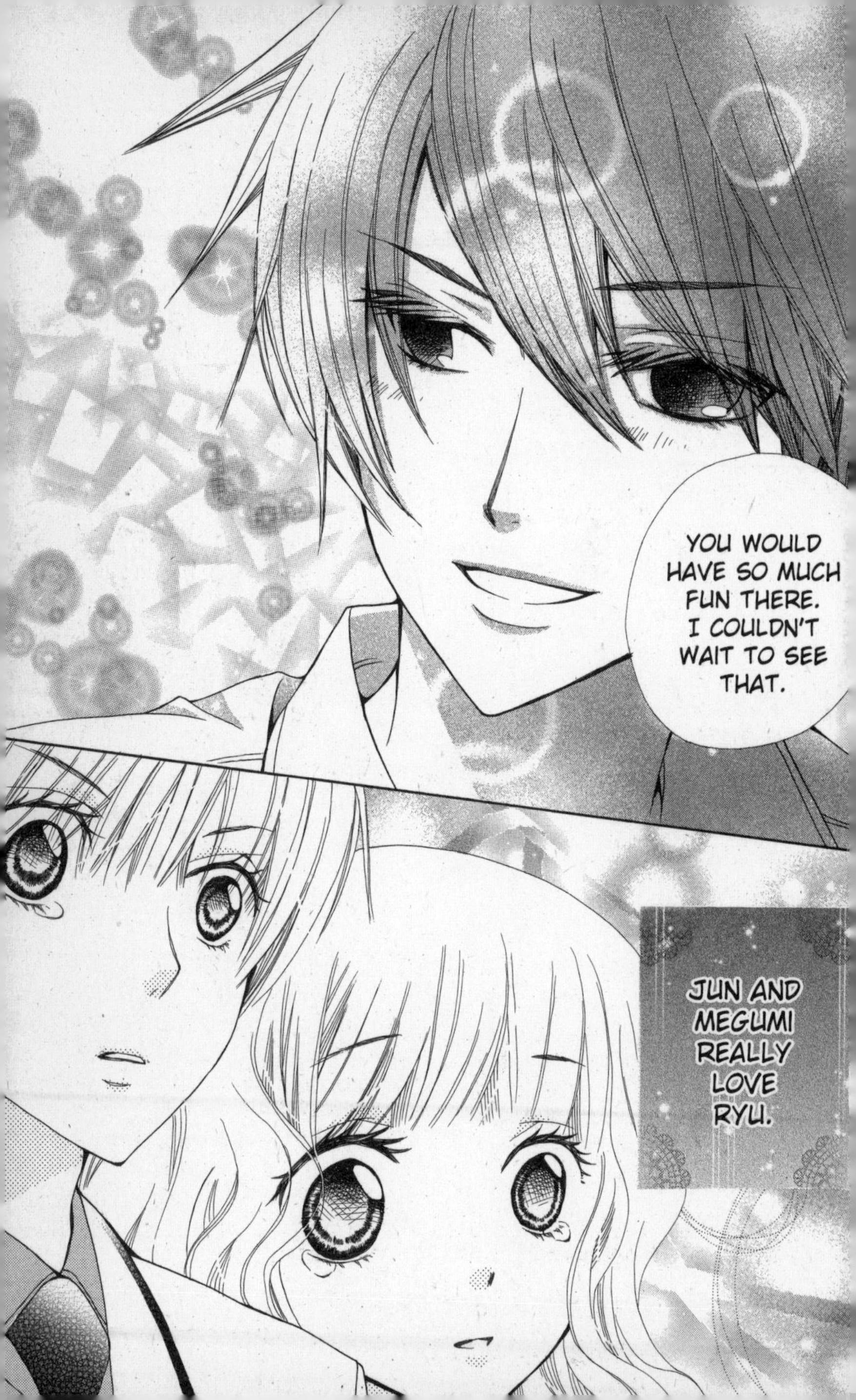
YOU WOULD HAVE SO MUCH FUN THERE. I COULDN'T WAIT TO SEE THAT.
JUN AND MEGUMI REALLY LOVE RYU.

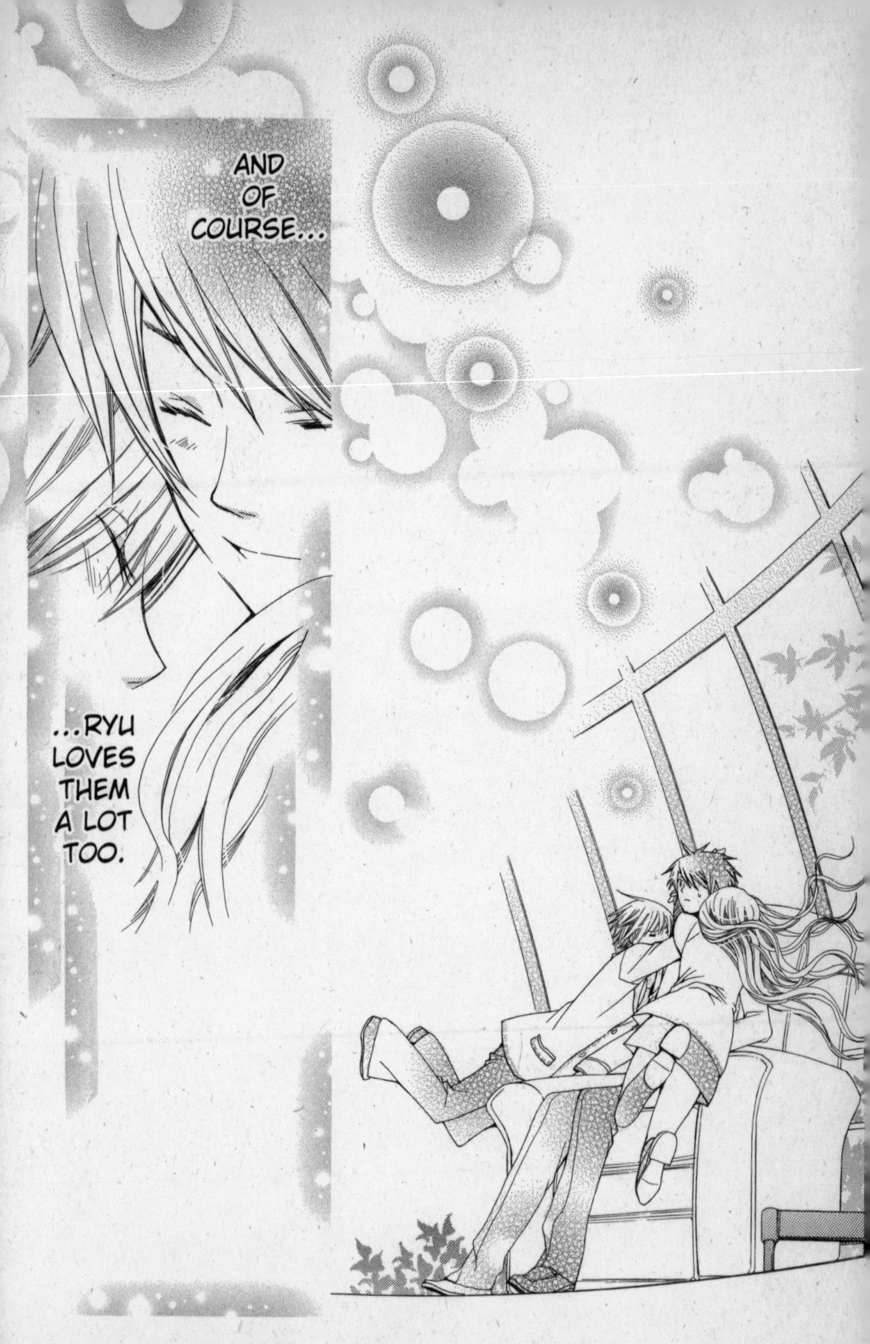
AND OF COURSE...
...RYU LOVES THEM A LOT TOO.

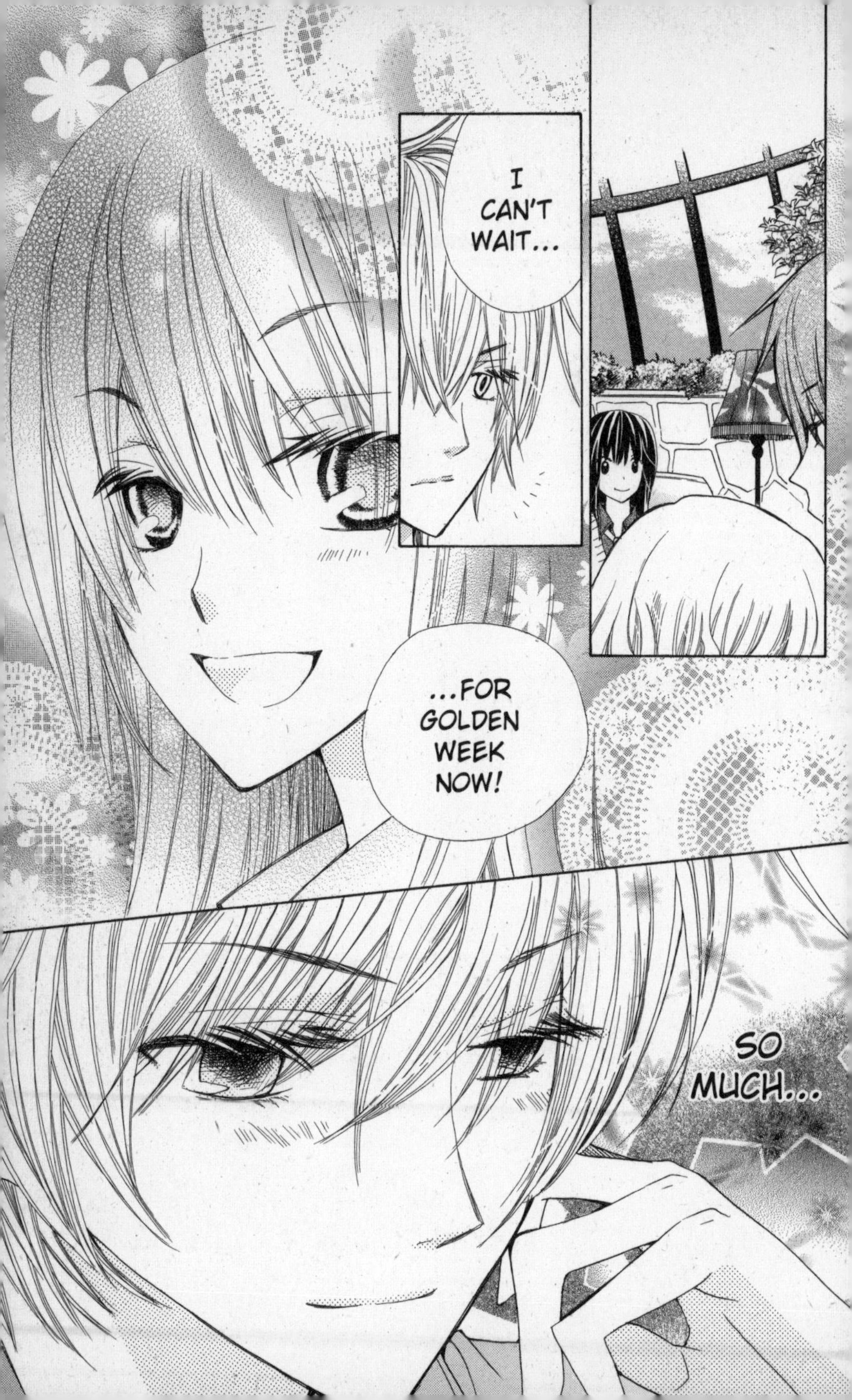
I CAN'T WAIT...
...FOR GOLDEN WEEK NOW!
SO MUCH...

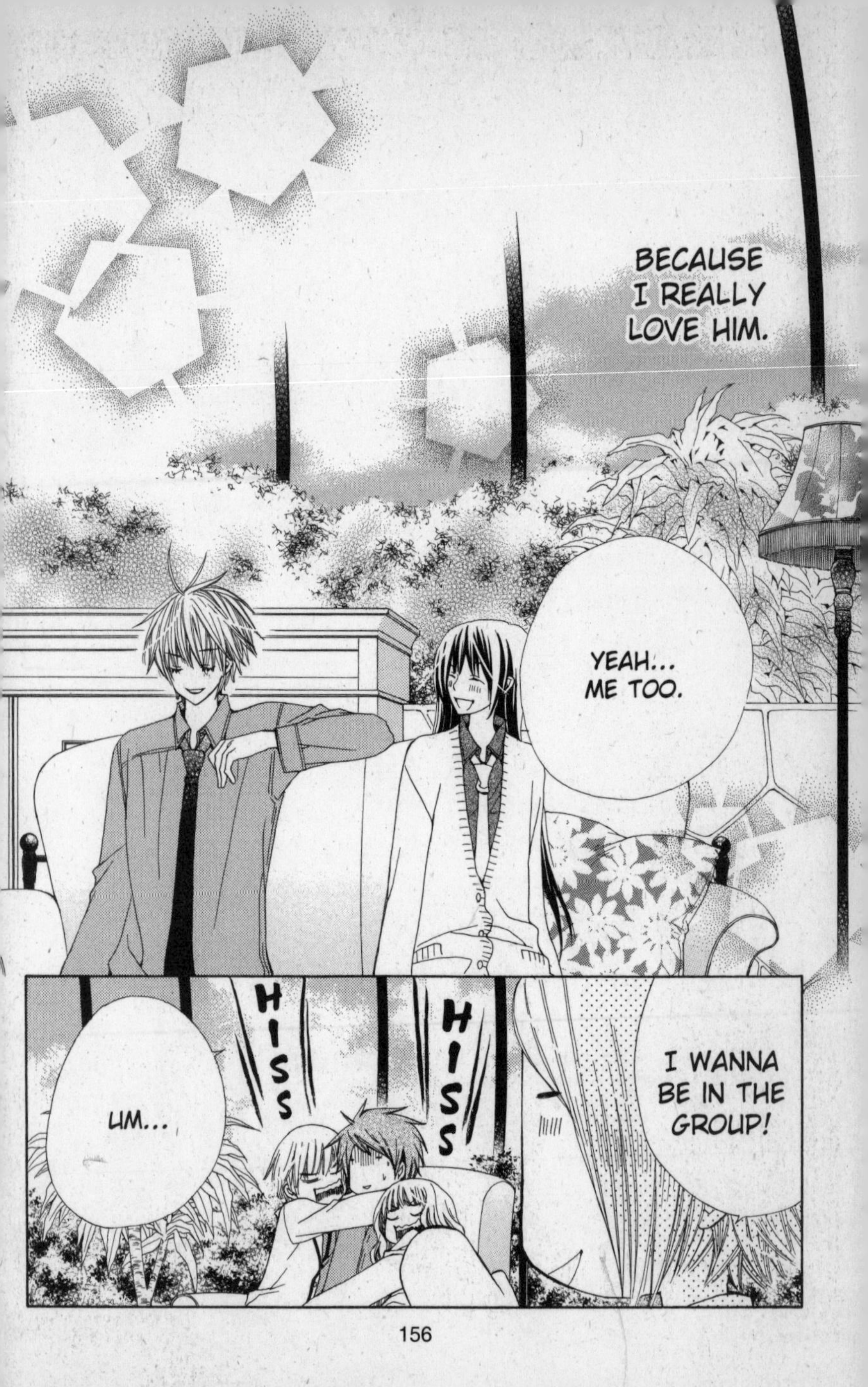
BECAUSE I REALLY LOVE HIM.
YEAH... ME TOO.
I WANNA BE IN THE GROUP!
HISS
HISS
UM...

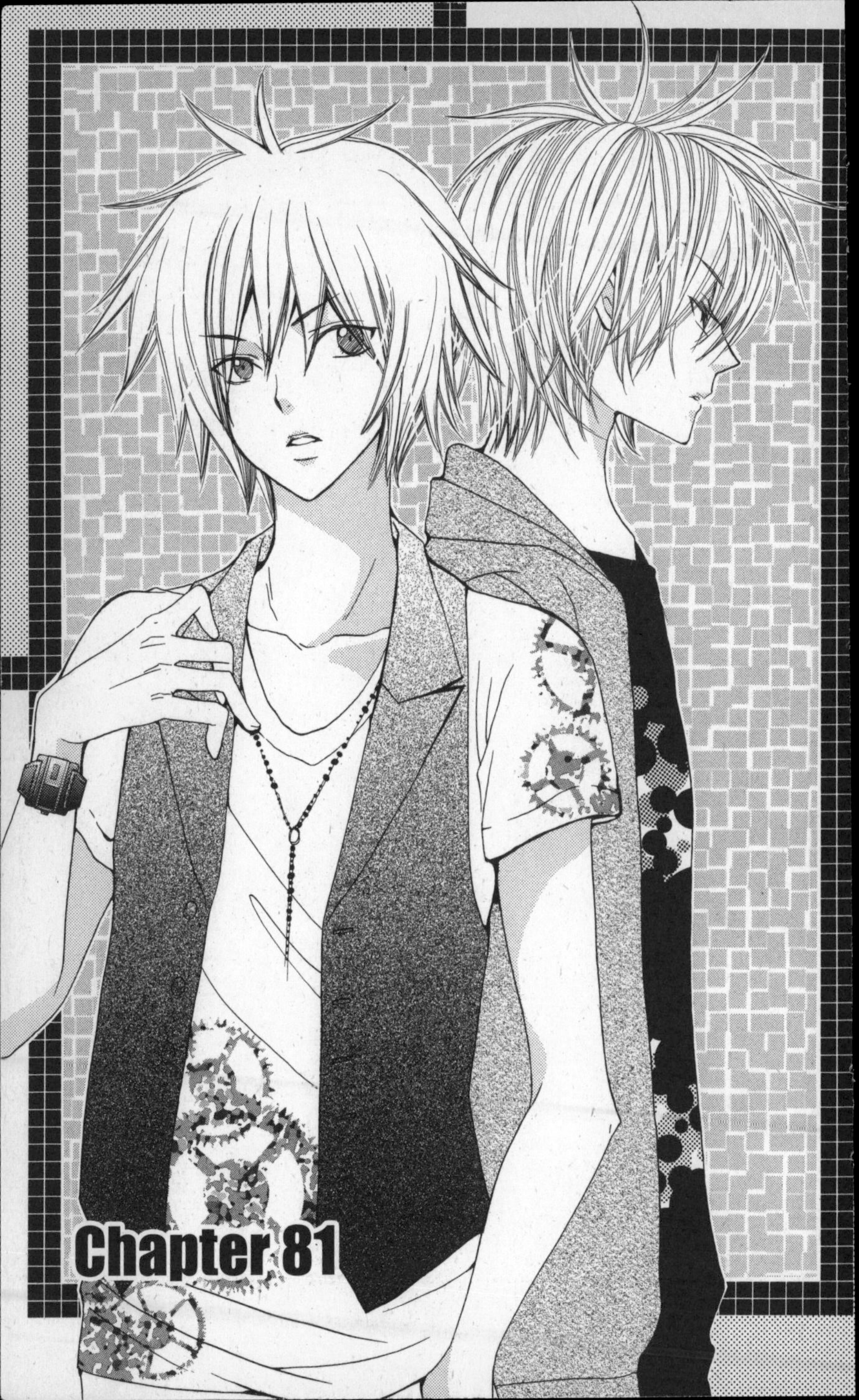
Chapter 81

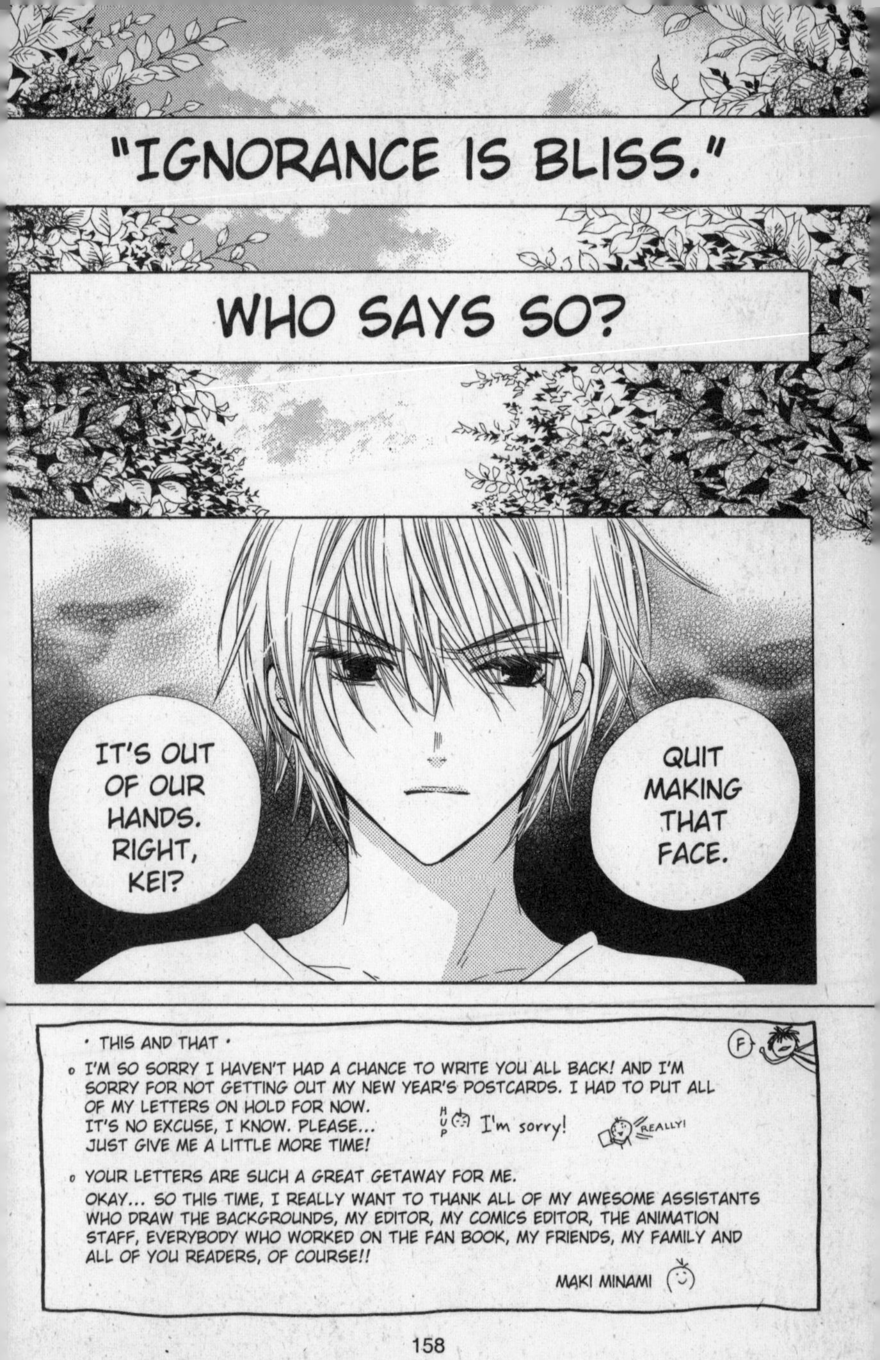
"IGNORANCE IS BLISS."
WHO SAYS SO?
QUIT MAKING THAT FACE.
IT'S OUT OF OUR HANDS. RIGHT, KEI?

· THIS AND THAT ·

- I'M SO SORRY I HAVEN'T HAD A CHANCE TO WRITE YOU ALL BACK! AND I'M SORRY FOR NOT GETTING OUT MY NEW YEAR'S POSTCARDS. I HAD TO PUT ALL OF MY LETTERS ON HOLD FOR NOW.
  IT'S NO EXCUSE, I KNOW. PLEASE... JUST GIVE ME A LITTLE MORE TIME! HUP I'm sorry! REALLY!
- YOUR LETTERS ARE SUCH A GREAT GETAWAY FOR ME.
  OKAY... SO THIS TIME, I REALLY WANT TO THANK ALL OF MY AWESOME ASSISTANTS WHO DRAW THE BACKGROUNDS, MY EDITOR, MY COMICS EDITOR, THE ANIMATION STAFF, EVERYBODY WHO WORKED ON THE FAN BOOK, MY FRIENDS, MY FAMILY AND ALL OF YOU READERS, OF COURSE!!

MAKI MINAMI

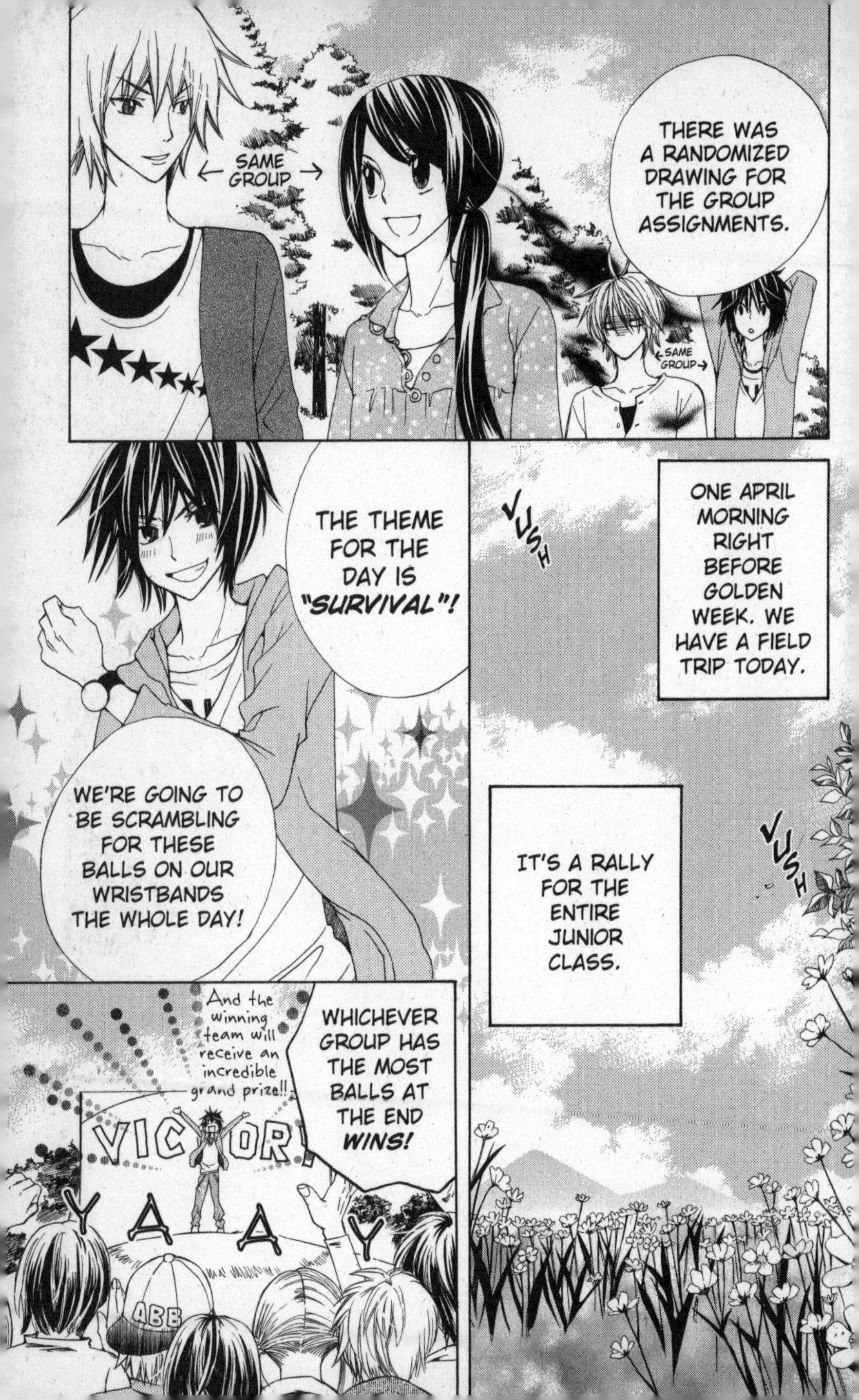
THERE WAS A RANDOMIZED DRAWING FOR THE GROUP ASSIGNMENTS.
← SAME GROUP →
← SAME GROUP →
VUSH
ONE APRIL MORNING RIGHT BEFORE GOLDEN WEEK. WE HAVE A FIELD TRIP TODAY.
VUSH
IT'S A RALLY FOR THE ENTIRE JUNIOR CLASS.
THE THEME FOR THE DAY IS "*SURVIVAL*"!
WE'RE GOING TO BE SCRAMBLING FOR THESE BALLS ON OUR WRISTBANDS THE WHOLE DAY!
WHICHEVER GROUP HAS THE MOST BALLS AT THE END *WINS!*
And the winning team will receive an incredible grand prize!!
YAAY
ABB

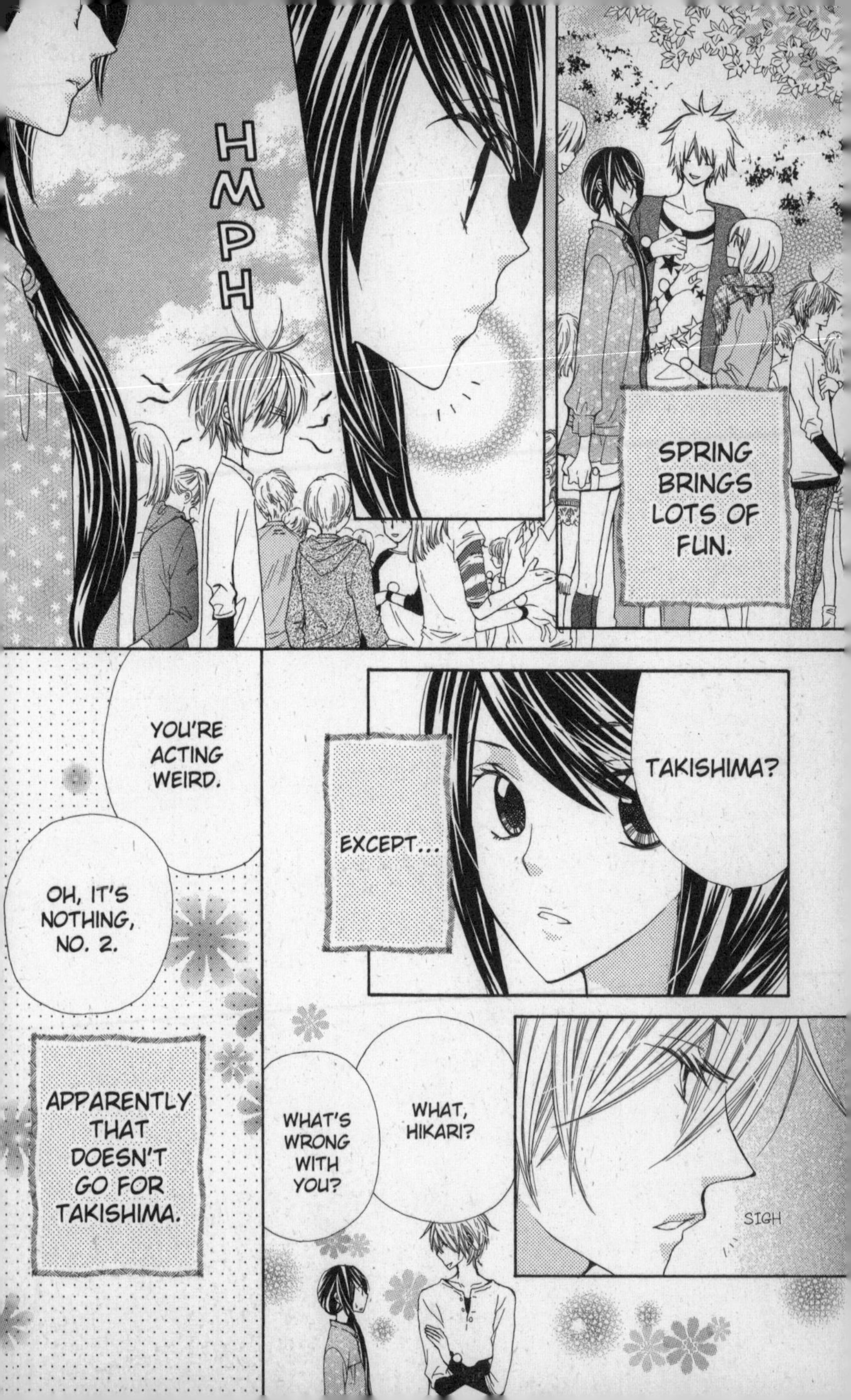
SPRING BRINGS LOTS OF FUN.
HMPH
TAKISHIMA?
EXCEPT...
SIGH
WHAT, HIKARI?
WHAT'S WRONG WITH YOU?
YOU'RE ACTING WEIRD.
OH, IT'S NOTHING, NO. 2.
APPARENTLY THAT DOESN'T GO FOR TAKISHIMA.

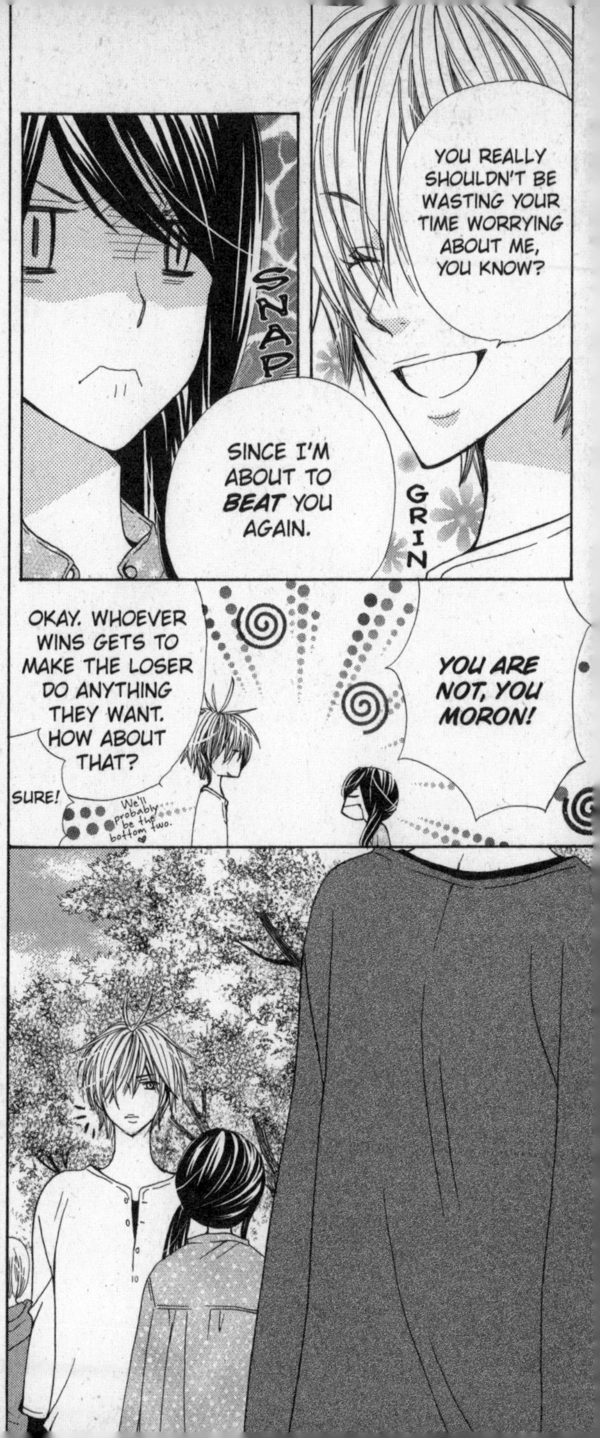
YOU REALLY SHOULDN'T BE WASTING YOUR TIME WORRYING ABOUT ME, YOU KNOW?
SINCE I'M ABOUT TO ***BEAT*** YOU AGAIN.
GRIN
SNAP
YOU ARE NOT, YOU MORON!
OKAY. WHOEVER WINS GETS TO MAKE THE LOSER DO ANYTHING THEY WANT. HOW ABOUT THAT?
SURE!
We'll probably be the bottom two.

6

∘THIS AND THAT∘

- THANKS FOR STICKING WITH ME THROUGH THE WHOLE BOOK AND ALL THESE QUARTER PAGES!
- "FAIRYTALES" WAS THE THEME REQUESTED THIS TIME. THANKS SO MUCH FOR ALL THE SUGGESTIONS!
- THE NEXT VOLUME WILL BE NUMBER 15... I CAN'T BELIEVE IT! AND IT'S REALLY ALL BECAUSE OF YOU! THANK YOU SO MUCH!
- IT'LL BE SUMMER BY THE TIME THIS BOOK HITS THE STANDS! ARE YOU PLANNING ANY VACATIONS?
- OKAY. WELL, THANK YOU SO MUCH FOR READING THIS FAR!

✿ IF YOU'D LIKE TO, LET US KNOW WHAT YOU THINK. ✿

MAKI MINAMI
C/O VIZ MEDIA
SA EDITOR
P.O. BOX 77010
SAN FRANCISCO,
CA 94107

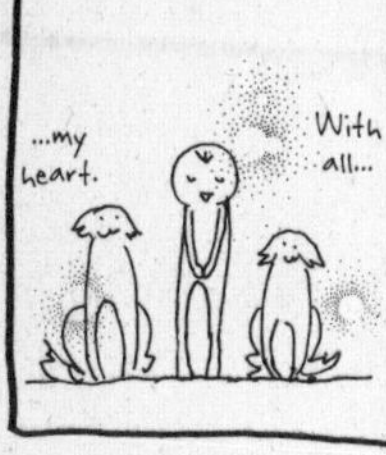
With all...
...my heart.

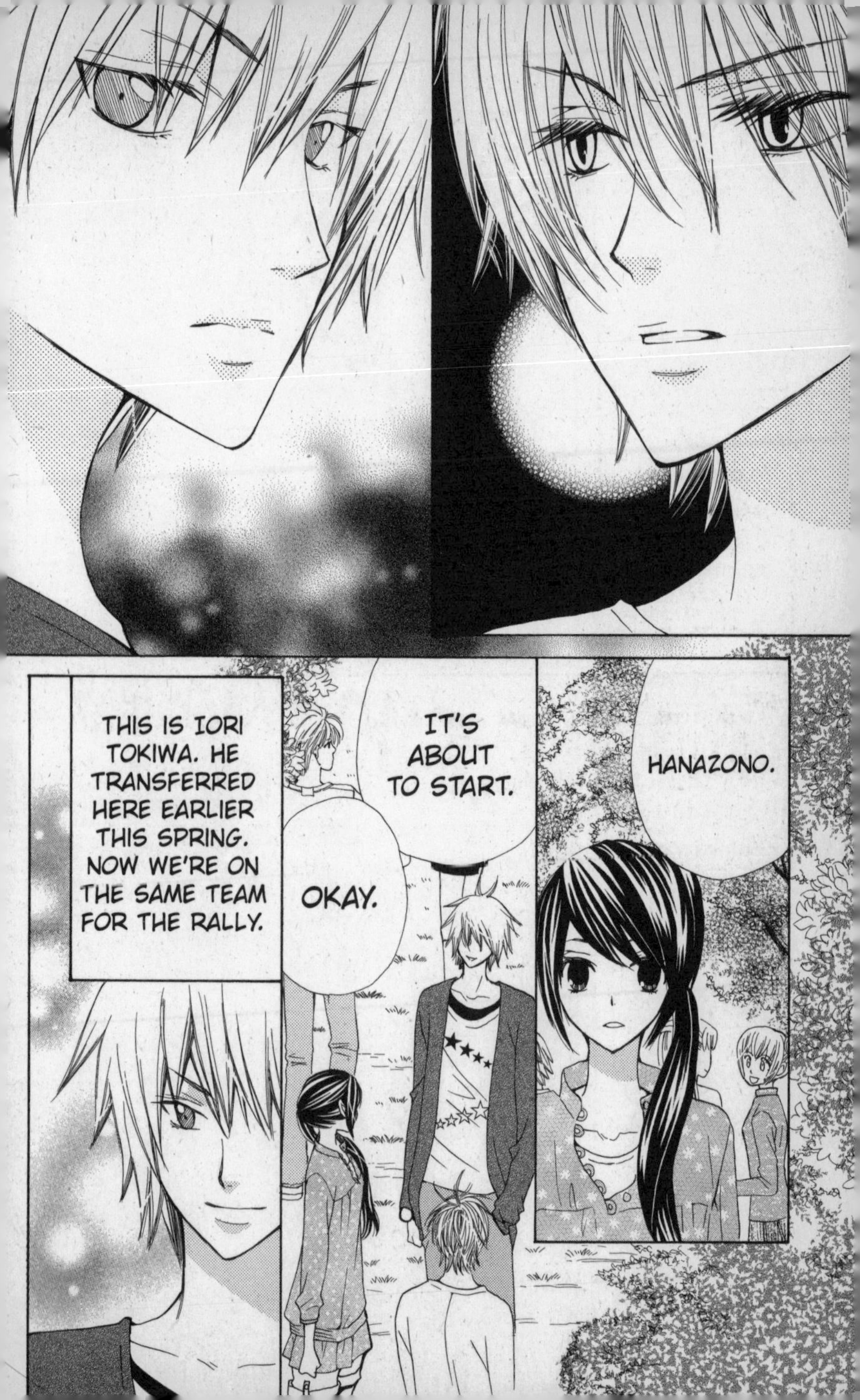
HANAZONO.
IT'S ABOUT TO START.
OKAY.
THIS IS IORI TOKIWA. HE TRANSFERRED HERE EARLIER THIS SPRING. NOW WE'RE ON THE SAME TEAM FOR THE RALLY.

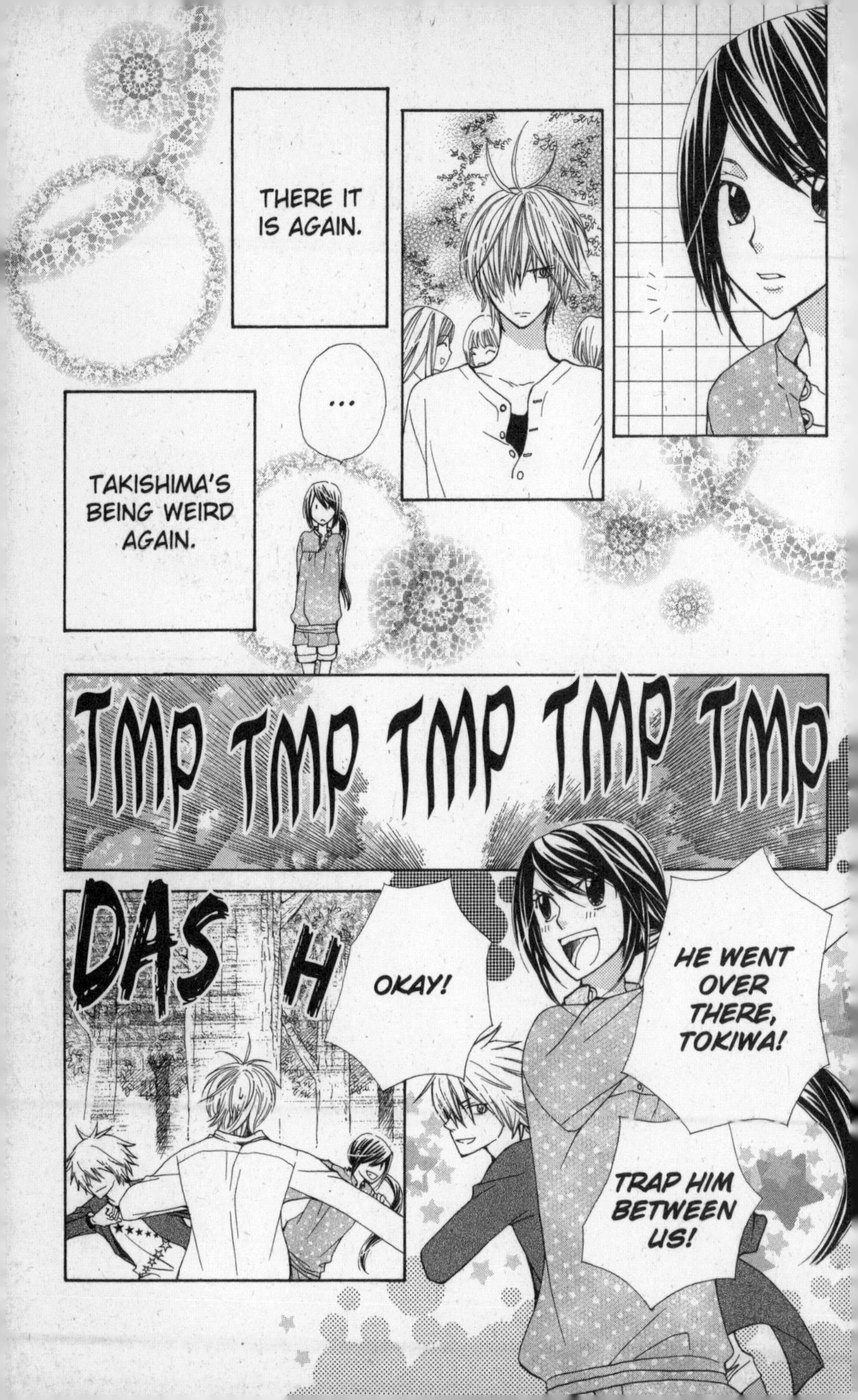
THERE IT IS AGAIN.
...
TAKISHIMA'S BEING WEIRD AGAIN.
TMP TMP TMP TMP TMP
HE WENT OVER THERE, TOKIWA!
TRAP HIM BETWEEN US!
OKAY!
DAS H

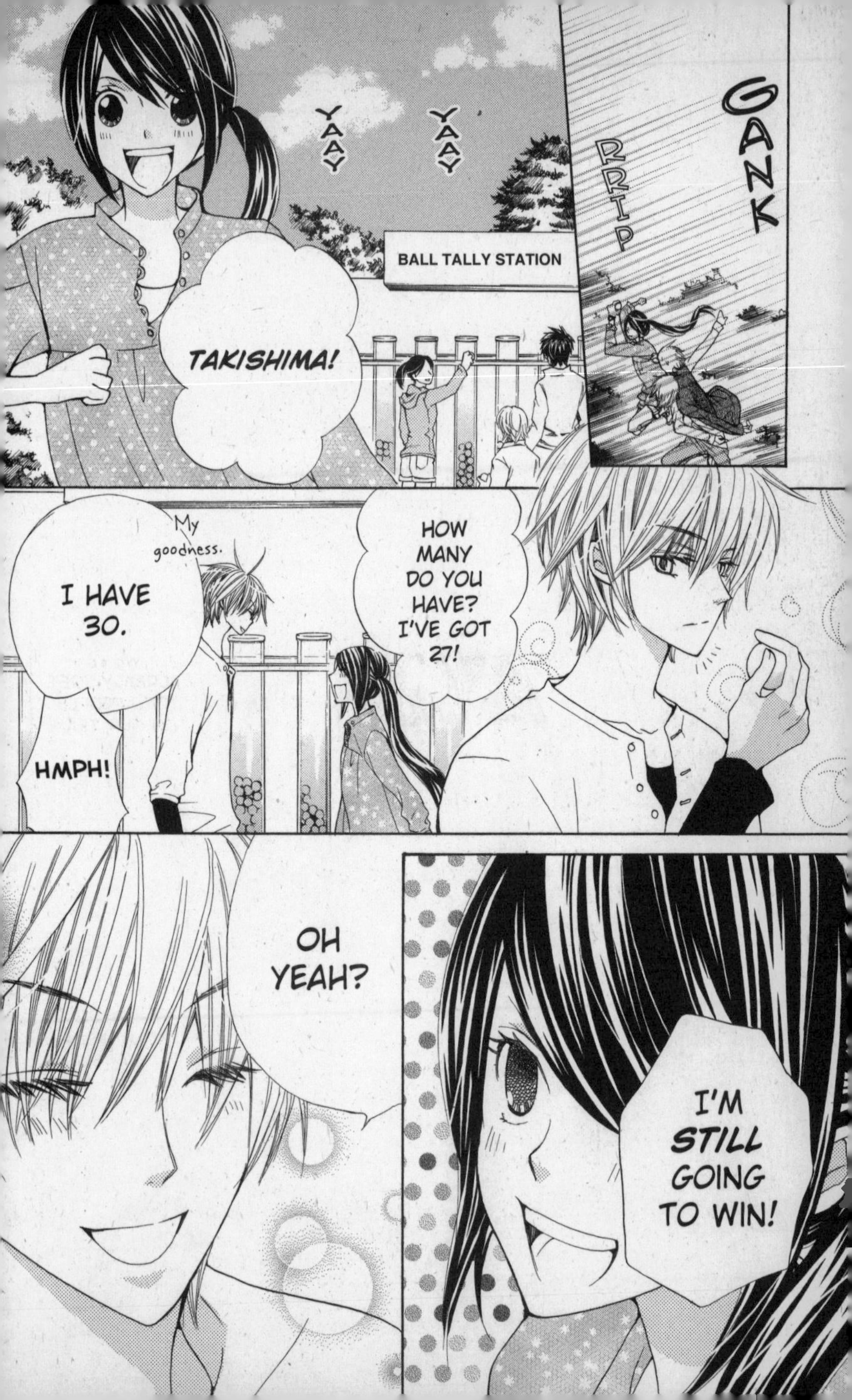
GANK
RRIP
YAAY
YAAY
BALL TALLY STATION
TAKISHIMA!
HOW MANY DO YOU HAVE? I'VE GOT 27!
My goodness.
I HAVE 30.
HMPH!
I'M STILL GOING TO WIN!
OH YEAH?

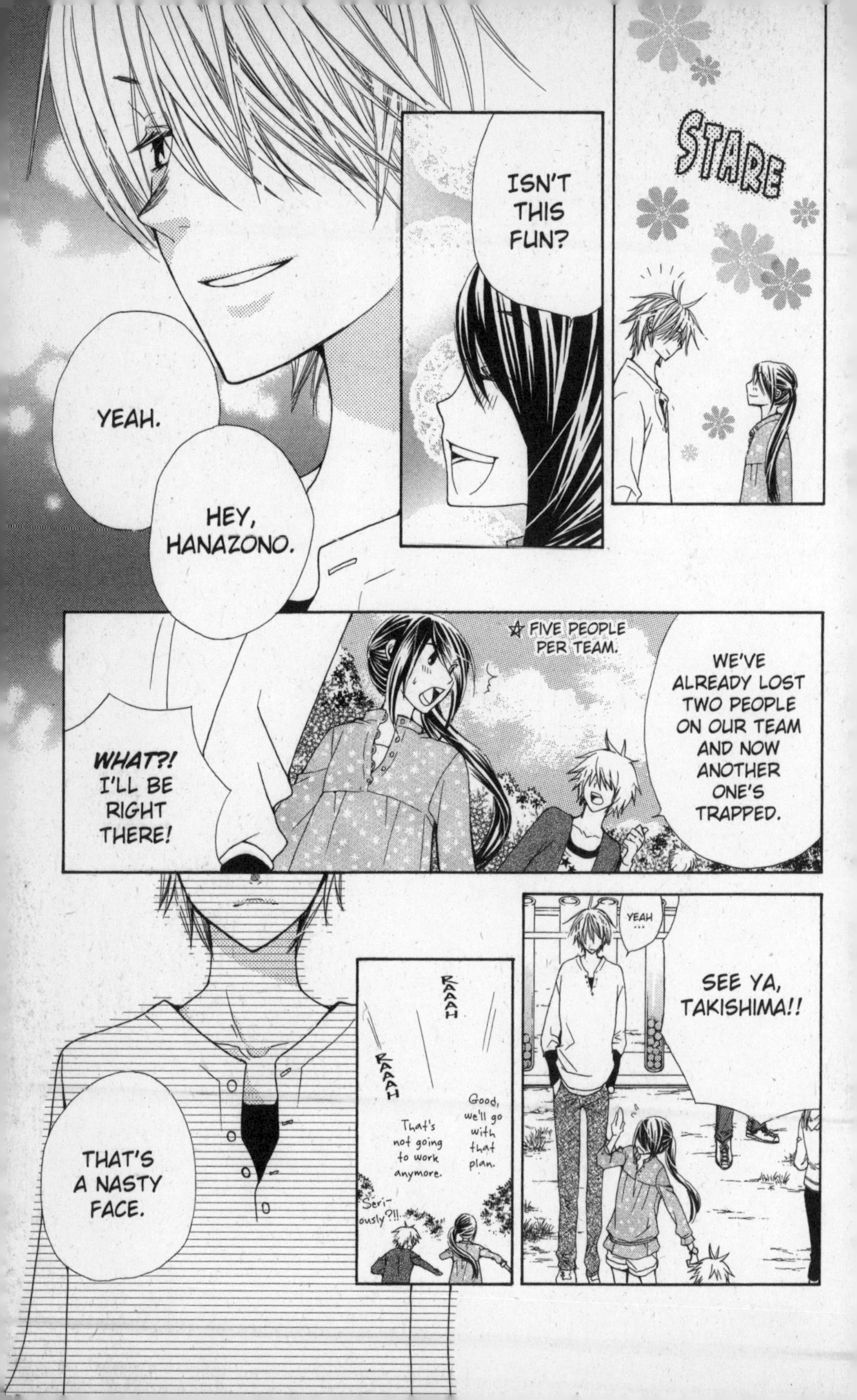
STARE
ISN'T THIS FUN?
YEAH.
HEY, HANAZONO.
WE'VE ALREADY LOST TWO PEOPLE ON OUR TEAM AND NOW ANOTHER ONE'S TRAPPED.
☆ FIVE PEOPLE PER TEAM.
WHAT?! I'LL BE RIGHT THERE!
SEE YA, TAKISHIMA!!
YEAH...
RAAAH
RAAAH
Good, we'll go with that plan.
That's not going to work anymore.
Seri-ously?!!
THAT'S A NASTY FACE.

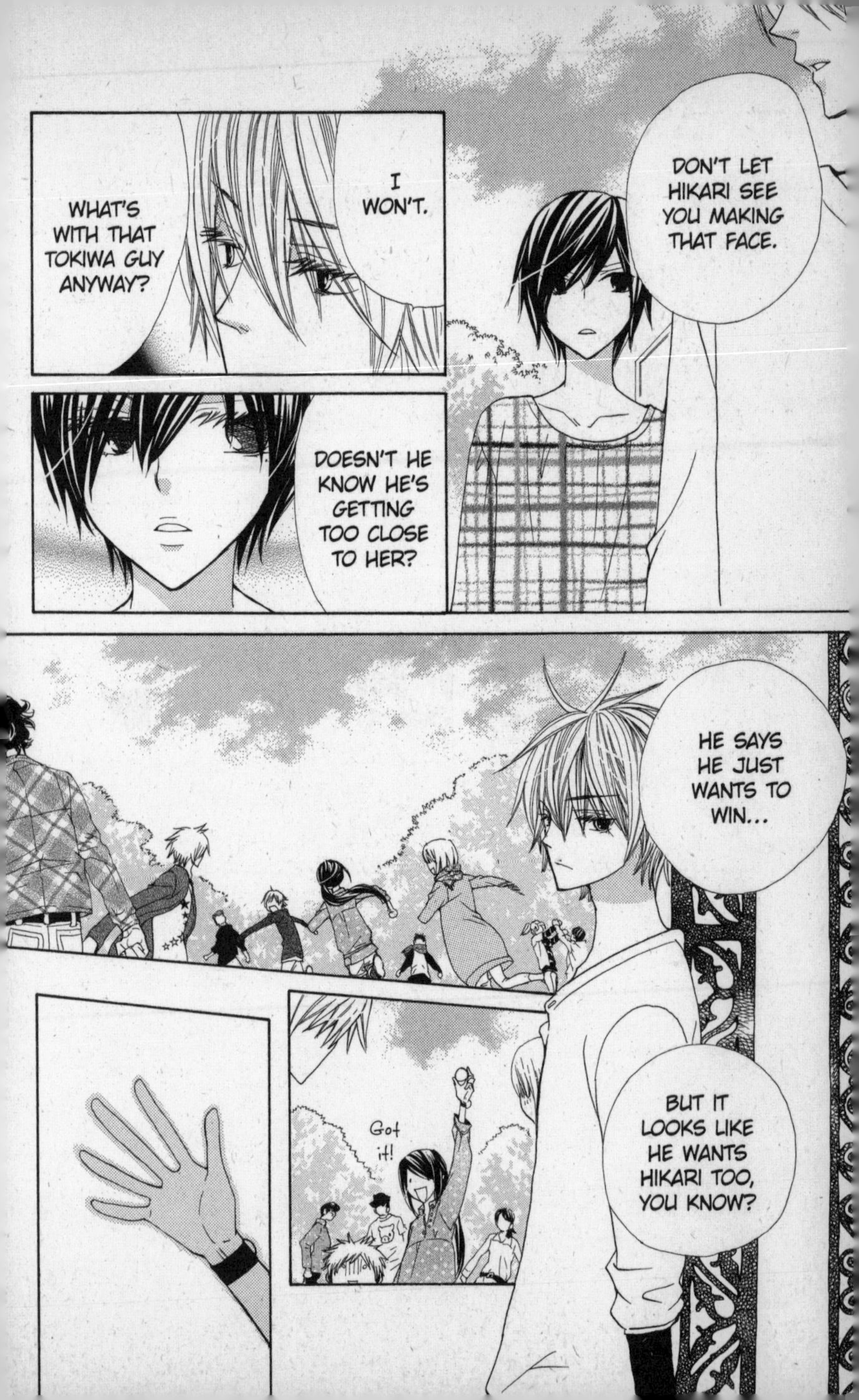
DON'T LET HIKARI SEE YOU MAKING THAT FACE.
I WON'T.
WHAT'S WITH THAT TOKIWA GUY ANYWAY?
DOESN'T HE KNOW HE'S GETTING TOO CLOSE TO HER?
HE SAYS HE JUST WANTS TO WIN...
BUT IT LOOKS LIKE HE WANTS HIKARI TOO, YOU KNOW?
Got it!

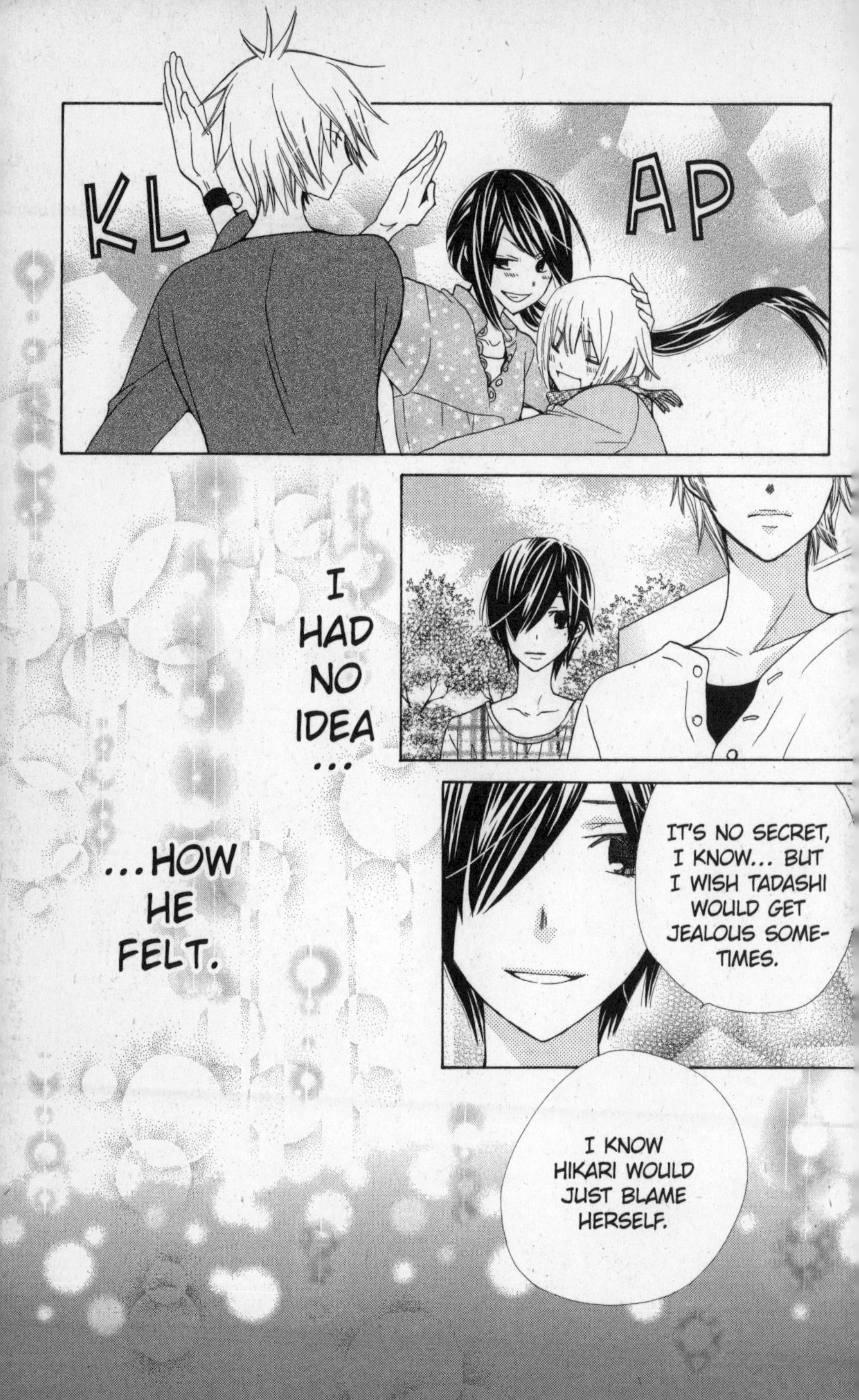
KL AP
I HAD NO IDEA...
...HOW HE FELT.
IT'S NO SECRET, I KNOW... BUT I WISH TADASHI WOULD GET JEALOUS SOME-TIMES.
I KNOW HIKARI WOULD JUST BLAME HERSELF.

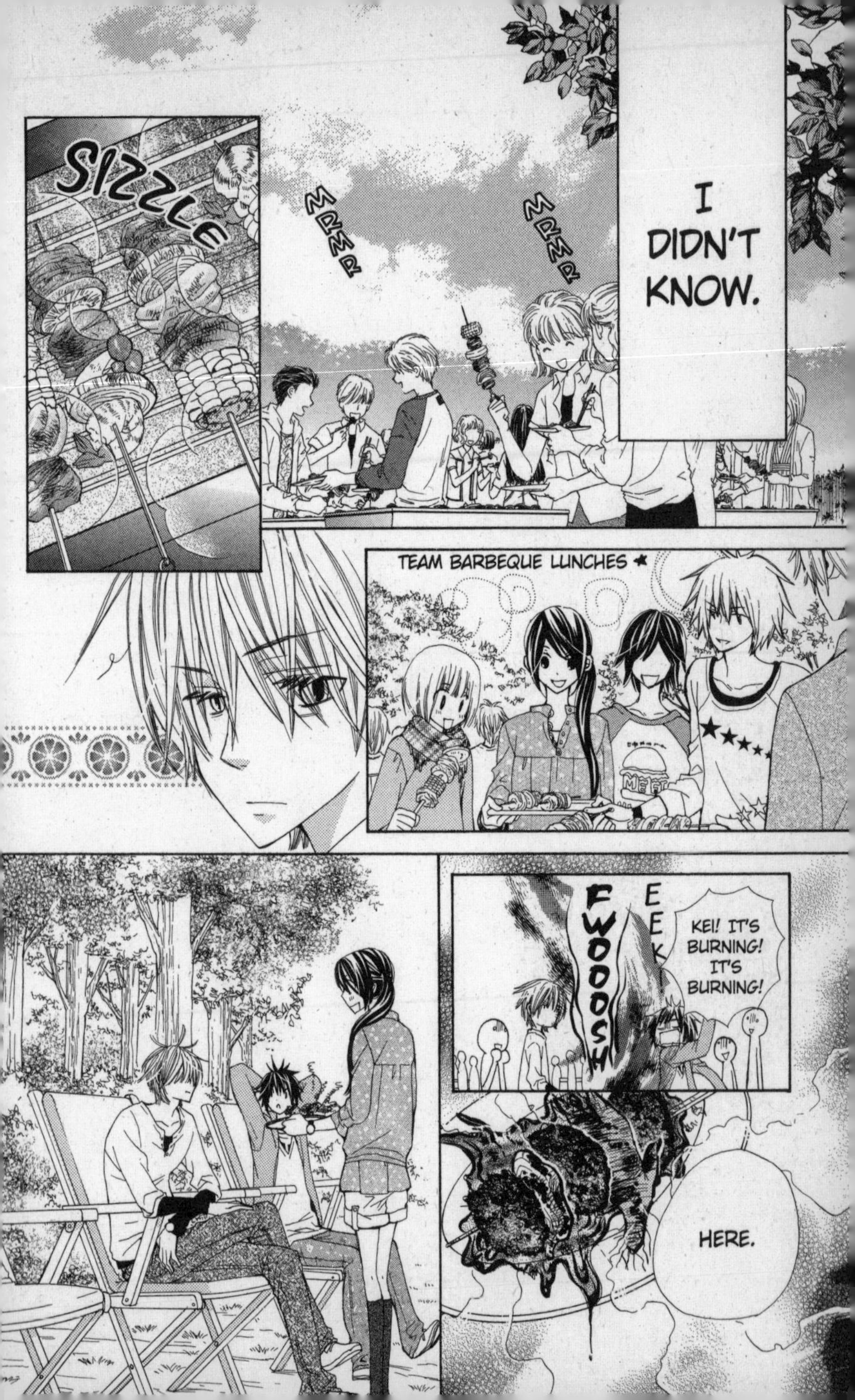
I DIDN'T KNOW.
MRMR
MRMR
SIZZLE
TEAM BARBEQUE LUNCHES ★
EEK
FWOOOSH
KEI! IT'S BURNING! IT'S BURNING!
HERE.

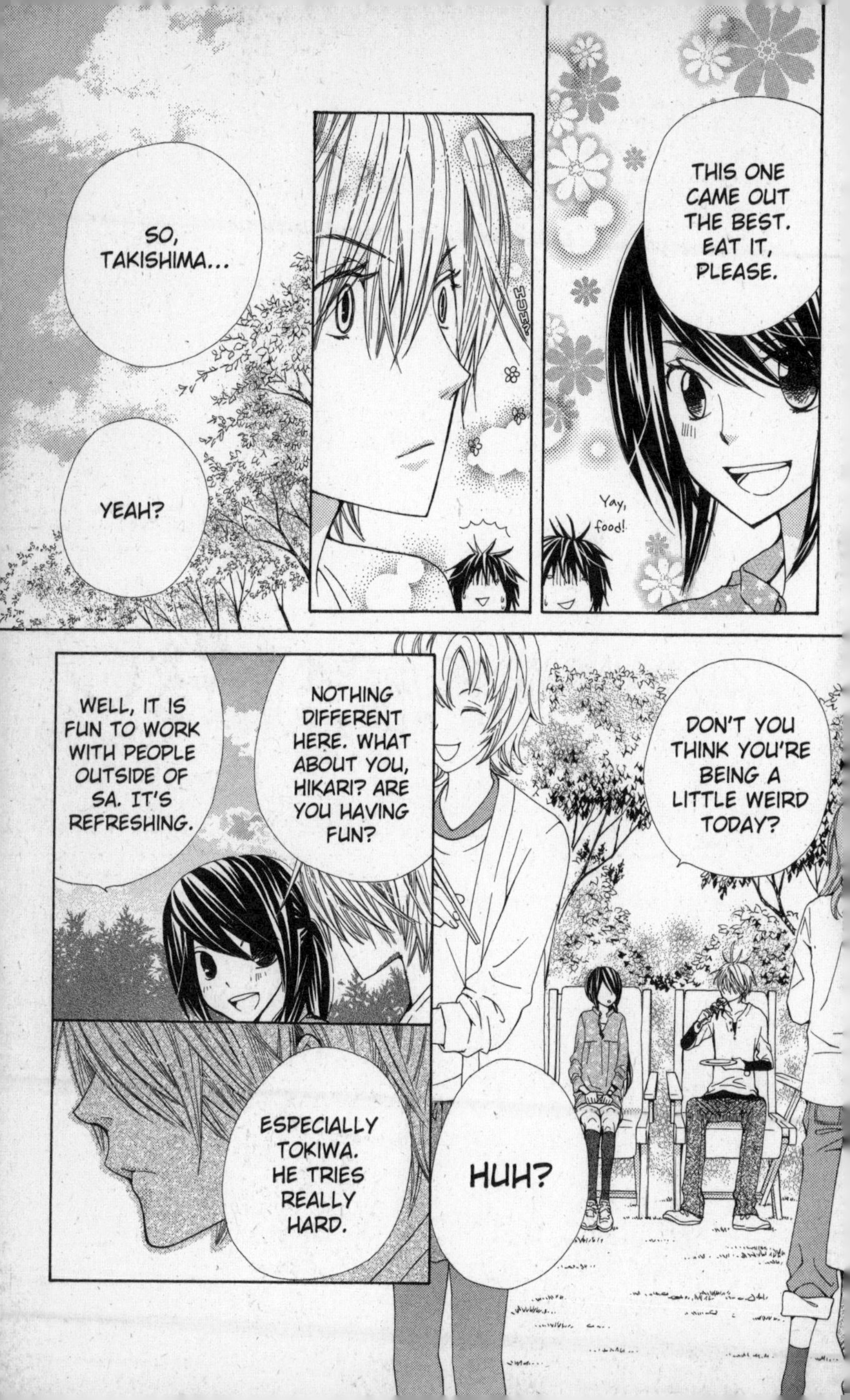
THIS ONE CAME OUT THE BEST. EAT IT, PLEASE.
Yay, food!
HUH?
SO, TAKISHIMA...
YEAH?
DON'T YOU THINK YOU'RE BEING A LITTLE WEIRD TODAY?
NOTHING DIFFERENT HERE. WHAT ABOUT YOU, HIKARI? ARE YOU HAVING FUN?
WELL, IT IS FUN TO WORK WITH PEOPLE OUTSIDE OF SA. IT'S REFRESHING.
HUH?
ESPECIALLY TOKIWA. HE TRIES REALLY HARD.

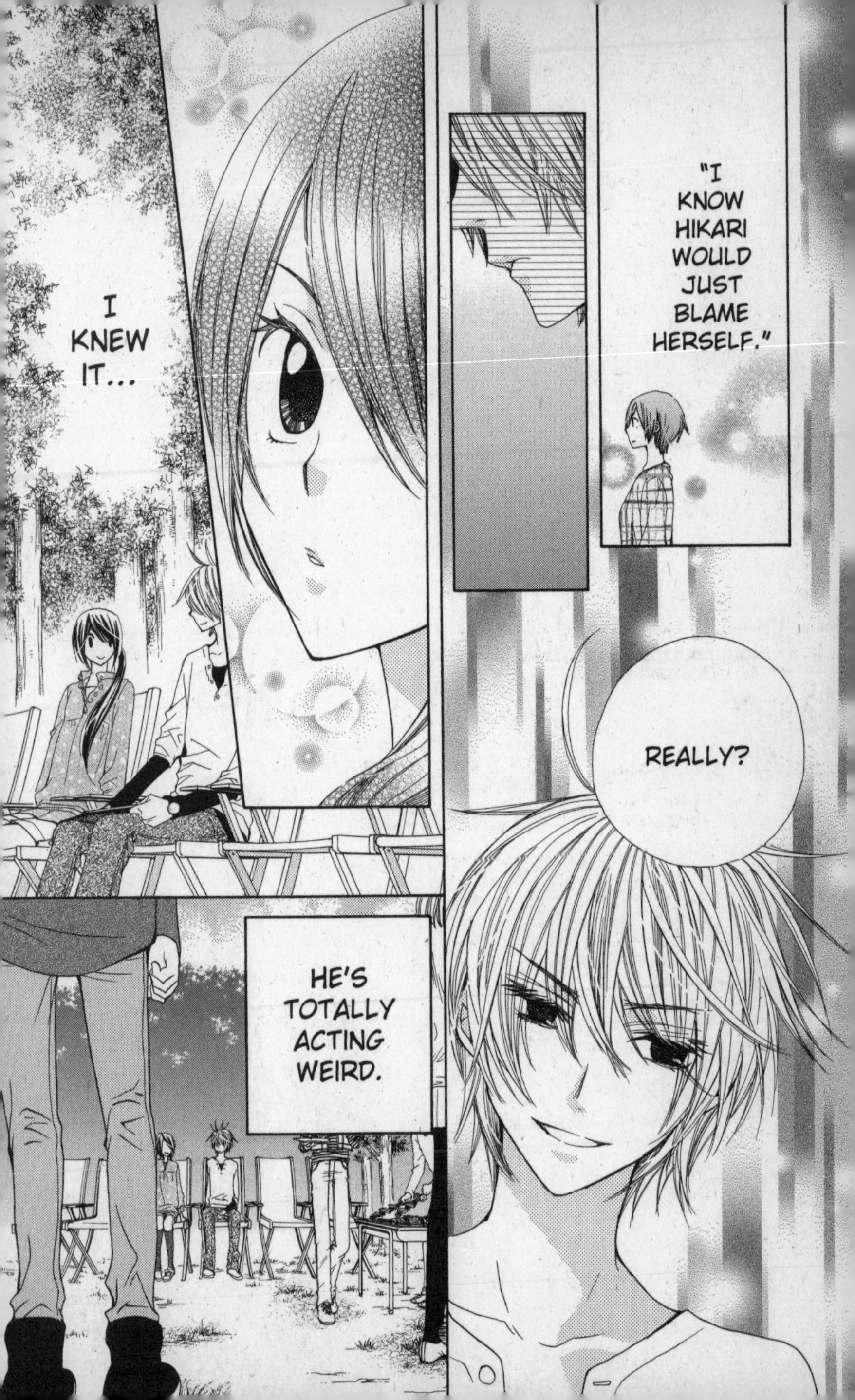
"I KNOW HIKARI WOULD JUST BLAME HERSELF."
REALLY?
I KNEW IT...
HE'S TOTALLY ACTING WEIRD.

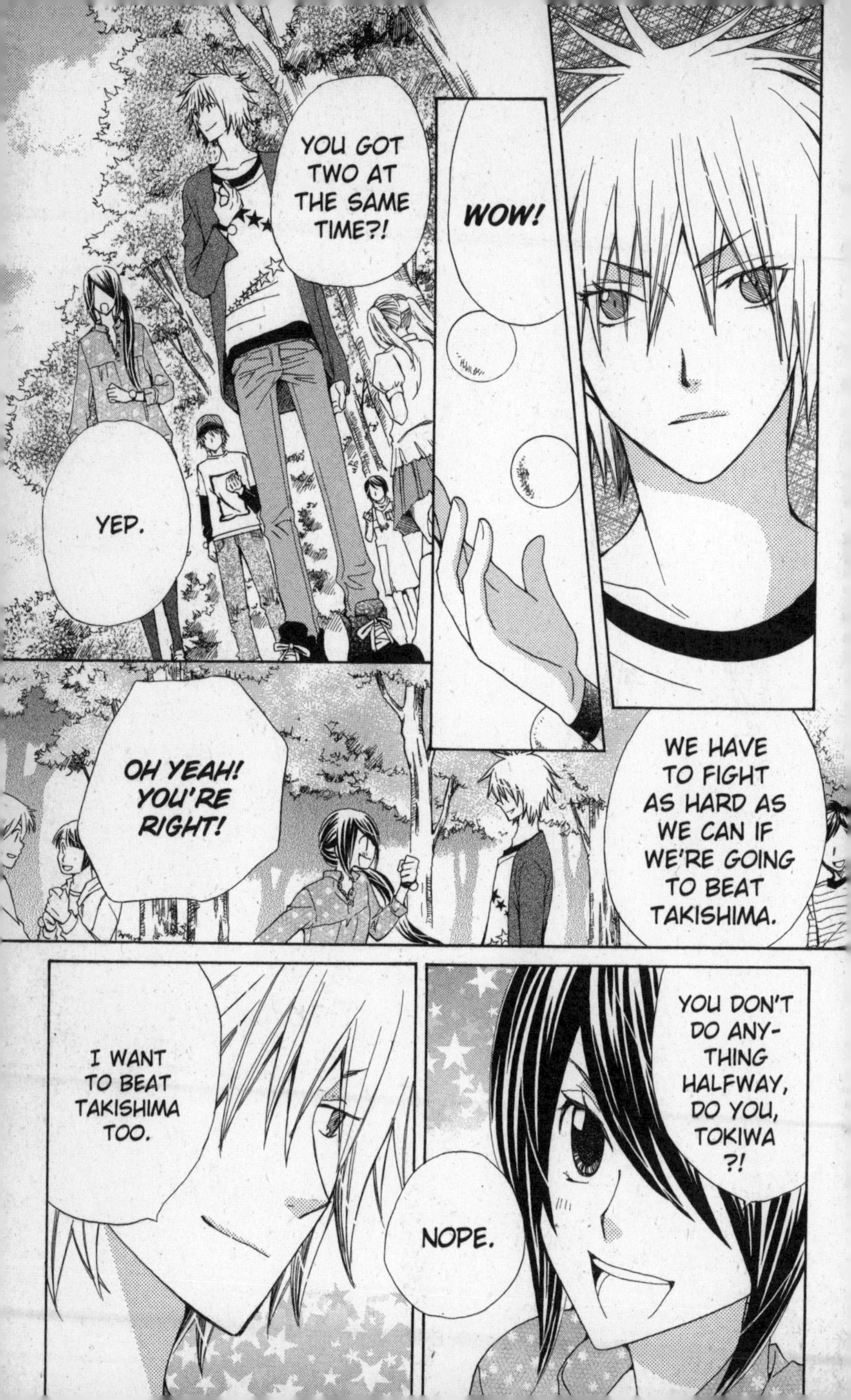
WOW!
YOU GOT TWO AT THE SAME TIME?!
YEP.
WE HAVE TO FIGHT AS HARD AS WE CAN IF WE'RE GOING TO BEAT TAKISHIMA.
OH YEAH! YOU'RE RIGHT!
YOU DON'T DO ANY-THING HALFWAY, DO YOU, TOKIWA?!
NOPE.
I WANT TO BEAT TAKISHIMA TOO.

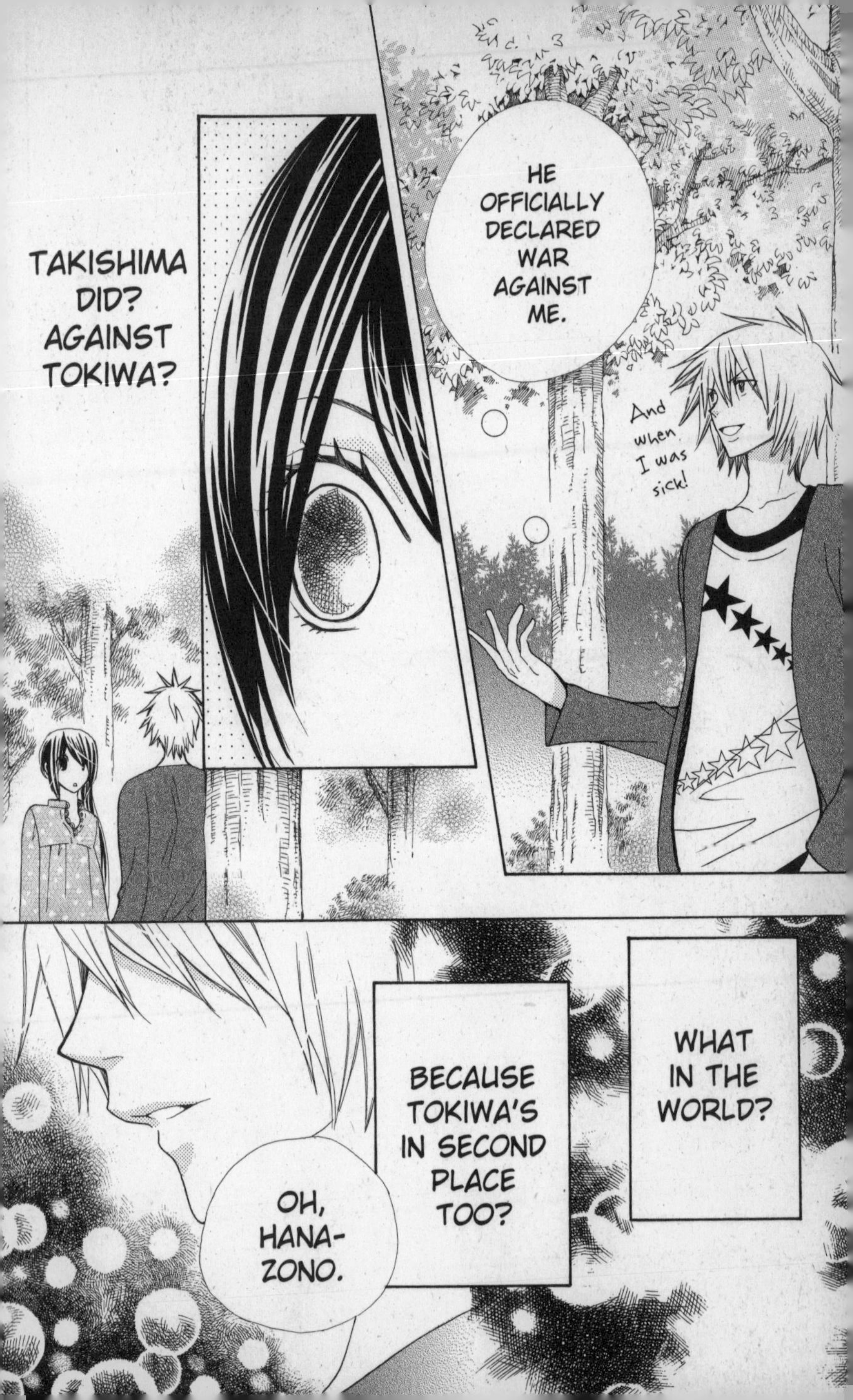
HE OFFICIALLY DECLARED WAR AGAINST ME.
And when I was sick!
TAKISHIMA DID? AGAINST TOKIWA?
WHAT IN THE WORLD?
BECAUSE TOKIWA'S IN SECOND PLACE TOO?
OH, HANA-ZONO.

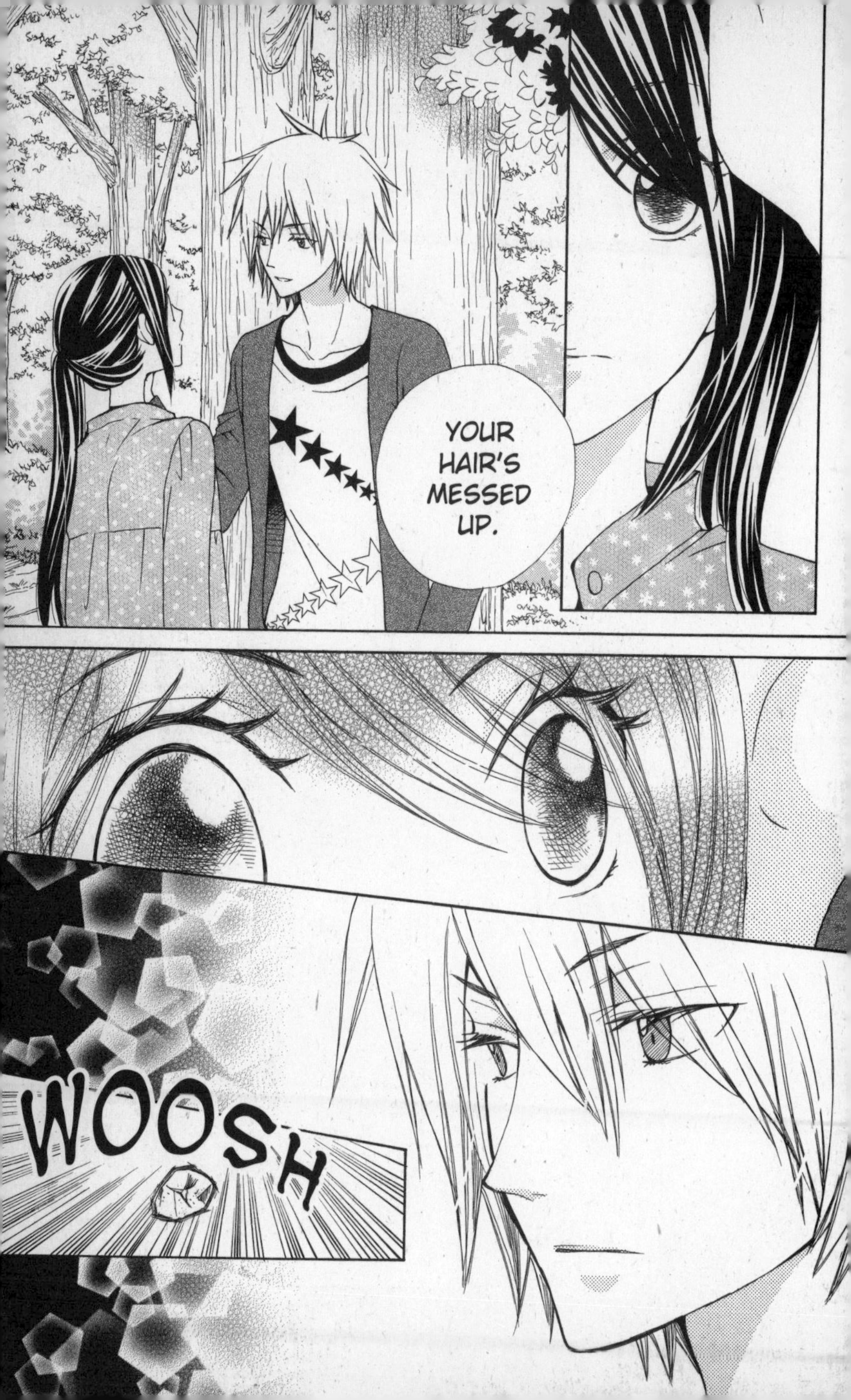
YOUR HAIR'S MESSED UP.
WOOSH

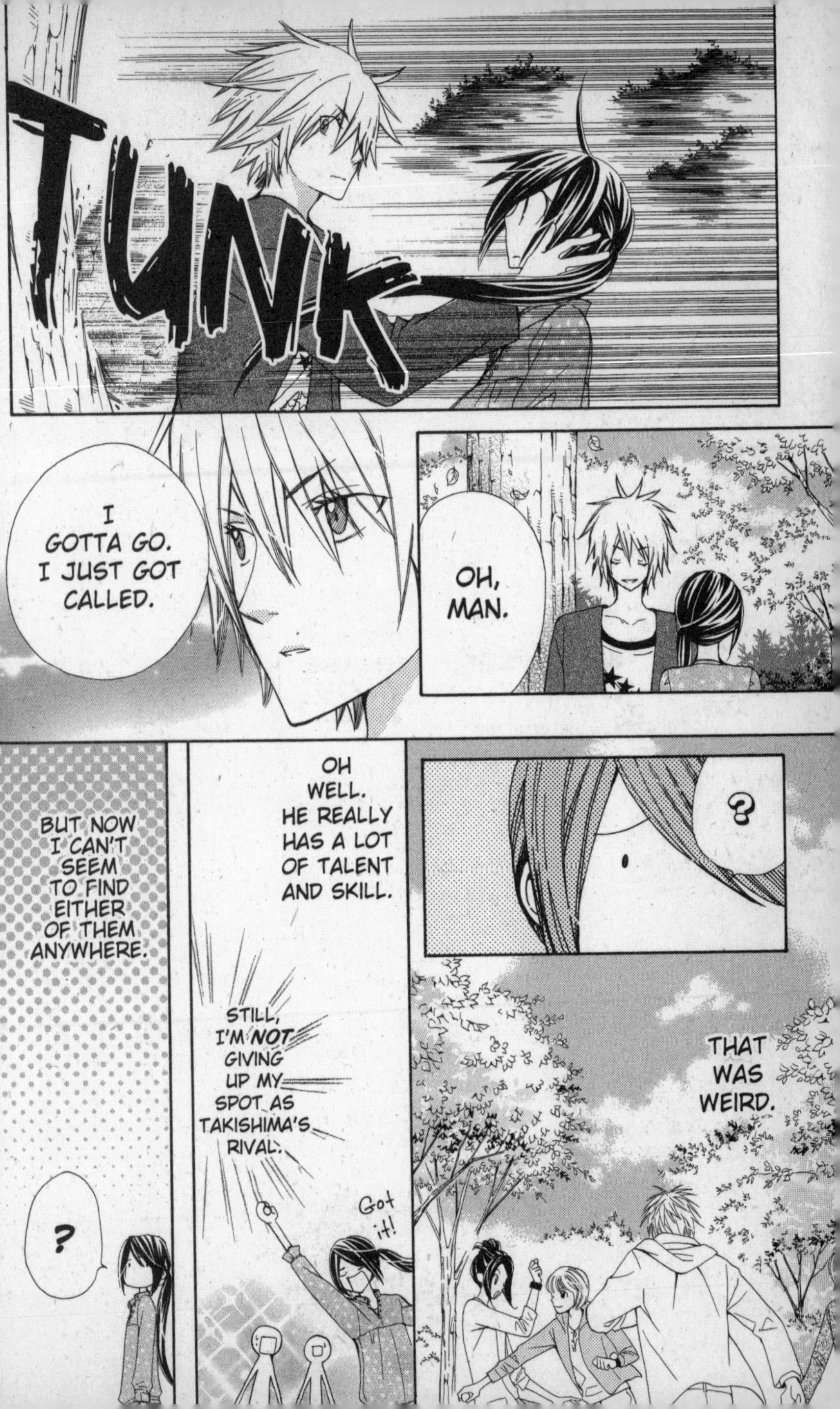
TUNK
OH, MAN.
I GOTTA GO. I JUST GOT CALLED.
?
THAT WAS WEIRD.
OH WELL. HE REALLY HAS A LOT OF TALENT AND SKILL.
STILL, I'M NOT GIVING UP MY SPOT AS TAKISHIMA'S RIVAL.
Got it!
BUT NOW I CAN'T SEEM TO FIND EITHER OF THEM ANYWHERE.
?

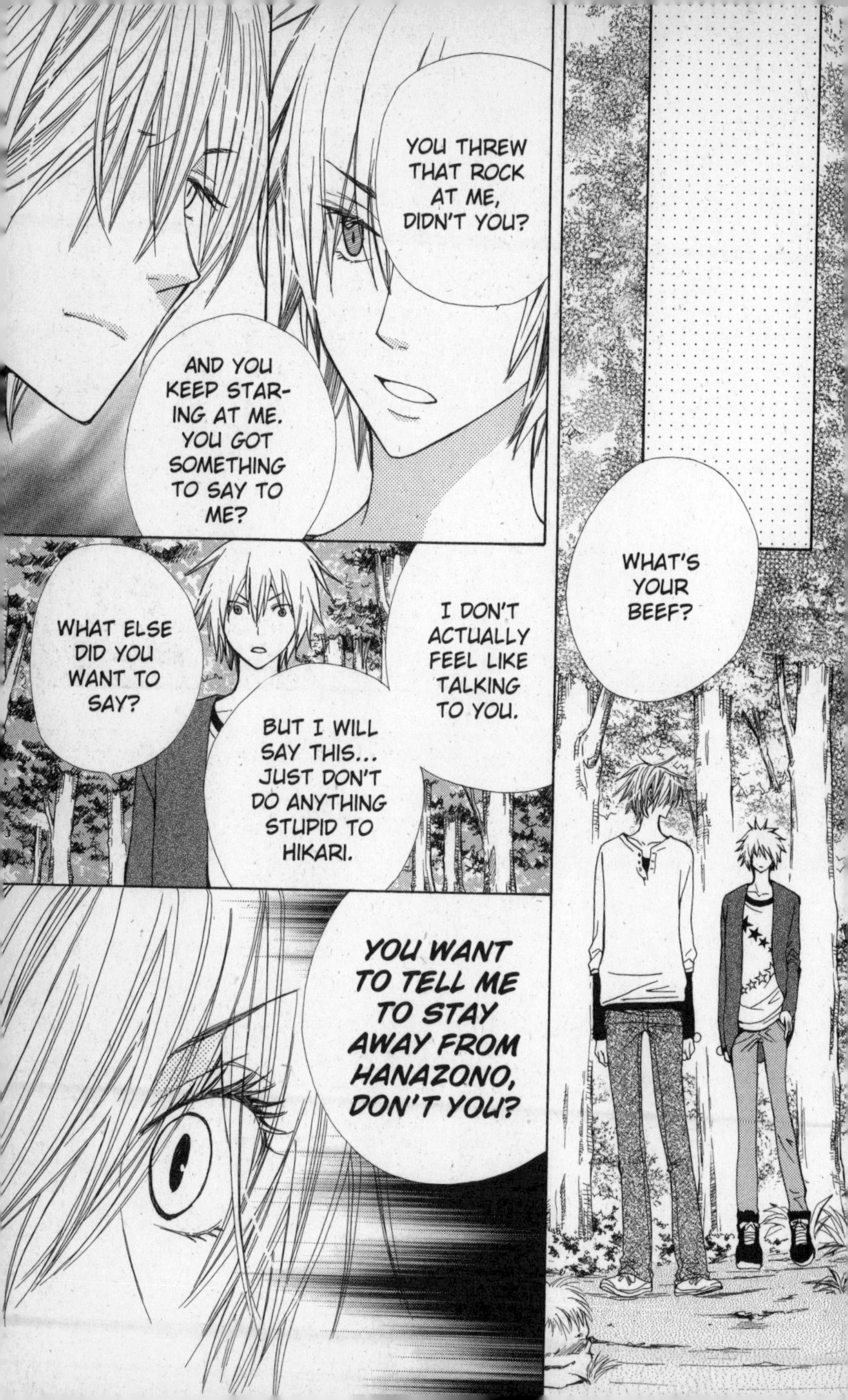
WHAT'S YOUR BEEF?
YOU THREW THAT ROCK AT ME, DIDN'T YOU?
AND YOU KEEP STAR-ING AT ME. YOU GOT SOMETHING TO SAY TO ME?
I DON'T ACTUALLY FEEL LIKE TALKING TO YOU.
BUT I WILL SAY THIS... JUST DON'T DO ANYTHING STUPID TO HIKARI.
WHAT ELSE DID YOU WANT TO SAY?
YOU WANT TO TELL ME TO STAY AWAY FROM HANAZONO, DON'T YOU?

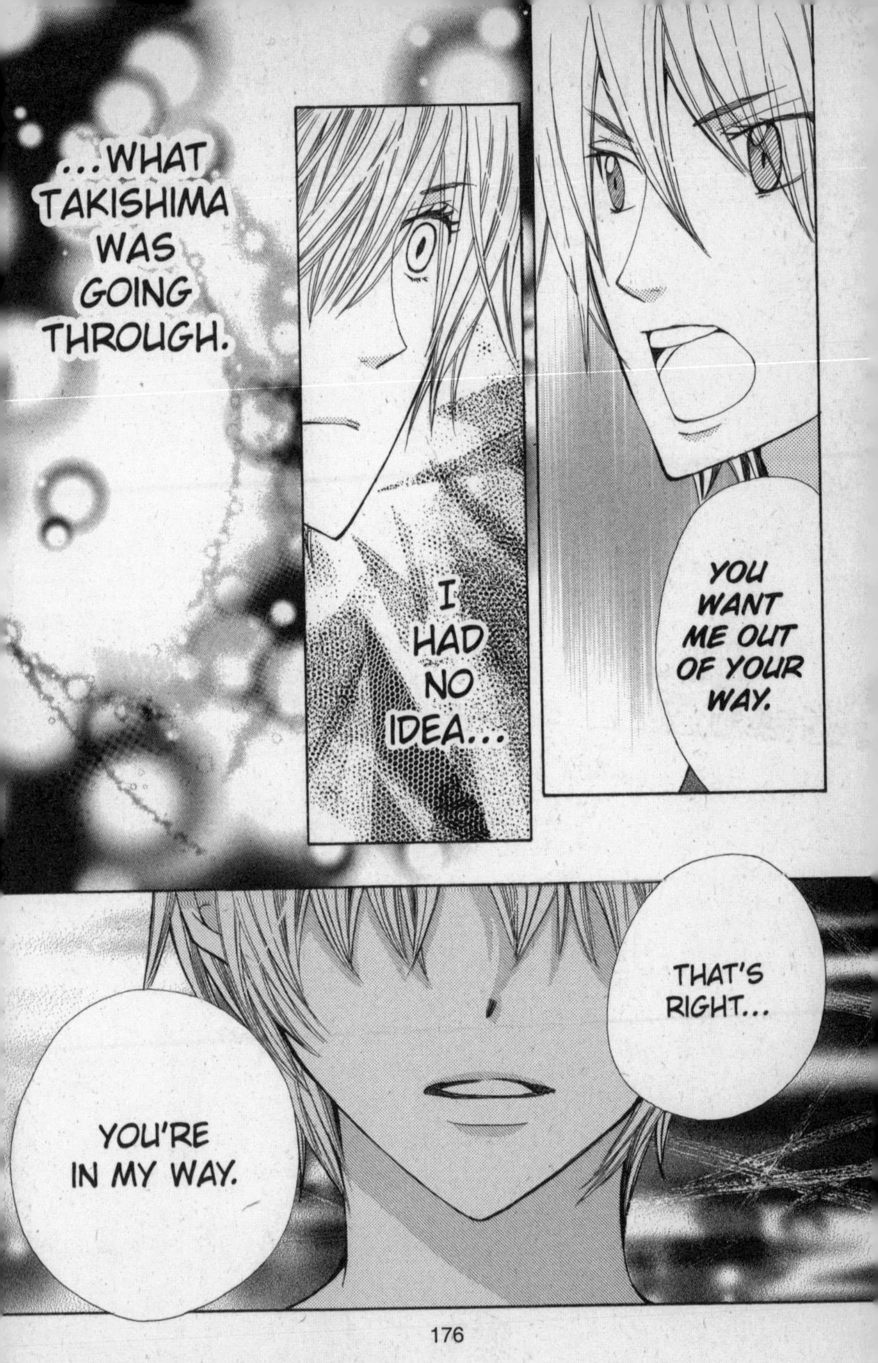
YOU WANT ME OUT OF YOUR WAY.
I HAD NO IDEA...
...WHAT TAKISHIMA WAS GOING THROUGH.
THAT'S RIGHT...
YOU'RE IN MY WAY.

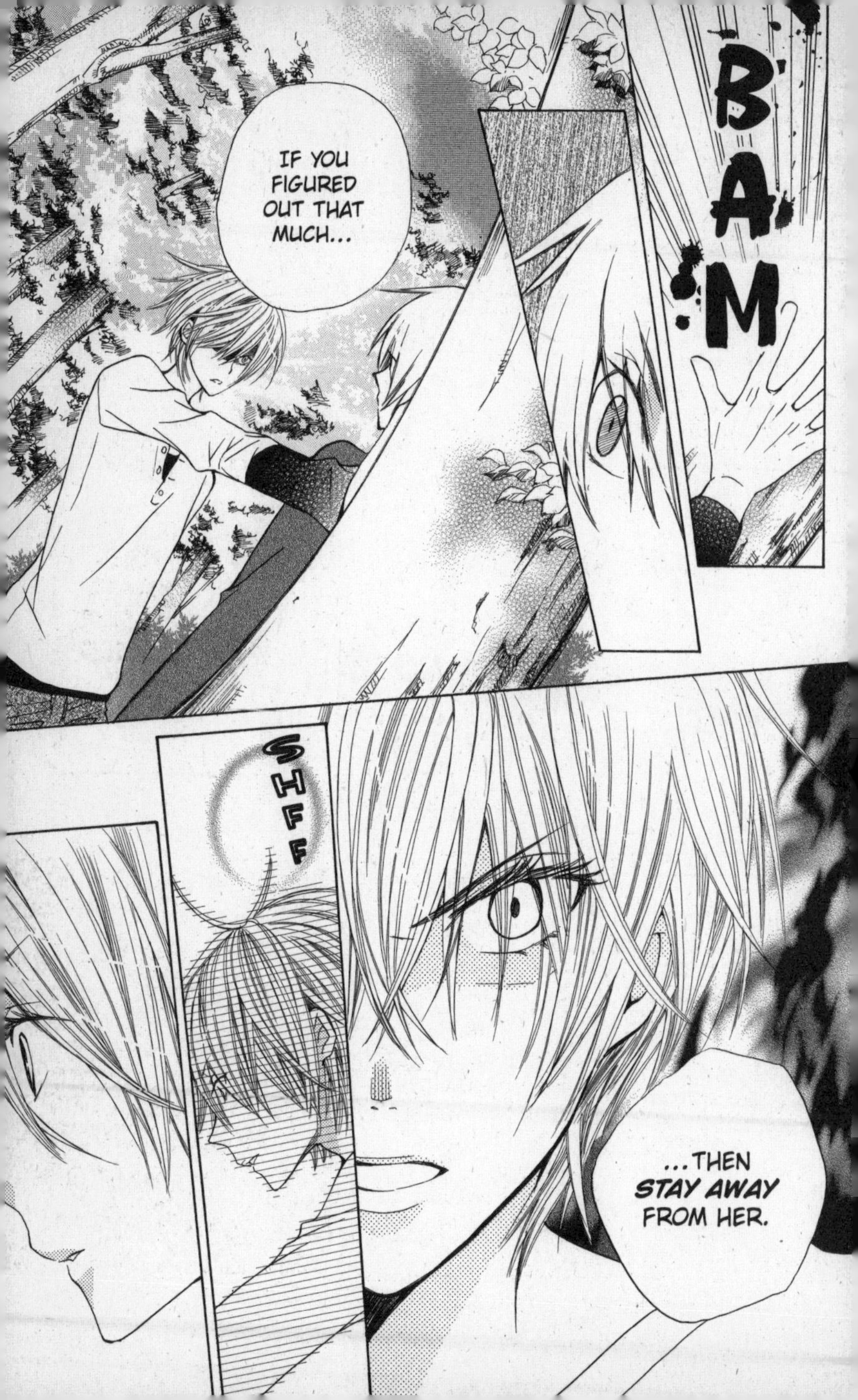
BAM
IF YOU FIGURED OUT THAT MUCH...
...THEN STAY AWAY FROM HER.
SHFF

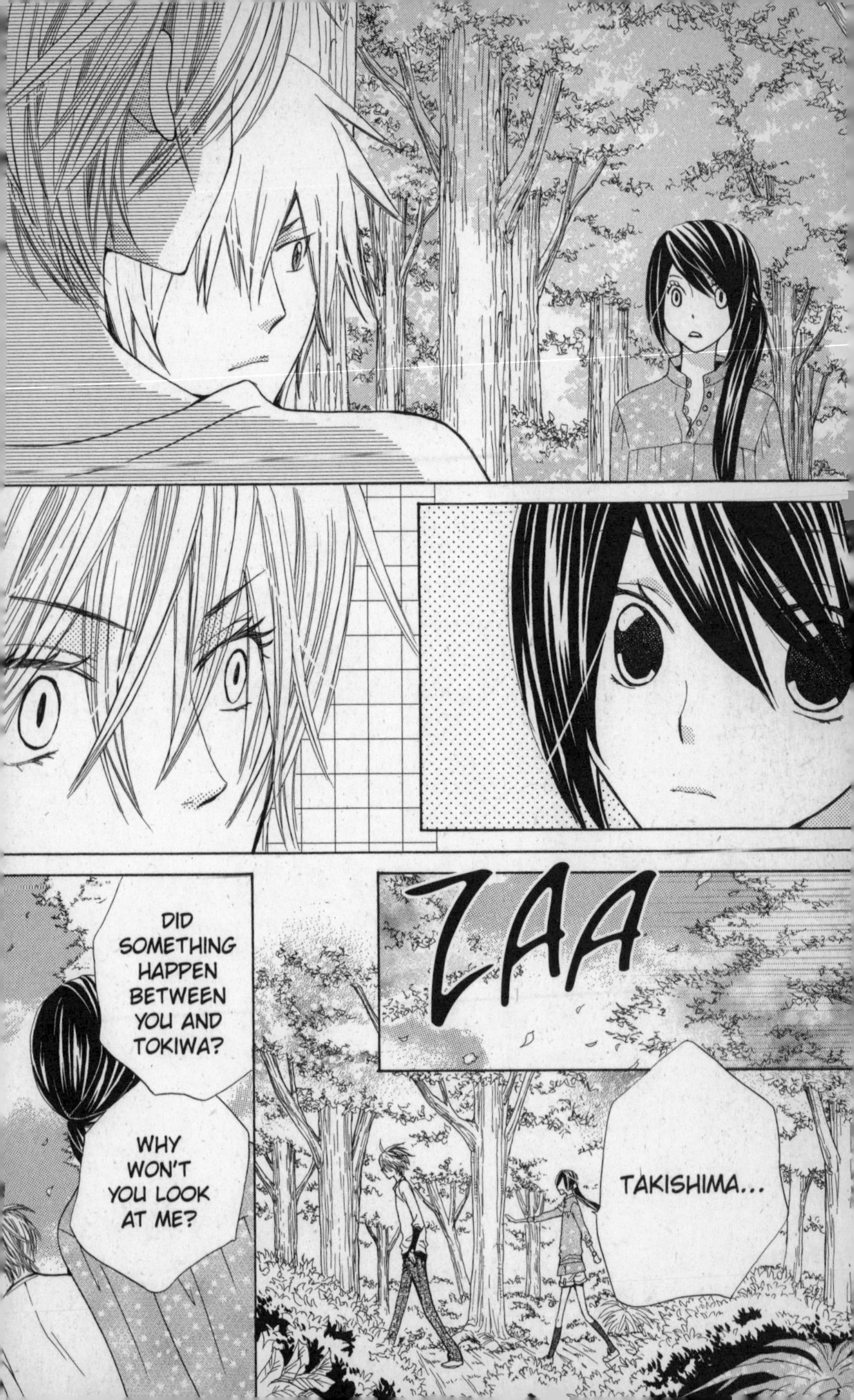
ZAA
TAKISHIMA...
DID SOMETHING HAPPEN BETWEEN YOU AND TOKIWA?
WHY WON'T YOU LOOK AT ME?

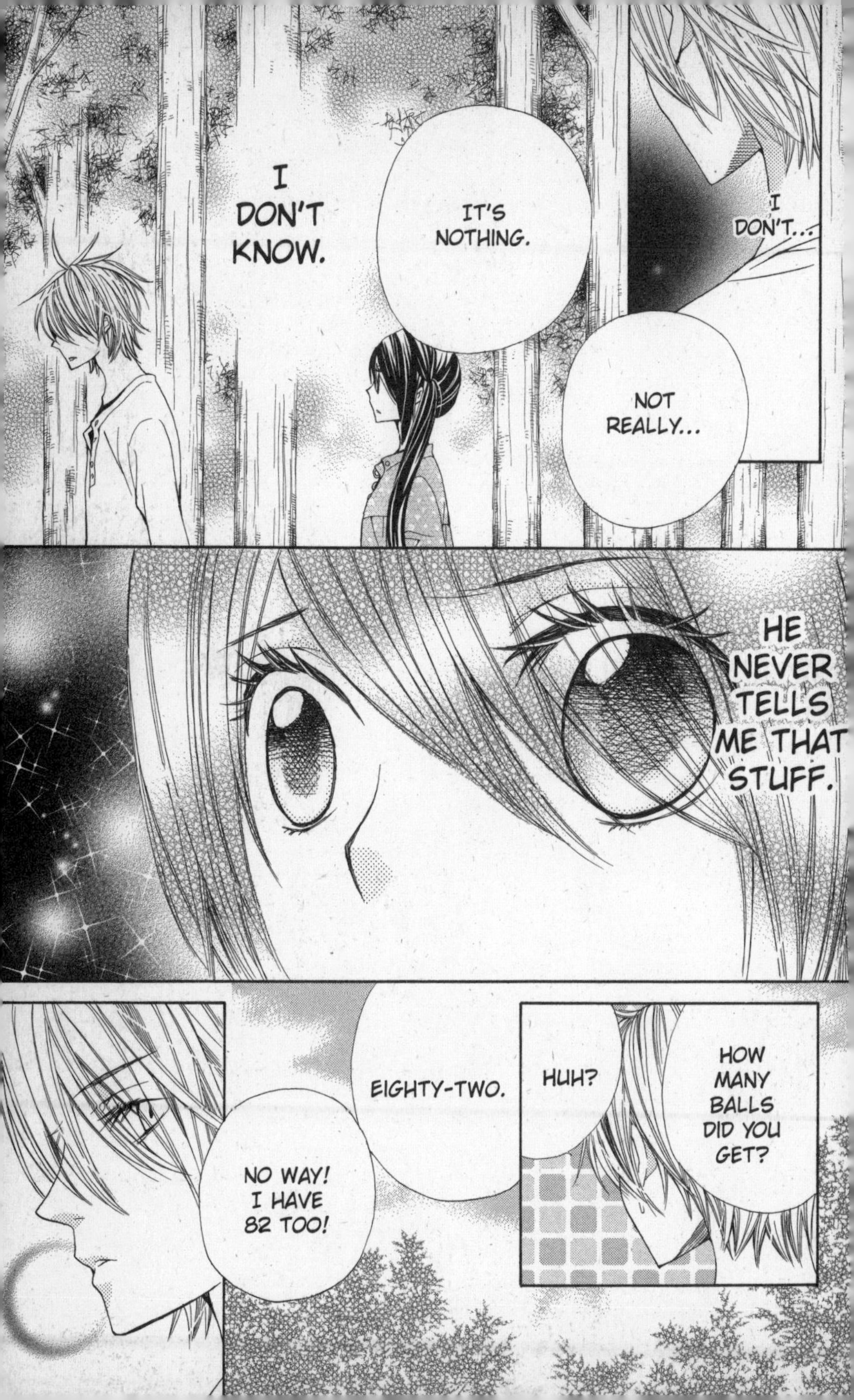
I DON'T...
NOT REALLY...
IT'S NOTHING.
I DON'T KNOW.
HE NEVER TELLS ME THAT STUFF.
HOW MANY BALLS DID YOU GET?
HUH?
EIGHTY-TWO.
NO WAY! I HAVE 82 TOO!

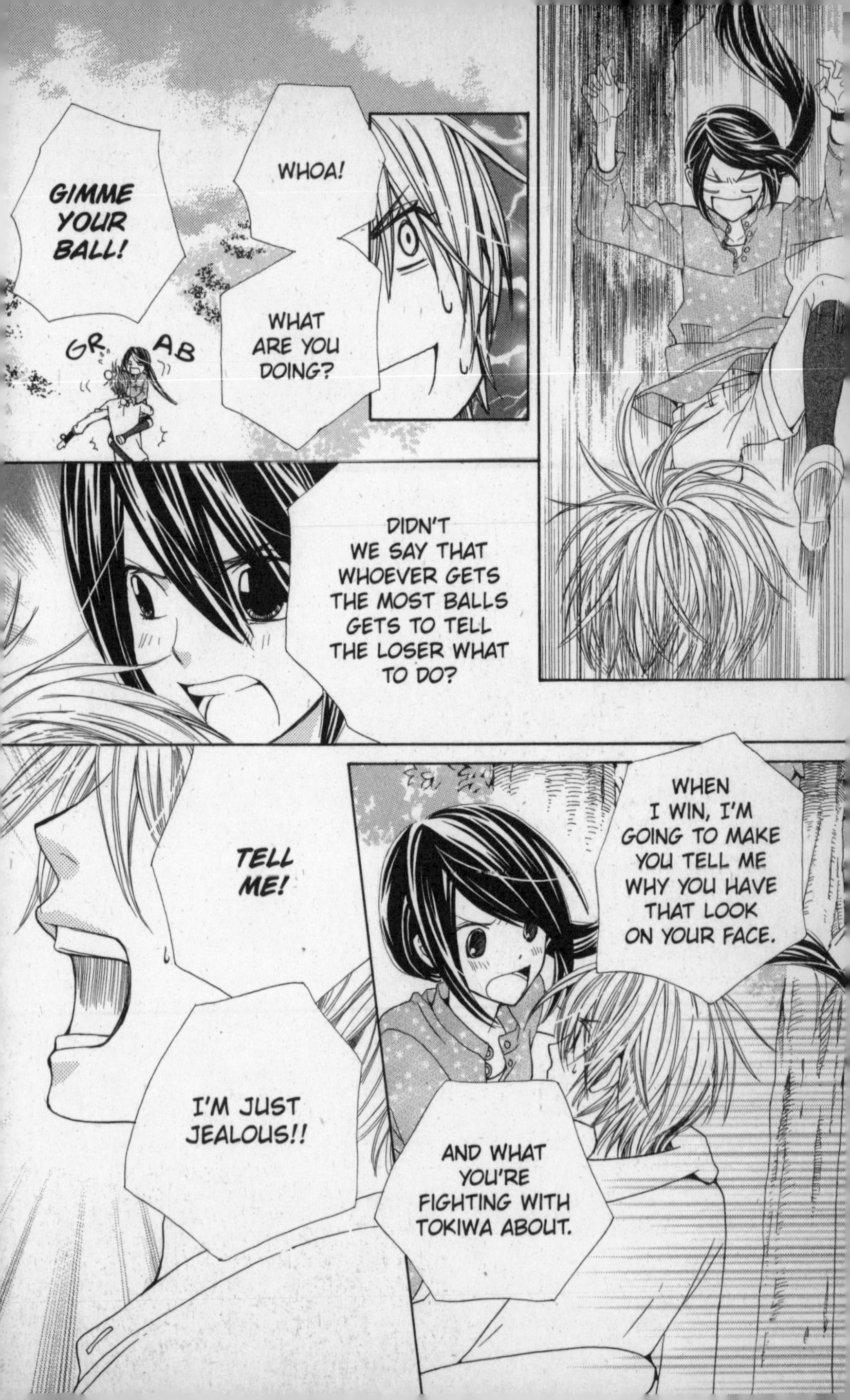
WHOA!
WHAT ARE YOU DOING?
GIMME YOUR BALL!
GR AB
DIDN'T WE SAY THAT WHOEVER GETS THE MOST BALLS GETS TO TELL THE LOSER WHAT TO DO?
WHEN I WIN, I'M GOING TO MAKE YOU TELL ME WHY YOU HAVE THAT LOOK ON YOUR FACE.
AND WHAT YOU'RE FIGHTING WITH TOKIWA ABOUT.
TELL ME!
I'M JUST JEALOUS!!

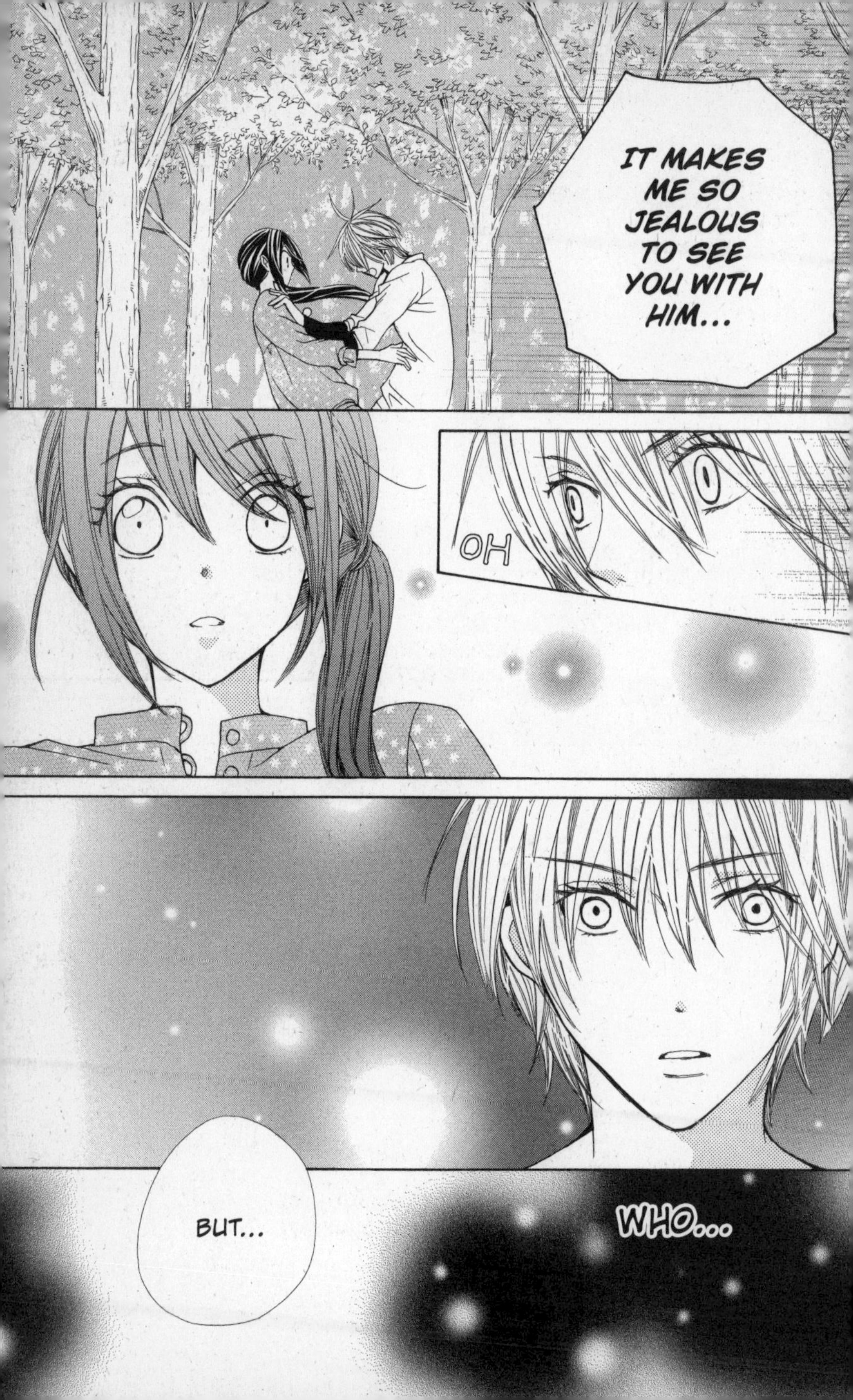
IT MAKES ME SO JEALOUS TO SEE YOU WITH HIM...
OH
WHO...
BUT...

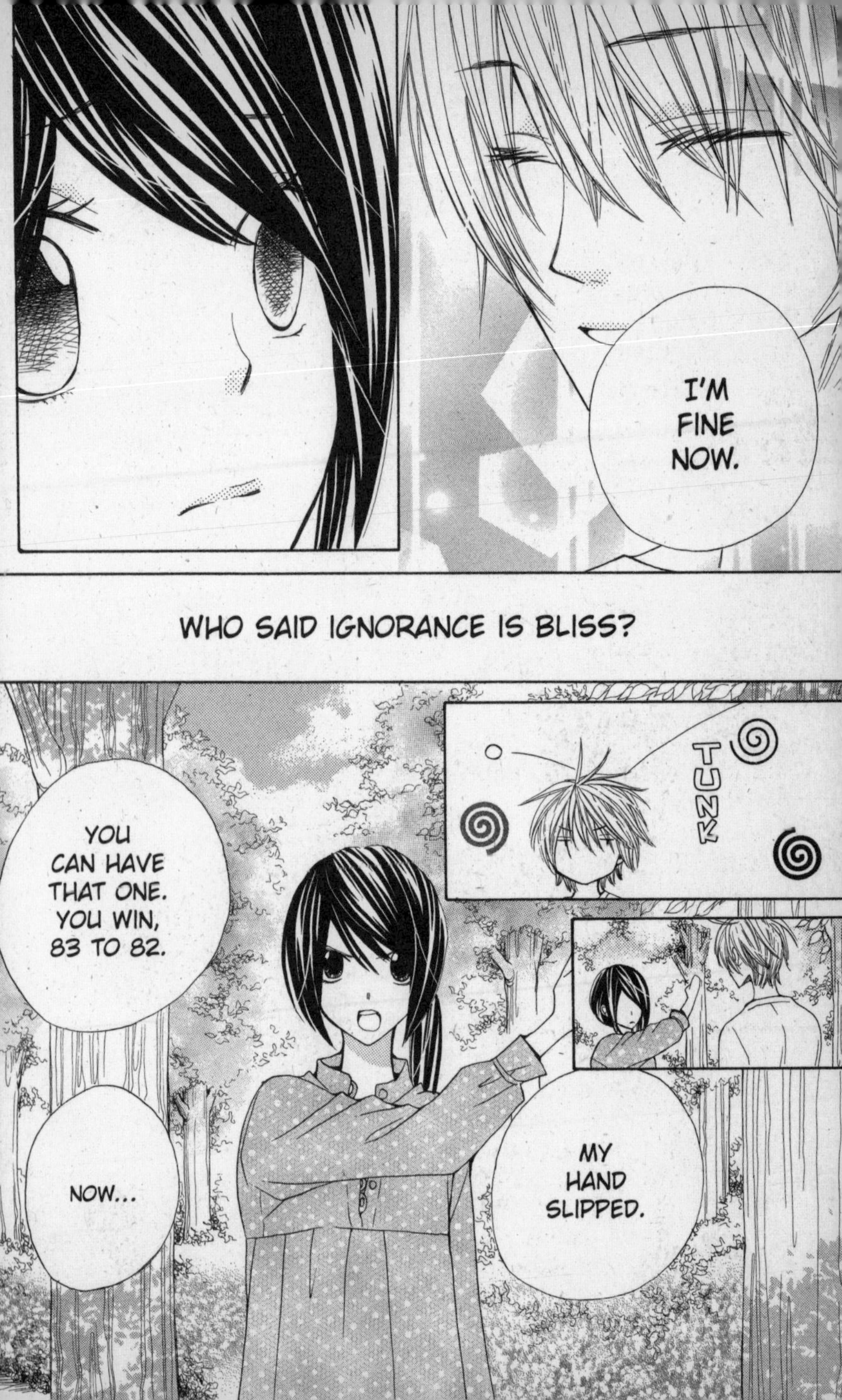
I'M FINE NOW.
WHO SAID IGNORANCE IS BLISS?
TUNK
MY HAND SLIPPED.
YOU CAN HAVE THAT ONE. YOU WIN, 83 TO 82.
NOW...

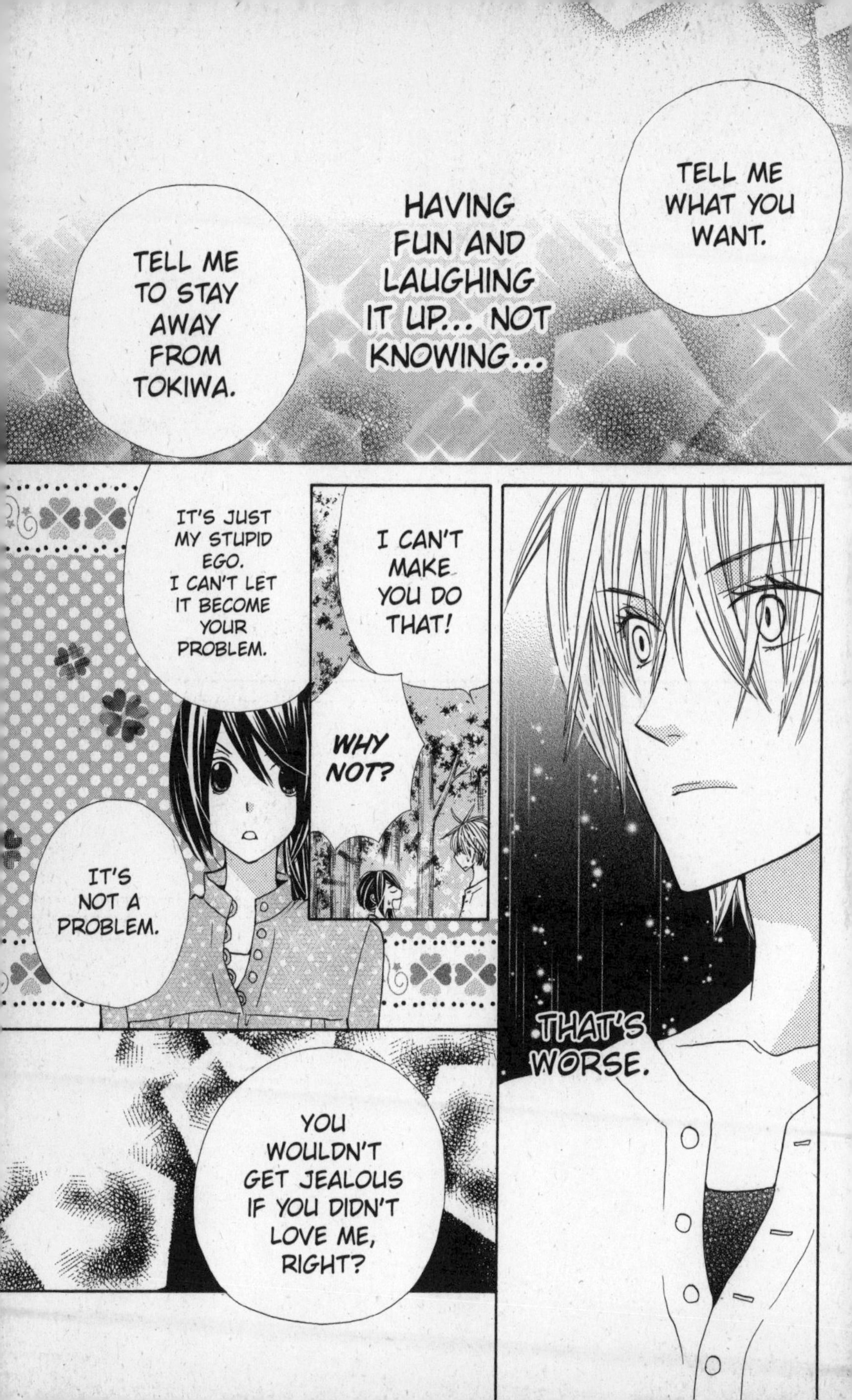
TELL ME WHAT YOU WANT.
HAVING FUN AND LAUGHING IT UP... NOT KNOWING...
TELL ME TO STAY AWAY FROM TOKIWA.
THAT'S WORSE.
I CAN'T MAKE YOU DO THAT!
WHY NOT?
IT'S JUST MY STUPID EGO. I CAN'T LET IT BECOME YOUR PROBLEM.
IT'S NOT A PROBLEM.
YOU WOULDN'T GET JEALOUS IF YOU DIDN'T LOVE ME, RIGHT?

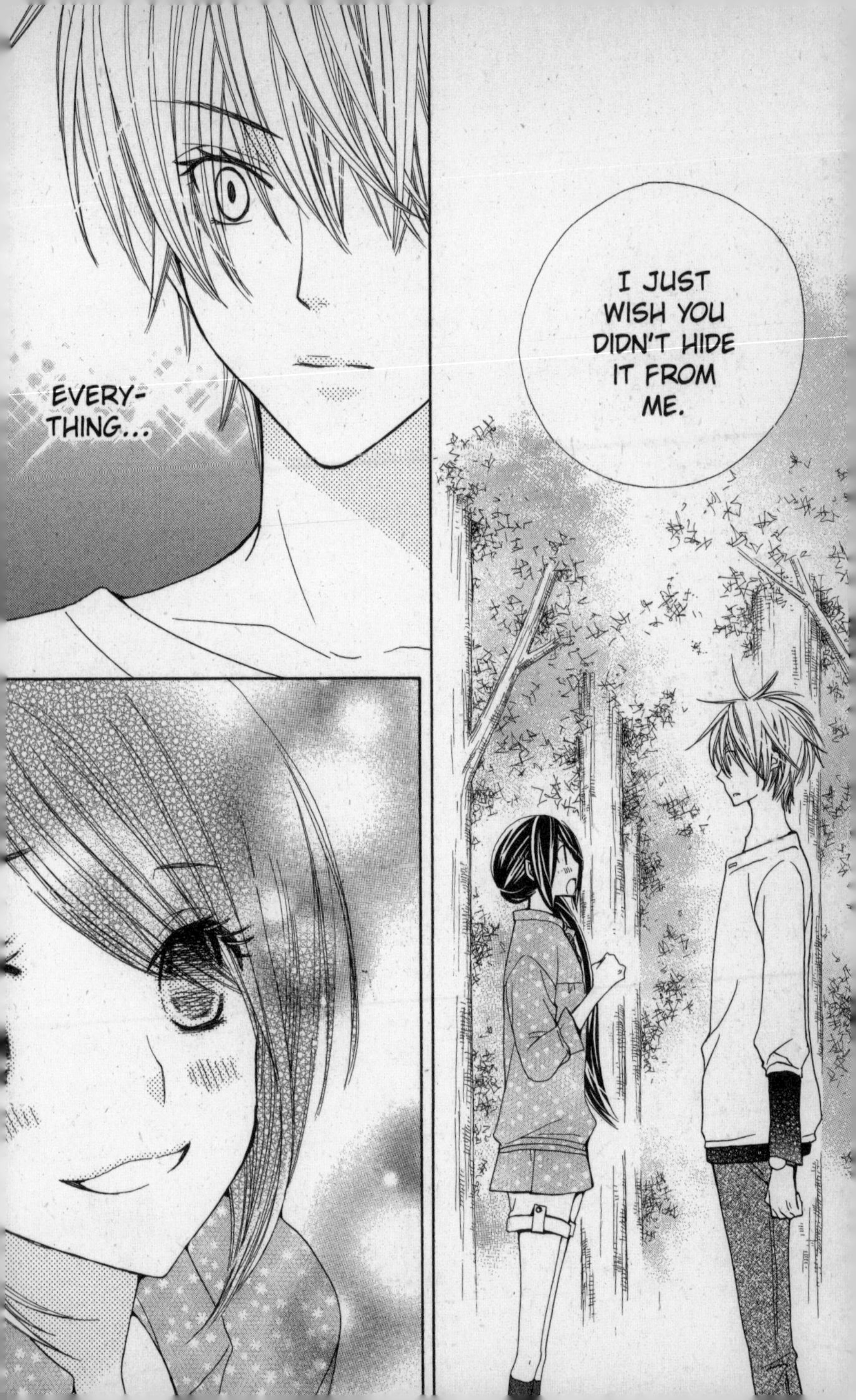
I JUST WISH YOU DIDN'T HIDE IT FROM ME.
EVERY-THING...

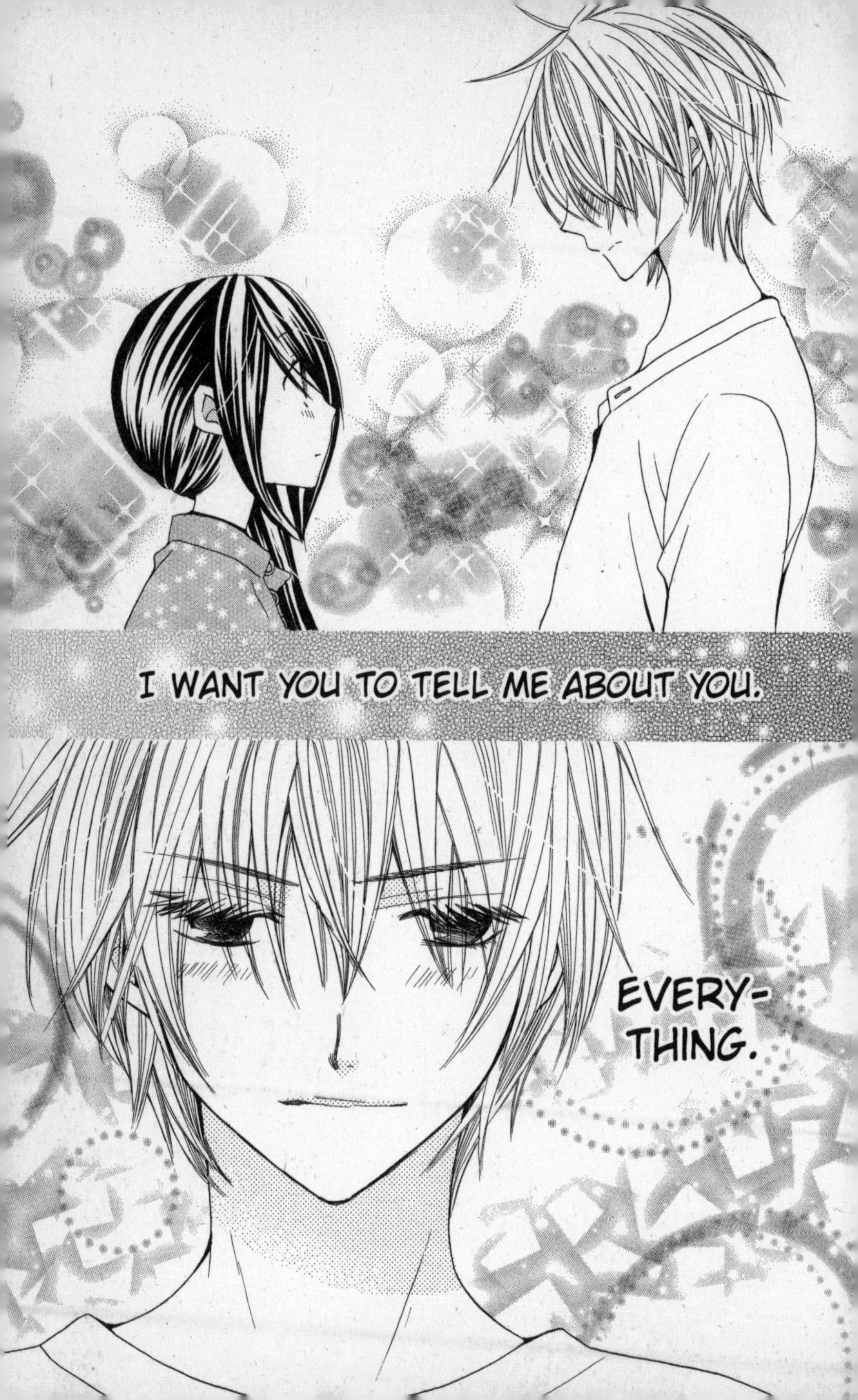
I WANT YOU TO TELL ME ABOUT YOU.
EVERY-
THING.

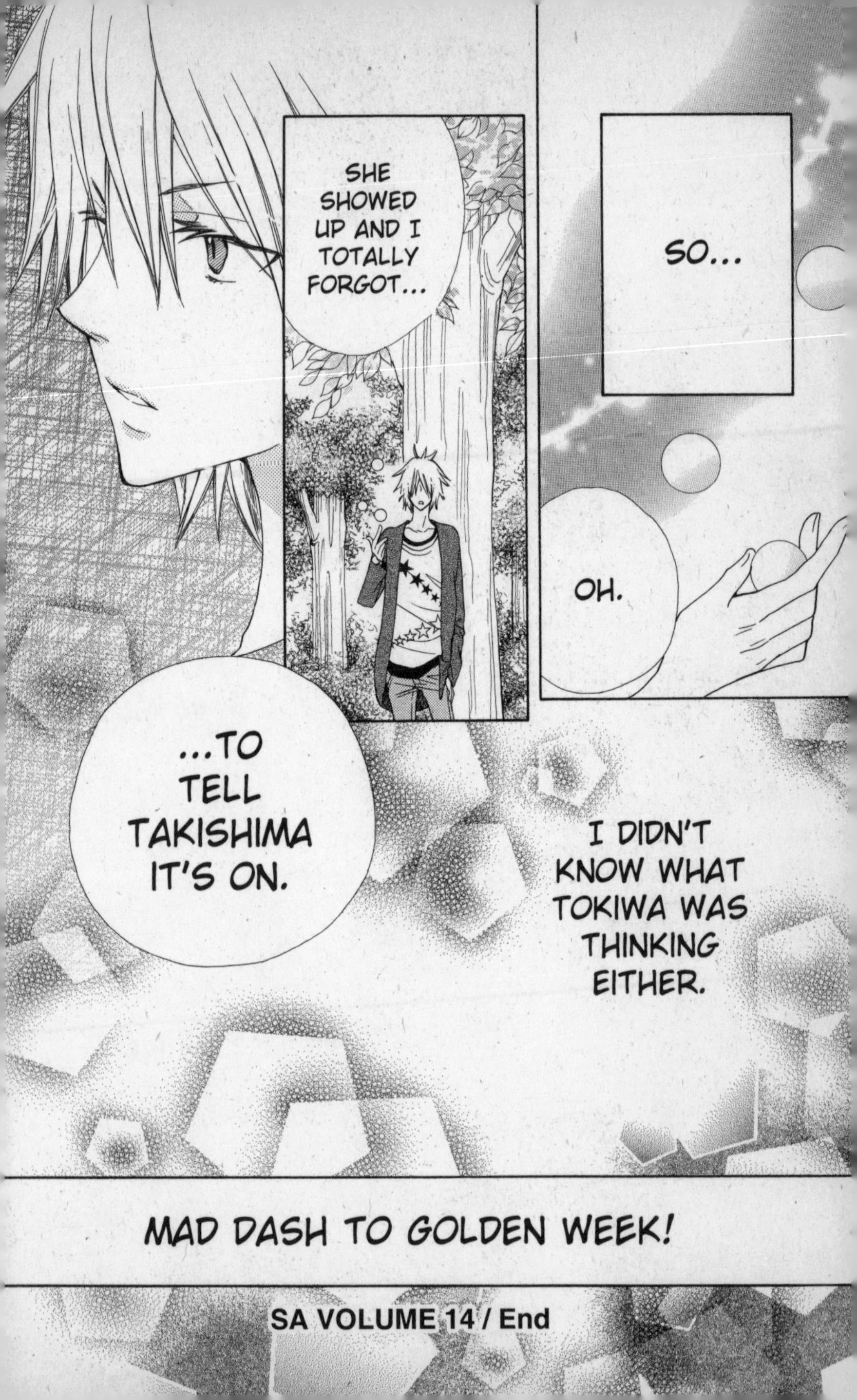
SO...
OH.
SHE SHOWED UP AND I TOTALLY FORGOT...
...TO TELL TAKISHIMA IT'S ON.
I DIDN'T KNOW WHAT TOKIWA WAS THINKING EITHER.
MAD DASH TO GOLDEN WEEK!
SA VOLUME 14 / End

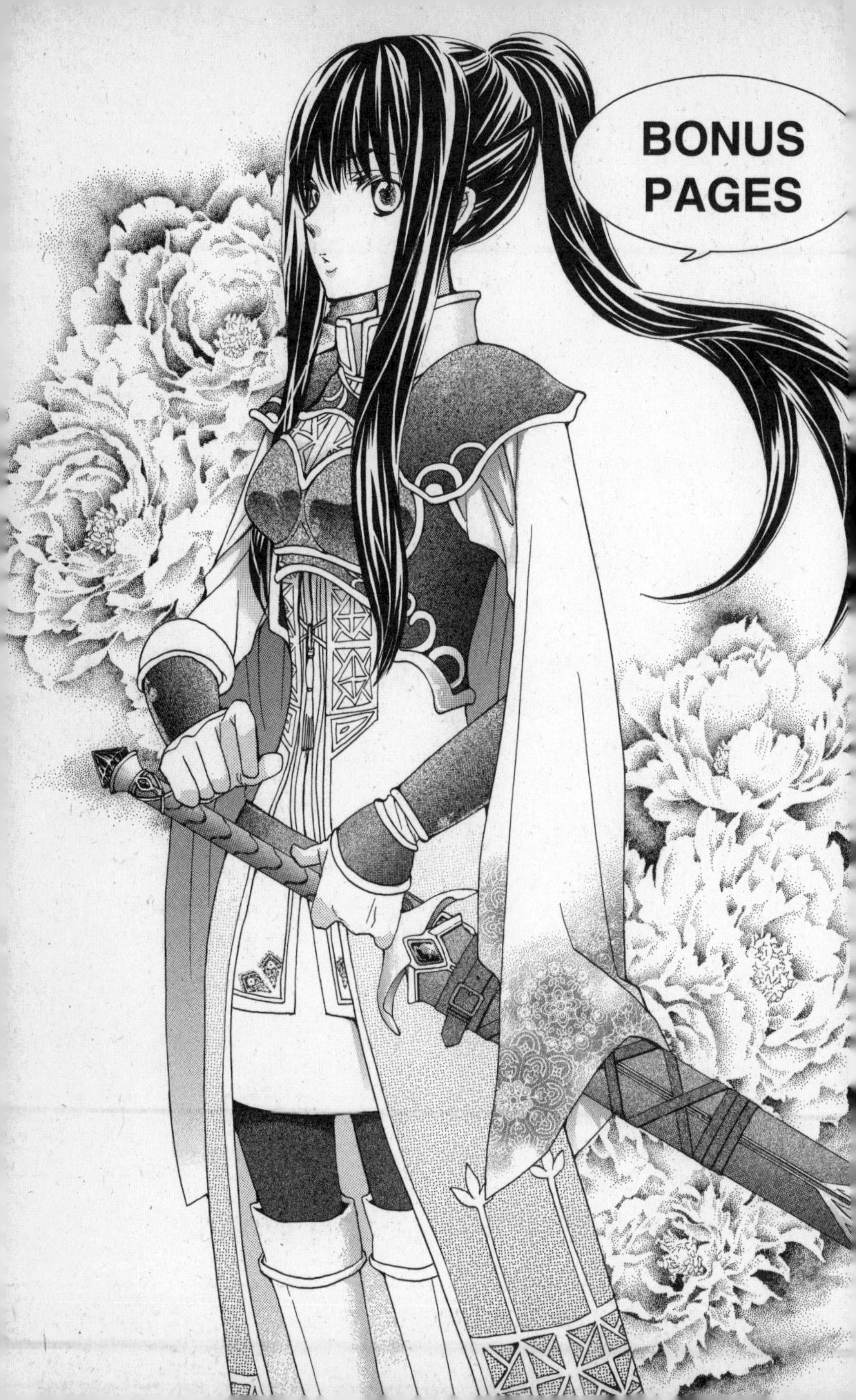
BONUS
PAGES

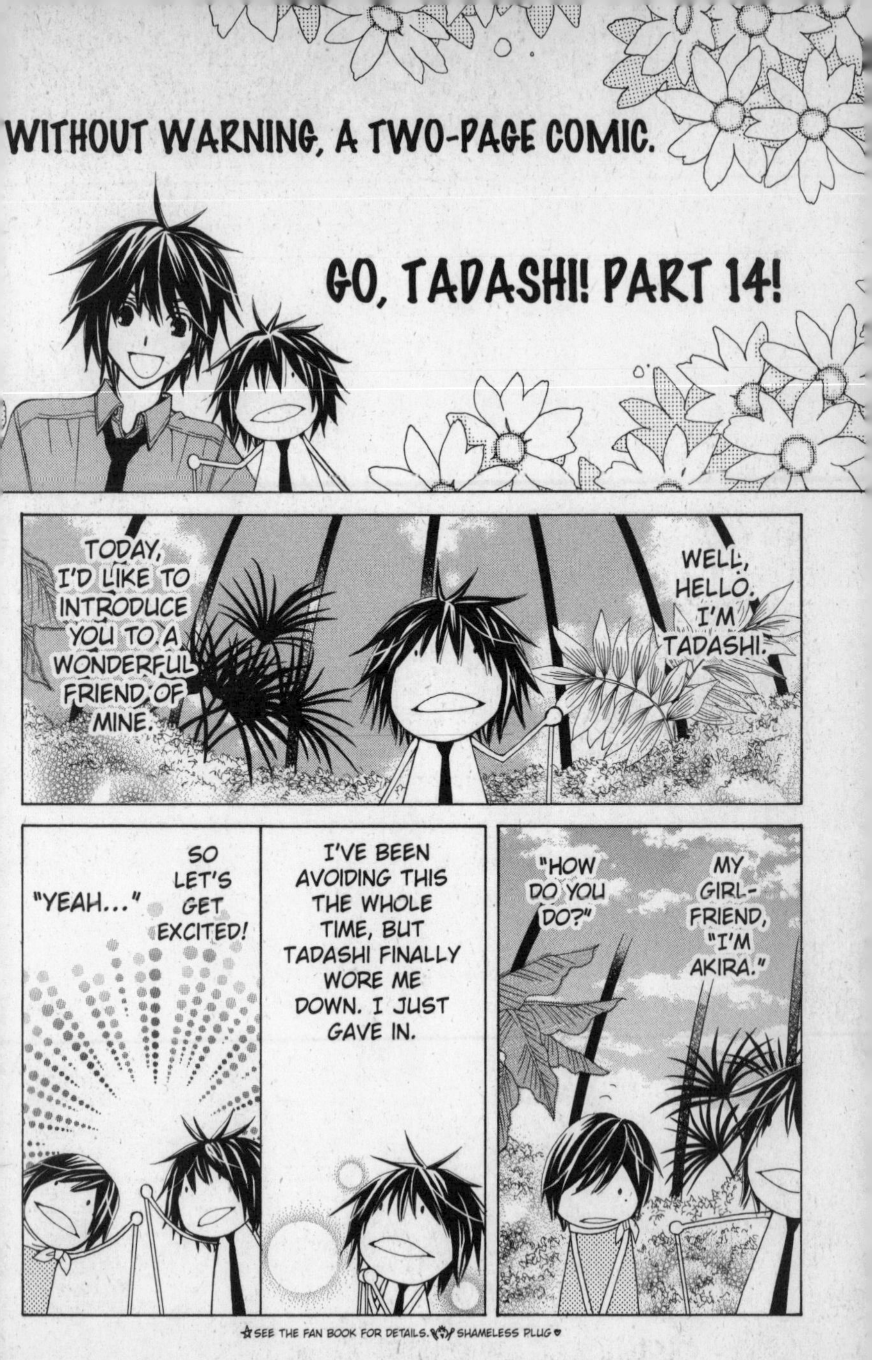
WITHOUT WARNING, A TWO-PAGE COMIC.
GO, TADASHI! PART 14!
WELL, HELLO. I'M TADASHI.
TODAY, I'D LIKE TO INTRODUCE YOU TO A WONDERFUL FRIEND OF MINE.
MY GIRL-FRIEND, "I'M AKIRA."
"HOW DO YOU DO?"
I'VE BEEN AVOIDING THIS THE WHOLE TIME, BUT TADASHI FINALLY WORE ME DOWN. I JUST GAVE IN.
SO LET'S GET EXCITED!
"YEAH..."

☆SEE THE FAN BOOK FOR DETAILS. SHAMELESS PLUG♥

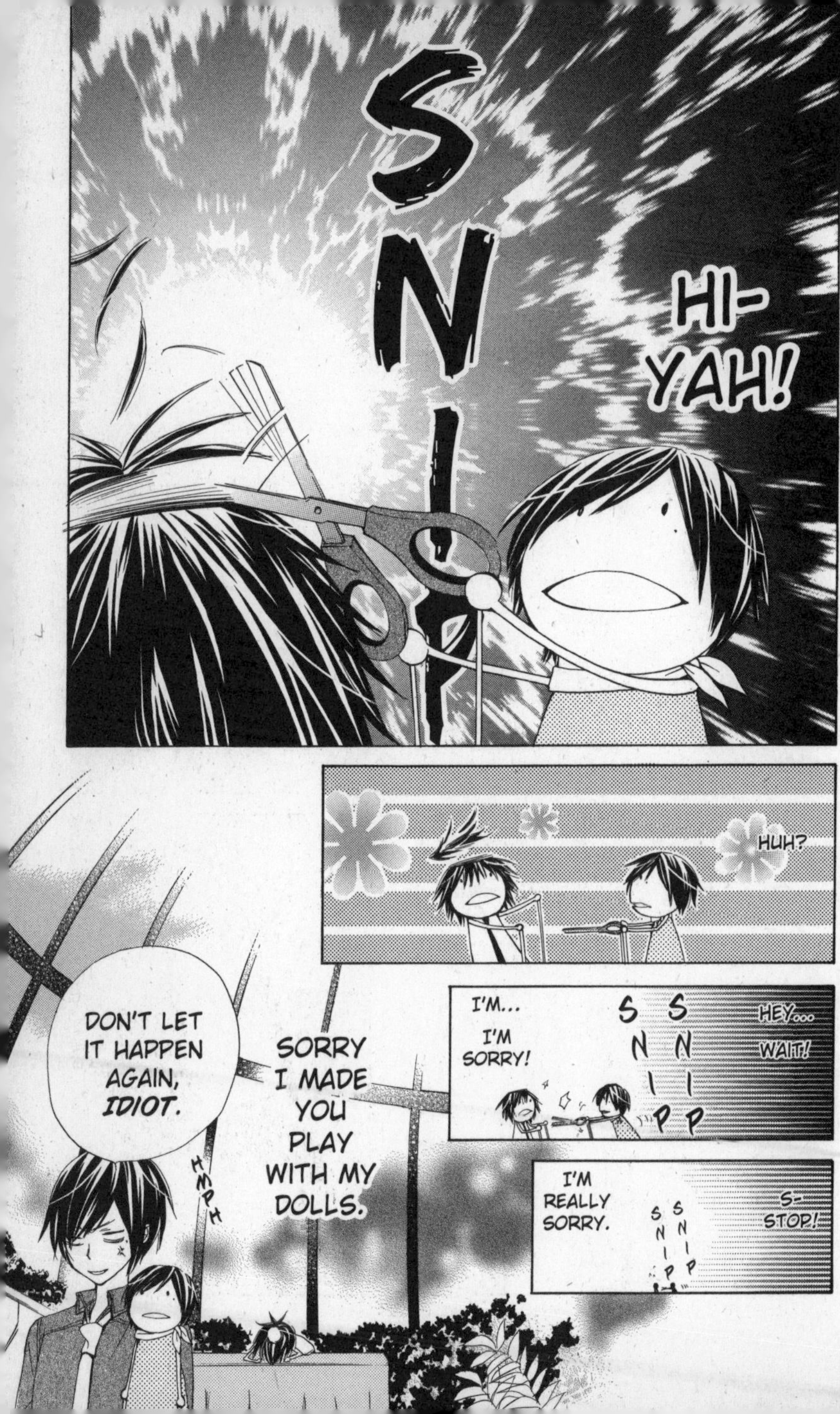
HI-YAH!
SNIP
HUH?
HEY... WAIT!
SNIP
SNIP
I'M... I'M SORRY!
S-STOP!
SNIP
SNIP
I'M REALLY SORRY.
SORRY I MADE YOU PLAY WITH MY DOLLS.
HMPH
DON'T LET IT HAPPEN AGAIN, *IDIOT*.

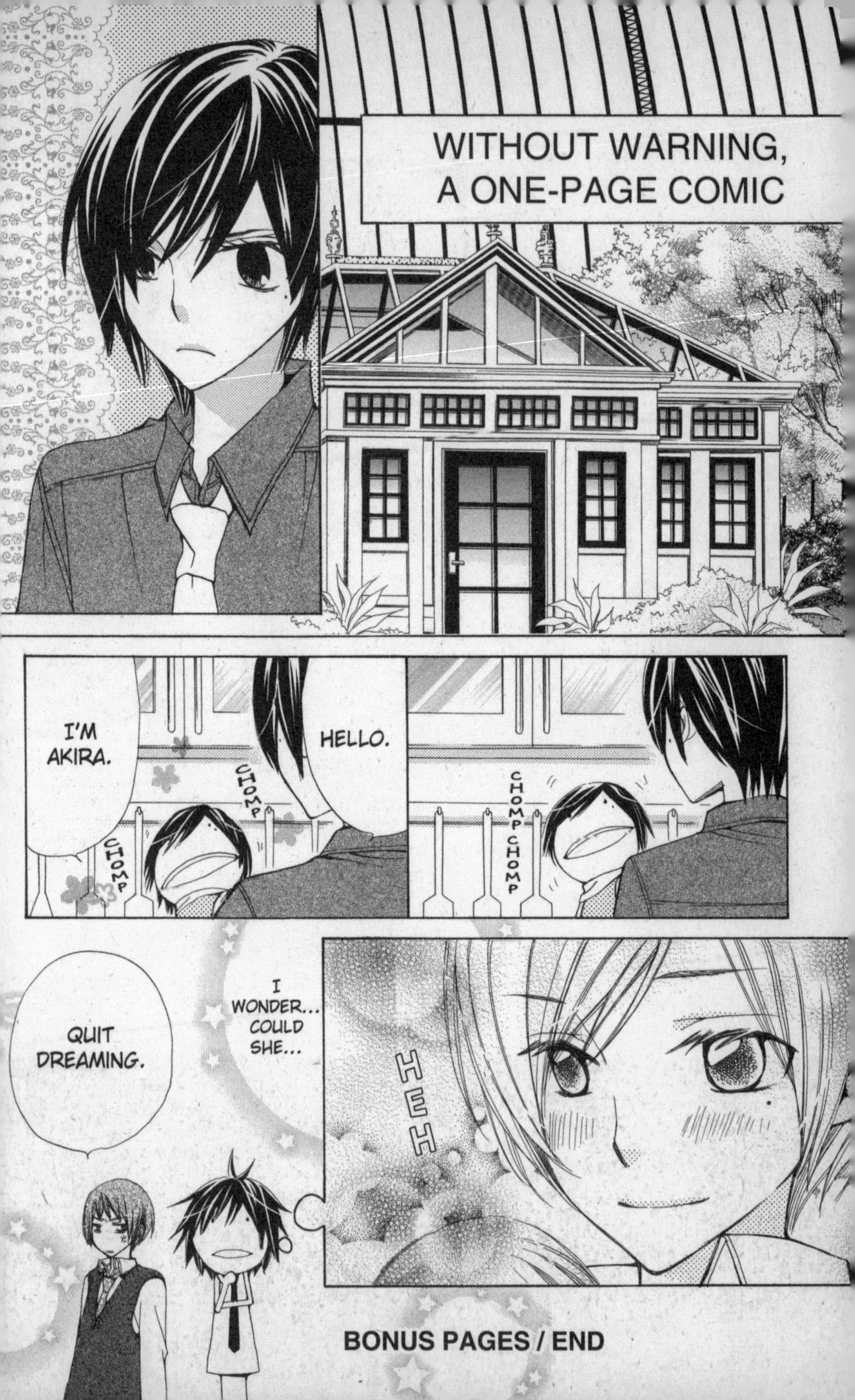
WITHOUT WARNING, A ONE-PAGE COMIC
CHOMP CHOMP
HELLO.
CHOMP
I'M AKIRA.
CHOMP
HEH
I WONDER... COULD SHE...
QUIT DREAMING.
BONUS PAGES / END

Maki Minami is from Saitama
Prefecture in Japan. She debuted
in 2001 with *Kanata no Ao*
(Faraway Blue). Her other works
include *Kimi wa Girlfriend*
(You're My Girlfriend), *Mainichi
ga Takaramono* (Every Day Is a
Treasure) and *Yuki Atataka*
(Warm Winter). *S•A* was serialized in
Japan's *Hana to Yume* magazine and
made into an anime in 2008.

S•A
Vol. 14
Shojo Beat Manga Edition

STORY & ART BY
MAKI MINAMI

English Adaptation/Amanda Hubbard
Translation/JN Productions
Touch-up Art & Lettering/Hudson Yards
Design/Deirdre Shiozawa
Editor/Jonathan Tarbox

VP, Production/Alvin Lu
VP, Publishing Licensing/Rika Inouye
VP, Sales & Product Marketing/Gonzalo Ferreyra
VP, Creative/Linda Espinosa
Publisher/Hyoe Narita

S•A -Special A- by Maki Minami © Maki Minami 2008. All rights reserved.
First published in Japan in 2008 by HAKUSENSHA, Inc., Tokyo. English
language translation rights arranged with HAKUSENSHA, Inc., Tokyo.

The stories, characters and incidents mentioned in this publication are entirely
fictional.

Printed in Canada

Published by VIZ Media, LLC
P.O. Box 77010
San Francisco, CA 94107

10 9 8 7 6 5 4 3 2 1
First printing, January 2010

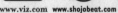

PARENTAL ADVISORY
S•A is rated T for Teen
and is recommended for
ages 13 and up.
ratings.viz.com

www.viz.com www.shojobeat.com